Duquesne Studies

LANGUAGE AND LITERATURE SERIES

VOLUME TWENTY

General Editor:
Albert C. Labriola

Advisory Editor:
Foster Provost

The Forms of Things Unknown

The
Forms of Things
Unknown

Renaissance
Metaphor
in *Romeo and Juliet*
and *A Midsummer
Night's Dream*

Mark Stavig

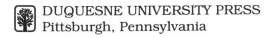

DUQUESNE UNIVERSITY PRESS
Pittsburgh, Pennsylvania

Published by
DUQUESNE UNIVERSITY PRESS
600 Forbes Avenue
Pittsburgh, Pennsylvania 15282–0101

Library of Congress Cataloging-in-Publication Data

Stavig, Mark, 1935–
    The forms of things unknown: Renaissance metaphor in Romeo
and Juliet, A midsummer night's dream / by Mark Stavig.
        p.   cm. — (Duquesne studies. Language and literature series
; v. 20)
    Includes bibliographical references and index.
    ISBN 0-8207-0264-1
    1. Shakespeare, William, 1564–1616—Style.   2. Metaphor.
3. Shakespeare, William, 1564–1616—Contemporary England.
4. Literature and society—England—History—16th century.
5. Shakespeare, William, 1564–1616. Romeo and Juliet.
6. Shakespeare, William, 1564–1616. Midsummer night's dream.
7. Renaissance—England.   I. Title.   II. Series.
PR3072.S78   1995
822.3'3—dc20   95–4407
                                                            CIP

For
Donna
Anne, Hal, Tom, and Rolf
and
my Shakespeare students at Colorado College

CONTENTS

CHARTS

PREFACE

This study began many years ago as an attempt to explain the backgrounds of Elizabethan culture to my Shakespeare students at Colorado College. It developed gradually into an explanation of Renaissance metaphor that tried to combine a traditional emphasis with an awareness of recent trends in modern criticism. When my teaching began to become more dependent on my charts, I realized that what has been helpful for my students might fill a need for other teachers as well. I also became aware that no detailed study of the close relationship between *Romeo and Juliet* and *A Midsummer Night's Dream* exists and concluded that my treatment of the patterns of Renaissance metaphor in the plays might also be of interest to scholars. That rather innocent beginning has led to a far more ambitious and complicated project than I first contemplated. Metaphor has become an increasingly important subject for scholarly analysis. The recent seminar on the topic at the Shakespeare Association meeting in Chicago suggests an encouraging interest in its study in historical context.

My debts to others are great. Colleagues in the English department at Colorado College—Tom Ross, Tom Mauch, John Longo, Ruth Barton, and Brenda Tooley—have read versions of the manuscript at various stages and have offered helpful criticism. Other members of the department—particularly Jane Hilberry, John Simons, Barry Sarchett, George Butte, and Neale Reinitz—have provided advice on more particular matters. One advantage of teaching at a small college is the opportunity for contacts with faculty in other disciplines. They have listened to trial runs of my ideas, both in jointly taught courses and in our interdisciplinary faculty discussion group—The Seventeenth Century Group—where they have been subjected to drafts of this study. I am particularly grateful to Bob McJimsey, Tim Fuller, Joe Pickle, Edith Kirsch, Carol Neel, Marie Daniels, and Marcia Dobson. The college has also provided me with generous financial aid and release time, and I want to thank Dean Tim Fuller for this support. Former colleagues at the University of Wisconsin—John Shawcross, S. K. Heninger, Jr., and Alan Dessen have also provided helpful advice, as have Tom Roche of Princeton University and Mary Beth Rose of the Newberry Library. I should also thank the staff of many libraries—notably the British Library, the Bodleian Library, and the Newberry Library and the libraries of Colorado College, the University of Colorado, Boulder, and Denver University. I also thank Todd Morrison, Terry Davis, and Tom Stavig for help with the design and execution of my charts and Donna Gianarelli for her assistance in reproducing the text on computer. Albert Labriola of the Duquesne University Press has been supportive and helpful in seeing the manuscript through to publication, and I am also grateful to the senior editor, Susan Wadsworth-Booth, and to my copy editor, Annie Barva, for their close attention to the text. More personal debts are expressed in my dedication.

INTRODUCTION

THESEUS. The poet's eye, in a fine frenzy rolling,
Doth glance from heaven to earth, from earth to heaven;
And as imagination bodies forth
The forms of things unknown, the poet's pen
Turns them to shapes, and gives to aery nothing
A local habitation and a name.
                    (*A Midsummer Night's Dream* 5.1.12–17)

In the primarily public and rational intellectual world of England in the 1590s, interest in the more personal and subjective dimensions of human experience was growing. A skeptical Theseus associates the imagination of the poet (and the reports of the lovers on their night in the wood) with the "frenzy" of madness, but Elizabethan writers were searching for meaningful ways to give "shapes" to the "forms of things unknown," the realm of experience that includes love and can be expressed best, or perhaps only, through metaphor. Describing the mysteries of the night and wood leads to emphasis on the ambivalent cyclical processes of nature rather than on the rational and more rigid structures of the diurnal world. Shakespeare's interest in dramatizing such topics reflects the period's shifting emphases rather than an entirely new course. The language of Theseus's speech

1

reflects familiar issues of philosophy and poetry—the ontological status of Platonic reality and Aristotelean universals, the validity of a symbolic art that uses implausible fictions to express deeper truths, and the ambiguous sources of love and madness in inspiration and illusion.[1]

The forms of "the natural" prove to be complex. Influenced by neoplatonism, writers such as Sidney, Spenser, and Shakespeare wanted to "glance from heaven to earth, from earth to heaven" in order to illuminate cosmic truths; but, influenced by Aristotle and by more empirical approaches to nature and society, they also strove to base their depictions of reality in "A local habitation and a name." The theology and moral philosophy of traditional thought were increasingly pushed to the background as writers sought a more flexible framework at once less controversial and more attuned to life in this world. The particular circumstances of the time encouraged such departures. The traditional gender analysis that privileged reason and masculinity was undergoing a revaluation, reshaping the old associations of femininity with the passion and disorder of nature and the night. Queen Elizabeth, cynosure of the aristocratic culture and ultimate patroness of its fashionable poetry, encouraged responses to both her femininity and her masculine qualities as monarch. Petrarchan sonneteers explored the psychology of love through describing the power of the elevated woman and the emotions of the courtier in love. Poets and playwrights writing about mutability and renewal often emphasized analogies to the cycles of nature. Neoplatonists sought the wisdom and truth that are beyond reason through contemplation of the "dark" mysteries.

In *Romeo and Juliet* and *A Midsummer Night's Dream*, both circa 1595, Shakespeare uses metaphorical structures patterned on the contrarieties and unities of cyclical nature to modify the more hierarchical understanding of people and society. In his use of metaphors of nature to express the complexities of existence, he reflects the period's changing emphasis from, in W. R. Elton's summation, "absolute natural *law* bestowed by God" to "relativistic *natural* law, recognized by man."[2] The old structures are still present, but the shift away from theological and philosophical categories encourages a revision of attitude toward hierarchy itself. Instead of privileging rulers, fathers, and males in general by identifying them with reason and God, Shakespeare relates the structures of the self, love, the family, society, and the cosmos to both the shifting cycles of nature and the longer lasting but still mutable values of hierarchy. Reason and authority are necessary but can become tyrannical, just as "the forms of things unknown" can express an illusory dream as well as a genuine vision. Both plays tell of a diverse group of characters (lovers, parents, rulers, friends, advisors) who struggle with analogous forces in themselves and their world. Shakespeare uses his art to clarify the oppositions of contrarieties but not to resolve their ambiguities.

Scholars have long recognized the connections between the plays: they tell similar stories of passionate young lovers who rebel against fathers dictating unwanted marriages; they both use the conventional love imagery that we think of as Petrarchan and neoplatonic; and they share parallels to the Pyramus and Thisby story presented by Bottom's company. But the tendency of recent scholarship has been to define their dramatic forms as opposite. Scholars praise *Romeo and Juliet* for its realism of plot and characterization and its brilliant poetic language, and *A Midsummer Night's Dream* for its unity of fantasy and symbolism.[3] Older readings of both plays commonly implied reservations while dwelling on their immense popularity, but in recent decades *A Midsummer Night's Dream* has profited from comedy's rise in critical esteem. Critics see the strength of the play in its symbolic attention to play and holiday, dream and nightmare, mythic rituals of renewal, as well as in its self-reflexive commentary on art. *Romeo and Juliet* continues to suffer from comparison with the major tragedies.[4]

We seem to be moving away from the old debate as to whether the tragedy is caused by the erratic passions of the lovers themselves, the destructive feud, or an intervening fate, but critics still charge that the lovers fail to achieve the maturity we expect of tragic figures, that their speeches are too often merely conventional, and that chance plays too large a part in their downfall. In contrast, descriptions of the play's strengths tend to be condescending: speeches that go beyond the conventional are said to foreshadow the mature characterization of the later tragedies, and the story is praised mainly for the emotional power of its linking of youth, love, and death. Attempts at restoring a Renaissance view are still apt to concentrate on the lovers, with the interpretations usually veering toward the medieval or the romantic. By now we have, among other readings, a medieval view of lovers (and feuding parents) as sinners in a fallen but still potentially orderly world, a romantic view of idealized tragic lovers in a chaotic world, and an existential view of maturing lovers trying to make their own meaning in an empty world. In much of the criticism allowances are made because it is "early Shakespeare."

I do not argue that the two plays need to be seen together as a diptych. The differences in setting and style plus Shakespeare's reluctance to link his plays, except in the histories, make that unlikely. *Romeo and Juliet* seems to have been designed for a diverse popular audience whereas *A Midsummer Night's Dream* was apparently first put on for an aristocratic wedding. Treating them together, however, reveals similarities that help us interpret the individual plays and understand the early Shakespeare's conception of tragedy and comedy. The tendency to study the comedies together and the tragedies together can lead to a bifurcated Shakespeare without a larger vision that includes both. In shaping a form for the plays Shakespeare finds ways of satisfying both those looking primarily for entertainment within a traditional framework and others expecting the theater to be a sophisticated place for examining the society's cultural assumptions. In both plays Shakespeare finds ways to criticize excess but also to work out resolutions that are at least not inconsistent with traditional assumptions.

When the plays are studied in this context, their characterization, imagery, and settings can be seen as contributing to similar effects despite their differences. The lightly sketched characters in *A Midsummer Night's Dream* invite a response to them as types while Romeo and Juliet, Friar Lawrence, the Nurse, Tybalt, Mercutio, and Capulet are all presented as sharply individual. But even these fuller depictions, partly the result of tragedy's need for audience involvement with specific people, are based on character types. Shakespearean characterization—even the fairly full development in *Romeo and Juliet*—moves outward to illuminate theme and inward to delineate a gender-based, faculty-oriented psychology of the self. The plays' poetic imagery also tends toward the representative and transforms the verbal into the dramatic.[5] More than in later Shakespearean plays, set speeches and elaborate metaphors call attention to poetic form and encourage reflection about larger frames of reference. Romeo not only sounds like the speaker in a Petrarchan sonnet sequence, he actually becomes the stage embodiment of the sonnet's sensibility as lyric poetry turns narrative and dramatic. Close attention to imagery tends to make the plays more dramatic as the verbal images become a part of a conception at once theatrical and emblematic. Times and settings take on parallel associations in the two plays. *Romeo and Juliet* describes four hot July days ending in predawn tragedy and *A Midsummer Night's Dream* four midsummer (if we think of summer as including spring and summer) days ending in reconciliation and renewal. Although the settings have the exotic appeal of being far removed from England, preclassical Athens and Renaissance Verona turn out to be remarkably similar to each other and to Elizabethan London.

Under the pressure of the critical movements of recent decades, historical study has become more sophisticated about its presuppositions and methods. Recent scholarship has helped us understand the nature of metaphor and the operation of metaphorical systems within the larger structures of philosophy.[6] To be metaphorical is to be symbolic, that is to say, what is signified can never be fully contained in the sign; to use metaphor is to imply a larger structure since the "idea" through metaphor has an inevitable relationship to other ideas. The obverse is also true: to be philosophical is to be metaphorical and therefore symbolic since the language of philosophical discourse requires metaphor for the communication of ideas. The study of the metaphor at the basis of both philosophical and literary texts needs to begin with the signs and structures that are its grammar and syntax and go on to the "immanent structures"[7] that underlie its discourse.

Gaston Bachelard, using an image particularly appropriate to these plays, states: "metaphors are not simple idealizations which take off like rockets only to display their insignificance on bursting in the sky, but . . . on the contrary metaphors summon one another and are more coordinated than sensations, so much so that a poetic mind is purely and simply a syntax of metaphors." He goes on to suggest that "Each poet should then be represented by a *diagram* which would indicate the meaning and the symmetry of his metaphorical coordinations."[8] What may be true of metaphor generally is particularly important for Shakespeare since he writes at a time when a system of metaphor going back to Plato and frequently depicted in diagrams still functioned. Shakespeare's "syntax of metaphors" depends on this familiar system but is modified by a creative imagination, making it a vehicle for fresh exploration that Shakespeare knows will also elicit differing responses.

The study of metaphor requires a historical orientation because metaphors, like the ideas to which they relate, have their own history. If we are to recover what Michel Foucault calls the "discursive formations"[9] that control the assumptions of any time, historical, structural, and semiotic criticism must come together in explicating metaphorical systems. Knowledge of the structures of political and social institutions, of the mind and gender, of myth and genre, and, perhaps most important, of metaphor and language itself leads to fuller awareness of the complexities and ambiguities of texts. Raymond Williams argues that a "dynamic," "complex" relationship exists between the "dominant" culture of a society, the "residual" culture that is passing away, and the "emergent" culture that is coming into being.[10] Since metaphors also have histories, they are subject to what Derrida describes as *"wear and tear"*[11] that erode their value and may eventually destroy their meaning. Finding their historical moment is difficult since both cultures and metaphors may reflect "traces of the lineage" of the past or provide "foreshadowings"[12] of the future.

In this study I have tried to get beyond the *"wear and tear"* to recover and revivify the structures of Shakespearean metaphor in two plays. To accomplish such an examination requires detailed attention to the language of the text in a way that is carefully historical but also makes use of modern scholarly techniques. Critics must try to avoid the tendency to explain the structures and signs of a different culture through modern strategies that distort its traditional insights; they must also question the assumption that the forms and terms of the period itself are the only adequate vehicles for analyzing its culture. Every study, whether based on historical or modern principles, is an experiment in criticism that can claim no final resolution. I want to take advantage of the vast reservoir of learning on Renaissance metaphor but apply it with the awareness that its vitality depends on an often ambivalent complexity resonating at levels from the personal to the cosmic. Shakespeare escapes the rigidities of traditional ideology without sacrificing the rich flexibility provided by conventional metaphor.

One of the virtues of the critical theory loosely termed deconstruction has been its exposure of the weaknesses of several time-honored approaches to Shakespeare: historicism too often seeks out grand syntheses without searching for the tensions that undercut unities; literary history may exploit our older authors in the service of modern liberal values; and literary formalism tends to ignore history altogether in its concentration on the work of art itself. Recent studies have increasingly emphasized breaks rather than continuities—a play's tensions about genre or gender, its self-conscious reflections on the artistic process itself, and its oblique or unconscious revelation of hidden presuppositions. A number of alternative Shakespeares have emerged. We have had plausible readings of these plays that pick out specific patterns and make Shakespeare a critic of the power structure, a spokesman for an emerging materialism, a sympathizer with feminist causes, an analyst of archetypal psychological and anthropological structures, a skillful manager of conflicting semiotic systems, a playful artist staging language games, and a precursor of modern nihilism. Practitioners of the "new history" have used Renaissance principles of analogy and sophisticated techniques of cultural analysis to explore how a seemingly inconsequential incident or episode of the time can sometimes reveal more than the generalizations of traditional scholarship.[13]

The interrogation of conventional assumptions leads toward a Shakespeare whose relationship to the structured views of his time is somewhat analogous to modern deconstruction's relation to structuralism. While Renaissance and modern structuralism differ fundamentally, they both represent attempts to find and express the rational principles that underlie society's institutions and culture. In his analysis of Elizabethan structures of thought, Shakespeare frequently seems to resist overly simple formulations that reinforce the patriarchal culture as he examines such topics as the gender identities of lovers, the justifications for order and rebellion, and the relationship of art to life. Such preoccupations lead Shakespeare to fashionable topics of our own time—gender issues (androgyny and bisexuality, shifting male and female roles, gender analogies in society and nature); the structures of the mind, the family, society, and nature; and the ways art and language both reflect and influence how we understand these relationships. Jonathan Culler describes the program of deconstruction in such terms: "Since deconstruction attempts to view systems from the outside as well as the inside, it tries to keep alive the possibility that the eccentricity of women, poets, prophets, and madmen might yield truths about the system to which they are marginal—truths contradicting the consensus and not demonstrable within a framework yet developed."[14]

How far Shakespeare's deconstructive impulse leads is at issue. His critique of his world runs deep in these plays. By his omission of references to a personal God and by his reluctance to impose moral categories on human behavior, he draws back from the specifically Christian version of traditional ideology. If there is no personal God who takes an active role in human affairs, then the existence of God-given structures is inevitably called into question. By presenting a Friar Lawrence who is more concerned about the natural than the supernatural and an Oberon with limited awareness and questionable motives, and by including rulers and fathers who are a major cause of the problems, Shakespeare encourages revaluation of the traditional society itself. By showing the significance of the feminine in every dimension of life and suggesting that each sex has gender components of the opposite sex, Shakespeare quite specifically opens up the whole question of gender identity. Although his retention of "masculine" and "feminine" as stable categories that are apparently more than just social constructions suggests a kind of essentialism, he might legitimately be regarded as having sympathy for an Elizabethan version of "male feminism."[15] When women are seen as having a masculine reason and men as having feminine passions, what constitutes their basic selves or their differences is open to discussion.

From a Renaissance perspective, Shakespeare's tendencies are clearly liberating even if not antiessentialist. His analytical mind seems constantly to be searching for ironies and ambiguities that undercut rigid formulations, and he might even agree with postmodern analyses that define societal structures by reference to cultural rather than natural forces.[16] Even though his metaphorical patterns have archetypal overtones apt to make postmodern readers uneasy, his intention seems to be to find a less controversial and more flexible framework that will encourage diversity of analysis and response. Metaphor is useful for communication but does not require belief. Since Shakespeare makes less detailed use of such patterns in his later plays, we should draw back from seeing them as providing his view of the world. What we can say is that his analogical approach helps redefine the relationships of marriage and the family and of social and political structures. From a modern perspective he helps deconstruct the forms of an excessively patriarchal society, but attention to the patterns of metaphor in the plays suggests that what Shakespeare actually does is valorize the feminine polarity of an older gender system based ultimately on the natural world.

Studying Shakespeare as an artist of the 1590s allows us to better understand the complexity of Elizabethan culture. London in the early 1590s was a bustling center of activity, but the older image of optimistic vitality needs to be balanced by the realities of threatening disorder. England as an international power was taken more seriously after the Spanish fleet's debacle in 1588, but concern about maintaining state power was mounting, partly because of the uncertain succession. Commerce was booming but was also bringing disruptive changes. In retrospect, we can see that literary London was thriving, but the struggle for aspiring young authors was considerable. The sonnet cycle that had started slowly in the 1580s with Watson and Sidney became a fashionable form. Narrative poetry influenced by Ovid, historical drama celebrating the English past, sophisticated court comedy in the tradition of Lyly, Roman comedy, romantic comedy, and Senecan tragedy were all competing for attention. Shakespeare, one of a large group of young poets and dramatists, was trying his hand in all of these areas and by 1595 had accumulated a remarkable and diverse list of contributions, but his preeminence was by no means assured.

If we are to understand the Shakespeare of *Romeo and Juliet* and *A Midsummer Night's Dream*, we should see him as a working professional responsive to the intellectual, political, and literary climate of his time. As Leonard Tennenhouse reminds us, "during the Renaissance, political imperatives were also aesthetic imperatives."[17] In the London of the mid-1590s this meant being sensitive not only to a Queen Elizabeth with strong personal views but also to an aristocracy looking for ways to please her. As Tennenhouse points out, dramatists responded with increased emphasis on active women like Juliet and Hermia who express their desires more openly and on rulers like Theseus who may have something to learn about the basis of wise government.[18] Shakespeare challenges and entertains his sophisticated audience without revealing his own views. We should expect the excitement of imaginative art that enriches through presenting fresh insights but ultimately puts them into what is at least formally a traditional context.

Impulses toward both diversity and unity characterize Elizabethan attitudes toward themselves, their world, and their cosmos. Diversity is apparent in the variety of

philosophical traditions competing for attention, and we
should not oversimplify their views in the name of some
coherent world picture. But to concentrate on contradictions may lead to underestimating the Renaissance
mind's facility for subsuming dualities in larger syntheses. We have heard so much about analogical thinking
and planes of correspondence that many think of them as
the cliches that original artists had to grow beyond.[19]
Such traditional ways of describing the world were,
however, undergoing a resurgence in combination with
revitalized strains of Petrarchism and neoplatonism.
Petrarch's English followers found ways of building
cosmological, political, and psychological implications
into their structure and language; the Petrarchan mode
became fashionable for more than literary reasons.
Frances Yates and others have helped us understand the
magical and spiritual side of Renaissance neoplatonism
that lies behind many attitudes toward love and mystery,
and we also need to remember that English neoplatonism
continues to be influenced by philosophical fusions as
ancient as Augustine.[20] Shakespeare was also deeply
rooted in the more popular influences of English tradition. Celebrating a periodic freedom from patriarchal
order and reason belongs to a heritage of holiday and
carnival appropriate for the theater.[21] Shakespeare is alert
to the follies of excess, irrationality, and illusion but also
understands that the release of natural impulses can
contribute to order. He writes as he does because he is
responsive to new ways of describing the world and because as artist he can relate fresh insights to old wisdom.

Other writers of the time reflect similar preoccupations. Even though both were dead by 1593, Sidney and
Marlowe remained influential in shaping the issues and
tone of intellectual discourse. Sidney contributed his
enormous authority to Petrarchan poetry and to the fusion of neoplatonic critical ideals with the practical concerns of the Aristoteleans. He retains the structure of
neoplatonic goals but self-consciously attempts to make

his writing relevant to the problems of this world. In "Astrophil and Stella" he seems more interested in probing the psychological states of lovers than in either philosophical analysis or moral judgment.[22] Marlowe is more interested in power than love, but his depiction of fascinating overreachers who challenge the old orthodoxies broadened the scope of the theater's role as a place for comment on the issues facing society.[23] Spenser and Donne are perhaps even better examples of the period's vitality: both examine the specific within a larger intellectual framework that they modify in their own ways. Spenser's shorter poetry, much of it published in the 1590s, and *The Faerie Queene* (1590, 1596) reflect an elaborate "structure of imagery" based on approaches that are often similar to the patterns described in this book.[24] Donne is more preoccupied with religious issues than either Spenser or Shakespeare, but his *Songs and Sonets*, many of which seem to be from the 1590s, reveals both the absurdities and the profundities of the Petrarchists and the neoplatonists.[25]

A full study of Shakespeare's relationship to these strains would require extended analysis of much of his early work. That is impossible here, but I do want to indicate their relevance to this study. In *The Two Gentlemen of Verona*, Shakespeare explores how to combine popular romance motifs with the imagery and themes of Petrarchan poetry. In *Love's Labour's Lost*, he satirizes the absurdities of young lovers but manages to suggest that love remains a positive value. Both *Venus and Adonis* and *The Rape of Lucrece* make extensive use of imagery of cyclical nature and describe without final judgment the contradictions and frustrations caused by analogous forces in our selves, the world, and the cosmos. The sonnets explore ways of overcoming time and mutability and of presenting the complexities of the self. My working assumption is that Shakespeare would have been aware of the new fashions in poetry and philosophy but that he was not advocating any particular point of view. We can never be sure whether he is taking advantage of an intellectual fashion or describing his own ideas. All we can do is pay attention to the various patterns that emerge in the works themselves.

All of this literary activity by Shakespeare and others establishes a context for *Romeo and Juliet* and *A Midsummer Night's Dream*. In part 1, I describe Shakespeare's version of the traditional metaphorical system based on the analogical relationships between the cycles in life and nature and the hierarchies that were thought to give the cycles meaning. My primary conclusions can be simply stated: these patterns provide a richer and more flexible description of the world than is commonly thought, even by scholars who accept that historical scholarship is essential for understanding Shakespearean drama; the underestimation of the metaphorical system's value results partly from failing to remember that it outlines patterns of analogies and metaphors that grew gradually over the centuries and were never intended as a scientific system; and the general scheme was used in widely different ways by artists and thinkers of Shakespeare's own time. Although the interaction of cycles and hierarchies is fundamental in Renaissance descriptions of the world, those supporting an absolute authority in politics and religion are more likely to emphasize the hierarchical and to rely on a masculine God-sun-monarch-father-reason paradigm. Those concerned about the dangers of patriarchal power tend to talk less about God's love and religion and more about earthly love and seeking out balances of masculine and feminine (ruler-subjects, parents-children, husband-wife) that will make society function effectively. Readers who know the Renaissance world well will be able to skip and skim after they have understood my method and the basic structure that I am outlining. For others, part 1 can serve as an introduction to Renaissance metaphor and a reference guide for help in understanding my readings of the plays themselves.

When I move to the plays, I show how Shakespeare uses these flexible patterns in developing the fundamental rhythms in the plays' structures. *Romeo and Juliet* (my subject in part 2) begins with the extreme behavior of Romeo and others in Verona (chapter 2), shifts toward illusory promises of resolution (chapter 3), hesitates between the joy of hope and the woe of disaster (chapter 4), and finally moves inexorably toward the final tragedy (chapter 5). *A Midsummer Night's Dream* (part 3) opens with frustrated Athenian attempts to resolve issues of law and love (chapter 6), introduces an analogously disrupted fairyland (chapter 7), depicts the chaotic night in the wood that results from these disorders (chapter 8), and finally reveals a restored though not entirely ideal order (chapter 9). In both plays, metaphorical patterns based on cycles and hierarchies shape our responses to the central themes of love and to the movements toward tragedy or resolution. Shakespeare proves to be highly skilled in developing dramatic forms suited to a sophisticated audience interested in issues of gender and power. His balanced approach may suggest a point of view but allows considerable diversity of response.

PART 1

Cycles and Hierarchies

ONE

Cycles and Hierarchies

In the springing of the dawning, flowres that be closed,
open: and hearbes and grasse, that wither and fade in
great heat, arise and reare vp theyr heads. In the
dawning vertue and strength of wit and of feeling be
comforted. In the dawning sicknesse of beasts is lighted
and abated. For in the dawning, sanguine humour hath
principall mastry.

> (Batman vppon Bartholome,
> *De Proprietatibus Rerum*, 1582, C4v)

S hakespeare may have used the patterns of cycles and
hierarchies that this study describes simply because
they provided an appropriate metaphorical context for
Romeo and Juliet's story of the revolt of idealistic young
lovers against the authority of their feuding families.
The preoccupation of both old and young with issues of
love and family honor, the lovers' clandestine night

19

meetings and dawn separations, and the central role of a practical friar in trying to fuse natural magic and traditional morality lead easily, perhaps almost inevitably, to the metaphorical stress on the cycles of nature and the interactions of gender. The themes of *A Midsummer Night's Dream* seem to be shaped largely by *Romeo and Juliet*: the continuing concern with similar patterns demonstrates the connection between the plays but does not indicate to what extent the patterns are the result of shared but largely unquestioned assumptions of the period or of Shakespeare's more self-conscious attempt to work out their implications. What is evident is that the play's metaphorical structures would be of particular interest to those who were alert to the intellectual issues of the day. As I will be demonstrating in my detailed analysis of the plays, Shakespeare retains a hierarchical basis for his analysis but modifies it in ways that allow the play to become in part a critique of his society.

My charts began inductively and developed gradually as a part of my attempt to describe Shakespearean patterns of metaphor for my students. They are based on charts of the period, but I include more detail than is present on any one chart, and I often depend on references to other texts. I am working with metaphor, not science, and the charts should be regarded as guides rather than as absolutes. Some items, for example some of the passions and virtues, could fit in more than one place, and some reshaping is necessary in order to clarify the analogies. The principles of hierarchy can be charted in different ways: although some conception of the great chain of being that links the natural to the supernatural is implied, I follow Shakespeare in being more concerned with analogies that exist within the human and natural realms.

The primary advantage of the charts is that I am able to define a framework that would have been easily accessible to an audience of the time but is likely to be overlooked or ignored by modern readers. Our modern or postmodern suspicion of structure can lead to skepticism about approaches that, viewed historically, helped to break down overly rigid conceptions. Most Renaissance writers working with analogical views of nature were interested in illustrating both the diversity and the unity of a cosmos that cannot be understood by scientific methods. They began with the assumption that we live in a complex universe that is governed by principles of plenitude and analogy. Metaphor was thought of as a necessary means of revealing the paradoxical relationships in an intricately constructed cosmos where order and harmony underlie apparent conflict and discord.[1] Any interpretation is ultimately subjective, but, as I have argued in my introduction, an approach through historical semiotics—the study of the signs and structures of a text in its own time—offers a promising method for combining cultural and linguistic scholarship. In this part, I describe the patterns of metaphor that are relevant to an interpretation of *Romeo and Juliet* and *A Midsummer Night's Dream*. After a discussion of time and love, I proceed to separate sections and charts on cycles (pp. 31–42) and hierarchies (pp. 42–53), and finally to an analysis of how the individual relates to the two together (pp. 53–56).

Reality in the Renaissance cosmos still included for most people both a material and a spiritual dimension. To explain the connections between the two requires facing the ultimate questions about the origins and purposes of the cosmos and our world's position in time and space. Theological and philosophical explanations inherited from classical and Christian thought remained influential even though changes in emphasis were appearing. Implicit in most views was a basic distinction between one realm that is temporal, mutable, and imperfect and another that is eternal, unchanging, and perfect. Various dualistic concepts and terms—time and eternity, becoming and being, nature and grace, and cycles and hierarchies—are ultimately based on this split. A relationship between the two realms is possible through the power of love, the divine force that initiates creation in time and space, motivates its continuing patterns, and overcomes its tendencies toward decay and destruction. Time is cyclical, linear, and horizontal, but love—both the divine *agape* that descends and the earthly *eros* that rises—is vertical and counteracts temporal emptiness through its higher values.[2]

Plato and Aristotle established the framework for the discussion of both time and love.[3] Plato believed that the regular motions of the heavens bring about the periodic return of the stars and planets to their original positions (the moon in a month, the sun in a year, the system itself in a great year). Even though he included no sense of linear progression because the cycles are repetitive, for Plato time is positive. As the "moving image of eternity,"[4] it suggests the order and perfection that guide people toward a fuller conception of beauty and goodness. Although our sublunar realm of change or becoming is a flawed copy of the perfect and timeless being of the eternal, we can progress toward knowledge of the eternal through an aspiring love (*eros*) that eventually leads to an understanding of the divine forms themselves. Aristotle tended to ignore the larger metaphysical questions about both time and love. Unlike Plato, who concerned himself with the correspondences between our universe and the divine ideas, Aristotle described reality as material and thought of Plato's forms as abstractions or generalizations without metaphysical being. He described the physical universe as a scale of being that rises from the inanimate to animals to people to spirits to some sort of prime mover but did not postulate any force (like love) that would allow people to rise above their place. He saw time as a measure of motion and directed his attention to the specifics of movement and continuity. Much of the story of Western philosophy has been the attempt to work out a fusion of these apparently irreconcilable theories. In the eclectic Renaissance the disagreement or tension between them was commonly overcome by giving each authority in his own acknowledged area.

The Judeo-Christian view, apparently residual in Shakespeare but no doubt still dominant in many in his audience, is reflected most clearly in Augustine, who draws a sharp distinction between the eternal realm of God and the temporal realm of the created universe and man. In Augustine's hierarchical scheme, people are inferior to everything eternal but superior to the sensible universe because their souls are immortal. Augustine makes God personal and good and sees time as primarily linear rather than cyclical: a loving God created the world in time, chose a people to work out His plans in history, sent Christ at a specific point in time to become mankind's savior, and will end the world and time itself with the second coming and the day of judgment.[5] Since God or Providence directs the whole pattern, the order of time is meaningful even though nature and mankind are fallen. The world is an arena where people can see God's power and goodness and can participate, with the help of God's loving grace (*agape*), in the divine plan. People have the opportunity, indeed the responsibility, to judge the temporal world and determine their roles in it. When they use the individual moments of time constructively (*eros*), life becomes a meaningful pattern that reflects the eternal. But people are ultimately dependent on God's grace; time, though potentially redemptive, remains destructive because of the continuing effects of the Fall. Augustine's formulations became normative and were still influential in the Renaissance, even among those for whom the explicitly Christian version required modification.

Some medieval thinkers, indebted to Averrhoes and Aristotle, tried to modify Augustine's view that time has become a part of the corrupted order of this world. They saw time as positive, with some even suggesting that the world itself is eternal. Scholastic philosophy secularized the concept of *aevum*, a term that describes the middle realm of the angels, who are neither co-eternal with God nor subject to the mutability of the world; and the emphasis shifted toward seeing time as a continuum both

endless and dynamic. Although the church opposed this
trend because it altered the Christian interpretation of
history, gradually the stress on time as positive and potentially creative fused with the orthodox belief in the
split between time and eternity. This emerging attitude
gave more status to *eros* and became the basis for a view
of individual action that stresses the continuity and reli-
ability of experience.[6]

This medieval discussion is reflected in the Renaissance debate about the role of love and the deterioration
of the world. Many saw no reason to change the traditional view. Christians with this perspective thought
that the only question was when God will choose to end
a world that has been corrupt since the Fall. Pessimists
developed a Christian version of the theory that the gold-
en age had descended through ages of silver and brass to
an age of iron as the world deteriorated.[7] They thought
the spread of sin would bring the world's destruction
and that God's redemptive love is meaningful primarily
as the means of salvation. Still others, including many
Christians, accepted a more positive view of time and
love and argued for a progressive view of mankind's possibilities. They believed we can begin to understand the
spiritual and material forces that underlie the cosmos
and apply this knowledge to the improvement of our
world. Such thinkers often stressed cyclical process—the
rhythms of a nature and universe filled with God's love
and concern. Since individual lives include these same
rhythms, people should seek an understanding of themselves and their world that will encompass this broad vision. Such an approach is less urgent about salvation and
more positive about this world. Despite their different
emphases, these Renaissance views remain similar in
important respects: they all trust in the efficacy of love
and think of the line of time as at once cyclical and
linear. The point of the present moves both linearly toward a final end and cyclically through the repetition of
seasons and years.[8]

I have developed three charts that describe how Renaissance thinkers and artists dealt with these issues: two concern the cycles of life in this world and one the hierarchies that relate this world to higher, ultimately eternal, values. (See the charts on cycles on pages 27, 29 and the Metaphors of Hierarchies chart on p. 31.) My charts are unabashedly syncretic and therefore more useful for my purpose, which is to explain a metaphorical system. Metaphors of analogy are particularly useful for dramatists because they call attention to similarities without asserting specific causal relationships; thus the cycles of life are like the cycles of the seasons and days largely because the same forces operate at all levels of existence. The metaphorical system also encourages the association of the passions with the humours, seasons, and ages of life, but the dramatist need not demonstrate the connection. For a working dramatist interested in depicting readily understandable characters and situations, the advantage of such analogies is apparent. Type characters—the melancholic lover, the bold knight, the wrathful father—will be recognizable as more than oversimplifications. Settings—a moon-lit orchard on a July night, dawn in a wood—will translate easily to significant metaphor. That dramatists make use of such expectations may tell us more about dramatic conventions and techniques than about their acceptance of the philosophical, physiological, and psychological bases of the theory, but they at least understood that analogical patterns can reinforce and broaden audience responses.

The first chart on cycles (Cycles) pulls together material from actual charts of the time. Their descriptions of the analogical structures of the physical world outline a psychological and cosmological system that influenced the Western world until well into the Renaissance. In Christianity the dualism of heaven and hell and of good and evil shaped ways of understanding the positive and negative dimensions of nature—day and night, summer and winter, and the sun and the moon. In more scientific

systems, traceable to early Greek thought but sharing
assumptions with the myths of many societies, the numerical basis of the analogical structures was more apt
to be four or seven even though a dualistic tendency remains. In my chart's inner circles (one through four) is
the ancient tetrad, which starts with the four elements
and develops analogies to other divisions into four—the
qualities, the humours, the seasons, the parts of the day,
and the ages of life. The second segment (circles five and
six) moves from the mundane realities of the tetrad to
describe the analogous order based on the seven planets.
The ages of life and the days of the week (see the small
inset)[9] as well as colors and metals are all linked to the
planets. The outer circle brings in the zodiac, whose description of the twelve constellations relates both to the
order of four (the seasons that govern the dating of the
signs) and to the order of seven (the association of the
signs with the sun, the moon, and the planets). While the
emphasis varied depending on the scheme being used,
eclectic Renaissance thinkers and artists shifted easily
from one numerical base to another, thus making a single chart possible.

Charts describing cycles will tend to be horizontal and
this-worldly since the line of time repeats itself without
any implication of vertical or transcendent meaning; recurring sunrises and springs are meaningless in and of
themselves. Although the more religious of the period
would of course accept the cyclical basis of life, their
tendency was to minimize gender issues and to see the
love of God as the only means of ascent to higher values.
The more secular were more apt to stress the importance
of the feminine and to see love as a spiritual but not exclusively religious force activated through the marriage
or balance of gender qualities. My second cycles chart
(Metaphors of Cycles) adjusts the first one in order to
relate these metaphorical associations to the chart on
Cycles: the left side becomes explicitly feminine, the right
masculine, the top positive, and the bottom negative.

CYCLES

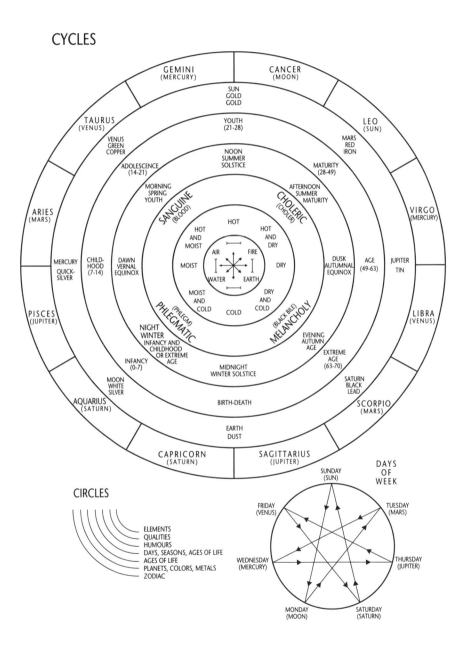

CIRCLES

ELEMENTS
QUALITIES
HUMOURS
DAYS, SEASONS, AGES OF LIFE
AGES OF LIFE
PLANETS, COLORS, METALS
ZODIAC

Turning the inner three circles of Cycles (condensed into circles one and two of Metaphors of Cycles) slightly to the right puts the most positive humour (the sanguine) and qualities (heat and moisture) at the top and the most negative humour (melancholy), element (earth), and qualities (coldness and dryness) at the bottom. Circle four of Cycles (circle three of Metaphors of Cycles) does not shift: the polar oppositions of noon and midnight (and the solstices) and the positive emphasis on youth and maturity need to remain. Turning circle six (circle four of Metaphors of Cycles) slightly makes Venus and the sun equally positive and supports the overall division into masculine and feminine. When we remember that the day and year are hottest after noon and the solstice, having the sun at the upper right seems appropriate.

In circles five, six, and seven of Metaphors of Cycles, I use slanted lines to indicate that the top can also be negative and the bottom positive. This distinction is of crucial importance in defining how the complexity of the Shakespearean metaphorical vision reflects Renaissance thought. The light, heat, and moisture of the physical world are only potentially positive since after the Fall they remain in perpetual danger of misuse by people who live openly by worldly values or deceive themselves that their illusions of a higher life have genuine validity. At the opposite pole darkness, coldness, and dryness, though basically negative, can encourage the purgation that leads to physical renewal and / or spiritual understanding. Melancholy and Saturn belong at the very bottom of the chart since both have strong metaphorical associations with all that is physically dark, dry, cold, empty, and dead or that is spiritually powerful and / or frightening. It is the metaphorical time for despair or for spiritual illumination.[10]

What becomes apparent in the Metaphors of Cycles chart is the need for fusing the positive feminine and masculine qualities: the moon and night must be in harmony with the sun and day; the combination of moisture

METAPHORS
OF
CYCLES

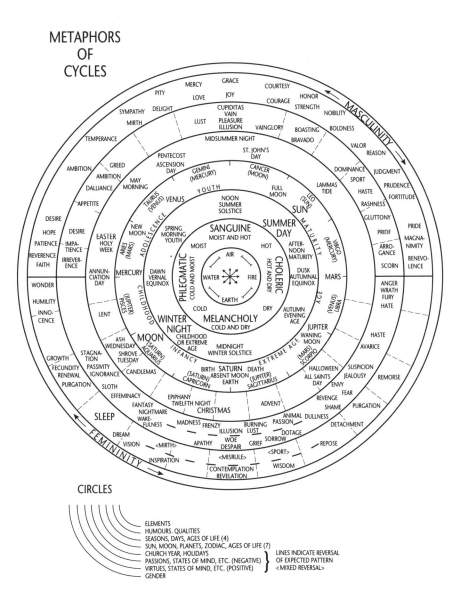

CIRCLES

ELEMENTS
HUMOURS. QUALITIES
SEASONS, DAYS, AGES OF LIFE (4)
SUN, MOON, PLANETS, ZODIAC, AGES OF LIFE (7)
CHURCH YEAR, HOLIDAYS
PASSIONS, STATES OF MIND, ETC. (NEGATIVE)
VIRTUES, STATES OF MIND, ETC. (POSITIVE)
GENDER

LINES INDICATE REVERSAL
OF EXPECTED PATTERN
<MIXED REVERSAL>

and heat is ideal; the freshness of the regenerating dawn and spring and the maturing fruition of noon and summer are both necessary. Blurring the exact analogy between the humours and the seasons or periods of the day is an unavoidable result of shifting sanguinity to the top, but my chart seems closer to Renaissance metaphor even if it departs somewhat from symmetry. (I should also add that not everyone agreed about which season belongs with which humour.)[11]

The third chart (Metaphors of Hierarchies, p. 31) is structured by similar assumptions about gender and light and is designed to be congruent with the Metaphors of Cycles chart. Nevertheless some differences are apparent. The Cycles charts suggest moral patterns that are clearly applicable to the cycles of the year and the ages of life but can be confusing when applied to a single day and night. Old people go into the winter (or night) of their lives, but young people, usually sanguine because of their age, are not usually associated with the debility of winter. Their qualities fit better with the moral associations of the Metaphors of Hierarchies chart, which concentrates on the moment of individual action rather than on longer cycles of time. In this scheme, darkness and night are linked to effeminacy, passion, and evil. If we think of these patterns as reflecting a different though related set of metaphors, we are less likely to be confused. That heaven and morality are bright, and hell and immorality dark is an overriding metaphorical conception frequently taking precedence over all other associations. Thus, lusty behavior, which from one perspective results from the vitality of youth, is placed morally in the realm of darkness defined by the lower left of the Hierarchies chart.

In general, the Cycles charts can be seen as more neutral morally since their patterns reflect nature itself, while the Hierarchies chart is more closely linked with specific cultural values. The hierarchies suggest a meaningful structure of analogical relationships within and

METAPHORS
OF
HIERARCHIES

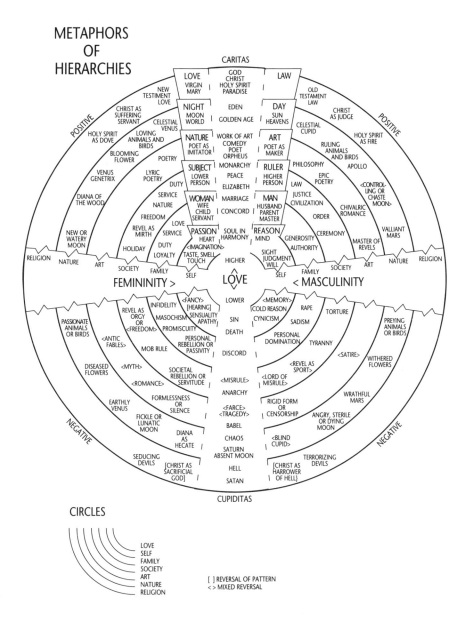

CARITAS

CIRCLES

LOVE
SELF
FAMILY
SOCIETY
ART
NATURE
RELIGION

[ ] REVERSAL OF PATTERN
< > MIXED REVERSAL

among the self, the family, society, nature, and the cosmos. The orientation is vertical but not necessarily otherworldly since the religious or supernatural level can be omitted (as Shakespeare does in most of his plays). While the whole scheme is based on traditional philosophical and theological thought that includes the concept of God, there is no necessary connection with a Christian God or divinely revealed religion. Many who attempted to find a rational basis for hierarchical structures deliberately ignored the supernatural or religious dimension, at least in their philosophizing. In implying that both cycles and hierarchies are this-worldly, Shakespeare follows this secular tradition.

CYCLES

The traditional tetrad of the elements and humours, depicted in the inner circles of my charts on cycles, forms the basis of the entire system. In the late sixteenth century, the scheme described here was both widely known and still generally accepted, and I do not propose to go into a detailed summary of matters that many modern scholars have explicated.[12] The basis of the scheme is cyclical. Since fire and water have no direct way of interacting positively, their qualities must achieve their fusion in other elements (air and earth). Water moistens the cold, dry earth and then is warmed by the heat in air, but drying from fire leads inevitably to a return to earth. Just as the macrocosm—the universe—is made up of four elements that ideally are in harmony, so people's bodies are sustained by four humours or fluids. Thus both water and phlegm are cold and moist, air and blood are hot and moist, fire and choler are hot and dry, and earth and black bile are cold and dry. Heat and moisture are the positive physical forces that vitalize both people and the universe; their opposites—coldness and dryness—result in inactivity and finally death. The combination of humours varies in each individual, thereby producing the different psychological types: phlegmatic, sanguine, choleric, and melancholic.

A complicated interplay of physiological, psychological, and ethical factors controls behavior.[13] The humours are affected by the blend of heat and moisture in the climate, food, and drink, by the level and kind of physical and mental activity, and by the changes in the body as it grows older. They in turn influence the passions. Someone sanguine in humour tends toward hot and moist passions such as love and joy; someone choleric, toward anger and rashness; someone melancholic, toward grief and fear. The humours are also influenced by the passions. Moved by the senses, the reason can initiate a passion and through the will dictate the sending of the appropriate humour to the heart. Joy causes the sanguine humour (blood) to open the heart and warm and moisten the body, whereas grief and melancholy close the heart and lead to cooling and drying. The body's response in turn encourages the passion that originally produced it, thus repeating the process and making a reversal more difficult. When the sanguine or choleric humour becomes excessive, it may undergo adustion (burning) that transforms the natural temperament to an unnatural melancholy. The result—melancholy adust—differs from natural melancholy in being hot and dry rather than cold and dry: it encourages passionate behavior that reflects in a more extreme way the heat of the sanguine and choleric temperaments. The victim of love-melancholy is often a basically sanguine person who has gone through adustion. Despite the power of these reactions, a new impulse from the reason can initiate another change: lovers like Romeo swing between the sanguine and the melancholic.

The scheme is not in theory deterministic since the reason remains capable of independent choice, but stressing the complexities of causation means that dogmatic answers are less possible. Inevitably, differences of

opinion will exist about which force—a person's natural
humour, humours influenced by outside factors such as
diet and climate, passions that affect the humours, or
free will controlled by reason—has the dominant influence. Moralists continue to emphasize people's responsibility for their choices, and Renaissance thinkers tend to
stay within that general framework.[14]

The passions and emotions (also, related virtues, vices,
and states of mind) are depicted in circles six and seven
of the Metaphors of Cycles chart. The two circles, one
positive and the other negative, help illustrate that, despite the power of humours and passions, people do retain their ability to choose. Someone influenced by a
sanguine humour may behave lustfully and selfishly or
lovingly and altruistically. The fire of the choleric can either purge the self of ties to the physical world or increase anger, envy, and rashness. Natural melancholy can
lead to sorrow and despair or to detachment, contemplation, and spirituality, and the unnatural melancholy that
results from adustion can produce destructive passions
such as lust and madness. (Such an account helps clarify
how passions can be associated both with the improper
use of the day and with the dark passions of an evil
night, conventionally the time when personal excesses
are most likely to occur.) The water of the phlegmatic
properly purges, restores, and prepares for new growth
but can also influence a lapse into sloth.

A proper relation to the cycles can lead to a healthy
and natural use of the seasons, days, and the various
stages of life, while an improper use can make each time
period disastrous.[15] People lacking commitment to higher
values will follow the negative circle of the passions. In a
fallen world all people must struggle constantly if they
are to achieve and maintain a place on the proper circle,
but in drama the simplifications of art are apt to lead to
clearer depictions of the motivations described in ethical
and psychological theory. If one's goals are unworthy or
illusory, the wheel of life that represents the ages of man

becomes a wheel of fortune.[16] Though youthful vigor or material wealth may bring about pleasure or apparent success, fortune will inevitably cause a fall, if not in this world, then in the next.

In the rising part of any cycle, people should involve themselves in achieving the natural fruition of positive personal and societal goals but stay off fortune's wheel by recognizing that a just evaluation is based on our motivation rather than on success or failure. In the falling part of the cycle, people should detach themselves from worldly decay and find values that either transcend this world or else emphasize the earthly renewal a new cycle will bring. Traditional winter festivities restore confidence about both this world and the next. Christmas transforms a cold, dark time into a spiritual triumph, but its celebrations also recognize the reviving life of the gradually lengthening days. The chaotic impulses of the dark and the renewed vitality of nature are both subsumed within a larger framework of order that at least in theory becomes stronger through allowing a release for passions that might otherwise threaten destruction.

Renaissance scholars do not always emphasize the cyclical nature of the tetrad of elements and humours because they are often more concerned with other issues, for example the ascent from base, heavy, and material earth to pure, light, and spiritual fire. But the order of the elements clearly suggests the cycle of the day and of the seasons (circle three of Metaphors of Cycles). People in all cultures and times have found a reassuring order in the analogies of days and seasons. The parallels between morning and spring, afternoon and summer, evening and autumn, and night and winter are apparent, and the more subtle parallels between noon = midnight and the solstices and between dawn = dusk and the equinoxes are apparent to close observers. The rains of spring and the dew of the morning bring renewed life to the cold, dry earth of winter and night. Then the sun of spring, summer, and day brings growth and vitality. Finally the gradual drying and cooling period of late summer and afternoon takes the world back to the dry and cold of winter and night.

Each life also follows a cycle through the humours. Children are at first naturally phlegmatic but, as heat and moisture increase, become sanguine in the prime of life. As people age, their bodies dry and cool, and older people are naturally first choleric and finally melancholic.[17] One's individual humour is of crucial importance in determining temperament, but cyclical process is also at work. Thus someone who is sanguine by nature may be as physically vital at 60 as someone melancholic is at 40. Women, because they are more moist than men, are apt to become rheumy and lethargic (phlegmatic) rather than choleric as they grow older, but they may also go through the masculine part of the cycle.[18]

The rhythm of the humours within the body reverses the expected analogical scheme. The cyclical pattern is still present, but day is associated with the consumption and depletion of energy, evening and night with its restoration through dining, digestion, relaxation, and sleep. From one perspective sleep is a little death because of the loss of consciousness, but from another it provides the revitalization of the body by increasing its moisture and heat. Thus it is appropriate to think of 6 P.M. to midnight as the phlegmatic time, midnight to 6 A.M. as sanguine, 6 A.M. to noon as choleric, and noon to 6 P.M. as melancholic. (In another version each period is moved up three hours so the phlegmatic time begins at 3 P.M., the sanguine at 9 P.M., the choleric at 3 A.M., and the melancholic at 9 A.M.) No doubt the different designations for time periods have something to do with a society's working, eating, and sleeping habits; each person's temperament will also have an effect. Shakespeare's depiction of a choleric Tybalt at 9 A.M. in the opening scene of *Romeo and Juliet* and of a sanguine Romeo and Juliet so energized by love that they skip both sleep and noon dinners becomes more meaningful in this general context.[19]

The most common division of the ages of life was into

four or seven periods, largely because of the analogies to
the four seasons and the seven planets.[20] The division
into seven—infancy, childhood, adolescence, youth or
early adulthood, maturity, age, and decrepit age—presents a fuller description of life's stages and permits references to the planets but loses the easy analogy to days,
seasons, and humours. The division into four always includes youth, maturity, and age, with the fourth, the period analogous to winter and night, sometimes being
childhood and sometimes extreme age. Both childhood
and extreme age fit the paradigm, though somewhat awk-
wardly since neither seems to need a full quadrant to itself. The disagreement parallels the old debate about
whether the day begins at midnight or dawn and the year
around the time of the winter solstice or the vernal equi-
nox. Seeing childhood as a period of predawn preparation
for life accords with thinking of the sun as beginning its
return journey at midnight and at the winter solstice, but
extending age and delaying birth have their own empirical logic in the facts of darkness and cold. In *The Shepherd's Calendar*, Spenser connects old age with February:
it fits "with the season of the month, the year now
drooping, and as it were drawing to his last age."[21]

I have already noted the relationship of the planets
(circle six of Cycles) to the ages of life (circle five), but I
also want to clarify the relationship of the planets and
stars to cyclical analogies in general and to the zodiac
(circle seven). Although belief in some ancient patterns,
such as the influence of the gods of the planets on the
hours or the days of the week, was fading, Don Cameron
Allen, in his authoritative summary, *The Star-Crossed
Renaissance*,[22] concludes that almost everyone agreed
that the heavens do have a significant influence on both
nature and people. Even such reputable scholars as Bacon
and Raleigh were careful not to dismiss astrological influence. But acceptance of its importance does not lead
automatically to acceptance of the judicial astrology
involved in horoscopes and predictions. Many took the

position that further scientific study would clarify the extent and nature of the influences. A widely accepted view was that, though the stars incline people in certain directions, they never determine human actions because outside forces cannot control moral decisions. Shakespeare is not much interested in the subtleties of astrology,[23] but he constantly refers to Renaissance beliefs about the cosmos and its influence.

As the dominant force in the physical universe, the sun is commonly associated with the most positive features of the cosmos, but examination from a cyclical perspective that emphasizes gender reveals the ambiguities of masculinity as well as the perfections of divinity.[24] Some limitations of the sun as a symbol seem inherent: its physicality makes it seem less plausible as the embodiment of the transcendence, spirituality, and wisdom of the divine; its intense heat makes it seem incomplete without the moisture associated with the feminine moon (or with masculine gods of storms and rain). It should ideally play a positive role analogous to that of God, the monarch, the father, and reason. Light, heat, power, and regularity do link it to the beneficence, strength, and order of divinity and patriarchy; and the literal and metaphorical illumination of its light and inspiration of its heat also embody central truths of the cosmos. Its life-engendering heat combines with moisture to produce the growth of sanguinity and then through the drying of the next stage of the cycle the bounty of harvest. But the sun governs the natural world imperfectly after the Fall: its heat too often becomes a threat rather than an aid to moisture. When the sun's role is viewed as only one part of the cycles of life, its power is diminished and can be seen as needing to join its efforts with those of the watery and feminine moon. Just as reason should direct but not subdue the passions, so the sun must work in harmony with the moon.

Treating the sun as less than perfect may seem vaguely heretical, but the moon has always had an ambiguous reputation.[25] Identified with the tides and with moisture generally, the cold and watery moon is associated with the phlegmatic humour. In its rhythms we meet a powerful force close to the femininity of creation itself: it suggests spring rains, morning dews, menstrual cycles, and a fecundity in women and nature that after the Fall repeatedly threaten to break out of orderly constraints. Nevertheless, like a woman properly insistent on being more than merely passive, the moon has a life of her own as well as a married role with the sun. In her different manifestations she is not only Luna or Cynthia (identified with the moon itself) but also Diana (a powerful and independent wood or nature goddess) and Hecate (the mysterious goddess of witchcraft and the underworld).

In sorting out the moon's contrarieties—moisture and dryness, dark and light, cold and heat—we illustrate the complexities of gender in women and nature. As the moon receives steadily increasing light from the masculine sun and thereby grows to fullness, it nevertheless remains cool since its light is reflected. As the elevated goddess Cynthia worshipped by a subservient and passionate male, the moon provides a visual image of neoplatonic beauty or of austere, haughty, domineering, and unapproachable chastity. The moon can be associated with nature's fulfilled femininity because of its union with the masculine sun, with chaste, elevated order since its cool light directs us to wonder at its beauty and seek the source of its illumination, but also with a self-sufficient, powerful, and dangerous independence that deceives with its illusory and changing light. It can be a magical revealer of love's mysteries or an alluring but fickle and uncaring temptress. It can be a controlling and ordering force or a disruption that brings chaos to both nature and people.

The other phases of the moon—the new or waxing moon, the waning moon, and the dark or absent moon—suggest the changing processes of nature as the moon takes on characteristics of other parts of the cycle. The new moon, a symbol of renewal and regeneration, is associated with love and growth, providing a propitious time for weddings and the planting of seeds. The cold and dry, waning moon is linked to a sterile chastity as well as to decay and aging. In the dark or absent moon's apparent withdrawal from the world, we confront the mysteries of death and lunacy; there is the potential for contact with either the divine and its promise of renewal or, through Hecate, with evil spirits and the horrors of hellish witchcraft. What each manifestation reveals is the moon's complexity as a metaphor: it can be associated with chastity and fickleness, love and infatuation, growth and sterility, orderly control and madness, ultimate reality and illusion, and good and evil.

The moon and sun rule only a single sign each (Cancer and Leo), but their signs link together at the height of summer, as if to suggest the union of powerful dualities—not only the moon and the sun but also the feminine and the masculine, and night and day. At this time, roughly July 12 (ten days earlier than the same date on the present-day calendar, since the revision of the Julian calendar in 1582 had not yet gone into effect in England), the six night houses (Aquarius through Cancer) end, and the six day houses (Leo through Capricorn) begin. The setting of *Romeo and Juliet* is the period in July just before Cancer and the night houses turn the rule over to Leo and the day houses. (The analogy to the play's difficult transitions from night to dawn is most likely not coincidental.) The mixed nature of the sun's influence is most explicit in the Friar's speech (2.3.1–8) but is implicit in the handling of masculinity in general. *A Midsummer Night's Dream* also establishes cosmic dimensions: Shakespeare links Theseus, Hippolyta, Oberon, and Titania in complex ways to the sun and the moon and develops other parallels to diurnal and annual cycles.

The placement of the planets—three (the moon, Mercury, and Venus: two feminine and one hermaphroditic) closer than the sun to the Earth and three (Mars, Jupiter, and Saturn: all masculine) farther from the Earth—helps clarify much Renaissance metaphor about the planets. An influential assumption in the sixteenth century was that all of the gods associated with the planets are beneficent if one can respond to their influence in the proper way. Not surprisingly, the astrological signs linked most closely with the circle of the planets on my chart provide the clearest material for metaphor, not only the sun in Leo and Saturn in Capricorn and Aquarius, but also Jupiter in Sagittarius, Venus in Taurus, and Mars in Scorpio. Along with the sun and the moon, Saturn and Jupiter are apt to be metaphors for larger cosmic dualities (day and night, summer and winter, good and evil). The two houses ruled by Saturn join at the depth of winter and are thus exactly opposite the houses of the sun and the moon. (Having these juxtapositions and oppositions at the solstices might seem more logical and natural, but summer is normally hottest and winter coldest at times after the solstices.) Saturn can be associated with destructive or contemplative melancholy and can be seen, in his identification with the end of the year and Time (Father Time), as a destroyer or as a revealer of truth. In Sagittarius, Jupiter can appropriately be the wise, detached philosopher who is growing old in the right way. The active Capulet, the more reflective Montague, and the angry Egeus have very different temperaments, but all lack the wisdom that should accompany age.

Because of their size and rapid movement Mars and Venus are more prominent in the sky than any of the planets except Jupiter. Not only do they rule the signs of the spring months crucial for growth and love, but they are also strong and clearly defined gods with mythological legends that associate them with both nature and each other.[26]

The signs associated with spring, and particularly with Taurus, when Venus rules and Mars is in decline, are of special interest to the love poets. In these plays, the force of Venus on the young lovers and the difficulty that young men have in achieving their manhood is apparent. Venus in Libra is a much less passionate influence. Mars in contrast is somewhat ambiguous in Aries but tends to be an unruly masculine force in Scorpio. The choleric Tybalt reveals his influence.

Mercury has ambiguous and even contradictory qualities. The planet and the god are sometimes thought of as feminine, sometimes as masculine, and sometimes as hermaphroditic. As young, cold, moist, and feminine, Mercury can be linked with fertility and with childhood as an age of life; as young, cold, dry, and masculine, he can be associated with quick wits, theft, exercise, and delivering messages; as hermaphroditic, he can be a mysterious god of transitions and transformations who deals with magic, fate, luck, philosophy, inspiration, and literature. Mercury attracted the interest of those who were delighted by ambiguity and complexity, notably the hermetists and the alchemists. Mercutio has some of Mercury's qualities: he is impulsive, playful, witty, cynical, and unpredictable. Puck has many of the same qualities, and the parallels between them prove to be useful links between the plays.

The imagery of alchemy is closely connected to the patterns I have been describing. Alchemists started with the optimistic assumption that all life reflects an underlying unity, and their views of the transmutation of metals tended to reflect the accepted relationships of the elements, the humours, the seasons, the planets, and the ages of man.[27] My intention is not to describe the alchemical process in detail but only to point out that the patterns of imagery in alchemy parallel the cyclical patterns I have been discussing. The alchemist attempts to fuse the opposing and apparently irreconcilable elements of water and fire by bringing mercury (liquid) and sulphur (brimstone) together. The imagery used to describe the fusing process recalls familiar metaphorical relationships. As John Read explains, sophic sulphur and sophic mercury "were known as Osiris and Isis, sun and moon,

Sol and Luna, brother and sister, masculine and feminine, active and passive, giver and receiver, seal and wax, fixed and volatile, wingless lion and winged lioness, lion and eagle, and so forth. The Stone, when conceived as the result of the union of masculine and feminine principles, was sometimes represented as an infant."[28] The imagery links the process to the larger patterns of death and rebirth in man and nature. Though imagery of alchemy is not pervasive in the plays, it appears in key contexts, notably in the gold imagery of *Romeo and Juliet* and in the dawn imagery of Oberon (3.2.388–93).

HIERARCHIES

The usual Renaissance way of dealing with the changes represented by the various cycles was to assert that there are hierarchical values associated with love that enable people to overcome mutability. Such values can be otherworldly, but most relate to life in this world. The underlying philosophy and theology are neoplatonic and Christian, so we can recognize a progression of understanding from the level of self to family to society to nature to religion. But the emphasis in Shakespeare is not on an ascent to higher knowledge or on a scientific understanding based on a conception of the great chain of being. Instead, no doubt partly because of the specificity of dramatic settings, he tends to think about individual responses to particular situations. A hierarchical structure provides, not a rigid code of behavior, but metaphors for describing relationships. We are dependent on others: cycles in themselves are without purpose, but hierarchies counteract emptiness by suggesting what can be meaningful patterns.

When adjusted to include the positive metaphors associated with the night, the chart on Metaphors of Hierarchies with its division into a positive upper half and negative lower half fits loosely on top of the chart on

Metaphors of Cycles. The positive personal qualities of the lower part of the chart on Metaphors of Cycles—vision, imagination, contemplation, detachment, repose—have a place in the upper part of the chart on Metaphors of Hierarchies. They inform the perspective of a structured, social world and become a part, usually the feminine part, of dualities (moon, sun; night, day) that require fusion to be meaningful. The controlling polarity is masculine-feminine, with the other dualities being understood by principles of analogy that see the right side of the chart as generally diurnal and rational, the left as nocturnal and passionate. The Hierarchies chart with its stress on defining the moment through moral decision tends to ignore some cyclical patterns of the Cycles charts (the seasons and the ages of life) and emphasizes instead the night's metaphorical associations with effeminacy, sensuality, and evil, not winter or the ages of life. The lower right of the Hierarchies chart defines masculine excesses usually unrelated to the natural cycles.

The inner circle depicts the force of love, at once physical and spiritual, that emanates from God, generates and animates the attractions of the polarities at each level, bonds the structures of existence, and governs the transformations of time. After the Fall people have trouble choosing between worthy objects and appealing illusions, thereby creating a countering force leading toward disorder. All of life becomes a struggle to distinguish between what Augustine calls *caritas* and *cupiditas*. *Caritas* is the powerful force of divine love, while *cupiditas*, properly understood, is a disruption or confusion of something positive rather than the product of an independent evil. Satan has no power except what God allows him. (When interpreted in this context, the absence of deliberate and active evil in both *Romeo and Juliet* and *A Midsummer Night's Dream* can be seen as reflecting a more traditional way of understanding the world.) Nevertheless, dualities exist: daemonic powers, angelic and devilish, express the polarities that shape people's lives; and each individual's choices depend on the ability to distinguish between them and to pursue proper objects of love.[29]

Love not only attracts the sexes; it motivates the relationships of the family and society, brings the renewal of spring, and orders the movements of the cosmos. If we think of love as a magnetic force, moving away from it weakens the attraction and threatens a fall. Parents, rulers, and husbands must give freely of themselves (*agape*) in order to pull others toward worthy ends without slipping themselves toward dogmatic rigidity. In contrast, young lovers give prominence to the feelings and must be wary of making passion dominant. In order to avoid these tendencies, masculine and feminine impulses must find the harmonious balance of marriages real and metaphorical.

The psychological interactions of love are best understood if we remember that the Renaissance conception of gender has an androgynous component: males have a feminine and females a masculine side. Although gender roles for males and females are analogous, they differ significantly because the dominant gender orientation controls basic responses. The Jungian anima and animus as well as Freudian, neo-Freudian, and feminist descriptions of the structures of the self are relevant and often helpful,[30] but the analysis is best carried out in a Renaissance framework. Neoplatonic and Christian interpretations of the self remain important even though the concepts had long since entered the metaphorical language of the popular imagination. Men and women in love relate hierarchically; the feminine in the male responds to the masculine in the female and vice versa. Friendship, which is nonhierarchical, can and should also develop but that is a different form of love (*philia*). Reflecting a paradox central to the Christian tradition, love involves both worship and grace (analogues of *eros* and *agape*). For a man to love in grace (*agape*) is comparatively easy psychologically since as a male he already understands himself as analogous to God, the sun, and reason, but he must grant his own inadequacy and incompleteness when he expresses his feminine side through worshiping something outside himself. For a woman, worship expresses her instinctive femininity as she looks to masculine reason for completion and meaning, but she also has to deal with her own independence and with the often confusing power that male courtship gives her.

When a male lover admires or worships a woman, he participates in the wonder of love, with his passionate (feminine) side caught up in a mystery that fills him with both physical and spiritual longing and with his rational (masculine) side striving to rise toward understanding of both the process and its goals. Both dimensions are versions of *eros* since they involve man striving for an experience of the divine. When Greek *eros* becomes Latin Cupid, the same mysterious force partly inside and partly outside the lover is operating, but allusions to Cupid tend to be more playful and to imply that lovers have less control over their behavior. Even when love is not interpreted theologically or philosophically, the traditional metaphorical structure remains, at least in the background. The woman becomes the emblem of the beauty and truth that ideally will provide a sense of meaning and completion, making the male feel at one not only with the woman but with himself, nature, and the cosmos. The divine quality of the virgin is conventionally represented by the chaste perfections of an independent Diana, but when she invokes and responds to the impulses of love, she becomes a Venus. Ideally the woman as wife fuses her Diana and Venus qualities and continues to inspire her husband's love.[31]

The danger of *eros* is that the physical, spiritual, and rational worship of love can easily become idolatrous and illusory and will therefore prove transitory. Physical or emotional longing may be misinterpreted or disguised as a higher love. Romanticism tends to blur such distinctions, but a society still emerging from the theological insistence that all love must lead to God will be more alert to distortions. The animal drive itself is positive in its impulse toward procreation but is negative if it has a merely sexual goal. We oversimplify love if we try to reduce it to either a divine or physical basis, or to describe physical love as proper or improper; after the Fall people are caught between divine aspiration and earthly desire, and so must struggle to achieve and maintain worthy love.

The second circle of the Metaphors of Hierarchies chart describes the self.[32] Each person has a soul with three sub-souls—the vegetative, sensitive, and rational souls—that communicate with the body through spirits distilled from the blood. People, animals, and plants all have a vegetative soul which manages nourishment and growth. People and animals have a sensitive soul that controls physical feeling and motion. Only people have a rational soul (reason): it contemplates, makes judgments, and serves as the masculine principle that governs the feminine senses and impulses in a marriage held together by love. The five senses are commonly arranged in a hierarchy with sight at the top and touch at the bottom. Sight can be the agent of rising toward the divine or of falling through lust toward destruction. Seeing is passive in that rays of light, usually from the sun, are reflected to the eye by objects that function like mirrors, but it is active in that we determine what we look at and must interpret what we see through our reason. Passive seeing that evokes wonder at the beauty of creation is analogous to hearing that values inner vision, the contemplative night, the divine Logos, and harmony. Hearing is commonly paired with speaking, with emphasis on human receptivity to the divine word: speech should function like *agape*, and analogy links hearing to "feminine" silence and obedience in response to patriarchal authority. Smelling, tasting, and touching, the most dangerous sense, are primarily physical and therefore in constant danger of excess, but the rational soul can transform

tendencies toward passion (the lower senses) and violence (the hands) into positive bonding.

The passions and states of mind recorded in circles six
and seven of Metaphors of Cycles could also be listed
here: their placement should be apparent from the qualities that I include in circles two and three. The positive
passions in each circle of Cycles should be elevated and
the negative passions lowered. The resulting scheme
looks very much like systems based on Aristotle, Cicero,
Seneca, and others, with many of the lower passions suggesting a defect or excess of the positive quality. Almost
any virtue can be seen in terms of defect and excess, and
the Renaissance was drawn to such patterns. Shakespeare seems to use such a scheme in *Romeo and Juliet*
in presenting the problem that the lovers and Friar Lawrence have in finding the prudence to fuse patience
with boldness. Patience without the willingness to act
(boldness) easily becomes fear while boldness without
the balance of patience becomes rashness.[33] Shakespeare
does not usually concern himself with virtues that are
already self-sufficient, such as the four cardinal virtues
(temperance, fortitude, justice, and prudence) and the
three theological ones (faith, hope, and charity). He may
have felt that they are less dynamic and therefore less
dramatic. I am not interested in defining virtues and
vices too schematically[34] because Renaissance poets and
dramatists generally, and Shakespeare in particular, were
not. Renaissance metaphor tends to be suggestive rather
than dogmatic.

The third circle describes familial and sexual relationships.[35] Women, wives, children, and servants were
thought to be subservient by nature whereas men in
their various authority roles and women as mothers and
as mistresses of households belong on the right side of
the chart. Young men have a difficult transition from
adolescence to manhood. The young woman changes less
since she primarily substitutes the authority of a husband for that of a father. Just as the individual combines

masculine and feminine traits, so too a relationship requires flexibility for different situations. Also individual differences in humours, age, lineage, and education produce behavior that resists generalization based on gender. Effeminate behavior, by either a man or a woman, can be a lapse into phlegmatic acceptance or into rebellion or sensuality. Since the woman is a person with reason (see circle two), she must be true to that side of her nature when male authority slips toward tyranny or irresponsibility. In an oppressive situation, passivity can be more damaging than rebellion. Understanding such hierarchies usually helps provide a framework for interpretation but seldom a clear moral reading. Shakespeare's women are almost invariably defined by their hierarchical relationships, but his men are usually seen in a broader context.

The fourth circle takes the analogies to the societal level.[36] A familiar analogy suggests that the ruler is reason, the head of the body politic, and father of the state as well as king, while the subjects are the rest of the body, passions that need ordering, and the king's children. When the ruler fails to respect his subjects, the bond is broken and he may become a tyrant. When subjects will not recognize authority, they become a mob, as in the first scene of *Coriolanus*. Since society itself is arranged hierarchically, people's roles are constantly shifting; there are times for ruling and times for serving. Success in fulfilling these roles requires balancing or marrying the positive qualities suggested by freedom, nature, and revel on the one hand and law, civilization, and order on the other.

The analogies between the poet-playwright, the work of art (circle five), and the other hierarchical levels are particularly helpful for understanding Shakespeare's conception of drama.[37] We have perhaps heard enough about the practical working dramatist concerned only with entertaining a diverse and largely unsophisticated audience. The more intelligent members of that audience were probably most important in influencing Shakespeare's

methods, and we should also remember that much of
what we struggle to understand would be easy for them
because the habits of analogical interpretation were built
into their approaches to life. That Shakespeare was know-
ledgeable about the essentials of the poetic theory of his
time is apparent, but whether his specific debt is to
Sidney or Puttenham or to conversation with his colleagues is impossible to determine. In his *Defence of
Poesie*, Sidney discusses the poet as seer, imitator, and
maker.[38] As seer, the poet would be divinely inspired, but
Sidney recognizes such a role only for David and other
biblical poets. We might expect the poet as imitator to
hold the mirror up to nature and the poet as maker to
use imagination and wit to shape his materials, but an
Aristotelean Sidney puts imitation at the center of his
theory by suggesting that the poet imitates Aristotelean
universals, not just the specifics of nature. Since these
universals resemble Plato's ideas, the traditional neoplatonic aesthetic can also function: the poet is an active
creator who, like God with his universe, embodies the
idea or form of his concepts in the material reality of his
work.[39] The more restricted conception of imitation
places that poet on the left side of my chart while the
poet as maker invents and transforms and thus belongs
on the active, masculine right side, where God as Creator
also fits. While only the poet as seer fits perfectly in the
middle of my chart, Sidney's ideal poet, who tries to
combine close attention to universal nature with the
creative embodiment of higher truths, aspires to that balanced fusion. Poetry is superior to both history, which
must limit itself to the specifics, and philosophy, which
deals with abstract precepts. In describing the superiority
of art to nature, Sidney says "Her world is brazen, the
poets only deliver a golden."[40]

Various analogies make fuller sense when seen in light
of these correspondences.[41] The created universe is a
work of art produced by God as Creator. In each of its
parts, according to the principles of the great chain of

being, there will be microcosmic evidence of the macro-cosm itself. In Augustinian terms, each object is a sign as well as a mere thing.[42] As sign it points to and partici-pates in the unified cosmos. In a cosmos where every ob-ject has meaning, the metaphors of the poetic maker will both reflect and creatively explicate the coherence of the larger system. As S. K. Heninger, Jr., says, "the essence of making is the framing of metaphors."[43] Each person should also be a poet: the rational soul should shape the self so that each thought and action will participate crea-tively in the whole. If nature is a work of art full of cos-mic metaphors, through proper reading we can interpret that work and achieve knowledge of both nature and God. If "all the world's a stage," it can be understood as a divinely produced play. Conversely the work of art should become what Heninger calls a "literary micro-cosm" that will embody in its form and meaning the metaphorical truths of the world and of the macrocosm itself. When literary form is understood in this way, the work of art embodies the metaphorical analogies of the entire system in its structure, settings, imagery, and characterization.

Tragedy and comedy are the dramatic forms most likely to be full literary microcosms. Although tragedy relates death and disaster, it often finds meaning in those depths; although comedy celebrates joy and resolution, it unmasks the emptiness of conventional platitudes. The vision of each is in turn masculine and feminine, ratio-nal and passionate, orderly and chaotic. Epic poetry as-serts the heroic values of mature masculinity (upper right). Satire aggressively defends the secure values of a confident masculinity, and farce emphasizes the chaos of life from a comic perspective. Romance (lower left) ac-centuates ritualistic patterns in archetypal tales of des-truction and regeneration.[44] *Romeo and Juliet* fluctuates between romance and tragedy and *A Midsummer Night's Dream* between romance and comedy, but both finally are about the possibility of achieving joyful resolutions (the top of the chart). I have also indicated the polarities of formlessness (or inarticulateness) and rigid form, and of freedom to speak and censorship. At the bottom is the lack of communication suggested by the chaos of Babel and the silence of death.

At the natural level (circle six), nature finds its harmony and balance through the proper blending of all forces described on the Metaphors of Cycles chart. While there is a God-given order implicit in the rhythm of the cycles, nature fell when man did, with a resulting disruption of the pattern at every stage. Moisture and heat should be positive qualities, but after the Fall excess and dearth interrupt in unpredictable ways. Personifying the forces as dualistic makes their patterns more comprehensible. The gods can be helpful or destructive. Venus appears in three forms: she can be the celestial Venus of an elevated love, the Venus Genetrix of positive generation, or the earthly Venus of corrupted passion. Mars can be an emblem of valor or of wrath. In her various guises Diana, as we have already seen, is as complex as the moon's changing manifestations; she can embody the fecundity of a wood goddess, the restraint and control of chastity, or the frightening mysteries of Hecate.[45] Animals, birds, and flowers fall into similarly polarized patterns that reflect moral readings of cyclical and hierarchical patterns.

The final circle, the circle of the supernatural, properly puts God, Christ, and the Holy Ghost directly in the middle, but each has roles that are masculine and feminine.[46] God has a masculine face of justice and a feminine one of love. But His role as love also has a masculine dimension: He is the active lover of the soul and the active principle that shapes the natural world. He is both transcendent and immanent, or, in the philosophy of Bruno (and later Spinoza), He is the *natura naturans* (creating nature) as well as the *natura naturata* (created nature). The Holy Ghost is the masculine spirit whose fire enlightens and impregnates and also the feminine dove that broods over the waters. Christ is both judge and suffering servant. The Virgin Mary like Diana is paradoxically the emblem of both chastity and fertility. The opposite of these powerful forces for good is Satan, so linking hell with darkness and chaos and with midnight and the winter solstice is appropriate.

CYCLES AND HIERARCHIES

An individual trying to relate behavior to cycles and hierarchies must first understand changing roles and times, then act in a way appropriate for that moment. Douglas Peterson distinguishes between "durative time," which describes the cycle of passing time, and occasion, which is time seen as the present moment that must be seized and turned to use.[47] This distinction fits easily with the Christian sense of each moment as providing a sacred time for moral evaluation and proper action. In a fallen world, mutability seems to rule: outside circumstances make timely action difficult, and results depend on many factors beyond the individual's control. When the conflict of contrarieties is apparent, as it often is in Shakespeare, we enter an atmosphere of breakdown and chaos that speaks directly to our modern world. Gloomy responses are possible, even inevitable, within the framework I have described since the stress now falls on the structures of nature rather than on the traditional religious hierarchy. People who see this natural structure as meaningful achieve a perspective that puts whatever happens in context, but interpretations of the implications of Renaissance contrariety can differ considerably.

The traditional governors of actions and results—God, fate, and fortune—function analogously.[48] God is personal and therefore reassuring: you can reach Him through prayer which can help both in reaching decisions and accepting results. He is at once detached from and active in the world. With the foreknowledge of His eternal perspective, He observes the whole continuum of time and grants people free will to determine their own actions. He also acts within time to grant the power of grace to people who seek His guidance. When tragedy occurs for whatever reason, He remains available to help people shape the new situation into something positive. His role should not be limited to these functions: He acts in mysterious ways that illustrate His justice and love but will always be beyond human comprehension. Fate is impersonal and vaguely ominous: it suggests the forces that govern the complicated interactions of the natural world and the cosmos and that affect people in ways they can neither control nor understand. It is usually viewed negatively when it is thought of as influencing or determining what people do; it then refers to the complex forces in a contingent universe (chance, etc.) and to forces within the self that seem impossible to control. Such references make the three Fates analogous to an unjust God and to Satan, but fate can also be thought of as passive, a description of results considered in retrospect. Once something happens, it becomes a part of the unchangeable order of time (fate) that the eternal God foreknows but does not predetermine. Believers in an orderly world are likely to see this passive fate as evidence of God's providence, while those who stress the active fate are apt to be pessimistic about both human free will and divine grace.

Fortune relates more specifically to what people think they are able to achieve and control in this world. When people act, the results are dependent on the notoriously fickle goddess Fortuna. No one escapes her power, but they can deal with it by planning actions wisely and by realizing that nothing can be certain in a mutable world. Something like Machiavelli's "virtu" joins with prudence in seeking an earthly success that may or may not be acceptable morally,[49] whereas a more traditional virtue encourages a boldness that increases power by its very detachment from results in this world. Although differences in emphasis lead to strenuous disagreements about the exact roles of God, fate, and fortune, these broad outlines establish the framework of their metaphorical and analogical functions.

Perhaps the most useful way to demonstrate the flexibility that the metaphorical patterns of cycles and hierarchies offered is to describe the variations in two other authors of the time, John Donne and John Davies. Along with Shakespeare, they came to maturity in the last decade of the century. All three are sensitive to the shifting literary and philosophical atmosphere, and all make extensive use of the patterns I have been discussing; yet each is profoundly different from the other two, not only in literary intention and method but also in his basic way of looking at the world. Shakespeare is the working dramatist, sophisticated and even learned, but caught up in his theatrical world and almost anonymous behind his company's plays. Donne is first the aspiring courtier and coterie poet hoping to make connections in London society and struggling with his personal problems, and later the great divine preaching traditional Christianity. Davies is the educated gentleman and philosopher-poet, comfortable in the Elizabethan world and perhaps a little too complacently outlining its conventional ideas and virtues.

In Donne, what begins in the dawn poems in *Songs and Sonets* as a witty celebration of the possible transcendence of earthly love later becomes the rejection of this world in the name of religious love in poems such as "A nocturnall upon *S. Lucies* day" and in his divine sonnets, hymns, and sermons. There are striking similarities between the dawn imagery of *Romeo and Juliet* and *A Midsummer Night's Dream* and that of "The good-morrow" and "The Sunne Rising," also between the last act of *Romeo and Juliet* and Donne's Christmas sermon for 1624, and his final sermon, "Deaths Duell." But the dawn that does not come in *Romeo and Juliet* and the dawn that arrives in *A Midsummer Night's Dream* reflect Shakespeare's concern with the days of this world whereas Donne's preoccupation with a spiritual midnight and noon in the 1624 sermon is otherworldly. Though Donne does not fully reject this world, even in the final sermon, and Shakespeare does not deny transcendence, their contrasting tendencies are clear.

Another version of the cycles is found in Sir John Davies' *Nosce Teipsum* (1599), a poem roughly contemporary with *Romeo and Juliet* and *A Midsummer Night's Dream*. Like Donne, Davies believes in immortality, but his justification is based less on divine revelation than on cyclical, analogical, and rational arguments. Earth and water are seen as the elements of the body and the physical world, but fire is an immaterial substance whose "sparks"[50] of immortal light are begotten in people by God. Rather than following life's cycle to decay and destruction, people can use "Reason's lamp (which, like the sun in sky, / Throughout man's little world her beams did spread)"[51] to rise to understanding, knowledge, and finally wisdom. The metaphor differs from Donne's early poetry in its emphasis on reason and from Donne's religious writing in its optimism about people's ability to achieve a steady ascent in light toward truth. People can depend on the analogous levels in the hierarchy as well—on "Nature's speech, / Which like GOD's oracle, can never lie" and on Queen Elizabeth, who makes it possible for her subjects to "Reason, Live, and Move, and Be." Davies sees a struggle between the world's darkness and God's light but no breakthrough to illumination.

Neither Davies nor Donne thinks and responds exactly like Shakespeare, but they help reveal both the habits of mind and the diversity of approach possible when dealing with the complicated questions of cycles and hierarchies. In this section I have tried to provide a noncontroversial description of the patterns of metaphors that form the background of *Romeo and Juliet* and *A Midsummer Night's Dream*. What should become clear as we move on to the plays is that these patterns help Shakespeare achieve scope, unity, and intelligibility without sacrificing complexity, flexibility, and vitality.

PART 2

Romeo and Juliet

Two

Every Thing in Extremity

(*Romeo and Juliet* 1.1–4)

SERV. Madam, the guests are come, supper serv'd up,
you call'd, my young lady ask'd for, the nurse curs'd
in the pantry, and every thing in extremity.

(1.3.100–02)

I n developing the familiar story of Romeo and Juliet's
tragic love, Shakespeare makes use of the traditional
metaphorical framework described in part 1. In analyzing
how Shakespeare shapes the play's development, I make
use of charts, one for each chapter based on the metaphorical structures described in part 1. (For help in reading the charts, see the instructions across from the first
chart for each play.) The society of Verona understands
itself in relation to regular cycles of life and nature and

Instructions for interpreting the charts in part 2:

Each chapter's chart combines features of part 1's charts on Metaphors of Cycles and Metaphors of Hierarchies. (See pp. 29, 31.) Hierarchies provide the underlying structure, with the positive masculine and feminine principles at each analogous level—individuals, the family, society, art, and nature—linked by love at the top and by negative forces at the bottom. The cycles—of the humours, seasons and days, and the ages of life—are indicated in the inner and outer circles. Each chart suggests how gender and analogy shape the patterns of metaphor in that part of the play. When reference to the chart is helpful for clarification of my analysis, I use abbreviations in the text: UL = upper left; UC = upper center; UR = upper right; LL = lower left; LC = lower center; LR = lower right. Since each moment in time has potentially positive or negative overtones, further discriminations are needed. When metaphors contradict the basic up-positive and down-negative form, I use brackets—[ ] to indicate a reversal and < > a partial reversal. Readers should remember that metaphorical associations are suggestive and complex, not exact. The charts should be thought of as providing a rough outline of the plays' metaphorical structure that my analysis fills out and makes more precise. Shakespeare had no need to develop charts to communicate with his audience since the metaphorical patterns I describe were built into the Elizabethan understanding of the world.

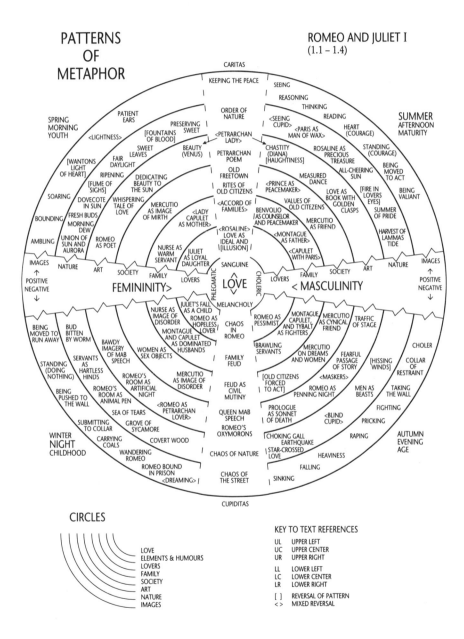

PATTERNS
OF
METAPHOR

ROMEO AND JULIET I
(1.1 – 1.4)

CIRCLES

LOVE
ELEMENTS & HUMOURS
LOVERS
FAMILY
SOCIETY
ART
NATURE
IMAGES

KEY TO TEXT REFERENCES

UL   UPPER LEFT
UC   UPPER CENTER
UR   UPPER RIGHT

LL   LOWER LEFT
LC   LOWER CENTER
LR   LOWER RIGHT

[ ]   REVERSAL OF PATTERN
< >   MIXED REVERSAL

to stable hierarchies of family and society, but harmony has been lost as individuals move to extreme positions and a renewal of violence threatens order. The play becomes not only the lovers' personal tragedy but also an account of a spreading chaos that has familial, societal, and even cosmic implications.

The prologue summarizes a story in which feuding families and an unfriendly cosmos generate tragic oppositions that allow the lovers only limited control over their lives. Their actions may be "misadventur'd," but the stress falls on the "ancient grudge" of the families and the "star-cross'd" (pro.7, 3, 6) nature of their love.[1] From my perspective, these causes function analogously: similar forces interact in the microcosm of the self, in the larger structures of the family and society, and in the macrocosm of the cosmos. The prologue's poetic language and open allusion to dramatic structure prepare us for a play in which the form itself will, as a literary microcosm, embody and reflect the other levels of meaning.

In creating the play's world, Shakespeare combines the primarily verbal introspection of the sonnet with the narrative excitement of romance and transforms that fusion into the more plausibly developed reality of drama. The sonnet form, conventional for Petrarchan love poetry, here describes death as well as love. Verbal wit complicates the story's themes with ambiguous, often ominous, meanings—not only "star-cross'd" and "misadventur'd" but also "civil," "fatal," "take their life," "bury," and "fearful passage"; metonymy makes "civil blood," "civil hands," "fatal loins," and "patient ears" both general and specific; alliteration reinforces oxymoronic oppositions in "From forth the fatal loins of these two foes / . . . lovers take their life" (pro.2–9). In the sestet Shakespeare plays with a journey image that draws a parallel between the "two hours' traffic of our stage" and the "passage" of the lovers to their "end" (pro.12, 9, 11). That the play must retell the story and that the company needs the audience's attention are conventional observations, but there is a further suggestion that the audience's "patient ears" and the company's "toil" (pro.13, 14) can prevent a disaster in the theater analogous to that of the characters. While the actors are unable to "remove" the "fearful passage" (pro.14, 11, 9) of the tragic story, they can in the microcosm of the theater resist analogy and come to a resolution that at least succeeds as drama.[2] The Chorus comments again only at the start of act 2 in a speech that puts more stress on the lovers' passions than on fate and the feud: the play is a dramatized story as well as a literary microcosm, and the rest of the story unfolds without interruption.

In the opening scene, Shakespeare signals the importance of the structures I have described by illustrating how gender polarities functioning at every level of the hierarchy create profound problems for Verona. Deeply ingrained masculine pride and aggression LR lead to yet another conflict between the Capulets and the Montagues. What starts with the servants quickly escalates to the young men and then to the masters themselves. Voices of cool reason <UR>—Gregory, Benvolio, Lady Capulet, and Lady Montague—sharpen our sense of the extent of masculine excess, and the restoration of order is achieved only through the intervention of some wise old men [LR] and the arrival of the Prince himself <UR>. The beginning of a new day should involve constructive activity, at least a secularized version of doing God's work in the world,[3] but on this morning people who should be sensible UR slip toward violence LR as the street becomes a place of chaos LC. If the basic units of civilization—the individual and the family—are governed by petty passions, the city-state of Verona has little chance of maintaining stability.

The opening dialogue of the Capulet servants introduces some of the play's main polarities as Sampson swaggeringly asserts his manhood despite undercutting from the more intelligent Gregory.[4] Gregory takes Sampson's refusal to "carry coals" as a pledge to avoid the collier's sharp dealing and Sampson's boast that he will "draw" when "in choler" as an attempt to save his neck from the "collar" (1.1.1–5) of hanging.[5] As we shall see, the play repeatedly considers the polarities of feminine passivity LL (carrying coals or accepting hanging) and masculine assertion LR (the deception of the collier, "choler," and the restraint of the "collar"). Further related punning follows: since moving can mean "being moved" <UR>, or "running away" LL while standing can mean "being valiant" UR or "doing nothing" LL. Sampson's claims about being moved and standing can mean just the opposite of what he intends. And his boast that in walking he "will take the wall of any man or maid of Montague's" LR can, as Gregory points out, imply weakness since "the weakest goes to the wall" LL (1.1.12–14). Sexual violence becomes a primary symbol of male disorder. Sampson is always one pun behind as Gregory tauntingly turns his boasts about women <UR> into cowardice LL—"The quarrel is between our masters, and us their men"; his masculine strength UR into rape LR—"the heads of the maids?"; and his sexual "stand"ing UR into impotence LL—"'Tis well thou art not fish; if thou hadst, thou hadst been poor-John" (1.1.19–20, 24, 30–31). No doubt their swords and bucklers, convenient images of male and female sexual parts, would reinforce these images on the stage.[6]

Disruption at a lower level requires decisive handling by people with authority. Benvolio, as his name implies, means well UR, but unfortunately his Capulet counterpart, "the fiery Tybalt," LR behaves like the foolish servants who Benvolio says "know not what you do" (1.1.109, 65). When Benvolio explains that he is using his sword to "keep the peace" and invites Tybalt's help, Tybalt reveals a different conception of both swords and peace: "What, drawn and talk of peace? I hate the word / As I hate hell, all Montagues, and thee" (1.1.70–71). To Tybalt "hate" LR is justified [LR], and his sword is an instrument of personal, familial, and even religious honor

UR. When Montague and Capulet themselves enter, ironic images of overturned hierarchies escalate. Both Montague and Capulet choose "choler" LR over "collar" <UR> and are prevented from joining the fight only by the restraint of their wives. While there are serious implications to the scene, comedy, already present in the absurd behavior of the servants, dominates in the conventionally ludicrous image of powerful men controlled by their women.[7] A production must balance the impulse toward comedy with the need to avoid caricature. Psychological differences between the two families might be apparent already. Even in this first scene Shakespeare shows how the Capulet approach to life contributes to the momentum toward disorder. Everyone connected with the Capulets has a level of energy, emotion, and activity <UR> in sharp contrast with the more reflective and passive <UL> Montagues. Perhaps we are to see that the contemplative, in some ways feminine <UL> Romeo is the product of such a household, while the lively and forceful <UR> Tybalt and later Juliet have Capulet traits. If so, Shakespeare combines an interest in heredity and environment with insight into the gender oppositions that attract lovers.

The people who prove most helpful to the Prince in restoring order are not the natural hierarchical leaders UR but a group of "Verona's ancient citizens" [LR] who must use "old partisans," like their hands quite naturally "Cank'red with peace, to part your cank'red hate" (1.1.92–95). Imagery of improper swordmaking accentuates the debasement: the fighters' personified weapons are said to be "mistempered" (1.1.87), that is, at once wrathful, improperly tempered when made, and figuratively marred by debased causes. The swords that should be used by a community of people acting with dignity and wisdom UR to preserve the peace UC have instead become "neighbor-stained" (1.1.82) with blood LR. If the old men are onstage at the start of the play and are dressed in "grave beseeming ornaments" (1.1.93) as part of a religious ceremony, perhaps related to the sun so important in the imagery of the opening scenes, they would shape audience response to the whole scene. We know that the play's first day is a Sunday only because of later mentions of days of the week, but Shakespeare's unusual explicitness about time suggests that he may intend some ironies about violent behavior on the Sabbath. If some observance is under way, the servants' transformation of a holy day into a wild holiday would have added point. Even without these specific associations, the contrast of the dignified old men—"grave" in appearance, seriousness, and nearness to death [LR]—with the brawling servants and with the feuding Capulets and Montagues LR would be emphatic.

When the Prince enters and finally succeeds in stopping the fight, he defines himself as the image of order <UR> once again halting a recurring cycle of violence: "Three civil brawls" have "disturb'd the quiet of our streets" (1.1.89, 91). In the imagery of the Prince, the four elements, by analogy present in the body politic and nature as well as in the humours of the men, are in conflict and disorder. The "civil brawls" are "bred of an airy word," and the fighters' "pernicious rage" has become a "fire" that they "quench" with "purple fountains" (1.1.89, 84, 85). The vital moisture that should sustain both self and community is wasted as "men" become "beasts," and a new start is possible only if their weapons are thrown "to the ground" (1.1.83, 88). Later, Benvolio uses analogous imagery when he ridicules "The fiery Tybalt" LR as someone whose behavior insults both the Prince and the winds UR, which "hiss'd him in scorn" [LR] (1.1.109, 112). Despite his temporary success, however, the Prince seems to be solving the problem with a "collar" <UR> almost as extreme as the "choler" LR (1.1.5, 3) of the participants.[8] Each time the Prince appears he is responding to an emergency: he is full of threats <LR> but never seems to have solutions. He requires Capulet and Montague to meet with him, but they apparently will not meet with each other. If we take seriously the need for love UL as well as law UR and for mutual respect UL as well as judgment UR, the prospects for this truce are not promising. Meeting at "old Free-town, our common judgment-place" UC (1.1.102) becomes ironic. Capulet later tells Paris: "But Montague is bound as well as I, / In penalty alike, and 'tis not hard, I think, / For men so old as we to keep the peace" (1.2.1–3). But what they have achieved seems to be a negative solution based on the penalty of being bound LL and on the withering of age LR rather than on the wise judgment UR and maturing growth UL of a higher love UC.

The patterns of metaphor described so far depend primarily on overturned hierarchies as men misuse the possibilities of the day and plunge instead toward conflict. When everyone except the Montagues leaves, the imagery of disrupted cycles implicit in the role of the old men becomes more significant. Benvolio's rhetoric links him to Montague, who also likes to think of himself as a part of the Prince's day world of peace and order. The Montagues as a family get little attention in the play, but Shakespeare uses this short scene to reveal Montague himself as opposite in manners and temperament to the impulsive Capulet. In this exchange the topic is Romeo and his habit of predawn walks followed by days spent in the "artificial night" (1.1.140) of his room. Benvolio has seen Romeo walking "westward" in a "grove of sycamore" <LL> "an hour before the worshipp'd sun / Peer'd forth the golden window of the east" (1.1.122, 118–19). To walk west is to walk away from the rising sun, and the "grove of sycamore / That westward rooteth from this city side" (1.1.121–22) suggests not only darkness but also perhaps "sick amour" LL that has its cause in the city.[9] When Benvolio arrives, Romeo goes even deeper into "the covert of the wood" (1.1.125).

Montague's reply reflects his conventional outlook in its patterns of metaphor and in its controlled, slow-moving dignity. His traditional views may seem to support the role of the old men, but his polarities are overly simple: night for him is a dangerous time LL best used for sleeping, while the "all-cheering sun" UR (1.1.134) is the bringer of health and order UC. He describes an ideal dawn UL in nature's relationship between the sun and Aurora, the goddess of the dawn, who is just waking from an apparently restful sleep [LL]. In the context of the fight he has joined on this Sunday morning, his praise of the sun seems naive or hypocritical. His views are complacently patriarchal in that he reinforces the analogy among sun, monarch, father, sight, and reason and associates the night with decay and corruption. He seems to have little sense of a positive night or a destructive day and only limited awareness of the conflicting impulses within himself.

To Montague, Romeo's salt tears and sighs pervert the helpful moisture of dew and clouds. His melancholy heaviness and furtive stealth contradict the natural "light" (suggesting both ascent and illumination) that he should get from the sun. His isolation as he "private in his chamber pens himself" (1.1.138) suggests in "pen" both a descent to the animal LR and to a self-conscious, destructive process of creation LR. (We should remember that men have also become "beasts" [1.1.83] through misuse of the day.) When he "makes himself an artificial night" (1.1.140), Romeo "makes" both himself and his chamber a "night." In Montague's view the only solution is to provide "good counsel" UR that will prevent his "humor" from becoming "Black and portendous" (1.1.141–42). In the following passage Montague describes the "secret" and "close" LL Romeo as being like a "bud bit with an envious worm, / Ere he can spread his sweet leaves to the air / Or dedicate his beauty to the [sun]" UL (1.1.149, 151–53). In philosophical terms, Romeo is ignoring Montague's traditional ideals. In psychological terms, he is a victim of love-melancholy LC whose natural growth UL is stunted by his negativism.

Romeo's speeches to Benvolio about love and melancholy

introduce one of the play's central interpretive problems. His elaborate rhetoric, particularly the oxymorons in his first major speech, establishes a connection to the similar language of the Petrarchists. Shakespeare clearly saw the possibilities of dramatizing the attitudes that by 1595 had built up around the sonnet cycles. Many scholars think Shakespeare reveals Romeo's callow immaturity by associating him with Petrarchan excess. From this perspective, Romeo's style is self-consciously imitative early in the play but improves as he matures, with his occasional lapses back into the old rhetoric revealing his still incomplete development.[10] Such judgments of his later speeches lead ultimately to the view that Shakespeare is not in full control of his materials and that the play is early and immature. Various aspects of the Petrarchan manner—the lover's abject passivity LL, the lady's unfeeling haughtiness [UR], the exaggerated use of conventional metaphor—are open to ridicule, as Shakespeare knows, but the various intellectual structures described in part 1 are expressed naturally and seriously through a Petrarchan treatment of paradoxes and polarities. They operate throughout the play and are crucial to the play's form.

How then does the rhetoric of the play function? To use Rosalie Colie's useful term, Shakespeare "unmetaphors" the sonnet's young lover by putting him in a play. According to Colie, "an author who treats a conventional figure of speech as if it were a description of actuality is unmetaphoring that figure."[11] Although Colie follows the conventional view in seeing Romeo and to a lesser degree Juliet as self-conscious poets and concludes it is "in many ways an apprentice-play," she finds that in certain scenes with Juliet, Shakespeare manages Romeo's "sinking of the conventions back into what, he somehow persuades us, is 'reality,' his trick of making a verbal convention part of the scene, the action, or the psychology of the play itself."[12] I would argue that the "unmetaphoring" is basic to the play's conception and should be thought of more positively as the creation of a character who becomes what might be called embodied or actuated metaphor. Lyric becomes drama: the detached introspection of the sonnet's speaker is transformed into dialogue that retains the advantages of poetry while gaining the intensity of the stage. Some of Romeo's preoccupations may result from the fashion. His life does imitate art: Benvolio seems to recognize the rhetorical approach; after their joint sonnet, Juliet says, "You kiss by th' book" and refers later to "a rhyme I learnt even now / Of one I danc'd withal" (1.5.110, 142–43); and Mercutio refers specifically to Petrarch in making fun of Romeo (2.4.38–41).

Romeo does think of himself as in some sense a poet: from his perspective, his poetry would be analogous to the dreams that he later tells Mercutio communicate "things true" (1.4.52). In a poetic drama, however, we should not think of his speeches as his poems. The fashion itself was popular because it expressed what many thought were more significant truths about the psychology and philosophy of love than what we hear from Montague. Romeo behaves as he does, not just because he follows a fashion, but because he is a sensitive and troubled young man struggling to relate the emotions of love to the rest of his world. Lovers will swing wildly between extremes and will seem foolish and immature in their lack of control, but that is how young men in love behave. He is poetical in the same way that Montague is philosophical in his earlier speech about the sun and the night. Both are more concerned with exploring their own immediate situations than with self-conscious literary and philosophical skills.

Benvolio is close enough to Romeo in background, age, attitude, and motivation to serve as almost an alter ego; he has been in the early morning wood because of melancholy <LC> and shares the poetic sensibility of the Petrarchist. As a result he is the perfect interlocutor for Romeo's transformation from sonnet speaker to dramatic character. The central topics of the conventional sonnet—time and love—are introduced casually through dialogue as Benvolio and Romeo discuss the time of day and the contradictory impulses of love. In his first lines Romeo reveals that one side of him is preoccupied with the sorrows of hopeless love LL that make time drag and life seem empty, while another more optimistic side <UL> wonders "Where shall we dine?" (1.1.173). Since unrequited loving and dining seem contradictory, we laugh and wonder about the depth of his despair. While noting that Romeo's swings between depression and optimism are extreme, we should not, however, conclude that Shakespeare is undercutting all that he says. Romeo himself has considerable self-awareness about the impression he makes. He concludes his first long speech with "Dost thou not laugh?" (1.1.183). Later he mocks himself and puns on "sadness" as "serious" and "melancholy" when he replies to Benvolio's "Tell me in sadness, who is that you love?" with "What, shall I groan and tell thee?" (1.1.199–200). Though he knows that his desperation LR makes him seem foolish LL, he cannot escape the role of unrequited lover <LL>.

In the first act, Romeo is defined by the contrarieties of love-hate and melancholy-sanguinity familiar from the sonnets. He claims to understand the "fray" (1.1.173) because he understands himself as the microcosm repeated not only in the society's disorder but in the universe itself. Love is the motivating force behind all action or movement in man and nature, and strong passions can pull toward creation or destruction. All is seen in terms of polarities whose linkages become paradoxical and oxymoronic—not only "loving hate," "cold fire," "sick health," and "Still-waking sleep" but also the more complex opposed meanings of "heavy lightness" (heavy and light in weight, gloomy and bright, melancholy and gay, plodding and nimble, profound and trivial) and of "serious vanity" (1.1.176–81) (weighty or profound and empty, deeply concerned and foolishly trivial, plodding and imaginative).

Montague believes that all works in harmony if nature's rhythms can be followed, whereas the disillu-
sioned Romeo justifies gloom by reference to views of
creation that are themselves contradictory: the cosmic
emptiness of the *ex nihilo* theory has merely changed its
appearance; the "well[-seeming] forms" UC have returned to their original "Misshapen chaos" LC (1.1.179).
Adding Benvolio's love will only "propagate" (1.1.187)
Romeo's grief. Love's sunlike power UR transforms the
earthy, cold, and dry grief LC by drawing up the smoke
(fire) LR of passion and the fume (water) LL of sighs. If
the "fume" LL is "purg'd," one is left with a fire LR in
the eyes; if the "smoke" LR is "vex'd," one is left with a
"sea" of "tears" LL (1.1.190–92).[13] In love's cycle "madness" can seem "discreet" because the "preserving
sweet" of the sanguine UC affects the "choking gall"
(1.1.193–94) of melancholy LC, but burning (adustion)
and weeping will only add to the gall. Whether this phe-
nomenon is seen as metaphor or physiology, it provides a
graphic description of the conflicts within a troubled
lover. Romeo's summation sounds almost existential:
"Tut, I have lost myself, I am not here: / This is not
Romeo, he's some other where" (1.1.197–98). But, as
Leeds Barroll has pointed out,[14] the self in Renaissance
theory was usually defined in relation to a transcenden-
tal philosophy based on cosmic harmony and meaning.
Romeo's self, society, and cosmos are governed by conflict rather than harmony. In short, if there is a spokesman for Renaissance contrariety in the play, it is the
Romeo of this opening scene.[15]

When Romeo goes on to describe Rosaline as a Diana
impervious to Cupid's arrow, we recognize a proud Petrarchan lady <UR> and a Romeo whose changing views
of love are reflected in the differing Cupids that he
thinks influence him. Cupid, the poetic image of love's
causes, has at least four faces: two can see and two are
blind, and we meet all of them in this scene. In the
mystical and neoplatonic traditions of love, the lover's

way to heaven can come either through ascending from the vision of beauty in this world to an understanding of divine beauty (the positive way governed by the Celestial Cupid UR) or through seeking detachment from the world through contemplation and spiritual illumination (the negative way of a blind Cupid with inner vision [LR]). The second seeing Cupid <UR> instigates a physical and earthly love that can also be positive if its object is not overvalued. The second blind Cupid LR is thoroughly disreputable: he shoots his arrows at random and causes the torments of passionate love.[16]

At the very beginning of their exchange, a hopeful Benvolio defines a seeing and generally beneficent Cupid whose "view" (suggesting both his appearance and his vision) is "gentle" even though the lover may find him "tyrannous and rough in proof" (1.1.169–70). But a gloomy Romeo describes a blind Cupid "whose view is muffled" and who "Should, without eyes, see pathways to his will!" (1.1.171–72). The point of the wit is that Benvolio is trying to get Romeo to grant that Cupid can see: Romeo must realize that his sight and reason UR can function. Benvolio cleverly invites a shift to a seeing Cupid when he says "A right fair mark, fair coz, is soonest hit" (1.1.207), but Romeo refuses to be trapped. He associates the seeing Cupid with his state of mind when he tried to court Rosaline. In my view, contrary to the usual reading, Romeo is making fun of these earlier attempts when he describes an ineffective Cupid LL who sees Rosaline but will never hit that "right fair mark" UR with an arrow from his "weak childish bow" LL (1.1.207, 211). A now wiser Romeo <UR> knows that the old methods will not work since the Diana-like Rosaline UC resists all temptation: "She will not stay the siege of loving terms, / Nor bide th' encounter of assailing eyes, / Nor ope her lap to saint-seducing gold" (1.1.212–14). Now Romeo claims to know that love is blind LR.

Romeo then proceeds to make the conventional case against the chaste woman who "Cuts beauty off from all posterity" (1.1.220). Romeo believes that beauty UL and chastity UR (Venus and Diana) should be reconciled: a place must be found for fecundity and married love or else the world will be left to the ugly and corrupt. Again we should think of this recourse to the arguments of the sonnet tradition more as "unmetaphoring" than as evidence of Romeo's imitative style. The argument is also topical. In a society in which Queen Elizabeth has become a public symbol of virginity and in which the neoplatonic tradition celebrates progression from the woman to the divine, justifying marriage is necessary. Shakespeare's first group of sonnets (1–14, 16–17) makes essentially the same point; and in *A Midsummer Night's Dream* Shakespeare finds a place for both Diana and Venus.[17] In this play he touches the theme only lightly since we never meet Rosaline and since Juliet, to Romeo's delight, quickly becomes a follower of Venus.

Despite his gloom, Romeo ends his speech by making a Petrarchan argument that depends on belief in a divine Rosaline UC. If she has the qualities of someone beyond earthly love, she would be "wisely too fair," that is, too just, to "merit bliss" (1.1.221) by following the letter of her vow of chastity. To make Romeo "live dead" LC (1.1.224) in spiritual despair despite his worthy love [LL] would link her to a legalistic Old Testament justice LR that denies New Testament mercy UL. If Romeo were to follow Benvolio's advice to "forget to think of her," he claims he would have to "forget to think" LL (1.1.225–26). When Benvolio responds by asking Romeo to give "liberty unto thine eyes" and "Examine other beauties" UR (1.1.227, 228), Romeo invokes his mind's memory of what he once could see. Like fair women with black masks, the dark makes the fair even more compelling. Romeo's image of a man "strooken blind" LL who "cannot forget / The precious treasure of his eyesight lost" UR (1.1.232–33) suggests both a beauty that the eyes can see UR and an inner vision [LC] that understands the profound illumination of the blind Cupid [LR].

As the next scene begins, a discouraged Benvolio has abandoned the claim of reason and turned to homeopathy: perhaps a cure can be found through introducing a "new infection" (1.2.49). Romeo denies that he is mad but unintentionally proves Benvolio's point with his raving that he is "bound more than a madman is, / Shut up in prison, kept without my food, / Whipt and tormented" LL (1.2.54–56). At this point Romeo is able to "read" UR only "mine own fortune in my misery" LL (1.2.57, 58), but he begins to recover when he first reads the servant's note about the Capulet party and then agrees to Benvolio's plan that Rosaline "be weigh'd" on "crystal scales" (1.2.96) along with the other beauties at the party. At the end of the scene, sight and reason UR are once again in control, and they lead a Romeo who trusts "the devout religion of mine eye" (1.2.88) to declare absolute fidelity to Rosaline. The sun he was avoiding is now the "all-seeing sun" UR who "Ne'er saw her match since first the world begun" (1.2.92–93). In act 1, scene 1, Romeo described cosmic and personal chaos LC but then at least indirectly claimed to be both loving UL and reasonable UR; in scene 2, he repeats the pattern as the pieties of the religion of love <UC> replace his metaphor of being tortured LL.

After the first scene we see little of Montague, but Capulet takes on a parallel role. In his talk with Paris about Paris's proposed "suit" (1.2.6) for Juliet's hand, he, like Montague, is full of conventional advice and at first seems genuinely wise UR. The rash LR Capulet of 1.1 now accepts a more patient UL role, though a hint of regret may be present in his comment that age <LR> should make it easy for him and Montague "to keep the peace" (1.2.3). He seems to understand the rhythms of life and of nature: he knows that "two more summers" need to "wither in their pride" before Juliet will be "ripe to be a bride" (1.2.10–11). When Paris tells him that girls as young as Juliet make happy mothers, Capulet expresses a wise caution that may stem from his own early marriage: "And too soon marr'd are those so early made" LL (1.2.13).[18] But when he invites Paris to come to his party to "woo her" (1.2.16) and goes on to disclaim his parental control over her choice, he is modifying his earlier position and beginning a process whose developing momentum leads directly to the tragedies.

Capulet seems to be rationalizing: he will create an atmosphere that will encourage the match but will avoid LL direct responsibility for pushing LR someone so young into marriage. Planning for the future is essential, but his gloomy LC reliance on Juliet seems excessive: "Earth hath swallowed all my hopes but she" (1.2.14). He makes an attractive case for his party, but we are bound to remain uneasy. In talking of plans for the "old accustom'd feast" (1.2.20), he reminds us that such traditions develop the family values that form the basis of Verona's societal structure UC. As he describes Juliet and the other young girls who will attend the feast and invites Paris to judge them, he reveals himself as another believer in the association of beauty with sight, reason, and virtue UR. But the dangers are apparent. Judging by sight (and hearing) and by "merit" (1.2.31) may through illusion [UC] lead to misvaluing, and youthful "delight" in the time of life "When well-apparell'd April on the heel / Of limping winter treads" may lead "lusty young men" <UL> (1.2.26–28) to treat very young girls <UL> as mature. The play takes place in July, at the height of summer. Instead of letting Juliet mature, Capulet is encouraging, later even forcing, her early spring UL self to play a summer UR role. One reason is that old autumn <LR> Capulet is desperate to retain his own vitality UR.

Not long before the feast begins, the young Juliet must sort out the marriage counsel of her well-meaning UL but officious LR mother and the warm UL but disorderly LL Nurse. In their enthusiasm over a possible wedding, they represent opposite images of the values and attitudes that a young woman needs to develop. The Nurse's earthy preoccupation with the natural rhythms of life suggests the threat of the passions LC but also includes something healthy UL that undercuts both Romeo and Juliet's naive idealism <UL> and the material concerns <UR> of the Capulets. She is linked to a positive femininity UL by her own former life with her husband and Susan, by her long service to the Capulets, by her motherly nurturing of Juliet, and by her colorful warmth and energy; but she lacks the qualities of mind UR that would give her a more independent view of her patriarchal society.

Lady Capulet, although only about 28 if we accept that "I was your mother much upon these years / That you are now a maid" (1.3.72–73), is much older LR in spirit and has become so manipulative and pragmatic LR that she lacks rapport with Juliet. She has lost much of her feminine vitality while taking on the more masculine concerns <UR> of the conventional wife and mother.[19] From her own perspective, her speeches fill out the idealistic philosophy of love and beauty <UC> presented earlier in different ways by Montague and Capulet. For her, Paris is an "unbound" page UL in a "precious book of love" UC, and Juliet can become the "gold clasps" UR that secure the book and thereby "share the glory" of the "golden story" UC (1.3.87, 91–92). References to love in material terms can suggest genuine value UR, as do Romeo's images of Rosaline as "precious treasure" and of Juliet in the balcony scene as valuable "merchandise" (1.1.233; 2.2.84).[20] Nevertheless, the implication is that Lady Capulet has become preoccupied with a worldly "glory" [UC]. She needs to remember that gold and beauty can become ends in themselves, and that the "clasps" that bind can result in a closed book and a rigid order LR.

In the play's final scenes, gold <UR> has associations with both real value and appearances. Standards of judging are made to seem important. To the Nurse, Paris is a "man of wax," and to Lady Capulet "Verona's summer hath not such a flower" (1.3.76, 77). We are apt to question their evaluation and Paris's virtues, particularly if we recall the judgment of the original Paris, whose choice of Aphrodite initiated the Trojan War.[21] Lady Capulet's hope that Juliet may "share all that he doth possess, / ... making yourself no less" deserves the earthy response of the Nurse that she will in fact be "bigger" since "women grow by men" (1.3.93–95). The Nurse's further advice to "seek happy nights to happy days" (1.3.105), with its relaxed acceptance of the natural cycles of life, sums up her conflict with Lady Capulet's values.

Some of what seems to be social comedy in the Nurse's talk gradually takes on more serious personal and even cosmic implications that parallel the chaotic LC world of the first scene. The Nurse's bawdy and rambling reminiscences describe how 11 years earlier she and young Juliet suddenly underwent a series of changes. On Juliet's third birthday, the very day when the Nurse, "Sitting in the sun under the dove-house wall" UL (1.3.27), decided to wean Juliet, there was an earthquake LR. Juliet's unpleasant experience "When it did taste the wormwood on the nipple" <LC> (1.3.30) is reflected absurdly in the cosmic disruption. A day earlier the "high-lone" UL Juliet had another negative experience in her new world of childhood when she "broke her brow" (1.3.36, 38) in a more literal fall LC. Her answer "Ay" to the Nurse's husband's "Thou wilt fall backward when thou comest to age, / Wilt thou not, Jule?" (1.3.56–57) is comically relevant to various falls (including the Fall in Eden), with the husband's good-humored cynicism <LR> about women adding an ambiguous image of masculine attitudes.[22] Juliet's age also has cyclical implications: she makes the transition from infancy to childhood at exactly three, and now she is almost 14, the age at which a young girl is supposed to pass from childhood to adolescence (young adulthood).[23] Also, her birthday will come on Lammas Eve, the night before Lammastide, August 1st. Lammastide, the harvest festival at which the first ripe corn (grain) was presented, has, as Barbara Everett suggests,[24] overtones of both the sacrifice <LC> of the young lovers and the renewal UL possible through the reconciliation of the families.

Astrology may also be significant. Shakespeare may expect an astrologically aware audience to realize that the reference to "A fortnight and odd days" (1.3.15) before Lammastide puts the present date and consequently the action of the entire play around the time when the month of Cancer (the moon) becomes that of Leo (the sun) on July 12 (Old Style). This astrological time of passage is analogous to both dawn and noon. In the transition from feminine moon to masculine sun and from the six night houses to the six day houses, it suggests dawn and the potential harmony of night and day. In the union of the powerful forces of sun and moon at the warmest time of summer there is an emblematic parallel to the summer solstice (high noon) of a month earlier. (In exact opposition the two houses governed by Saturn [Capricorn and Aquarius] meet at the depth of winter, one month after the winter solstice.) If the audience is made aware that the play's first day is Sunday, then the placing of Romeo and Juliet's first meetings on Sunday evening and early Monday also reflects this union of powerful masculine (sun) and feminine (moon) forces.[25] The harmonious fusion of opposites usually leads to order, but in this play the transitional times reflect the difficulties of a mutable world. In Romeo and Juliet's personal world, early afternoon and dawn are times of promise but also of danger. The time just after noon brings marriage and then death in act 3, and the time before dawn is repeatedly significant for love and then separation.

In the Queen Mab scene (1.4) the metaphorical patterns shift slightly, with the theme of masking serving as the vehicle for presenting love in a more active guise. Maskers belong to a traditional, old-fashioned world of romance <LL> in which lovers are outsiders who must disguise themselves in mock-frightening [LR] ways in

order to gain entry and pursue their elaborate court-
ships.[26] In this case the actual situation is closer to the
convention since the intruders really are interlopers
who threaten the order of the Capulet household. From
one perspective such invasions are necessary since the
Capulets cannot continue as a family without renewal
through new blood, but a visit by Montagues strains
manners and the masking tradition itself to their limits.
Each young visitor defines himself by his attitudes toward masking. The conventional Romeo <UL> seems to
want them to do whatever tradition dictates, but he insists that his own role will be that of a torchbearer-
observer <LL>. Benvolio ridicules any thought of having
a silly, armed blind Cupid <LR> who would reduce their
undertaking to absurdity. In his calm, rational (measured) way <UR> he proposes that they present themselves quietly UL but directly UR in an orderly dance UC
that will allow others to judge their good intentions: "let
them measure us by what they will," and "measure
them a measure and be gone" (1.4.9–10).

Mercutio, making his first appearance, takes on a role
of advisor to Romeo opposite that of Benvolio. While
Benvolio is the spokesman UR for a Petrarchan idealism
about love and beauty UC, Mercutio ridicules <LR>
submission to any hierarchical values. Like his name-
sake Mercury, he is "mercurial" in the complexity of
attitudes associated with him. (The name comes from
Brooke's poem, but the role there is not defined.)[27] Preoccupied both with the fun UL of being maskers and
with bringing Romeo out of his depression, he presents
a different view of love and proposes a different kind
of movement. While Benvolio defines women by their
beauty UC, Mercutio sees only their sexuality <LL>.
Benvolio expects a passive <LL> Romeo to see and judge
UR the women at the party, but Mercutio tells Romeo
to assert himself so that he can control <UR> Cupid instead of being controlled LL. He should "borrow Cupid's
wings, / And soar with them above a common bound"

(1.4.17–18). (A more active Romeo UR follows this advice and even this image [2.2.66] when he gets into Juliet's orchard.) When Romeo describes being wounded by a "rough," "rude" Cupid LR and sinking LL under his "heavy burthen," the flexible Mercutio bawdily invokes a "tender," even feminine, Cupid [LL] who would sink under the weight of Romeo: "If love be rough with you, be rough with love; / Prick love for pricking, and you beat love down" (1.4.22–26, 27–28). When Mercutio asks for a "case" or "beetle brows" to cover his "deformities" (1.4.29, 32, 31), his implications seem to be at once sexual (the feminine "case") and violent (the "beetle brows" as an image of death itself). In this context Benvolio's "Come knock and enter" (1.4.33) as they approach the Capulet house takes on a crude meaning LR that a gesturing Mercutio might communicate. If we recognize the Capulet house as a private family place UL, analogous to Juliet's orchard UL, the violation becomes apparent.

Despite Mercutio's provocative encouragement, Romeo remains an earthbound victim. His puns on "ambling," "heavy"-"light," "soul"-"sole," "soar"-"sore," "bound," "prick," "light," "senseless," and "dun" (1.4.11, 12, 15, 18–20, 26–28, 35, 36, 39–41) reinforce his self-image of being weighed down and tied up, staked to the ground, tortured by wounds, and sinking in the mud LL while others are dancing, running, soaring, and loving UL. Nevertheless, Romeo claims a strength related to a positive vision of light and maturity. His role as torchbearer allows him both to worship passively [LL] and to see and strive UR for some kind of higher illumination UC or, more modestly, to be the wise observer whose active life is over [LR]. For Mercutio, Romeo's torch that burns for no useful reason is analogous to burning lights in the day and wasting time in talking [UR]. But Romeo still hopes to achieve a transcendent and unmoving love UC that can triumph over time and mutability LC.

In the Queen Mab section of the scene, Mercutio's

dominant metaphor is generation—of love, of dreams, of desires of all kinds. In Mercutio's view, Romeo is dominated by what the Renaissance thought of as the fantasy <LL>—the internal sense that presents the random and chaotic images of the five senses to the common sense and the judgment UR.[28] When Romeo takes Mercutio's "we burn daylight" literally, Mercutio asks him to "Take our good meaning, for our judgment sits / Five times in that ere once in our [five] wits" (1.4.43, 46–47). The point is more serious than it seems: Mercutio thinks Romeo fails to use his judgment UR to correct the impression of the senses <LL> (just as later he accepts unreliable dreams as truth). Mercutio delights in the fancy or fantasy, as the Queen Mab speech illustrates, but thinks that love without control becomes delusion. Mercutio is convinced that lovers in their dreams "often lie" by inventing polarities of airy illusion [UC] and melancholic despair LC, but Romeo thinks that they lie "In bed asleep, while they do dream things true" (1.4.51–52). For Romeo the vision of love and of dreams [LC] comes from a powerful force UC outside the self. From the traditional perspective described in part 1, each view contains some truth. Love can be illusion [UC] or vision UC; dreams can be wish fulfillment LC or a genuine communication [LC] from the beyond.

In the Queen Mab speech itself, Mercutio develops an imaginative myth that challenges traditional assumptions about love's dualities by expanding the Cupid stories in a way that parallels Shakespeare's handling of Puck in *A Midsummer Night's Dream*. Mercutio's flying Queen Mab turns out to be the feminine counterpart of the winged Cupid that soars and shoots the pricking arrow. From my perspective, critics have misread the implications of the speech through romanticizing its opening section. In his account of a fairy queen and her tiny chariot, Mercutio charmingly captures the fantasy of love and dreams <UC> but also includes an undercurrent of bawdiness that reveals love as a very physical desire

LL. Scholars recognize that "Queen Mab" includes references to "quean" ("slut") and to Mab as a common name for a prostitute[29] but ignore the sexual innuendo of the gestures that might accompany Mercutio's description. His Mab seems to be a bawdy "midwife" (1.4.54) generating or, more precisely, delivering dreams that are sexual fantasies of female genitalia. If the "forefinger" and "men's noses" are phallic; if the "agot-stone" ring and the "empty hazel-nut" "chariot" are vaginal; if the "joiner squirrel" and "old grub" are a pimp and a bawd; if the "waggon-spokes of long spinners' legs," the "traces of the smallest spider web," the "whip of cricket's bone" and "the lash of film" are pubic hair (with comically sadistic overtones); if the "cover of the wings of grasshoppers" and the "collars of the moonshine's wat'ry beams" are moist vulva; and if the "gnat, / Not half so big as a round little worm / Prick'd from the lazy finger of a [maid]" is a maidenhead, with the "round little worm" also suggesting a clitoris stimulated by the maid's "lazy finger" (1.4.55–69), the impulse of the dream of love becomes clear.

Parolles' claim in *All's Well That Ends Well* that "Virginity breeds mites" (1.1.141) (cf. the "atomi," the gnat, and the worm), the bawdiness of Romeo's rejoinder that "Thou talk'st of nothing" (1.4.96) (the vagina), and Mercutio's often obscene manner make allusions along these lines likely. To say that this female chariot "gallops night by night / Through lovers' brains" (1.4.70–71) makes the chariot an active force <UR> generating images in man's passive <LL> imagination. Galloping through the air can be seen as a metaphor for sexual arousal in both sexes: in her later account of another chariot's journey, Juliet tells the masculine "steeds" of the sun UR to "Gallop apace" (3.2.1) so Romeo can join her on their wedding night. Also relevant is Freud's view that dreams of flying often have a disguised sexual content.[30]

The satire finds other objects in the second part of the Mab speech. The glances at the lawyer, courtier, parson, and soldier add scope by suggesting that the illusions of dreams LC encourage other self-serving desires, and there may be further humor in implying that Mab's enticing chariot has no erotic effect on a "courtier's knees," a "lawyers' fingers," a "courtier's nose," or even with the help of a "tithe-pig's tail" on a "parson's nose" (1.4.72, 73, 77, 79–80). (A "courtier's knees" that respond with "cur'sies" [1.4.72] might seem sexless except that Mercutio puns bawdily on "cur'sy" and "courtesy" in a later scene [2.4.50–57]; possibly the courtier may dream of what he can no longer do.) The fun of the soldier's response is largely that this image of masculinity can be made fearful by tiny Mab, but there may also be gibes at someone whose dreams of "blades" and "breaches" (1.4.84) have only military overtones.

In Mercutio's final images we see Mab affecting women's sexuality as well. An "angry Mab" who earlier touched "ladies' lips" and made them "straight on kisses dream" now "plagues" them "with blisters" "Because their breaths with sweetmeats tainted are" (1.4.74–76); the image seems to suggest how sampling sexual "sweetmeats" brings on venereal disease.[31] Here the noble manes of horses are turned into "foul, sluttish hairs" (1.4.90). Then, continuing the horse motif, the "hag" (nightmare) "presses them [the maids] and learns them first to bear, / Making them women of good carriage" (1.4.92–94). This image returns us to more explicit linking of sex and dream, with "good carriage" perhaps suggesting among other puns the earlier "chariot." Here the woman, like the "tender" Cupid <LL> that Romeo was to "burthen," is learning to "bear" (1.4.23, 24, 93) as she should. She will bear the man (and bare herself?) now and children later.

When Romeo follows up his bawdy response that Mercutio "talk'st of nothing" (the vagina) with the suggestion that Mercutio's talk [UR] of "nothing" LL has produced "nothing," LC Mercutio replies that fantasy (ironically LR) and the "idle brain" (1.1.96, 97) (here LL) inevitably produce only the nothingness of dreams LC. He goes on to describe the "vain fantasy" [UC] of dreaming lovers as being as "thin of substance as the air, / And more inconstant than the wind" (1.4.98–100). In his airy courtship of the "frozen bosom of the north" [UC], the wind, like any lover, will become frustrated when he gets no response and "being anger'd" LR will turn to the "dew-dropping south" <LC> (1.4.101–03). The personified directions become a further analogy to women Mercutio sees as dominating the masculine imagination—the cool goddess <UC> who excites him and the earthy whore <LC> who satisfies him. Benvolio indirectly backs Romeo when he implies that Mercutio's windy talk [UR] has itself been fantasy [UC] without action or result, a wind that has blown them from their purposes and therefore from themselves.[32] Since Mercutio prides himself on being decisive and has urged that they not waste time, the point is telling. But from another perspective Mercutio's windy words provide a satirist's view <LR> that tells more truth than the elevated language of love <UC> or the "airy word" (1.1.89) of the brawlers in the opening scene.[33]

Romeo's view of the forces working on him remains somewhat ambiguous. He never does relate his ominous dream, and the power "yet hanging in the stars" (1.4.107) that he refers to in his speech at the end of the scene may or may not be connected to the dream. As always, Shakespeare remains vague about causes and thereby creates a complexity that we should recognize as central to his vision. Romeo at first sounds gloomy about the forces affecting his "despised life" (1.4.110), but he soon recovers. When he speaks of becoming a passenger on a metaphorical voyage, he remains a passive figure <LL> but is now resolved to leave the struggle to another force UR that he instinctively trusts: "But He that hath the steerage of my course / Direct my [sail]!" (1.4.112–13). Douglas Peterson argues plausibly that the allusion is to Cupid rather than God. References to Cupid as helmsman were common, and the play's imagery remains consistently in a secular context. But while an earthly Cupid is notoriously unreliable,[34] this Cupid seems to be celestial UR. To Romeo, trusting Cupid and trusting God are not that different. He leaves the struggle to cosmic forces: on the one hand a force "hanging in the stars," which, like a Satanic landlord LC in an inauspicious time for Romeo, will demand the "vile forfeit of untimely death," and on the other, a Cupid who will steer, presumably also by reference to the stars, Romeo's "course" (1.4.107, 111–12) to an earthly and heavenly harbor of love UC. Romeo's passivity, here as earlier, is ambiguous since giving up control of one's life can mean either rationalizing an abdication to passion and illusion [UC] or devoting oneself to a genuinely higher love UC. In the context of the play larger forces are at work: dreams do prove to tell truths, and mysterious cosmic forces do function. People must be wise enough to know when to drift and when to steer: Romeo's decision to yield control on this matter can be defended, but abdicating free will altogether is never wise.

At this point in the play, there can be little optimism about the party, particularly since the prologue has given us foreknowledge that the harbor of Romeo's voyage will be premature death. The advisors close to Romeo and Juliet represent opposed views. Romeo must evaluate Benvolio's Montague-influenced vision of an ideal patriarchal order based on beauty, sight, and reason <UR> on the one hand and Mercutio's cynicism <LR> about power and love on the other. Juliet is pulled between Lady Capulet's pragmatic concern with status and money <UR> and the Nurse's warm enthusiasm and earthy femininity <UL>. Both Romeo and Juliet seem unready or unable to take active control of their own lives. The upcoming feast seems even more threatening when we remember Capulet's self-indulgent idealism <UR>, Tybalt's proud, choleric honor LR, the maskers'

impulsiveness <LR>, and the developing competition between Paris and Romeo (though both are unaware of it).
The servant's comment about "every thing in extremity"
LC (1.3.102) seems like an apt summary of what has pre-
ceded and a forecast of what is to come.

THREE

Extreme Sweet
(*Romeo and Juliet* 1.5–2.6)

But passion lends them power, time means, to meet,
Temp'ring extremities with extreme sweet.

(2.Chorus.13–14)

T he opening of *Romeo and Juliet* is dominated, as we
have seen, by extreme views and behavior. In the
next section of the play (1.5–2.6) several characters, notably the young lovers but also Capulet and the Friar, try to
change the situation by "Temp'ring extremities with extreme sweet." For a time their various plans have a real
chance of success because the "passion" UL that "lends
them power" UR seems robustly natural and because the
power itself is directed by both patience UL and planning
UR. Capulet somewhat surprisingly proves to be a good
host, and his feast becomes an image of the possibilities
for familial and societal order UC. In the balcony scene,
Romeo and Juliet soar in their passion UL but also

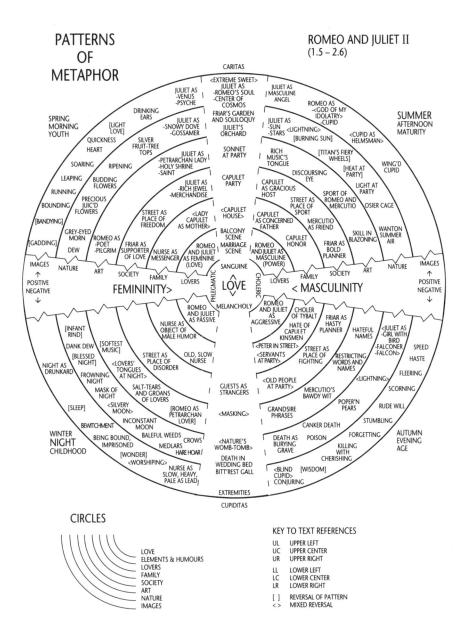

manage to achieve a remarkable balance of diverse roles
UC. As the new day dawns, we meet Friar Lawrence,
who proves in this initial stage to be a wise counselor
UR for Romeo and a bold advocate UR for love and reconciliation. In the street scene (2.4), a contagious spirit
of fun <LC> endangers order but ends up furthering the
image of potential harmony UC. At the end of this section, the dream of love <UC> comes closer to realization as Romeo and Juliet meet at the Friar's cell for their
marriage (2.6). Threatening forces remain, but for a short
time we are caught up in the hope that the "extreme
sweet" <UC> of the lovers can lead to a transformed reality as a mood of optimism spreads.[1] As my chart suggests, all times and places are potentially positive, but
the danger of slipping into illusion [UC] is also present.
We see an evening house, a night orchard and balcony, a
dawn garden, a late morning street, and an early afternoon cell, all of which promote love and joy UC, but we
also sense the fragility of the characters' hopes.

The party scene suffers from our inability to see the
original staged version, but we can discover some of Shakespeare's likely intentions through a willingness to consider possibilities suggested by the metaphorical patterns.
The staging of the scene can be divided into four sections
shaped by contrasting treatment of light and movement:
1) lines 1–25: the comments of the servants, the entrance
of the maskers, Capulet's welcome, and a lively dance; 2)
lines 26–87: Capulet's call for "More light" (1.5.27), a
more restrained dance, Romeo's observation of Juliet,
and Tybalt's angry response; 3) lines 87–110: Capulet's
call for "More light, more light!" (1.5.87), and the lovers'
sonnet; 4) lines 111–end: the parting of the lovers, the departure of the guests, and a return to darkness.

Capulet himself reflects the opposing poles of the
scene's metaphors. His impulse toward an idealized and
dignified world of beauty, light, and order UC conflicts
with his fascination for the spontaneity and vitality
<UL> that he sees in the maskers and remembers as a

part of his own youth. He sincerely wants the best for Juliet, and he seems aware that the family's renewal depends on avoiding both the rigidities of Tybalt LR and the chaotic tendencies of the first dance <LC>. His "ancient feast" (1.2.82) celebrates not only community and family UC but also the regeneration that comes through youth. Women of all ages are present and encouraged to participate, and Capulet himself nostalgically recalls his own masking days. Such deception can breed the illusions of love <UC>, and Lady Capulet later charges Capulet himself with being a "mouse-hunt in your time" LR (4.4.11), but it also promotes the vitality of a vigorous society. Both the upper class and the servants take part in the feast. We are reminded of the artisans' participation in the wedding celebration at the end of *A Midsummer Night's Dream*. Capulet recognizes the need for community and seems to understand that the feud has led to excessive reliance on the inner family circle. In contrast, the Nurse, always a useful guide to dangerous tendencies in Capulet manners, comments with apparent relief at the end of the evening, "the strangers all are gone" (1.5.144).

If the maskers behave as they have earlier said they will, the first part of the scene should take on more structure. Benvolio has stressed the judging of the beauties UR and presumably becomes an unobtrusive participant in the dancing. Mercutio has talked of a more active, even outrageous, role <LR> but apparently manages to stay within the limits of decorum, or at least to escape detection. The threat of a confrontation with Tybalt LR could be prominent on the stage, and Mercutio might also have some contact with the Nurse that would prepare us for their wild meeting in act 2, scene 4. If Will Kempe is playing a servant role,[2] as seems likely, he could promote an undercurrent of chaos <LC> in the opening section of the scene. If he clowns with the musicians, he prepares us for his later scene (this time as Peter) with the musicians (4.4). If he is the servant who

makes the odd comment (1.5.43) that he does not know
Juliet, he may intend a comic thrust at Romeo as an
intruding masker LR. The servants are always worth
watching for patterns: when the second servant regrets
the absence of "good manners" "in one or two men's
hands, and they unwash'd too" (1.5.3–4), he introduces
the prominence of "manners" UR and "hands" <LR> in
the party scene as a whole.

During the more proper dance UC of the second section, the judging theme UR so central in the expectations
of Paris, Juliet, and Romeo would be developed. Paris has
no lines but is almost certainly present: enough actors
were available to avoid requiring Paris to miss this important scene. Juliet should be the center of everyone's
attention, particularly Paris's and Romeo's. If Paris is the
"yonder knight" whose "hand" Juliet is said to "enrich"
and if Rosaline is assumed to be one of the "crows"
(1.5.41–42, 48), the fulfillment of the judging theme becomes apparent. Romeo should be passive <LL> but dignified UR: his role is prominent enough to attract
Capulet's attention and praise UR and to allow Juliet to
identify him as the one "that would not dance" (1.5.132).
Only a Tybalt obsessively concerned with Capulet decorum takes Romeo's refusal to dance as evidence of rude-
ness LR. He calls him a "villain," that is, a base person,
three times and a "slave" who "cover'd with an antic
face" has come "To fleer and scorn at our solemnity"
(1.5.62, 64, 75, 55–57). The kind of insulting behavior Tybalt defines here LR is characteristic of Mercutio rather
than Romeo and prepares us for the conflicts of 3.1.

Capulet's handling of Tybalt, while effective at the
time, does not resolve our questions about his wisdom.
After watching Capulet's behavior in the first scene, we
might expect him to support Tybalt, but their views of
honor differ considerably. Capulet treats Romeo well for
several reasons UR—the recent truce, Romeo's good
reputation, the honor of a host, and the fear of disrupting
the party.[3] In language that recalls the earlier description

of the "fiery Tybalt," Capulet sees Tybalt as a disruptive natural force LR: "wherefore storm you so?" (1.1.109; 1.5.60). (Tybalt even sounds like lightning itself when he wants "To strike him [Romeo] dead" [1.5.59]). But when his plea for patience UL has little effect, Capulet's terms for Tybalt become contemptuous LR. In his reply Tybalt defines an almost allegorical struggle between "Patience" UL and "willful choler" LR, and he speaks of a future transformation from "seeming sweet" <UC> to "bitt'rest gall" LC (1.5.89, 92). His words are ominously suggestive since most of the men in the play prove unable to control their "choler" and since Romeo has already described his own "choking gall" and "preserving sweet" (1.1.194).

The comparatively harmonious feast establishes a favorable atmosphere for Romeo and Juliet's first encounter. In the dance we see the balance of a societal order UC that includes the horizontal or earthly movement a vertically oriented Romeo has been denying.[4] The start of Romeo's opening speech recalls his earlier debate with Benvolio and is also relevant to the light-heat imagery. That "she doth teach the torches to burn bright!" fulfills Benvolio's hope that "one fire burns out another's burning" (1.5.44; 1.2.45) and suggests that Romeo's inner torch is bringing the heat of passion <UL> as well as light for Petrarchan observation UR. When Juliet "hangs upon the cheek of night / As a rich jewel in an Ethiop's ear," Juliet is the "jewel" UL (a proleptic pun by Romeo) whereas Paris is the "knight"-"night" who to Romeo is an unworthy "Ethiop" LR (1.5.45–46, 42). When Juliet is "a snowy dove trooping with crows," we can imagine a procession of dancing young ladies, including Rosaline, who like Paris are at least metaphorically dark; we should also recall Romeo's insistence to Benvolio that he would never think Rosaline his "swan a crow" (1.5.48; 1.2.87). As the speech continues, Romeo begins his transformation from a passive observer <LL> of beauty to a forceful suitor UR. In the conventions of the mask, the torchbearer <LL> is becoming an active masker UR; in the context of literary genre, the "unmetaphored" speaker <LL> of the sonnet is now an "unmetaphored" knight UR from the romance. The adolescent UL is becoming a young man UR as he takes on the qualities of the Cupid <UR> that he has described to Mercutio as "too rough, / Too rude, too boist'rous" [LR] for his "tender" <LL> (1.4.25–26) nature. Love itself <UC> is the transforming power, and as the play proceeds, we see Romeo (and Juliet) take on other roles shaped by the cyclical processes that govern the experiences of love and life itself.

When Romeo breaks into poetry upon meeting Juliet, the transition is made more smoothly since Romeo's first speech in his new role is part of his joint sonnet with Juliet: the romance hero can without inconsistency retain the lyric intensity of the sonnet speaker. Like the dance, the sonnet UC combines the form of measured art UR with the exuberance of youthful courtship UL and Capulet's call for "More light, more light!" (1.5.87) implying staging that will emphasize the visual beauty. It also combines wit, reason, epigrammatic balance, and formality UR with the spontaneity and emotion of the natural UL. Most striking, though, is its combination of worship [LL] and action <UR>, as in Romeo's images of "rough" hands <LR> that "profane" and "tender" <UL> (1.5.96, 93) kisses that purge. While Juliet is more passive in that she is a responder rather than an initiator, she too contributes to love's fanciful logic. Even her undercutting comment—"You kiss by th' book" (1.5.110)—is more an invitation UR to further ingenuity than a criticism LR of his style or an attempt at retreat LL. The formality of the sonnet allows the lovers to venture without great risk, for the elaborate logic of the argument could be dismissed by either of them as playful gallantry. The artificiality of the rhetoric should refute the notion that the language of love must be simple to be sincere. Eighteen lines do the work that in a realistic presentation would require much longer. Although Romeo and Juliet are together on stage for a fairly short time in the play,[5] poetic language gives their meetings an intensity that makes their love convincing. Their fluency identifies them not as skilled poets but as true lovers to whom poetic convention grants heightened expression.

In the final part of the scene, ominous references remind us of the threats to Romeo and Juliet's love as the stage gradually returns to darkness. What from one perspective is a natural love UL is from another a horrible mistake LR, and an uneasy Juliet has trouble in defining her attitude. She first worries that Romeo might be married and introduces a major motif, that her only "wedding-bed" UC may be "My grave" LC (1.5.135). (The "antic face" [1.5.56] Romeo is wearing may contribute to her image of death.) Then, in perceiving "My only love sprung from my only hate," she describes this "birth of love" UL as "prodigious" LR (1.5.138, 140) (that is, monstrous or unnatural). We are reminded of the diverse factors that contribute to the outcome. Their love is not the product of some divine force UC striking in a magically spiritual way but the result of a complex series of causes that Shakespeare is at some pains to explicate. The momentum caused by the family pressure on Juliet to marry, by the society's assumptions about love, and by the romantic atmosphere of the dance itself is powerful. Chance <LC> also plays a part. If Capulet had seen Romeo's actual approach to Juliet instead of his earlier reticence, if Tybalt had not exited just before Romeo speaks to Juliet, or if Romeo and Juliet had known each other's real identities, the encounter may not have taken place.

The Chorus in the prologue to act 2 presents a candid assessment of this new love and of the building momentum toward disaster. The less flattering side of the lovers' motivation gets more attention than earlier, but the Chorus maintains a detached manner that recapitulates without passing judgment. In recounting Romeo's switch from Rosaline to "tender Juliet," the Chorus implies that

the "heir," "young affection," is not much different from
his dying father, "old desire," and even calls the lovers
"bewitched by the charm of looks" LC (2.pro.4, 2, 1, 6).
Such comments echo Mercutio's views, but the Chorus
then goes on to concentrate on the "power" UR of their
"passion" UI. (2.pro.13) to overcome the difficulties
caused by the impossibility of a normal courtship. As
my choice of chapter titles suggests, viewing the lovers
as "Temp'ring extremities with extreme sweet" <UC>
(2.pro.14) sums up this section's tone. The lovers use
some form of "sweet" ten times in the balcony scene,
and later Juliet tries her own magic <UC> by imploring
the "sweet, sweet, sweet Nurse" (2.5.54) for good news of
her meeting with Romeo.

Just after the Chorus's summary and before the balcony scene, Mercutio, the cynical critic LR of sweetness,
presents his view of love's earthy goals LC and conjuring
language. When Mercutio playfully tries to conjure up
Romeo, he combines bawdy references to physical love
with descriptions of the lovers' elevated, and to him non-
sensical, rhetoric [UC]. Romeo may invoke the beloved's
(in this case Rosaline's) "bright eyes, / . . . high forehead
and . . . scarlet lip," but Mercutio thinks that her "quiv-
ering thigh, / And the demesnes that there adjacent lie"
(2.1.17–20) are his unstated goal LL. The metaphorical
structure of the Queen Mab scene is repeated, with conjuring LC replacing dreaming [UC] as the image of how
the mind of the lover functions. In Mercutio's parody,
Romeo's silence LL proves the failure of his rhetoric to
win Rosaline or raise himself and demonstrates his lapse
into inactivity LC. The natural place for such a pitiful
figure is the ground LC, where he can indulge himself
with more honest but equally hopeless wishes that
Rosaline were a "medlar" LL and he a "pop'rin pear" LR
(2.1.36, 38). Benvolio's explanation recalls the opening
scene: "Blind is his love and best befits the dark"
(2.1.32). According to both Benvolio and Mercutio,
Romeo is in a world of melancholy night and Blind
Cupid LC.

But we know better. Juliet has replaced Rosaline and a new activity is apparent: the running, leaping UL Romeo (as he makes his escape) that Benvolio describes is no longer the standing, watching Romeo <LL> who went to the feast or the wandering, melancholy Romeo LC of 1.1. But Romeo is still troubled: "Can I go forward when my heart is here? / Turn back, dull earth, and find thy centre out" (2.1.1–2). The most apparent meaning is that Romeo's body is "dull earth" LC without the heart that he has left with Juliet, but there are other overtones. His "centre" Juliet is the emblem of divine beauty and therefore the center of the universe UC. On the other hand, the literal center of the earth has a core of fire traditionally associated with destructive passion and with hell itself LC.[6] If Mercutio is right, Juliet's "centre" is thus sexual, and Romeo's impulse toward love is both physical and foolish.

In the balcony scene Shakespeare's art creates a microcosmic setting whose analogical implications suggest the full scope of the play's levels of meaning. This part of the house and the adjacent orchard are Juliet's, and her counselor here is that emblem of one kind of femininity, the Nurse <UL>. The balcony and orchard, the physical extensions of Juliet's bedchamber, embody her femininity UL and the openness of her consciousness. Such a place complements but also threatens Capulet's masculine household. He can allow "strangers" (1.5.144) and even Montagues at his festive party but would see any masculine intrusion into this feminine space as an outrageous violation of family honor. When Romeo enters, the setting becomes the traditional garden of love, identified with both the sacred love that directs the earthly toward the divine UC and the profane love LC familiar from Mercutio's speeches.[7] The metaphors of the scene associate the lovers with the impulses of both gardens. Each of the lovers is at once a supplier of love's grace (*agape*) and an aspiring lover (*eros*).

Shakespeare organizes the scene around the lovers' shifts between masculine and feminine roles. In the first

part of the scene (ll. 1–32) Romeo, after boldly entering UR the orchard, is a passive [LL] but articulate UR
worshiper [LL] of a sunlike UR but silent [LL] "winged
messenger of heaven" UR (2.2.28). When Juliet speaks,
Romeo listens and accepts her revelatory word UR (33–
49). When Romeo himself speaks, he remains a worshiper but becomes a suitor identified with Cupid himself
UR, while a very human Juliet, at first a frightened
daughter <LL>, soon becomes the passionate mistress
<UR> of an ambiguously dark garden <LL> (49–135). In
this long central section the Petrarchan worship <LL> of
the beloved, so often leading to the lady's rejection [UR]
of the wooer, is transformed into mutual love UC.[8] Finally, in the last part of the scene a practical Juliet, with
impulses toward a domination that is in turn maternal
UR and possessive <LR>, directs a compliant but less assured Romeo <UL> toward marriage (136–end). But she
also remains passive in her pledge to "follow thee my
lord throughout the world" (2.2.148).

The opening of the scene suggests a Petrarchan context different from the first scene,[9] with Romeo now
looking "east" UL (2.2.3) toward the dawn rather than
walking west LR to escape it. His changed attitude results from seeing Juliet as a "fair sun" UR (2.2.3) whose
metaphorical rising removes the darkness of his melancholy LC and provides form UR for the passive UL side
of his nature. He asks the Juliet-sun to "kill the envious
moon," her former goddess, whose whiteness is now to
Romeo not the strength of chastity <UR> but the paleness of "grief" LC (2.2.4, 5) and whose green livery as
Diana now suggests not self-sufficiency UR but illness
and folly LL. Masculine images of Juliet dominate, but
fusing them with feminine images keeps Juliet from losing her natural gender. Her "eye discourses" UR (2.2.13)
actively with the stars, but her eyes and cheek are also
praised for a brightness UC that signifies beauty UL as
well as power UR. To be "star-cross'd" (pro.6) by such
eyes is to be governed by a beneficent cosmos UC.
Romeo longs to be a "glove" UL on her "hand" UR,

thereby being able to "touch" UR her "cheek" UL (1.2.24–25). When Juliet speaks from the balcony, she becomes a masculine "bright angel" who, like a "winged messenger of heaven" (2.2.26, 28), elicits mortals' wonder <LL>. Romeo's response, however, perceives the angel-messenger in relation to images of femininity—the clouds as his horse and the air as a bosomy sea—that make Juliet's power seem more natural and balanced. Her "word" UR about a name change leads an eager Romeo to talk about being "new baptiz'd" UL into a religion of love that has Juliet as his "dear saint" UC (2.2.49, 50, 55). His love seeks a power to serve, and Juliet becomes for him a mediator of the divine word UC.

In her overheard soliloquy, Juliet is to herself no angel, saint, or divine messenger; nevertheless, she fantasizes a power UR over Romeo that he is eager to accept. Her fanciful revolt depends on making love more important than family. In her attacks on names and forms <LR> and in her defence of natural love UL, Juliet sounds like a philosophical nominalist criticizing the structures of neoplatonic realism and like a woman more concerned with real emotions than with the rigid systems of the patriarchal mind. That these two positions coalesce so easily helps explain why Juliet gets the same high praise from both modern "nominalist" and feminist critics for her maturity and insight.[10] When we read the passage analogically and link it to her later implied criticisms of masculine tendencies LR—spying, violence, perjury, laughing at broken vows—her position has some force. A Renaissance playgoer would be more apt to interpret her views as a feminine view of masculine excesses than as a sweeping indictment. Romeo's search for structures is the justified if not always wise occupation of active, creating, philosophizing man <UR>.[11] What Juliet wants is the revitalization, not the overthrow, of traditional hierarchies. She sees herself as a young girl struggling between her natural impulse UL toward love UL and the moral duty UR of a chaste daughter.

The Romeo of the scene's central section combines

continued worship with a masculine boldness that he claims comes from Cupid himself. If we identify Juliet with Psyche, their story takes on mythic overtones.[12] Juliet has seen Romeo only at the party and never does see him during the day except in the Friar's dark cell. Her trials, including a descent to the underworld, parallel Psyche's, and Romeo, like Cupid, not only suffers a "wound" but also regards her as his "soul" UC (2.2.1, 164). Romeo transforms Mercutio's mocking LR reference to winged Cupid (1.4.17) into an image of power UR: "and what love can do, that dares love attempt" (2.1.68). He makes the connection with Cupid explicit after Juliet questions how he found his way: "By love; . . . He lent me counsel, and I lent him eyes" (2.2.80–81). Cupid, earlier a helmsman UR (1.4.112–13) and winged UR (2.2.66), has become a blind counselor [LR] of a higher love UC directed by Romeo's clear earthly vision UR. When Romeo goes on to say that he is "no pilot" (2.2.82) but will venture anyway, the implication is that Romeo's eyes, the blind Cupid's higher love, and the seeing Cupid's skill as a helmsman can come together to make the journey successful. Juliet becomes the goddess UC who makes the sea journey rewarding: "My bounty is as boundless as the sea, / My love as deep" (2.2.133–34). The sea becomes the image of a feminine fullness UL both cosmic UC and personal.[13]

When Juliet, the emblem of bright beauty, welcomes "the mask of night" that hides her "maiden blush," her paradoxical justification depends on formulating the positive truths of "dark night" [LC] (2.2.85, 86, 106) and criticizing the deceiving appearances of masculine day [UR]. She "fain would . . . dwell on form" but implies that truth UC is more natural than the proper lady's false "compliment" [UR] (2.2.88, 89). A "gentle" Romeo must feel the true emotions of love UL, and "pronounce" them "faithfully" UR, and "trust" UL (2.2.93, 94, 100) her truth UR. What may seem like "yielding to light love" [UL] is actually her "true-love passion" UL (2.2.105, 104). Romeo's attempt to swear by the moon despite his earlier attack on it suggests he is about to continue the punning paradoxes on light; he invokes neither the chaste moon of Diana UR nor the fickle moon [UR] that Juliet thinks of but rather a moist moon UL associated with the fecundity of "fruit-tree tops" and the value of "silver" (2.2.108). Juliet, though, chooses to pursue another reading—the moon's fickleness—as a way of continuing her points about false light and swearing oaths. Her response is less a repudiation of Romeo's language of love than a playful way of complimenting this "god of my idolatry" UC who should "swear by thy gracious self" (2.2.114, 113). Judging by her elaborate rhetoric, the moon and the hyperbolic language of worship are not to be off limits.

Using the lightning LR as another image of light she dislikes, Juliet changes the argument itself by drawing back from her night vision to a more sensible Capulet daytime view. She worries that their "lightning" love will disappear before anyone "can say it lightens" UL (2.2.119, 120); her mention of "lightning" is the first reference to what becomes a dominant image cluster LR linking lightning, firepowder, and rash love. She advocates instead a return to the light of summer and the sun UR, which will allow the gradual "ripening" of their "bud of love" UL into a "beauteous flow'r" UC (2.2.121–22). Her call for patience reminds us of Capulet's fear of forcing April buds and his wish for "two summers" to "wither" so Juliet will be "ripe" (1.2.10–11) at marriage. Juliet now finds a new virtue in night: sleep is seen as the extension of the "sweet repose and rest" [LL] (2.1.123) that she feels within herself and wishes to communicate to the restless Romeo. Romeo still believes in their "blessed, blessed night!" [LC] but has his own fears that "Being in night, all this is but a dream, / Too flattering-sweet to be substantial" (2.2.139–41). At the scene's end Romeo longs to be the "sleep and peace" [LL] (2.1. 187) Juliet has invoked, but he must leave to escape detection.

The sense of intrusive outside forces LR, which has

been almost entirely lost in the middle section of the scene returns in the last part. After the Nurse's calls, associated with the Capulet world and its threats LR, Juliet begins to think in practical terms about what can be done today. Surprisingly, in light of her earlier call for patience UL, she boldly UR proposes an immediate marriage. Apparently she already feels under pressure to marry Paris: "Bondage is hoarse, and may not speak aloud, / Else would I tear the cave where Echo lies, / And make her airy tongue more hoarse than [mine], / With repetition of my [Romeo's name]" (2.2.160–63). The overtones are ominous. If Juliet, forced like Echo into whispers LL by a Juno-like Lady Capulet LR, is unable to communicate with her Narcissus, Romeo, she will lose the power UR to control him. When Romeo hears her voice but not her frantic words about tearing the cave of Echo, he responds with a reference to Juliet as Psyche UC, the soul UC that gives spiritual meaning to life: "It is my soul that calls upon my name" (2.2.164). These ironic allusions suggest the complexities and confusions that influence the rebellious but naive lovers. Earlier, Romeo juxtaposes another reference to Juliet as his soul UC—"So thrive my soul"—with a schoolboy image that calls attention to his youth <UL>: "Love goes toward love as schoolboys from their books, / But love from love, toward school with heavy looks" (2.2.153, 156–57). Both seem to be hoping for an ending that will, like the story of Cupid and Psyche, show the lovers overcoming all objections and achieving a marriage both human and divine UC. But a Renaissance audience might also be expected to remember the tragic story of Echo and Narcissus and the associations of Cupid with death LC.[14]

In the last part of the scene, Juliet is the one who asks the questions and makes the plans <UR>. Romeo, knowing nothing of Paris's courtship, has no reason to push a quick marriage, but under Juliet's urging he agrees as if it were a natural UL progression. Juliet's assertiveness also reflects a passionate woman's natural desire <UL> for love and marriage that becomes even stronger in her soliloquy in 3.2. A possessive Juliet <LR> worries about a wandering LL Romeo. When Romeo has left for the first time, she says in soliloquy (this time not overheard): "O, for a falc'ner's voice, / To lure this tassel-gentle back again!" (2.2.158–59). Later, while talking directly to him, she uses another bird image, this time of "a wanton's bird" that is her "poor prisoner" <LL> controlled <UR> by a "silken thread" (2.2.177–80). Juliet as the powerful little girl has some of the impulses of the Petrarchan lady <UR> with her suitor. We remember that in 1.2 Romeo spoke of himself as "Shut up in prison, kept without my food, / Whipt and tormented" LL (1.2.55–56). When Juliet hopes that she will not "kill thee with much cherishing" (2.2.183), the natural impulse of possessive love takes on an undercurrent of sadism LR. As she awaits Romeo on their wedding night, she herself becomes a falcon with "unmann'd blood" <LR> (3.2.14) eager for her prey. Implicit is the difficulty of finding a balance so that the impulse of both sexes to find peace UC, partly through sexual death, does not become death itself LC. The Romeo who identified with the singing birds UL (2.2.22) has now become Juliet's helpless but willing plaything <LL>.

Despite the references to classical myth, Romeo and Juliet are presented throughout the scene as human beings whose gender responses are spontaneous. Their sexual identities are secure because they are willing to follow apparently conflicting but actually natural instincts that balance their selves and their love through a harmonious fusion of masculine and feminine qualities. Romeo can be a venturing sailor or a winged Cupid UR on the one hand and a dreaming schoolboy or Juliet's little bird <LL> on the other; Juliet can be a falconer and a messenger of heaven UR but also a blushing maiden and a submissive would-be wife UL. Shakespeare seldom shows them as equals outside of hierarchical structures. Complex emotions demand diverse expression: while their impulses are at times foolish, they are natural and therefore convincing. Together they achieve a fusion UC that brings the security of personal identity and mutual love.

In the dawn scene that is our first view of him, Friar Lawrence speaks wisely about the forces that influence the relationships of people, society, nature, and the cosmos.[15] That this major speech is in soliloquy suggests Shakespeare is less concerned with Romeo as a tragic figure whose choices and education are central than with the larger patterns of meaning an audience should understand. (Romeo enters during the last eight lines, but there is no indication that he hears anything.) The balcony scene opened with Juliet as a metaphorical rising sun UL and closed with a threatening dawn [UL] that parts the lovers. Now the Friar uses dawn imagery to explicate a philosophy that provides a larger context for what has been happening. He is full of the wonder of the dawn and of a garden filled with the mixed blessings of the natural world. Just as the positive associations of Juliet's orchard UL are balanced by references to illusion [UC] and sensual fruit [UL], so the Friar's garden participates in the ambiguities of nature and life. The cell of his later scenes is, in contrast, isolated and dark, a suitable place for spiritual illumination [LC] or for plotting LR.

His opening words sound at first like an attempt at conventional description.[16] Our impression is of an unruly night LC and beneficent day UC: "The gray-ey'd morn smiles on the frowning night" and "fleckled darkness like a drunkard reels"; but in line four there is an ominous suggestion that the drunkard LL night better move quickly or "Titan's [fiery] wheels" LR (2.3.1, 3, 4) will get him. A similar ambiguity is present in the next lines: "the sun" will "advance his burning eye" <UR> in order "to dry" "night's dank dew," LL but the heat requires timely action and an "osier cage" UR to preserve the vitality UL of both the "baleful weeds and precious-juiced flowers" (2.3.5–8). The Friar describes two sides of both the night and the day; and the dawn seems to be a magical time when those who understand nature's polarities can effect beneficial fusions. The complexities of cyclical process underlie existence: "The earth that's nature's mother is her tomb; / What is her burying grave, that is her womb" (2.3.9–10). Night and winter bring death LC but also prepare for the renewal UL of life. A constantly changing but wondrously creative feminine earth is linked not just to the diurnal and seasonal (night and winter) but also to cycles of the four elements and the ages of life.[17] All "children" (2.3.11) of nature contain at least some good, and each contributes uniquely to some larger whole that, read properly, reveals God's grace UC. As a friar, Friar Lawrence would presumably believe in God's transcendent grace, but here he describes the "powerful grace" UC (2.3.15) that works within nature.

The Friar understands that after the Fall both motives and results are mixed: a well-meaning UR bungler, "stumbling on abuse," LR may cause disaster LC; and someone using questionable means LR may achieve, perhaps unintentionally, a "dignified" UC (2.3.20, 22) result. In the play itself, these principles of nature are illustrated: the lovers' "virtue" is "misapplied" (2.3.21), and through deception the Friar and the lovers almost achieve their worthy ends before stumbling. The potion from an "infant rind" <LL> almost brings the "medicine" of renewal UC but instead becomes indirectly the "poison" LR (2.3.23, 24) of tragedy LC. In the references to the "rind" as "infant" and the "flower" as "weak," the need for nurturing control UR suggested earlier by the "osier cage" (2.3.23, 7) is implied. In his final lines, Friar Lawrence explains that in both man and nature "grace and rude will" are like "opposed kings" (2.3.28, 27) who struggle for dominance. This more conventionally moral division reflects the Friar's hope that people will be able to translate knowledge into effective action, but his main point is that when "rude will" LR takes control, avoiding disaster becomes almost impossible. Implicit in the whole speech is the analogy between man, society, nature, and the cosmos, all of which work by hard to manage natural processes. From the Friar's perspective, Romeo's alternating moods and the Capulet / Montague conflict are dangerous both to themselves and their society. But if masculine and feminine principles are in balance, then by analogy there can be stability within the self, love and friendship in personal relationships, and concord in society UC.

The Friar is more comfortable with practical analysis than with theoretical philosophy and helps direct audience reactions toward Romeo's love. When he criticises Romeo's earlier love for Rosaline, the Friar uses the familiar imagery of Petrarchism, but he is talking about love, not poetry. As in the first scene of the play, Romeo's language <LL>—"sighs" that cloud the sky, "salt"-tears that "season love," "sallow cheeks," and "old groans" (2.3.70–74)—identifies him with the emotion of a speaker in a sonnet rather than as a self-conscious follower of a literary tradition. When the Friar says Rosaline "knew well / Thy love did read by rote that could not spell" (2.3.87–88), he sees Rosaline as a wise Diana UR who rejects Romeo for schoolboy attitudes [UL], not literary posturing. Critical of Romeo "For doting, not for loving, pupil mine" (2.3.82), he implies just what we would expect from a friar—that love can be the positive force UC Christianity, neoplatonism, and Petrarchism have traditionally celebrated but can also lead to trouble. When Romeo says, "I stand on sudden haste," Friar Lawrence replies, "Wisely and slow, they stumble that run fast" (2.3.93, 94). But the Friar has his own reason for hasty action <LR>: the hope that a marriage will resolve the feud. He knows that, if he can achieve that resolution, he will bring "extreme sweet" UC not only to Romeo and Juliet but also to the feuding families, the Prince, Verona, and himself. Like Capulet and the young lovers, he is in danger of pursuing an unwise course LR because he so eagerly wants a "sweet" result.

Before we again see Romeo and Juliet together, an intervening street scene (2.4) not only relaxes the atmosphere through Mercutio's wit and some farcical fun with
the Nurse but also shows us a Romeo who might be able
to survive in this world of extremes. Before Romeo arrives, Mercutio's satiric spirit <LR> controls the tone as
he criticizes both Romeo and Tybalt. From Mercutio's
perspective, Rosaline's domination LR has turned Romeo
into an emasculated fool LL. He is "for the numbers that
Petrarch flow'd in" (2.4.38–39) and thinks his lady
greater than the loveliest ladies of legend. Like the Friar
earlier, Mercutio is commenting more on Romeo's state
of mind than his literary interests. His sight, hearing,
and emotions have all been affected. Since he has been
"stabb'd with a white wench's black eye, run through the
ear with a love-song, the very pin of his heart cleft with
the blind bow-boy's butt-shaft" (2.4.14–16), he can be no
match for the very real sword LR of Tybalt. While Romeo
has adopted the manner of the lover, Tybalt has taken up
a new fashion of swordplay. Tybalt "fights as you sing
prick-song, keeps time, distance, and proportion; he rests
his minim rests, one, two, and the third in your bosom"
(2.4.20–23). In Mercutio's view, Romeo's style tends toward vapidity LL while Tybalt's becomes ridiculously
precise and emphatic LR.

But the Romeo who enters is very different. His high
spirits of the balcony scene have survived the coming of
the day, and the conflict with Mercutio identifying them
as opposites is worked out in a way that makes Romeo
seem more masculine UR and Mercutio more likely to
have his fun <LC> without destroying the peace. Romeo
proves himself able to trade quips in Mercutio's most
witty and obscene style; we are able to imagine that the
extremes of the preceding scenes might be fused in a
flexible society where old conflicts LC are forgotten and
where friendship and love UC, wit UR and passion UL,
and satire <LR> and romance <LL> are all given value.
Mercutio himself is delighted with Romeo's transformation: "Why, is not this better now than groaning for love?

Now art thou sociable, now art thou Romeo; now art thou what thou art, by art as well as by nature" (2.4.89–91). What Mercutio means by art is the ability to be rational, witty, and detached UR. His spirit does foster a healthy satiric impulse <LR> that exposes merely conventional values, but he denies the claims of sensitivity UL and restraint UR. When he talks, the meaning is often incomplete until the bawdiness emerges. Exact readings can be hard to find: much of the fun comes in the leering innuendo that can take the meaning in various ingenious ways.

Defining the atmosphere of the street is perhaps the best way to define Mercutio, who embodies both its strengths and weaknesses. We might expect the street to be a working place of commerce and activity <UR>, as in *The Merchant of Venice*, and Benvolio does describe the street as "the public haunt of men" where "all eyes gaze on us" (3.1.50, 53). In fact it is more a place where young men and servants can get away from the authority of their houses and express themselves openly <UL>. Shakespeare presents Mercutio as detached from the community of both family and state. We learn nothing of his family and discover only after his death that he is related to the Prince (3.1.189) and also to Paris (5.3.75), his polar opposite who makes the forms of society the basis of his life. Mercutio is never seen talking to anyone older except when he bullies the Nurse. Depicting male friendship as his one natural bond is appropriate, for friendship, though traditional, is not defined in hierarchical terms. It depends on no inherent obligation of kinship, marriage, or status and encourages a sense of equality between the friends. For many in our less hierarchical age, Mercutio's independence helps make him the play's most sensible character. Certainly his role as satiric observer is important, but his limitations are also sharply delineated.

When the Nurse joins the street scene as the self-important messenger of Juliet, she is an easy target LL for male sport <UR>. The fun that the young men have with her has thematic relevance in its exposure of her pretentious social values [UR] and in its reminder of the fine line that separates elevated love UC from foolish lust LC, but the scene seems most important for its spirit of farce <LC>. Mercutio and the Nurse are both engagingly outrageous, with the clowning of Will Kempe as Peter no doubt contributing in ways that are now hard to determine. Puns, both verbal and visual, suggest opposed perspectives, but an atmosphere of good feeling dominates. If the metaphors of the rest of the play are picked up, the reference to "a sail" (2.4.102) might be developed to suggest that the Nurse is on an incongruous sea journey with Peter ironically as her pilot (Cupid). (The nautical metaphor comes up later in the scene in a specific context of love when Romeo talks of using a corded ladder to climb to the "high top-gallant of my joy" UC [2.4.190].) Peter and Mercutio refer to an emblematic "fan," possibly with an ornamental clock motif ("her fan's the fairer face" [2.4.106, 107–08]), that provides material for their gross puns.

Imagery of hunting LR a "hare hoar" LL and of drawing weapons LR demeans but also delights the Nurse as she struggles to be a "lady" UL rather than a "bawd" LL (2.4.134, 143, 130). Not surprisingly she has doubts about Romeo: an eager but frightened Nurse swings between sentimental enthusiasm <UL> and a guardian's fear <LR> that Romeo will "deal double" LR (2.4.168). Her own language and behavior comically undercut her moral authority, but her warning about a "fool's paradise" [UC] (2.4.166) reminds us that the lovers' search for "extreme sweet" has a foolish dimension. A confident Romeo UR handles her reassuringly, and the Nurse slips into easy talk that seems inconsequential. When she associates Romeo with "rosemary" (2.4.206–07), our awareness of approaching tragedy might, however, prompt the reflection that rosemary can be a flower for either a wedding UC or a funeral LC.

Before that tragic story unfolds, two short scenes bring
the young lovers' hopes to their peak. The air of impatient urgency is quickly restored as Juliet waits for the
Nurse's return; then both the lovers and the Friar experience the high expectations <UC> of the approaching
marriage. While the slow moving LL Nurse provides a
link to the lassitude of the street scene, the Juliet who
waits for her and the Romeo and Juliet who meet at Friar
Lawrence's cell seem ready to soar beyond all physical
limitations <UC>. The Nurse was sent forth at 9 A.M. but
has dawdled all morning even though she promised to be
back in half an hour; for her, noon is a time to collapse in
exhaustion and think about getting some dinner. Dinner
is a time for rest and renewal, but Romeo and Juliet, unlike the Nurse and also unlike Mercutio (2.4.140–41),
have a sweet, sanguine love UC and apparently need dinner as little as they need sleep.[19]

Earlier, both Capulet and Juliet have spoken of the
need for the ripening of passing summers; now Juliet describes time as a cycle, not of years and seasons, but of
this single day. To Juliet morning is a time for action
even though she was up until dawn; her frustration
mounts as "the highmost hill / Of this day's journey"
(2.5.9–10) approaches. Time and the world should function at her level: "Love's heralds should be thoughts, /
Which ten times faster glides than the sun's beams"
(2.5.4–5). The Nurse, far from gliding, is "lame" LL
(2.5.4). If she were still young, Juliet and Romeo could
"bandy" her between them "as swift in motion as a
ball," but her time is past: "old folks—many feign as
they were dead, / Unwieldy, slow, heavy, and pale as
lead" LC (2.5.13–17). Instead the Nurse fears she will
"catch my death with jauncing up and down!" (2.5.52).
The July sun is already too slow for Juliet, and a Decem-
ber Nurse is infuriating. By calling the Nurse "honey"
and "sweet" UC (2.5.18, 21), Juliet tries to make her and
her news sweeter. After she hears the "sweet news" of
her approaching marriage, her images of light, speed, and

elevation combine to provide a sense of paradise UC: "Hie to high fortune!" (2.5.78). The Nurse, like Mercutio with Romeo, reasserts life's physical realities when she notes the coming of the "wanton blood up in your cheeks" <UL> and reminds her that the ascent by which Romeo "Must climb a bird's nest" <UC> will take place in the "dark" <LC> (2.5.70, 74) and depends on having the Nurse get a ladder. But no disagreement about expectations exists: Juliet eagerly anticipates physical love, and the Nurse shares Juliet's emotional excitement.

At the Friar's cell, here a place for both spiritual aspiration [LC] and this world's love <UC>, Romeo and the Friar are directly preoccupied with love's relation to time and eternity. Romeo believes that linking "hands with holy words" UC will make them superior to "love-devouring death" LC (2.6.6, 7). The more practical Friar deplores extremes: "These violent delights have violent ends, / And in their triumph die, like fire and powder, / Which as they kiss consume" LC (2.6.9–11). In Juliet's earlier image their "contract" is "Too like the lightning, which doth cease to be / Ere one can say it lightens" (2.2.117, 119–20). Lightning at least provides a momentary illumination, but the "kiss" [UC] of "fire" [UR] and "powder" [UL] is destructive LC even as it happens.[20] It is passion UL translated to rash action LR, and "Too swift arrives as tardy as too slow" (2.6.15). That the "sweetest honey / Is loathsome in his own deliciousness" (2.6.11–12)[21] relates specifically to the "extreme sweet" <UC> the lovers have been seeking. But the Friar, himself split between polarities of emotion and reason, is strongly drawn to Juliet's lightness and airiness <UC> and allows himself to speculate about a foot so light that the street will not be worn down, so bright and long lasting <UC> that its spark will need no relighting from the "everlasting flint" (2.6.17). Its "vanity"—in the positive sense of a lightness approaching transcendence <UC>— prevents a "fall," but it remains physical, like "gossamers" in "wanton summer air" (2.6.18–20). Romeo and

Mercutio used similar language in the Queen Mab scene: what Mercutio considers "vain fantasy," "the children of an idle brain" [UC] (1.4.98, 97), is for Romeo and now the Friar a vision of higher reality UC. First the lovers and now the Friar, who later stumbles LR despite his warnings of the danger, are acting as though defying gravity is possible.

When Romeo and Juliet meet, they exchange kisses that do not explode and speak in metaphors that describe love as weighty and full [LC] rather than light and soaring UC. Romeo refers to the "heap'd" "measure" (2.6.25, 24) of his joy and playfully asks Juliet's help in finding some literal means of expressing it. At issue is whether skill in language and art UR can somehow express the paradox that love is at once "heap'd" and airy. In her response Juliet accepts the image of their wealth of love but denies the importance of the "ornament" <UR> of language: "Conceit, more rich in matter than in words, / Brags of his substance, not of ornament" (2.6.30–31). This mild rebuke to Romeo's hope has been taken as her continuing suspicion of Romeo's language of compliment, but she seems rather to be making the conventional point that language can never express love adequately. Those who want to stress Juliet's natural language should notice that she builds on Romeo's earlier image with another hyperbolical image: "my true love is grown to such excess / I cannot sum up sum of half my wealth" (2.6.33–34). They understand each other perfectly and express a love both weighty and soaring.

In this section of the play, Shakespeare presents characters who seize occasions they think will allow them to achieve "extreme sweet" UC. Each decision to act creates both a problem and an opportunity for someone else. Capulet, because he wants a marriage that may help renew the family, pressures a vulnerable Juliet to permit Paris's courtship. As a result, she meets Romeo and falls in love. Because of the Capulet plan to marry her to Paris, Juliet suggests an immediate marriage to Romeo.

Because his own love demands it, Romeo agrees to marry her even though marriage to a Capulet will be dangerous. The Friar, because he wants to end the families' feud and is convinced that the lovers will act without him anyway, decides to marry them. All act partly because of the pressure of the situation LL as each understands it, but largely because of an optimistic belief UL that people can determine UR or at least influence their own lives. At each point, a refusal to act would stop or at least slow the momentum: Romeo, Juliet, or Friar Lawrence could resist an immediate marriage, but all three and Capulet share the same impulse—to take risks that not only might resolve a problem but that might accomplish a great good UC.

Shakespeare shows all of these forces at work but seldom shows us the inner process of evaluation and decision. The method fits the story: Shakespeare is writing about people who are driven by inner and outer forces that they understand imperfectly, and he invites our attention to how the analogous forces described on my charts interact with each other. Capulet, Romeo, Juliet, and the Friar are all aware of the dangers of haste and rashness LR but are caught up in a momentum of hope <UL> that makes patience UL difficult. In the next section of the play, the movement toward tragedy LC, which we as an audience have been expecting, takes over. As the characters try to find resolutions to their increasingly desperate problems, they swing wildly between polarities of joy UC and woe LC as events pull them toward the paradisal UC and the disastrous LC.

Four

Mortal Paradise

(*Romeo and Juliet* 3.1–4.4)

JULIET. O nature, what hadst thou to do in hell
When thou didst bower the spirit of a fiend
In mortal paradise of such sweet flesh?

(3.2.80–82)

I n the scenes discussed in chapter 3, achieving "extreme sweet" <UC> (2.Chor.14) seems possible because of individuals' decisive actions. Capulet prevents
Tybalt from attacking Romeo and transforms his party
into an image of celebration, order, and renewal UC.
Romeo finds Juliet, forgets Rosaline, and together with
Juliet moves toward a fulfilling love. Friar Lawrence undertakes a bold plan <UR> that has some chance of rec-
onciling the feuding families. Even Mercutio in the street
scene (2.4) seems controlled more by the spirit of fun
<LC> than satire <LR>. At the end of act 2, scene 6,
Romeo and Juliet begin a promising marriage. In the next

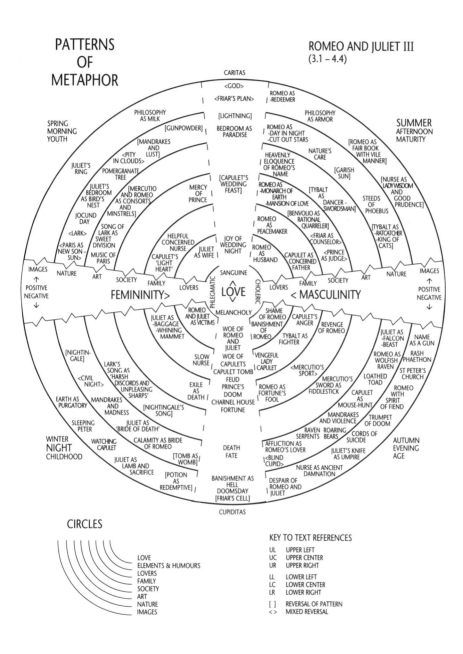

PATTERNS OF METAPHOR

ROMEO AND JULIET III
(3.1 – 4.4)

SPRING
MORNING
YOUTH

SUMMER
AFTERNOON
MATURITY

WINTER
NIGHT
CHILDHOOD

AUTUMN
EVENING
AGE

FEMININITY>

< MASCULINITY

LOVE

IMAGES
↑
POSITIVE
NEGATIVE
↓

CIRCLES

LOVE
ELEMENTS & HUMOURS
LOVERS
FAMILY
SOCIETY
ART
NATURE
IMAGES

KEY TO TEXT REFERENCES

UL   UPPER LEFT
UC   UPPER CENTER
UR   UPPER RIGHT

LL   LOWER LEFT
LC   LOWER CENTER
LR   LOWER RIGHT

[ ]   REVERSAL OF PATTERN
< >   MIXED REVERSAL

section of the play, the optimism is shattered by death, and the increasingly desperate characters try to find ways of turning the momentum back toward resolutions. Everyone seems enveloped by situations and emotions that are out of control Paradise UC at times still seems within grasp, but human passions and unfortunate events reassert a powerful awareness of mortality LC.

The early afternoon street scene (3.1) parallels the destructive opening scene of the play rather than the wild but optimistic scene (2.4) around noon of the same day. Both of these later street scenes include a sense of youthful, volatile energy—of "mad blood stirring" [UR] (3.1.4)—caused by the heat of the July day and the passions of the young men. In the earlier scene, playfulness dominates; in the second, petty squabbling LR escalates to tragedy. The actions fit the time of day, with the sanguine time around noon being appropriate for the polarities of both genuine and illusory ascent <UC> and with the hot afternoon suitable for the choleric outbursts LR that destroy the fragile order. From the start of 3.1, the subject is quarreling, and the humor, even between Mercutio and Benvolio, has a nasty edge LR missing earlier. For Mercutio, Benvolio represents another extreme. When he wants them to "retire" since "The day is hot, the Capels [are] abroad, / And if we meet we shall not scape a brawl" (3.1.1–3), Mercutio treats his preoccupation with the prevention of quarreling UR as proof of his tendency to quarrel LR. His self-righteous interference turns reason UR to choler LR and encourages rather than prevents trouble. With "two such, we should have none shortly, for one would kill the other" (3.1.15–16). The point of the exaggerated attack seems to be that Mercutio thinks Benvolio is a conformist [UR] who needs the irreverence and fun [LC] his sober approach destroys.

Mercutio, on the other hand, proves unable to recognize that the jesting and "bandying" LR (3.1.89) barely permissible with the Nurse become inappropriate with Tybalt and Romeo. His intention in fighting for Romeo

seems to be partly to show him how humiliating his
yielding LL to Tybalt is, partly to enjoy an exhilarating
fight <LR> with an insulting enemy, and partly to ridicule the whole situation [LC]. Although Tybalt does not
intend to kill him, Mercutio underestimates the potential for trouble, apparently because self-assertion and
sport <LR> take priority over reason UR. His own sardonic view, apparent in his repeated "A plague a' both
your houses" (3.1.99–100, 106, also 91), is that the feuding atmosphere LR and the conventional attitudes [UR]
of both sides make his more natural style of living impossible. When Romeo refers to him as "the Prince's near
ally" and Benvolio calls him "thy kinsman" (3.1.109,
145) in his report to the Prince, they identify a connection made more significant after his death than it has
seemed in life. The link helps explain the Prince's anger
<LR> and gives an added force to Mercutio's curse <LR>
"a' both your houses."

Benvolio remains associated with restraint and con-
formity <UR>, Tybalt with choler and rigidity LR, and
Mercutio with satire and sport <LR>, but Romeo is
harder to categorize. There is some justice in Mercutio's
description of him as the foolish lover LL, and some evidence of a Benvolio-like peacemaker <UR> in his statement of love for Tybalt and in his ineffectual attempt at
stopping the fight. Romeo also experiences a short period
of rage after Mercutio is killed when he laments his effeminacy LL and, after the manner of Tybalt, charges
forth to assert his masculinity and defend his honor
<LR>. Romeo tries to justify his attack on Tybalt in a
wild speech full of "fire[-ey'd] fury" LR but after having
slain him calls himself "fortune's fool" (3.1.124, 136):
"fool" suggests some personal responsibility for trying to
rise <UL> on fortune's wheel, but "fortune" also invokes
the mystery of forces LC beyond his control. Apportioning blame becomes impossible. Those forces include the
original feud, the taunting interchange between Tybalt
and Mercutio, the sudden transition from church to

street, Romeo's misunderstood plea for peace, Romeo's guilt and shame at Mercutio's death, Benvolio's ill-timed praise of Mercutio, the societal values that lead young men to act as they do, and something mysterious Romeo calls "This day's black fate" and Benvolio calls "the unlucky manage of this fatal brawl" (3.1.119, 143). The causes, at once personal, familial, societal, and cosmic, operate analogously and imply complexities that make both moral judgment and reductive references to the feud or to fortune and fate unwise.[1]

Having Mercutio as the kinsman of the Prince not only suggests the spreading of the tragedy beyond the families to the larger community but also raises the question of the Prince's fairness and wisdom in handling the case. From a dramatic point of view, Shakespeare no doubt wanted a quick judgment to end the scene so he could get on to other matters, but as usual he manages to combine dramatic exigency with thematic subtlety. What seems to govern his shaping of the scene is a sense of how rising emotions and bias affect all of the responses. Lady Capulet and Montague have obviously one-sided views, but even the more objective Benvolio slants his account by leaving out both Mercutio's role in starting the fight and his own plea that Romeo flee to avoid the Prince's judgment. Nevertheless, by stressing Romeo's peaceful intentions UR, by referring to Romeo's "newly entertain'd revenge" <LR> as a sudden thought, and by describing Tybalt and Romeo's fight as being "like lightning" <LR> (3.1.171, 172), he defends Romeo effectively. Lady Capulet asks the Prince for Romeo's death "as thou art true" (3.1.148), and Benvolio and later the Friar see death as the expected sentence of a ruler following the law UR. Earlier, I questioned the Prince's effectiveness in settling the dispute in 1.1.[2] While separating the factions and avoiding further death may now be the only course, the Prince again fails in his princely and fatherly role of promoting peace. Perhaps we should understand that his kinship with Mercutio rouses his passion and respect him for admitting it. Settling the matter quickly has obvious advantages for the Prince as well as Shakespeare, but exploring the Prince's motivations results primarily in our increased awareness that dispensing justice is as hard as apportioning blame.

In the next two scenes (3.2, 3), set in late afternoon and early evening, first Juliet and then Romeo fluctuate between joy UC and woe LC as they examine the prospects for their marriage. Both are preoccupied with the night, which in various guises is now approaching, and both interpret their personal situations in relation to analogous patterns in the cosmos. Juliet's soliloquy, an unconventional variation on the epithalamium, emphasizes ideas already familiar from the balcony scene[3]—the importance of love in a cosmos full of contrarieties, the shifting but complementary masculine and feminine roles of lovers, the struggle of love to express itself in a hostile social context, the lover's sense of time's subjectivity, and the contrasting impulses of physical and spiritual love.

Shakespeare's mythographical technique allows Juliet to express the complexities of her own feelings while at the same time relating them to the cosmic interactions of a gender-charged universe. Basic to the metaphorical pattern is the image of dusk as the time when the masculine sun moves toward union with the feminine night. Just as Juliet must wait for Romeo, so the night itself must passively await the sun's arrival. Phoebus's journey is unfeeling, and for Juliet painfully slow LR. After first urging his "fiery-footed steeds" to "Gallop," she speculates about an eager young "waggoner ... Phaeton" <UR>, by analogy Romeo, who would "whip you to the west" and "bring in cloudy night immediately" (3.2.1–4). Juliet's fantasy inverts the gender roles of Mab's chariot, which I have argued is a male fantasy of a feminine sexual journey.[4] In the previous scene, Romeo has acted like a young Phaethon LR and followed a passionate course to tragedy. Remembering Phaethon's disaster (though not death) and Romeo's role in the deaths that Juliet as yet knows nothing about, the "west" where the sun arrives takes on overtones of actual LC as well as sexual <UC> death. Behind her "close curtain," the "love-performing night" (3.2.5) <LC>, like Juliet, is ready to entertain the arriving charioteer UR and his horses, conventionally associated with male control both of their own phallic power and of unruly femininity <LL>, and an eager Juliet wants to enlist her as an ally and advisor. The controversial "runaway's eyes" that Juliet wants to "wink" (close) (3.2.6) seem at first to refer to the runaway (galloping at Juliet's request) horses <LR> of Phoebus, but in Juliet's flexible mythography they then belong to the runaway Cupid LR who could report the lovers to Venus, with perhaps an additional oblique reference to runaway (disobedient) stars that in their youthful enthusiasm <UL> make the night too bright for clandestine love.[5] Runaways in revolt are not surprisingly on Juliet's mind.

Juliet attempts to sort out how a woman can be both chaste UR and sexually aggressive <LR> by inviting "civil night," a "sobersuited matron" who is at once fully respectable and experienced in the arts of love UR, to teach her (and Romeo), both initiates UL, how "to lose a winning match, / Play'd for a pair of stainless maidenhoods" (3.2.10–13). Night understands femininity and can serve as a falconer UR who will "Hood my unmann'd blood" <UL>: her restraint UR will allow "true love" UC "bold" expression UR in "simple modesty" UL (3.2.15–16) through the purifying power of married love UC. Seeing Romeo UR as "day in night" brought in as "new snow" UL on the "wings of night" <LC> begins as a parallel image of sexual power and chastity but turns ominous when the "wings" become the "back" of a "raven" LC (3.2.17–19), an evil competitor whose passion brings the darkness of death. This leads Juliet to flatter "gentle night" [LC] (3.2.20) and even to bargain that night can have Romeo back after her death. Night can "cut him out in little stars" that will be so impressive the world will turn away from an unholy "worship" LL of the "garish sun" [UR] (3.2.22, 25) to the night.[6]

In such an Ovidian transformation, masculine light UR would become permanent and make night itself an emblem of the ideal fusion [LC] of masculine and feminine. In the last part of the speech, Juliet is both aggressive owner UR—"O, I have bought the mansion of a love, / But not possess'd it"—and passive property UL—"though I am sold, / Not yet enjoy'd" (3.2.26–28). Her language is full of the imperatives of authority UR, but she can also be the eager child UL longing for the festival day's UC "new robes" (3.2.30). Throughout the speech, Juliet's daring and often inverted imagery communicates the oppositions and fusions present in both cosmic night and femininity as a gender.

When Juliet gets the Nurse's report of Tybalt's death and Romeo's banishment, her response picks up the grim side LC of the paradoxical attitudes toward night that she has been exploring. Her exaggerated rhetoric <LR> is functional both in revealing her despair LC and in helping an audience find a sufficiently large context for evaluating the whole tragedy. Juliet is no self-conscious poet; rather, art imitates life as Shakespeare gives her language that moves from her own feelings and thoughts to generalized, almost choric, comments about the larger implications of her situation. At first she sees the Nurse who talks of Romeo as speaking "heavenly eloquence" UC (3.2.33). But when she thinks he is dead, she asks: "Can heaven be so envious?" LR and adds, "What devil art thou that dost torment me thus? / This torture should be roar'd in dismal hell" LC (3.2.40, 43–44). To believe that Romeo is dead destroys any sense of personal identity: "I am not I, if there be such an ay, / Or those eyes [shut], that makes thee answer ay" (3.2.48–49). Here, the dislocated language reflects her own psychological fragmentation LC but also calls into question the vision of a masculine universe that should reflect

heavenly justice UR but is instead dominated by violence LR and death LC.

If Romeo and Tybalt are both dead, "Then, dreadful
trumpet, sound the general doom, / For who is living, if
those two are gone?" LC (3.2.67–68). When she finds out
that Romeo has killed Tybalt, even Romeo's worth is
questioned in a speech whose metaphors <LC>—"Beautiful tyrant! fiend angelical! / Dove-feather'd raven! wol-
vish ravening lamb!" (3.2.75–76)—remind us of Romeo's
oxymoronic speech in 1.1. Diction that reveals the polarities of Juliet's chaotic world is directly connected with
cosmic evil LC: "serpent," "dragon," "fiend," "damned,"
and "hell" (3.2.73–75, 79, 80). Heavenly appearances UC
cover a hellish reality LC, and nature itself is implicated
in a journey to hell to "bower the spirit of a fiend / In
mortal paradise of such sweet flesh" (3.2.81–82); "bower"
suggests a garden, but it is a garden of corruption LC, not
a paradise UC. Romeo himself is guilty: he "justly
seem'st" [UR] (3.2.78). "The mansion of a love" UC
that Juliet had "bought" "But not possess'd" is now a
"gorgeous palace" occupied by "deceit" LC (3.2.25–26,
84–85).

Juliet soon swings to Romeo's support. When the
Nurse picks up Juliet's attack by generalizing on the corruption of all men LR, her exaggerated language, particularly her hope that "Shame come to Romeo!" (3.2.90),
helps impel Juliet to the opposite extreme. Romeo's brow
is for Juliet a suitable "throne" UR where "honor may
be crown'd / Sole monarch of the universal earth" UR
(3.2.93–94). The palace imagery of the preceding speech
has been inverted. Now Juliet sounds like a loyal wife
UL who believes that any questioning of her husband's
authority (his voice, word, or name) UR is a revolt that
destroys her properly passive femininity UL and transforms her into something subhuman. A loving Juliet pursues a positive view—that Romeo lives and that Tybalt
failed to kill him—until she remembers that Romeo is to
be banished. From her radically personal perspective, the

banishment of Romeo LC is a woe that goes beyond any earthly tragedy: "'Romeo is banished,' to speak that word, / Is father, mother, Tybalt, Romeo, Juliet, / All slain, all dead" (3.2.122–24). She expresses her point in terms of both time and place: since banishment separates them, "There is no end, no limit, measure, bound, / In that word's death" LC (3.2.125–26); it is a cosmic disaster LC that is eternal and infinite. In her "wedding-bed" UC, "death" LC will "take my maidenhead!" (3.2.136–37). But her lapse toward despair and death is overcome suddenly and dramatically through the nurse's promise to bring Romeo, a "true knight" UR (3.2.142) who is the polar opposite of this night that has proved false. Sexual death with Romeo may be only a "last farewell" (3.2.143), but Romeo remains for her a romance hero UR who as a bridegroom will bring an ecstasy UC that death cannot.

In the parallel scene that follows, Romeo is anything but heroic as he slips into gloom LR about the hierarchical forces LC shaping his future. According to the Friar, a passive Romeo LL also has a horrible lover LR—"Affliction is enamor'd of thy parts"—and a frightening marriage—"And thou art wedded to calamity" LC (3.3.2–3). The first half of the scene builds toward the desperate Romeo's attempted suicide LC, but in the last half Friar Lawrence's philosophizing and planning UR and the Nurse's bringing of Juliet's ring transform his spirits. The whole scene has an emblematic quality with gender-based analogical patterns carefully designed to shape audience response. Romeo's imagery of banishment LC makes Juliet's cosmic pessimism LC both more graphic and more sweeping. To Romeo, there is an explicit analogy LC among individual death, separation from Juliet, the "Prince's doom" that banishes him from Verona, and the "dooms-day" (3.3.9) that sends the damned to hell. When Romeo talks of his own banishment from paradise, the expulsion of Adam from Eden also becomes relevant. For Juliet, banishment is a death that spreads without end or limit. For Romeo, everything meaningful UC is in Verona and the only time is now: "There is no world without Verona walls, / But purgatory, torture, hell itself" (3.3.17–18). Romeo's banishment from Juliet becomes his expulsion to hell, and Juliet is left in a grotesque heaven [UC] (or fallen Eden) LC where she is the only remaining perfection UC: "carrion flies ... may seize / On the white wonder of dear Juliet's hand, / And steal immortal blessing from her lips" (3.3.35–37). Life will be death-in-life for Juliet, too.

Romeo's disaster forces the Friar into some new roles. He has been both spiritual advisor and father-substitute UR: when Romeo and the Friar call each other "Father" and "dear son" (3.3.4,7), both of these roles seem implicit. But now the Friar becomes a spokesman for Verona's societal order <UR> as he defends the Prince's judgment: "the kind Prince" "hath rush'd aside the law, / And turn'd that black word 'death' to 'banishment.' / This is dear mercy, and thou seest it not" (3.3.25–28). Romeo wants him to carry out his roles UC as "a divine, a ghostly confessor, / A sin-absolver, and my friend" (3.3.49–50), but the Friar takes on a more severe legal and philosophical role that adds justice <UR> to mercy UL. Such "philosophy," though designed to be at once "armor" UR and "sweet milk" UL (3.3.54–55), will inevitably seem ineffective to a lover. When Romeo states the case for feeling UL—"Thou canst not speak of that thou dost not feel" (3.3.64)—we recognize his immaturity but sympathize. Their short exchange on eyes and ears helps clarify the point. When Romeo tells the Friar to "Talk no more" (3.3.60), he replies: "O then I see that [madmen] have no ears" (3.3.61). Romeo responds: "How should they when that wise men have no eyes?" (3.3.62). Less rational people like the young and the mad need receptive ears UL since they lack mature understanding UR, but "wise" people need insight [LC] and sympathy UL if their talk UR is to be effective. Without them, sight and language are useless.

The extremes of Romeo and Juliet are defined by their physical actions. Romeo's effeminacy LL and despair LC find visual expression in his lying helplessly on the ground (earth) LC of the Friar's cell despite the Friar's repeated calls to "Arise" (3.3.71, 74). The Nurse urges him to "Stand up, stand up, stand, and you be a man" (3.3.88). Earlier, trying to "be a man" has led Romeo to rash action LR against Tybalt; now the Nurse suggests, with the help of functional anatomical puns ("in my mistress' case," "rise and stand," "into so deep an O" [3.3.84, 89, 90]), that Romeo's despair has emasculated him LL.[7] She also reports Juliet's similar actions. As a Capulet she "starts up, / And Tybalt calls"; as a lover she "on Romeo cries, / And then falls down again" LL (3.3.100–02). The Nurse's mention of Juliet is more effective than philosophy in rousing Romeo, and he asks tentatively about whether she thinks him "an old murtherer" LR who has "stain'd the childhood of our joy / With blood removed but little from her own" (3.3.94–96). To ask a virginal Juliet to shed more Capulet blood with her cousin's murderer on their wedding night would require that she see him as a husband and not as a Montague. When he learns that Juliet has called out both his name and Tybalt's, he imagines that his "name's cursed hand / Murder'd her kinsman" (3.3.104–05). Metonymy here reflects his fragmentation: they may have thought he was "new baptiz'd" UL as her love, but his Montague side LR has reasserted itself and thereby murdered the "joy" UC (2.2.50; 3.3.95) of their approaching consummation, their identities as lovers and people, and their future marriage. Othello-like <LR>, he determines to find and "sack" the "vile part of this anatomy" LR (3.3.107, 106) that has disgraced his honor. In their imagery they reinforce each other: the body that Juliet once called the "mansion of a love" becomes for a time a "gorgeous palace" occupied by "deceit" (3.2.26, 84–85). Now Romeo desperately hopes that his "hateful mansion" <LR> (3.3.108) can be purged by his dagger LR.

In the second half of the scene, the Nurse and Friar Lawrence take on almost archetypal feminine and masculine roles as they bring Romeo out of his despair LC. When Romeo draws his dagger, he is disarmed by the Nurse (if the stage direction of the first quarto is given authority): this may suggest that Romeo's attempt itself is half-hearted, but the Nurse's instinct for preserving life UL looks forward to her role in 3.5 as Juliet's protector UR against Capulet. The Friar follows up with an elaborately developed analysis of how to deal with destructive masculine and feminine oppositions. Rhetoric in the play should usually be taken seriously and in this case proves to be highly effective in defining the Friar's philosophy. First, the Friar denies Romeo's claim to honor UR: the opposite courses of "womanish" "tears" LL and the "unreasonable fury of a beast" LR produce an "Unseemly woman in a seeming man, / And ill-beseeming beast in seeming both" (3.3.110–13). In killing himself, Romeo would also kill the Juliet joined to him by marriage; in linking "heaven and earth" in death LC rather than "birth" UC (3.3.119–20), he would deny himself as a living microcosm.

In the long speech that follows, the Friar goes on to a more positive statement of the need to fuse masculine and feminine qualities: "Thy noble shape is but a form of wax, / Digressing from the valor of a man" <UR> and "Thy dear love sworn but hollow perjury" <UL> unless through the "ornament" of his "wit" UR (3.3.126–28, 130) he can fuse them meaningfully UC. If his wit is "misshapen," he will be like the "skilless soldier" who "set afire" LR the "powder" LL through his "ignorance" and "dismemb'red" his potentially noble form UC (3.3.131–34). Instead of understanding that both he and Juliet are alive and that "exile" is better than death, a passive Romeo refuses to see that an active UR, though still feminine UL, "Happiness courts thee in her best array" and instead continues to play the effeminate role of a "sullen wench" LL (3.3.140, 142–43). According to the

Friar, the extremes of either masculine or feminine responses lead to disaster LC, but thoughtful evaluation
UR and appropriate action UR can bring happiness UC.

When the Friar tells Romeo to "Ascend her chamber"
(3.3.147) and explains his plan for bringing about a
reconciliation, he shifts to the practical action that must
accompany moral philosophy if Romeo is to be revived.
The Friar's confident manner and detailed planning for
the next stage imply that a change is already evident in
Romeo even though he remains silent. The Friar is less
the generator of new impulses than the spokesman of
forces already within Romeo. If we think of Romeo as
also having an inner voice of reason UR and as subsuming the Friar's wisdom within himself, we get closer to
the emblematic quality of the scene. No depiction of the
process of psychological change in Romeo is necessary.
Romeo has found himself and remains a confident lover
UR throughout the next section of the play. The Nurse,
too, seems relicved, and we should note that Romeo has
already decided to go to Juliet before the Nurse gives him
the ring, another feminine "O" UL, that Juliet has sent
as a pledge UR of her love. Nevertheless admiration of
the Friar's wisdom is undercut somewhat by the Nurse's
praise: "O Lord, I could have stay'd here all the night /
To hear good counsel. O, what learning is!" (3.3.159–60).
No learning that the Nurse admires can be entirely wise!
We can grant the validity of the Friar's analysis while
still recognizing that Romeo himself must act effectively
and that even then positive results are far from certain.

In the next section of the play, Capulet and the Friar
become central to the unfolding of the plot. Capulet is
the initiator with his plans for Juliet's wedding, and the
Friar is put in the position of finding ways of responding.
Although they are working at cross purposes and do not
meet until the final scene, they share a number of attitudes UR that would seem to make them natural allies.
Both are believers in hierarchy, optimists about their
ability to influence events, and pragmatists who see that

marriages can help them accomplish their goals. If they were able to make effective use of the institutions (state, church, family) UC they both support, satisfactory resolutions might be found, but faulty communication proves to be one of the society's basic problems. Just as the Prince rejects counseling with Capulet and Montague together and instead resorts to warning them individually, so the Friar seems to assume that any discussion about reconciliation would be fruitless until Romeo and Juliet's marriage is a fait accompli. If the Friar had the relationship with Capulet that he has with Romeo, he would know something of Capulet's tentative steps toward peace, but they are not close, and the momentum of events LR takes priority over calm reasoning UR. Both Capulet and the Friar are behaving like typically well-meaning but flawed people, and their conflicting plans put them on a collision course that makes disaster more likely.

Controlling events proves to be most difficult: images of lateness LR, haste LR, and chance LC become increasingly and ominously prominent.[8] Their metaphorical function is closely related to the concept of occasion: people need to understand and respond to the rhythms of cycles and hierarchies and act only when the time is right. Misfortune may have no clear cause, but the human tendency is to blame chance LC or luck [LC] for what results from other factors. The causes of misfortune are not only general—passion within people, conflicts between people, and mysterious forces in the cosmos—but also specific—secrecy, overconfidence in reason or in one's ability to control situations, misplaced reliance on God, a longing to create better lives, desperation as a situation gets beyond control, bad planning, lack of sleep, and haste. Any of these causes, or a host of others, can lead to acting when the occasion is not right.

After his initial decision to marry the lovers in secrecy, a choice he would perhaps rightly see as seizing occasion, the Friar's haste is largely in response to a changing situation over which he has limited control, but he maintains a confidence that we are less and less likely to trust. The Nurse combines imagery of haste and lateness LR when she says, "Hie you, make haste, for it grows very late"; the Friar soon after repeats, "'Tis late" (3.3. 164, 172). When he details his plans for keeping Romeo informed through Balthazar about "Every good hap to you that chances here" (3.3.171), his assumption that all that "chances" <LC> will be fortunate must sound naive, particularly to an audience that knows the story. Capulet opens the next scene with another reference to chance: he tells Paris that "Things have fall'n out, sir, so unluck-ily / That we have had no time to move our daughter" (3.4.1–2). We are reminded both that fortune can be un-lucky and that the chance motif linking the Friar and Capulet is becoming increasingly prominent.

The themes of haste, lateness, and rashness are picked up in Capulet's response to Tybalt's tragedy and his plans for Juliet's wedding. In contrast to Lady Capulet, who took the lead in calling for Romeo's death, the more con-structive Capulet promotes Juliet's marriage to Paris. While Lady Capulet continues to be driven by vengeance LR, Capulet's motives <UR> include his concern for a Juliet who seems to be mourning excessively for Tybalt, his own admiration for the noble Paris, whom he now begins to think of as "my son Paris" (3.4.16), his hope for his family's future, and his longing for some happiness in his old age. Because of Tybalt's death that day (Monday), Friar Lawrence assumes that the Capulets' "heavy sor-row" LC (3.3.157) will encourage them to go to bed early. Instead Capulet is up late talking to Paris. When the scene begins it is "very late"; by the end it is "so very late that we / May call it early by and by" (3.4.5, 34–35). Their original topic is Capulet's regret that Paris has not been able to pursue his courtship of Juliet, but his com-ment in reference to Tybalt's death—"Well, we were born to die" (3.4.4)—seems to suggest his overeagerness <UL> to move beyond that tragedy. (In the previous scene, the Nurse was also a little too eager to get on with life: "Ah sir, ah sir, death's the end of all" [3.3.92].) When Capulet gets the idea of an early marriage, it quickly becomes an obsession. While he still recognizes a role for Juliet, he is about to deny it: "I think she will [be] rul'd / In all respects by me, nay more, I doubt it not" (3.4. 13–14). He is more concerned about the propriety <UR> of a marriage so soon after Tybalt's death than with genuine sorrow: the wedding will be on Thursday, not Wednesday, and will be small since "It may be thought we held him carelessly, / Being our kinsman, if we revel much" (3.4.25–26). Recognizing the danger of "haste" (3.4.22), he tries to restrain himself, but rashness LR is taking over.

Romeo and Juliet's wedding night is already underway while Capulet, Paris, and Lady Capulet are talking in scene 4, so his instruction to Lady Capulet to "Go you to Juliet ere you go to bed, / Prepare her, wife, against this wedding-day" (3.4.31–32) threatens their immediate discovery. The whole second "balcony" scene accentuates the danger LR of their situation and their desperate longing to be in harmony UC with the cycles of nature. Metaphors of hearing and seeing, and of night and day, provide the controlling patterns.[9] Juliet's reference to a nightingale [LL] singing on "yond pomegranate tree" UL recalls images of fecundity UL in the first balcony scene, but a more realistic Romeo identifies the song as that of a lark <UL>, "the herald of the morn" (3.5.4, 6). Romeo wants to reassure Juliet that a natural transition to "jocund day" UC is possible, but his own uneasiness is suggested by the ambiguous image of the "envious streaks" <LR> that "Do lace the severing clouds in yonder east" (3.5.9, 7–8); "lace" fits with the mood of "jocund day," but "envious" implies a malicious force actively splitting the clouds and by analogy the lovers themselves. (Earlier, the Friar's dawn description refers to "Check'ring the eastern clouds with streaks of light" in the context of a smiling but ambiguous sun's "burning eye" <UR> [2.3.2,

5].) Although Juliet has thought of the sun as "garish" [UR] (3.2.25), she now implausibly tries to see it as a friend UR who has provided the light of a meteor to "light thee on thy way to Mantua" (3.5.15). A witty, even teasingly playful, Romeo claims to be ready to delay and thus "be ta'en" and "put to death" if Juliet "wilt have it so" (3.5.17–18), but his real point is that they cannot resist such a powerful natural process <UC>. His sense of a vast nature stresses both sight UR and hearing UL: he will say the coming of light is "the pale reflex of Cynthia's brow" and that it "is not the lark whose notes do beat / The vaulty heaven so high above our heads" (3.5.20–22).

The grimness LC of a death they both know as a real threat leads to a frightened response from Juliet, and the harmony with a higher nature they both have struggled to find disappears. Now she admits the bird is a lark and thinks it "sings . . . out of tune, / Straining harsh discords and unpleasing sharps" LC (3.5.27–28). Juliet muses about switching the eyes and voices of the lark <UL> and a toad LR, which has added point since she has earlier associated Paris with a toad (2.4.202–03). The conventionally positive image of a dawn song UL with its celebration of life and with overtones of a bridal awakening has become an unwelcome song LR, "Hunting thee hence with hunt's-up to the day" (3.5.34). (Cf. the more positive hunting scene in *A Midsummer Night's Dream*). Now both night and day seem disordered, with the light of day serving only to illuminate their troubles LC: "More light and light. More dark and dark our woes!" (3.5.36). Time itself is no friend. Their too short night is ending, but their time apart, as in the first balcony scene, will seem endless (2.2.169; 3.5.44–47).

When Romeo descends from the balcony, Juliet's speeches look backward to the first balcony scene and forward to the ending. Juliet describes the various roles in their relationship: Romeo is "love, lord, ay, husband, friend!" (3.5.43). Calling him "love" and "lord" recalls her earlier description of both her worship in love [LL] and his dominion as lord UR (2.2.147–48), but "husband" and "friend" have new, more intimate overtones. Hierarchy is still present in "husband," but love makes their bond deeper than duty. In coming last, "friend" gets most emphasis: friendship was usually thought of as existing between men or women, and to assert it between wife and husband adds an easiness and warmth not always present in Renaissance marriages. Juliet's final image foretells the horror of the ending and adds a sense of mysterious forces LC at work: "O God, I have an ill-divining soul! / Methinks I see thee now, thou art so low, / As one dead in the bottom of a tomb" (3.5.54–56). Even Romeo's attempt at reassurance UR—that "Dry sorrow drinks our blood" (3.5.59)—unintentionally increases the sense of approaching disaster LC. Juliet's half-serious plea that the fortune "all men call . . . fickle" LC (3.5.60) may return her faithful lover suggests that she feels the pressures not only of family and society but also of what she fears is an unfriendly universe LC.

In the last part of the scene, Juliet, at once exultant over her wedding night UC and distraught about Romeo's departure LC, confronts parents full of plans for her wedding to Paris. In her verbal sparring with her mother, we sense Juliet's self-confidence UR and share the advantage in awareness that she has over a vengeful Lady Capulet LR, who thinks Juliet is weeping LL over Tybalt's death. When Lady Capulet attacks Romeo as a "villain" and speaks of someone in Mantua who "Shall give him such an unaccustom'd dram / That he shall soon keep Tybalt company," Juliet deflects her revenge through cleverly offering to mix a poison that would make Romeo "sleep in quiet" (3.5.79, 90–91, 99). The speech introduces a central motif of the last part of the play: the Friar's potion for Juliet, Romeo's later dream of dying and being revived by Juliet's kisses (5.1.6–9), and the later roles of the apothecary and Balthazar are hauntingly parallel. When Juliet says she wants to "wreak the love I bore my cousin / Upon his body that hath slaughter'd him!" (3.5.101–02), she wants to be an aggressor in love [LR] rather than in revenge LR. The passage's analogical overtones encourage us to recognize the significance of the play's recurrent images of liminal areas—not only sleep and death, and love and sex, but also dreams and waking visions, and illusion and reality. Through such iteration, metaphors of death, poison, and tombs LC on the one hand and of sleep, kisses, and renewal UC on the other gradually become the archetypal expression of the opposing forces that move events through illusory dreams LC and true visions UC toward the realities of death or life.

Juliet is put on the defensive by Lady Capulet's next revelation, the proposal of her "careful father" for a quick marriage to Paris—"a sudden day of joy" UC "to put thee from thy heaviness" LC (3.5.107–09). When Juliet is reluctant, Lady Capulet assumes her stubbornness and tells Capulet contemptuously "I would the fool were married to her grave!" LC (3.5.140). Desperate, Juliet picks up this image in her final speech to her mother after her father's tirade: she prefers a "bridal bed / In that dim monument where Tybalt lies" LC (3.5.200–01) to marriage to Paris. The cool Juliet who has kept Lady Capulet at a distance by repeatedly calling her "Madam" now frantically tries to reestablish a closer bond with "O sweet my mother" UL (3.5.198), but Lady Capulet's response only serves to increase the gulf between them: "Do as thou wilt, for I have done with thee" LR (3.5.203).

At first friendly and hopeful UR, Capulet becomes the outraged father LR when Juliet challenges his authority. His speech to Juliet about her excessive grief is full of warmth and even some gentle ridicule <LR>, as if he expects to win a smile through his exaggerated depiction of Juliet as a microcosm. The speech has been criticized as an example of the play's immature style,[10] but its imagery serves to recall major patterns of metaphor that link Capulet to the day and optimism <UR>. His playful comment that the "earth," like Juliet, "rains down-right" for "the sunset" of Tybalt but "doth drizzle dew" (3.5.126–28) for the setting of the sun suggests that Tybalt's death is merely a lesser sunset in a cyclical world where dew and rain are natural phenomena and where sunrises always follow the night. When Juliet proves to be rebellious LR as well as tearful LL, Capulet's tone changes as he speaks the language of patriarchal righteous indignation LR against a "mistress minion," "green-sickness carrion," "baggage," "tallow-face," "wretched puling fool," and "whining mammet" LL (3.5.151, 156, 157, 183, 184). Capulet justifies himself by claiming his fulfillment of obligations to the full range of the cycles and hierarchies: "God's bread, it makes me mad! Day, night, work, play, / Alone, in company, still my care hath been / To have her match'd" (3.5.176–78). The communion oath seems ironic in the context of his sacrifice of Juliet, a lamb who will not be allowed to "Graze" (3.5.188) with him.

When Capulet exits and Lady Capulet, despite a plea from Juliet, follows soon after, Juliet has only the Nurse. Calling on the Nurse to "Comfort me, counsel me!" and lamenting that "heaven should practice stratagems / Upon so soft a subject as myself!" (3.5.208–10), a childish LL Juliet makes the Nurse an authority figure UR capable of replacing her parents and heaven itself. Since the Nurse knows the whole situation, Juliet has every right to expect love and understanding UL, even if not wisdom UR. In some ways, the Nurse's failure is more shocking than that of the Capulets, who know nothing of Romeo and are convinced they have a wise proposal.[11] Shakespeare could easily have softened the impact, but he chooses a presentation more emblematic than psychological. We see in her a "counselor" whose worldly advice to view Romeo as already dead is cynically practical LR and whose favorable description of Paris is based on appearances [UR]. Realizing that the hierarchies of her childhood have failed her, a maturing UR Juliet knows she must depend on herself. Her judgment of the Nurse is severe but just: the Nurse is "Ancient damnation! O most wicked fiend!" LC (3.5.235). Juliet will go to the Friar for "remedy" (3.5.241) but will follow him only if he supports her. Her consolation is that "If all else fail, myself have power to die" <LR> (3.5.242).

Opening the next scene with Paris and the Friar making plans <UR> for Juliet's second wedding emphasizes the increasing pressure on the Friar: both Paris and Juliet are potential victims LL of his plans. Like Demetrius in *A Midsummer Night's Dream*, Paris has chosen to rely on the father, and a skeptical Friar suggests the difficulties of a courtship when "you do not know the lady's mind" (4.1.4). When Paris calls Capulet "My father Capulet" <UR> and the Friar "father" <UR> (4.1.2, 21) and gives a plausible explanation of his situation, he identifies himself as a conventional young man <UL> who believes implicitly in the traditional system. While Paris is not the paragon the Capulets describe, he is a decent person whose preference for a direct courtship has been sacrificed to Capulet's haste LR and whose happiness is now threatened by the secret marriage. Nevertheless, our sympathies lie with Juliet, and we are likely to ignore that her talk with Paris is a sham LR and that neither she nor the Friar even considers revealing she is already married. Perhaps the only results would be disgrace and separation LC; since no one raises the issue, we probably should not either.

Juliet still wants to place her faith UL in the spiritual and temporal values UC of her society, now represented for her by the Friar, at once a "holy father" who represents God's eternal values, a surrogate father for both her and Romeo, the minister who has "join'd . . . our hands," and the counselor whose "years and art" can bring "remedy" (4.1.37, 55, 64, 67). In their marriage, the heart UL (love, emotion, and the spiritual) fuses with the hand UR (law, action, and the material) to produce a permanent bonding. If, however, the Friar can find no way to maintain this unity of opposites in "true honor" UC, Juliet's "bloody knife / Shall play the umpeer" LR (4.1.65, 62–63). Juliet implies that her suicide would recognize the failure of all the Friar represents and the need for a logic based on the supremacy of death LC. Her combination of love UL, detachment [LC], and courage UR convinces the Friar that she is strong, and he proposes a plan <UR> that "craves as desperate an execution / As that is desperate which we would prevent" (4.1.69–70). Out of the gloom of despair LC can come the boldness of effective action UR. The battle has become for both of them a struggle between death LC and life UC that raises larger issues of the meaning of existence. The Friar will need the "wisdom" and "wits" UR of "long—experienc'd time" [LR] if his "counsel" UR is to provide "remedy" UC (4.1.52, 47, 60, 61, 67). Juliet will need masculine qualities UR—"resolution," "strength of will," "valor," and "strength"—if she is to escape "shame," "fear," and "Death" LC (4.1.53, 72, 120, 125, 74, 119, 75). Juliet is ready to place herself where the demonic forces LC are most powerful: she will "leap" "From off the battlements," "walk in thievish ways," face "serpents" or "roaring bears," or join the dead in a "charnel-house" or "new-made grave" if it will allow her "To live an unstain'd wife" UL (4.1.77–81, 88).

In the Friar's solution, the rhythms of nature and the sacraments of religion fuse UC. The Friar's potion will work according to the dualities within the larger cycles of nature. First her lips and cheeks will fade like roses or like dying fires as death LC "shuts up the day of life" (4.1.101). Then she will "awake as from a present sleep" from "this borrowed likeness of shrunk death" (4.1.104, 106). Her state, neither death nor sleep, will be like the wintry tomb of nature [LC] that mysteriously becomes the womb of a new spring UL. His power UC over nature is the stuff of folklore, but his intellectual framework is that of traditional religion and philosophy. The grip of death on Juliet is to be overcome by a potion that reflects the Christian belief that death and hell LC are conquered through Christ's body and blood [LC]. The relevance of this level of meaning is reinforced when Juliet speaks of being brought back from her two-day death by a Romeo who will "redeem" (4.3.32) her. In the biblical parable (Matthew 25.1–13), Christ, the son-sun who brings light and renewal UR, is the bridegroom who comes in the night, invites the five wise virgins to the marriage (symbolic of life) UC, and keeps the five foolish virgins away (symbolic of death) LC. As a bridegroom with Christlike redemptive power [LC], Romeo contrasts with Paris, the new "son" of Capulet but a helpless "bridegroom" [UR] who will find her "dead" when he "in the morning comes / To rouse thee from thy bed" (3.4.16; 4.1.107–08). Earlier Juliet implies that Paris is a bridegroom who both brings death and marries it LC when she tells her mother to delay the marriage or "make the bridal bed / In that dim monument where Tybalt lies" (3.5.200–01). In the last half of the play, Juliet's "marriage" to Death itself LC becomes a repeated image (3.2.136–37; 4.5.35–39; 5.3.103–05). Achieving the marriage to renewed life UC becomes the Friar's goal.

Juliet's soliloquy before taking the potion again exhibits the opposite extremes struggling for dominance in all of the characters.[12] Including her dismissal of Lady Capulet and the Nurse at the start of the scene reminds us again of their failure LR and her solitude LC: "My dismal scene I needs must act alone" (4.3.19). When Juliet tells the Nurse about needing "orisons / To move the heavens to smile upon my state" UC since she is "cross and full of sin" LR (4.3.3–5), she reveals her preoccupations. Is she "cross," that is, perverse, because of her own sin or is she "crossed," in the sense that the prologue's "star-cross'd" (pro.6) implies, by "heavens" [UC] that refuse to "smile upon my state?" The Juliet who feels abandoned by her family has spreading doubts that the power in herself, the Friar, and the heavens will be sufficient to overcome "death and night" LC (4.3.37).

The Friar has told Juliet that she will not meet "Death himself" (4.1.75), but for her the distinction between death and its images blurs. First a fearful Juliet worries that the potion the Friar has "minist'red" (4.3.25) may be a device for killing her LR. Then, after overcoming this suspicion, she wonders what will happen if she revives before Romeo arrives to "redeem" (4.3.32) her.

Juliet's imagined descent into the Capulet tomb also reflects continuing conflict between her love for Romeo UL and her guilty preoccupation with Capulet honor <UR>. In the play's last scene, one image of the tomb is of a monster of hell LC complete with mouth and stomach; here the analogous image is of a horrible Capulet vault LC that, like the Capulet house itself, allows her little room for life. The personified vault, like death, has a "foul mouth" LC that "no healthsome air breathes in" and that threatens to leave Juliet "stifled" or "strangled" LC (4.3.33–35). Her vision of the "terror of the place" LC is graphic: Tybalt and her "forefathers" (4.3.38, 51) are tormented and tormenting spirits as well as lifeless bodies. She recalls the belief that "spirits resort" to the vault and imagines "loathsome smells" and "shrikes like mandrakes' torn out of the earth" (4.3.44, 46, 47). The mandrakes, here associated with fertility <UL>, are, like Tybalt (and Juliet), victims LL who are "green in earth" (4.3.42) but are also conventionally thought to be the cause LR of sexuality, madness, and death in others.[13] The "pack'd" "bones / Of all my buried ancestors" (4.3.40–41) seem to be the leavings of death's feast LC even though the only explicit food reference is to Tybalt's body "spit . . . / Upon a rapier's point" (4.3.56–57) by Romeo. When she imagines that she might "madly play with my forefathers' joints," another food reference is likely; since an angry Capulet told her to "fettle your fine joints" UL (4.3.51; 3.5.153), fears of depraved sexuality may also be present. When she imagines that she might use "some great kinsman's bone" to "dash out my desp'rate brains" (4.3.53–54), there may be an added sense of punishing herself LL for her disregard of Capulet honor.[14] Finally drinking the potion, she responds to a vision of the ghost of Tybalt "Seeking out Romeo" (4.3.56) as he comes to rescue Juliet. In one sense, drinking the potion is a triumph of courage UR over fear LR as she tries to help Romeo, but her courage is linked to a frenzy bordering on madness <LC>. An Elizabethan audience that remembers her earlier vision of Romeo in the tomb and that has a stronger sense than we do of the "horrible conceit of death and night" LC (4.3.37) would understand her terror.

Capulet's preparations for the wedding feast <UC> are juxtaposed with Juliet's vision of a feast of death LC and prove to be as frantic as Juliet and the Friar's countermeasures. Like the Friar, he has plans <UR> to save Juliet from her grief and to use her for his own purposes. Like the Friar, he acts hastily <LR> but with full confidence that his plans are solidly based UR. In his response to Juliet's change, Capulet combines authority <UR> with enthusiasm <UL>. When Juliet pledges that "Henceforward I am ever rul'd by you," a paternal <UR> Capulet speaks of having "this knot knit up" <UC> (4.2.22, 24). At the same time Capulet allows his emotions the kind of expression <UC> that we associate with young lovers UL: "My heart is wondrous light / Since this same wayward girl is so reclaim'd" (4.2.46–47). Other images reinforce these patterns. He moves the wedding up a day and gives orders to everyone; but he will also stay up all night to get the feast ready: "I'll not to bed to-night; let me alone, / I'll play the huswife for this once" (4.2.42–43). When we see Capulet again in 4.4, his "light" (in all senses) <UC> mood is even more apparent as his household prepares for the wedding. Gone is any concern for Tybalt's memory, for his own sleep, or for what others think is properly masculine. The Nurse tries to send him to bed: in her view he is a "cot-quean" taking on a woman's role [UL] and will "be sick tomorrow" (4.4.6, 7). Capulet's refrain in the scene is "Make haste;" LR he says it five times in 13 lines (4.4.16, 26, 27, 28). Though he is well-intentioned, he illustrates the disaster that can result when autocratic power [UR] combines with unquestioning zeal LR.

Allusions in scenes 3 and 4 suggest some mythic implications. Imagery of contrasting feasts—death's feast LC on Juliet and the Capulet wedding feast <UC> provides ironic parallels to the Last Supper; references to different kinds of "watching" (4.4.8) at night—Juliet getting ready for the tomb, the Capulets staying awake to prepare for the wedding, and Capulet's watching (and chasing) women contrast with Christ's meditation in the Garden of Gethsemane [LC]. Juliet has feared both the spiritual death of a marriage to Paris LC and the physical "death" of the tomb's feasting LC but hopes for escape and renewal UL through the potion and Romeo. Capulet has overcome his grief for Tybalt and now anticipates a wedding feast UC that will regenerate his family. In the first line of scene 4, in ironic juxtaposition to Juliet's image of entering a closed up place of "loathsome smells," Lady Capulet asks the Nurse to "take these keys and fetch more spices" (4.3.46; 4.4.1). The fancy food <UC>— "bak'd meats" as well as "dates and quinces"—contrasts with the "fest'ring" (4.4.5, 2; 4.3.43) flesh in Juliet's vision of death's feast LC. The stage direction even tells us that the servants bring in "*spits*," thereby visually recalling Tybalt's body "spit . . . / Upon a rapier's point" (4.1.sd after 13; 4.3.56–57). When Capulet claims experience in "watching," Lady Capulet reminds him that it has come from being "a mouse-hunt in your time" LR (4.4.8, 11), that is, a woman-chaser. When she adds, "I will watch you from such watching now" (4.4.12), the reiteration punningly contributes to a developing image cluster that has an earlier example in the Friar's assurance to Juliet that he and Romeo "Will watch thy [waking]" (4.1.116).

If we compare these different watchings and Juliet's preparation for her "death" with the meditative watching that occupies Christ through the night of Maundy

Thursday [LC], their inadequacy becomes apparent. Juliet, like Christ, raises questions but has trouble maintaining her attitude of trust UL; here Capulet's watching is hasty LR rather than reflective [LR]. The allusions to the second crowing of the cock and to Peter as an absent (sleeping?) expert on finding drier logs for their fire (4.4.5, 18–20) may be oblique allusions intended to recall that same night. The biblical Peter was tested and failed: he fell asleep LC three times while Christ was praying and, while warming himself before a fire, denied Him three times before the cock crowed twice (Mark 14.12–72). The connection between Christ's sacramental feast and sacrifice [LC] and Capulet's ill-fated and hasty wedding feast [UC] is alluded to when Capulet asks that Juliet herself be prepared: "go and trim her up" (4.4.25). (Earlier he says he will "walk myself / To County Paris, to prepare up him" [4.2.45].) His mild oaths contribute to the irony: he swears earlier by "God's bread" and in this scene by the "Mass" (3.5.176; 4.4.19), but his actions lead inadvertently to his daughter's sacrifice LC. In the next scene the sacrificial dimension implicit earlier (1.3.3; 3.5.188) is again apparent when the Nurse calls Juliet "lamb" <LL> (4.5.2).

The actions of Capulet, the Friar, and the lovers have become increasingly desperate as they are forced to extreme measures that might achieve their different though analogous paradises <UC>. The son and "bridegroom" Paris, who has promised to "be here with music straight" (4.4.27, 22) at dawn, brings only a day of discord LC. Death and night and their companions—despair, haste, rashness, and chance—have frustrated renewal, and the last movement of the play is toward the darkness and woe of tragedy LC.

FIVE

Womb of Death

(*Romeo and Juliet* 4.5–5.3)

ROMEO. Thou detestable maw, thou womb of death,
Gorg'd with the dearest morsel of the earth.

(5.3.45–46)

A t the end of the play's third section, both Capulet
and the Friar's conflicting plans seem to have some
promise of success, but the mood changes dramatically
with Juliet's "death." In the reactions of the Capulets,
Paris, and Romeo to her apparent death, we get a fore-
taste of the total tragedy of the last scene LC. In the Friar's insensitivity to the Capulets' grief and his blun-
dering in informing Romeo of his plans, we sense the
ineffectiveness LR of renewal's key figure. Until almost
the end, the tomb could be the womb or dawn of a restored love UL rather than a "womb of death" LC, but
that is not to be for reasons that we understand better than anyone in the play. As the disaster gradually

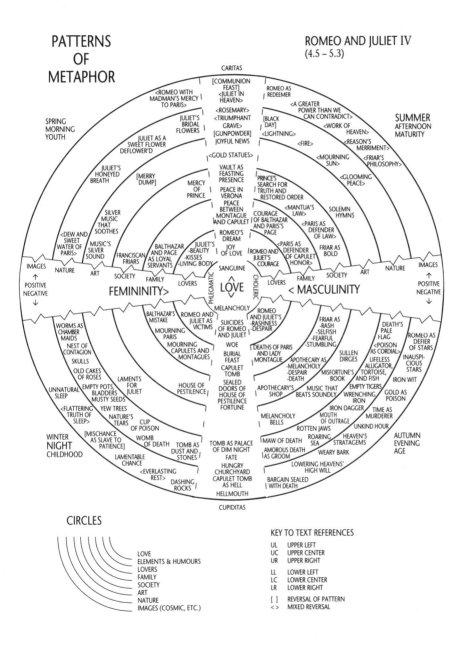

PATTERNS
OF
METAPHOR

ROMEO AND JULIET IV
(4.5 – 5.3)

CARITAS

[COMMUNION FEAST]
<JULIET IN HEAVEN>

ROMEO AS REDEEMER

<ROMEO WITH MADMAN'S MERCY TO PARIS>

<A GREATER POWER THAN WE CAN CONTRADICT>

<ROSEMARY>
JULIET'S BRIDAL FLOWERS
<TRIUMPHANT GRAVE>
[GUNPOWDER]
JOYFUL NEWS

[BLACK DAY]
<LIGHTNING>

<WORK OF HEAVEN>

SPRING
MORNING
YOUTH

SUMMER
AFTERNOON
MATURITY

<REASON'S MERRIMENT>

JULIET AS A SWEET FLOWER DEFLOWER'D

<GOLD STATUES>

<FIRE>

<MOURNING SUN>

<FRIAR'S PHILOSOPHY>

JULIET'S HONEYED BREATH

[MERRY DUMP]

MERCY OF PRINCE

VAULT AS FEASTING PRESENCE

PRINCE'S SEARCH FOR TRUTH AND RESTORED ORDER

<GLOOMING PEACE>

SILVER MUSIC THAT SOOTHES

PEACE IN VERONA

PEACE BETWEEN MONTAGUE AND CAPULET

<MANTUA'S LAW>

SOLEMN HYMNS

COURAGE OF BALTHAZAR AND PARIS'S PAGE

<PARIS AS DEFENDER OF LAW>

<DEW AND SWEET WATER OF PARIS>

MUSIC'S SILVER SOUND

ROMEO'S DREAM

JOY OF LOVE

ROMEO AND JULIET'S COURAGE

<PARIS AS DEFENDER OF CAPULET HONOR>

FRIAR AS BOLD

FRANCISCAN FRIARS

BALTHAZAR AND PAGE AS LOYAL SERVANTS

JULIET'S -BEAUTY -KISSES -LIVING BODY

IMAGES

NATURE

ART

SOCIETY

FAMILY

LOVERS

PHLEGMATIC

SANGUINE

^
LOVE
v

CHOLERIC

LOVERS

FAMILY

SOCIETY

ART

NATURE

IMAGES

↑
POSITIVE
NEGATIVE
↓

↑
POSITIVE
NEGATIVE
↓

FEMININITY>

< MASCULINITY

MELANCHOLY

ROMEO AND JULIET'S -RASHNESS -DESPAIR

BALTHAZAR'S MISTAKE

ROMEO AND JULIET AS VICTIMS

SUICIDES OF ROMEO AND JULIET

FRIAR AS -RASH -SELFISH -FEARFUL -STUMBLING

DEATH'S PALE FLAG

ROMEO AS DEFIER OF STARS

MOURNING PARIS

WOE

<POISON AS CORDIAL>

INAUSPICIOUS STARS

WORMS AS CHAMBER MAIDS

MOURNING CAPULETS AND MONTAGUES

BURIAL FEAST

DEATHS OF PARIS AND LADY MONTAGUE

SULLEN DIRGES

NEST OF CONTAGION

APOTHECARY AS -MELANCHOLY -DESPAIR -DEATH

LIFELESS ALLIGATOR, TORTOISE, AND FISH

IRON WIT

SKULLS

CAPULET TOMB

MISFORTUNE'S BOOK

OLD CAKES OF ROSES

LAMENTS FOR JULIET

HOUSE OF PESTILENCE

SEALED DOORS OF HOUSE OF PESTILENCE FORTUNE

APOTHECARY'S SHOP

MUSIC THAT BEATS SOUNDLY

EMPTY TIGERS WRENCHING IRON

GOLD AS POISON

UNNATURAL SLEEP

EMPTY POTS, BLADDERS MUSTY SEEDS

MELANCHOLY BELLS

IRON DAGGER

MOUTH OF OUTRAGE

TIME AS MURDERER

<FLATTERING TRUTH OF SLEEP>

YEW TREES

NATURE'S TEARS

CUP OF POISON

ROTTEN JAWS

ROARING SEA

HEAVEN'S STRATAGEMS

UNKIND HOUR

WINTER
NIGHT
CHILDHOOD

[MISCHANCE AS SLAVE TO PATIENCE]

WOMB OF DEATH

TOMB AS DUST AND STONES

TOMB AS PALACE OF DIM NIGHT

MAW OF DEATH

AMOROUS DEATH AS GROOM

WEARY BARK

AUTUMN
EVENING
AGE

FATE

LAMENTABLE CHANCE

HUNGRY CHURCHYARD

LOWERING HEAVENS' HIGH WILL

<EVERLASTING REST>

DASHING ROCKS

CAPULET TOMB AS HELL

BARGAIN SEALED WITH DEATH

HELLMOUTH

CUPIDITAS

CIRCLES

LOVE
ELEMENTS & HUMOURS
LOVERS
FAMILY
SOCIETY
ART
NATURE
IMAGES (COSMIC, ETC.)

KEY TO TEXT REFERENCES

UL   UPPER LEFT
UC   UPPER CENTER
UR   UPPER RIGHT

LL   LOWER LEFT
LC   LOWER CENTER
LR   LOWER RIGHT

[ ]   REVERSAL OF PATTERN
< >   MIXED REVERSAL

unfolds, the characters struggle with what we know is a discrepant, actually radically wrong, view of the facts.[1] Our superior knowledge allows our close attention as "death and night" LC (4.3.37) exert their power and actual tragedy replaces its illusion.

Shakespeare once again uses setting to establish the changed mood. In chapter 3, I described the positive settings that make bold action UR promising: Capulet's feasting hall, Juliet's balcony and orchard, Friar Lawrence's garden and cell, and Mercutio's boisterous street. In the next section, discussed in chapter 4, the same settings have become places of increased tension and desperation, but order still seems possible: the lively street is linked to chaos LC but also to the Prince's restored order <UC>, Capulet's house to frantic but hopeful planning for another feast <UC>, the Friar's cell to lament but also schemes for renewal <UC>, and Juliet's balcony and chamber to separation but also a consummated marriage <UC>. In the final section, the settings create an atmosphere of impending disaster LC. Except for a brief glimpse of the dreamer Romeo in Mantua before he learns of Juliet's death and a moment in the tomb when he seems vaguely aware of light and love <UC>, the settings are all grim and hopeless LC. In Capulet's house, the only repeated setting, a wedding UC becomes a funeral LC. In the remainder of the play, we hear reports of two settings associated with death and disease—the apothecary's shop and the house of pestilence—and get a full presentation of a third—the churchyard and tomb that dominate the play's ending. The survivors' attempt to understand what has happened and somehow bring life UL out of death LC proves to be very difficult.

Most scholars think that the scene showing the Capulet response to Juliet's death fails because of the overwrought rhetoric, and some suggest a satiric intention.[2] Since the Capulets have handled Juliet's marriage insensitively, their ritualistic laments may seem to be a further depiction of their inability to respond adequately;

but my approach through patterns of metaphor suggests that such a reading misinterprets both the Capulets and the scene's style. While deeply at fault, they are misguided, not villainous or unfeeling; they are agents LR of Juliet's plight LL but also victims LL of a spreading disaster LC. Suffering for Juliet's death may be a fitting punishment for their brutal treatment of her, but, as so often in the play, the tragic result exceeds the cause. In finding a style for their responses, Shakespeare draws together the imagery and attitudes already associated with death and despair LC. While reinforcing major themes, he also avoids a dramatic problem: he does not want a serious analysis of the Capulet view of what has happened. Believing that Juliet has died of grief over Tybalt's death, the Capulets blame Romeo. Since they know nothing of the secret marriage, they are not fully responsible for the desperate position they have forced upon Juliet. The Friar says vaguely that "The heavens do low'r upon you for some ill" (4.5.94), but he, and Shakespeare, cannot press home their guilt for something the Capulets do not know they have done.

Instead of criticizing the rhetoric, we should pay attention to what the characters are saying. When Capulet regrets the impossibility of communicating deep feeling through language (4.5.31–32) but then delivers a long lament, we should note a poetic convention and not deplore an inconsistency. Language may not finally be adequate, but the choric ritual, the polarized abstractions, and the familiar patterns of metaphor help communicate the spread of desolation LC. The tragedy has unmasked Lady Capulet's cool exterior: "my child, my only life! / Revive, look up, or I will die with thee!" (4.5.19–20). Capulet's image LC—"Death lies on her like an untimely frost / Upon the sweetest flower of all the field" (4.5.28–29)—is often regarded as an isolated felicity but takes on resonances from the allusion to broken cycles of nature. Later he picks up the death and flower images and relates them to the bridegroom motif:[3] "There she lies, / Flower as she was, deflowered by him. / Death is my son-in-law" (4.5.36–38). Cosmic pessimism LC is spreading. Capulet makes time a villain LR: "Uncomfortable time, why cam'st thou now / To murther, murther our solemnity?" (4.5.60–61). Juliet has described herself as the "soft" victim LL of heaven's "stratagems" LR (3.5.209–10). Death and now Time have become for Capulet the representatives of an unfriendly cosmos LC.

As the Capulets fall to the extreme of woe LC, the Friar shifts to the opposite extreme in stating the rational response of a believing Christian <UR>: "she is advanc'd / Above the clouds, as high as heaven itself" (4.5.74–75). His theology may be sound and he grants that "[fond] nature bids us all lament" LL, but his language and tone betray an insensitive emphasis on a rigid reason [UR]: "all the better is it for the maid" to have died; "she's best married that dies married young"; and "nature's tears are reason's merriment" (4.5.82, 68, 78, 83). He is full of a confidence that comes, partly from genuine Christian consolation UR, but also from the bold role he has undertaken and from knowing that Juliet is still alive. Capulet's response is a dignified lament [LC] of the change from wedding UC to funeral LC that reiterates the theme "all things change them to the contrary" (4.5.90), while the Friar has instructions <UR> and warnings <LR> for everyone. His dogmatic confidence in shaping the views and actions of others ironically identifies him with the very extremes LR he has opposed and contrasts sharply with his fear LL in the tomb. His swing to one extreme is followed by a disastrous counterswing to the other.

In the rest of the scene, Peter, played by Will Kempe, proposes a cure for sorrow that ludicrously parallels the earlier solutions of Capulet and the Friar. Capulet's confidence that Juliet's marriage will cure family grief leads him to language and actions [UR] that ignore Juliet's feelings LL, and the Friar's theology asserts the Christian triumph over death as "reason's merriment" <UR> (4.5.83).

When the doubting musicians refuse to play a correspondingly inappropriate "merry dump" [UC] that will assuage Peter's sorrow, he too becomes dictatorial and uses both the metaphorical "iron wit" LR (4.5.107, 124) of his language and an actual knife LR in an attempt to get his way. His claim to authority as a member of the household and his pseudological arguments, which turn to outright assertions of power, burlesque the inflexible methods of Capulet and the Friar.[4] Since Capulet has now become a victim LL, the Friar would be the main target of the burlesque. With parallel staging and imitative gestures, the comparison could be made clear.

Earlier, Peter's name has been ironically associated with Saint Peter by Juliet in opposing marriage to Paris: "Now, by Saint Peter's Church and Peter too, / He shall not make me there a joyful bride" (3.5.116–17).[5] The point of Juliet's oath is her refusal to sanction a marriage that goes against both the rebellious boldness <LR> she shares with their servant Peter and her desire for freedom from the patriarchal society <UR> of which the church of Saint Peter <UR> is a part. If Peter with the musicians serves as a parody of the authority that Peter the founder of Catholicism represents and that the formerly warm Franciscan UL Friar Lawrence has now assumed, the scene has satiric bite <LR> as well as the broad humor <LC> expected from Will Kempe. The surprisingly comic tone is more appropriate since we know, even if Peter does not, that Juliet is alive, but making the Friar an object of satire <LR> encourages our growing awareness that he is an unlikely agent of renewal.

In the rest of the scene, the methods and motivation of artists also attract Peter's attention. He seems to be making the realistic point that musicians who claim to be decorous servants UL of their employer's needs use their skills both to manipulate people's emotional responses LR and to gain their own personal ends LR. The point turns out to be more descriptive than moral: the same self-centered motives that influence friars and fathers affect artists, but artists have much less control over both their performance and their audience's response. They may be there because of compulsion or financial necessity LL and cannot explain what they are doing anyway. Peter himself plays teacher-critic <UR> as he tries to get the musicians to interpret how music's "silver sound" (4.5.128) assuages grief. One gives the conventional response in identifying "silver" with "sweet" <UC> (4.5.131), but another supports Peter's apparent point by taking "silver" as an allusion to the wages <UR> that will alleviate their own grief. Since drama is an analogous art, Shakespeare may also be commenting ironically on the relationship of his own company to their material. Like these musicians, actors work for money, not because of devotion UL to their employers or for the fulfillment of contributing to societal or cosmic unity UC. If we look at *A Midsummer Night's Dream* from the same undercutting perspective, Bottom's company is more concerned about the reward they will receive for their play than about contributing to hierarchical harmonies.[6] Shakespeare presents both views and commits himself to neither.

The references to iron and silver depend in part on conventional Renaissance metaphorical interpretations of metals[7] and help establish a context for the important references to iron and gold in the last act. Iron, traditionally associated with Mars and violence LR, is present here both in Peter's "iron dagger" and metaphorically in his "iron wit" (4.5.124). Earlier, both Romeo and Juliet have brandished presumably iron daggers while considering suicide as a way of escaping their woes LC. In the last act, Friar Lawrence wants an "iron crow" and Romeo a "wrenching iron" (5.2.21; 5.3.22) to break open the tomb; and Juliet kills herself with Romeo's dagger. Crude iron, linked to violence LR by these references, contrasts with ambiguous silver <UL>, inactive lead LC, and valiant steel UR. Silver, used here for both money <UR> and sweetness <UC>, has had polarized meanings earlier as well. In the balcony scene, Romeo swears by the "blessed moon" that "tips with silver all these fruit-tree tops" UL, but Juliet protests that the moon is "inconstant" LL (2.2.107–09). Later Romeo says, "How silver-sweet sound lovers' tongues by night" <UL> just after Juliet in an aside has spoken of her desire LR to "tear the cave where Echo lies" (2.2.165, 163). Lead, Saturn's metal, comes up three times in the play, always with a connection to slowness and heaviness LC (1.1.180; 1.4.15; 2.5.17). Steel, inevitably associated with swords, is linked with valor, both actual (1.1.82; 3.1.158–59) and metaphorical UR (2.4.198; 3.1.115). Romeo follows a cycle of metals that reflects his changing state of mind. He starts with a "soul of lead," turns to ambiguous silver in the balcony scene, laments after Mercutio's death that Juliet's beauty "in my temper soft'ned valor's steel" and then uses a sword to kill Tybalt, and finally in his despair turns to a dagger and a "wrenching iron" (1.4.15; 3.1.115; 5.3.22). When he kills himself, he uses a cup of poison that relates to other metaphorical patterns, but Juliet completes the cycle by using his dagger for her suicide.

Romeo is not identified with gold, the sun's metal <UR>, until near the end; by then repeated allusions have made gold seem highly ambiguous. In the first part of the play, gold is associated with the champions of an idealistic but also materialistic day world <UR>. According to Montague, the sun rises from the "golden window of the east," and the Friar says that in untroubled youth "golden sleep doth reign" (1.1.119; 2.3.38). From this perspective, both day and night are "golden" UR when they are used in conventionally approved ways. When Lady Capulet speaks of Juliet's "book" that "in gold clasps locks in the golden story" (1.3.91–92) of Paris, associations with wealth and appearances <UR> creep in. When Romeo tells the Friar "Thou cut'st my head off with a golden axe" (3.3.22), gold suggests a fine appearance for a horrible act LR. In the scene with the musicians, Peter associates gold with money <UR>: musicians have "no gold for sounding" (4.5.141). These comments prepare us for key references later. In the apothecary scene, gold takes on literal as well as metaphorical significance as Romeo uses it to buy the poison LR but also speaks of it as "worse poison to men's souls" (5.1.80). In the final scene, the gold statues that express the families' mourning provide an ambiguous culmination <UR> to this pattern of metaphor and to the play itself.

Romeo's joy <UC> in Mantua as he reflects on his curious dream <LC> parallels the Capulets's hope for Juliet's wedding. Romeo's depression over his banishment LC has been overcome by several factors <UC>— his wedding night with Juliet, the initial success of the Friar's plan, and now a dream in which Juliet's kisses revive him from his metaphorical death in Mantua.[8] He has Juliet's love and now a dream to remember and a future to imagine: "Ah me, how sweet is love itself possess'd, / When but love's shadows are so rich in joy!" (5.1.10–11). Familiar punning images of light and elevation <UC> reinforce the sense of a Romeo soaring in illusion <UC>: his "bosom's lord sits lightly in his throne" and "all this day an unaccustom'd spirit / Lifts me above the ground with cheerful thoughts" (5.1.3–5). An alert audience will remember other dreams and recognize the tantalizing parallel to what would actually happen if the Friar's plan were carried out successfully: Romeo's kisses should awaken the "dead" Juliet. If Romeo were somehow able to overcome his fears and trust the dream's almost accurate vision instead of Balthazar's incorrect facts, tragedy might be averted. A more ironic reading notes that Juliet does kiss the dead Romeo but only to try to get some poison for herself. Read in that way, the dream would be another reminder of the forces [UR] that in Juliet's words "practice stratagems / Upon so soft a subject as myself!" (3.5.209–10). A more optimistic interpretation sees the revival as an eternal awakening: life in this world is but a shadow of the eternal light UC. If we can remain undogmatic, these contradictory responses add complexity to our understanding of a play that refuses to be reduced to an either / or reading.

Romeo's response to Balthazar's news is to swing back to despair LC and make immediate plans to join Juliet in death. If we remember Romeo's earlier doubts about "the flattering truth of sleep" <LL> and "flattering-sweet" dreams <LC> (5.1.1; 2.2.141) and his pessimistic assumptions LC about cosmic polarities, this response is not surprising. When Balthazar, speaking more truly than he knows, tries to soften the impact of his message by saying that "Her body sleeps in Capels' monument" and adds that "her immortal part with angels lives," Romeo's impulsive response is "Then I [defy] you, stars!" (5.1.18–19, 24). To defy the stars <LR> as Romeo does is to accept their larger control over his life LL and to maintain only one limited power—that of killing himself <LR>. The play encourages conflicting reactions: like Balthazar, Romeo speaks more truly than he knows, for something—malevolent fate, unfortunate chance, or just bad luck LC—has kept him from getting the message.

The context for evaluating Romeo's defiance includes some supporting evidence for Romeo—the "star-crossed" and "death-marked" references in the prologue, his concern since early in the play that the stars and fortune are working against him, Juliet's fear that some power above is plotting against her, and the audience's superior knowledge that the Friar's plan is going awry LR. Yet we also know that the Friar's bold, well-intentioned plan <UR> could work if only these final obstacles could be overcome and that Romeo has repeatedly jumped to extreme conclusions. From another perspective, he is an unmetaphored character who is unaware that the play has changed genres in the Friar's plan [LC] for Juliet's "death" and "resurrection." If he could read the signs that make this clear to us, he could become the romance hero UR instead of a tragic victim LL, but we cannot expect that. There must be admiration for Romeo's courage UR, regret that he is losing patience UL at the time when he most needs it, and above all pity <UL> that he does not know Juliet is alive. Romeo does ask whether there is a message from the Friar but then quickly vows: "Well, Juliet, I will lie with thee to-night" (5.1.34). Such a union LC will bring no ecstasy UC.

The appearance of the apothecary and the description of his shop accentuate imagery of death and the death-in-life that accompanies melancholy LC. With his ske-leton-like frame, "worn" "to the bones," and his "over-whelming brows" (5.1.41, 39) he seems to personify death itself. Thereby he reminds us of the earlier person-ification of death as a lover and of Juliet's willingness to "undertake / A thing like death"; Juliet "cop'st with Death himself to scape from it" (4.1.73–75). As Joan Hartwig has shown,[9] the apothecary is also an emblem of *melancholia*, linked conventionally to the despair of the would-be suicide LC. Romeo's generalization—"O mis-chief, thou art swift / To enter in the thoughts of desper-ate men!" (5.1.35–36)—applies to both Romeo and the apothecary. We should also note the contrast between the apothecary's shop LC and the Friar's garden UL. The Friar looks for "baleful weeds and precious-juiced flowers" from which he can bring life, while the apoth-ecary undertakes his "Culling of simples" (2.3.8; 5.1.40) for herbs from which he can bring death. The apoth-ecary's wares include a stuffed alligator, a hanging tor-toise, and the "skins / Of ill–shap'd fishes" (5.1.43–44); all are water-dwellers now dry and lifeless LC. Romeo has turned from a counselor of life UC to an embodi-ment of despair and death LC.

In their curious dialogue, the apothecary is also re-vealed as a victim LL of a world that has made him "bare and full of wretchedness" (5.1.68). Romeo is also a victim of that world but becomes its representative LR when he uses forty ducats to corrupt a "needy" (5.1.54) man. In persuading the apothecary to sell, Romeo outlines a jus-tification for revolt by people not favored by society: "The world affords no law to make thee rich; / Then be not poor, but break it, and take this" (5.1.73–74). Romeo may see himself as a fellow victim LL of law [UR] because of his banishment. At least he understands the plight of the apothecary, who is faced with an awkward choice. If he sells the poison, he is threatened with death both by society's law and by God's law <UR>. If he does not sell, he sinks toward death by nature's law <UR> that man must eat to live. In his reply, the apothecary, probably with some irony since he has no doubt been selling poison for some time, replies: "My poverty, but not my will, consents" (5.1.75). Both seem aware of the difficulty of following a traditional morality that ignores economic necessity, but Romeo is less interested in political philosophy than in getting the poison.

In his final speech, with the poison now in hand, Romeo reverts to a traditional moral paradox that reverses his stated view of the apothecary's situation: gold means life for the body <UC> but death for the soul LC, while this poison will bring death to his body LC but life to his soul UC. To a modern mind, Romeo's point may sound like facile moralizing or even like a rationalization that the poor are better off without money, but a Renaissance playgoer would be more apt to assume that Romeo (like the trickster hero of romance <UR> who outwits the forces of evil?) has used a deceptive argument to persuade the apothecary and is now speaking his mind openly in calling for a "cordial" (5.1.85) that will bring him union with Juliet <LC>. Whether Romeo sees that union as an ironic release from a now grim physical life LC or as a promise of eternal marriage UC is unclear. His hope coexists with his despair.

The house of pestilence LC where Friar John is delayed is only briefly described, but it too becomes a setting with symbolic significance.[10] Pestilence LC, like poverty and death, is a problem that resists solution. Walling it off through quarantine <LR> is analogous to the locking of the tomb; and the apothecary's shop is also closed up, ironically for a holiday UL in which the apothecary takes no part. But in all of these cases something living is also enclosed—the apothecary, the friars and the well members of the house, and Juliet, in the Friar's words a "Poor living corse, clos'd in a dead man's tomb!" LL (5.2.30). The two friars' poverty, in their case a vow based on a philosophy of life that accords with Romeo's attack on gold, leads them, not to fear death and lead others to it as the apothecary does, but to risk themselves UR in order to bring spiritual comfort UC. In sharp contrast "the searchers of the town, / Suspecting" "infectious pestilence" "Seal'd up the doors and would not let us forth" (5.2.8–11). No doubt quarantines are necessary, and the spread of death would be very real in a London that experienced regular outbreaks of plague LC; but in such a world early death is a common fate, and acting boldly can make life fuller and richer. Friar Lawrence, another Franciscan dedicated to love and service UL, shares Friar John's willingness to take risks but also his inability LL to carry out his mission. While Friar Lawrence may not be responsible for Friar John's failure, he has made a serious mistake LR in not informing Balthazar of his plan. Shakespeare makes clear that Balthazar is the designated intermediary (3.3.169–71) and that his decision to inform Romeo is natural.[11]

By the time we reach the churchyard and tomb, the forces LR pushing the play toward disaster—poverty, pestilence, corruption, haste, rashness, bad planning, desperation, despair, chance—have taken on an inexorable power that makes resistance to them seem almost impossible. Friar Lawrence has blundered and seems increasingly indecisive, Romeo is plotting a defiant and bloody resolution LR, and no one seems to have the patience UL and the power UR to reverse the momentum. To attribute the disaster only to fate or chance LC is to misread the piling up of metaphorical patterns associated with disaster. While there is bad luck or misfortune in the failure to get the message to Romeo, what delays it is analogous to the factors that have made Romeo and

Juliet's situation difficult from the very start of the play. Ultimately the causes of the deaths include chance and human error as only a part of the personal, familial, societal, and cosmic forces that determine what happens in the world.

The first bridegroom to arrive at the tomb is a calm but naive Paris whose mission is a courtly one—to conduct what he calls "true love's rite" <UC> (5.3.20) outside Juliet's tomb. He tries to assimilate the contrarieties of his experience as natural to the Petrarchan mode that continues to express his manners. Imagery of seeing, speaking, and hearing, of light and dark, of life and death, and of the four elements help establish the atmosphere. When he imagines his "Sweet flower" in her "bridal bed," he implies that Death is the bridegroom who has "deflowered" her, as Capulet has said earlier (5.3.12; 4.5.37); but his thoughts are mainly of the role a grieving lover LL must play. He swings between the optimistic thought <UR> that the "dew" of his "sweet water" [LL] can keep his "flowers" and her bed fresh and the gloomy recognition LC that the "canopy" of her bed is of "dust and stones" (5.3.12–14). The illusions of his role-playing <UR> keep him once removed from the grim facts of the graveyard and tomb LC.

Paris's formal manners contrast sharply with Romeo's, whose first words are "Give me that mattock and the wrenching iron" LR (5.3.22). Romeo tries to frighten Balthazar by telling him he will "take" from Juliet's "dead finger / A precious ring," presumably a wedding ring; that ring seems now to token her obscene marriage LC to what he later describes as "amorous" death, and he determines to restore it to his own "dear employment" (5.3.30–32, 103). If an assertive Balthazar comes back to "pry" (as a more assertive Romeo pries open the tomb), a Romeo claiming heavenly sanction will "tear thee joint by joint, / And strew this hungry churchyard with thy limbs" LR (5.3.33, 35–36). Romeo describes both "The time" and his "intents" as "savage-wild, / More fierce and more inexorable far / Than empty tigers or the roaring sea" LR (5.3.37–39). Admittedly, he is trying to scare Balthazar, but his later images are just as strong, though the emphasis has shifted from death and violence to food and sexuality: the "churchyard" remains "hungry," but the Capulet tomb becomes a satiated, dragonlike monster whose hunger and lust LR have been "Gorg'd with the dearest morsel of the earth" LL (5.3.46). When Romeo calls it not only "Thou detestable maw" LR but also "thou womb of death" LC (5.3.45), death becomes bisexual. Forcing entry into a feminine monster suggests a rape that Paris, the protector of Juliet's honor, is unable to prevent. The association with eating seems stronger, however. When a powerful Romeo breaks open the tomb's (death's) appropriately "rotten jaws," locked into rigor mortis LC or just repletion, he will "cram thee with more food" (5.3.47–48) and bring about his own death. Earlier, Juliet spoke of the tomb's "foul mouth" (4.3.34) and imagined herself in its stomachlike interior. If Romeo could enter the Capulet tomb with the same spirit UR that motivated his earlier entry into the Capulet house and Juliet's orchard, he could free Juliet from her Capulet confinement, but despair now dominates his perspective.

An analogy of the tomb to hell LC is also implied by the mouth references. The Hellmouth had been used in the harrowing of hell scenes in the miracle plays, and a Hellmouth is listed as a prop for a London company as late as the 1590s.[12] Whether Shakespeare's company actually used a recognizable Hellmouth is less important than the metaphorical resonances suggested by the imagery. Hell as a cosmic setting is analogous to the tomb as the destination of the physical body, as well as to night and winter as parts of the cycle of nature. The Romeo UR who breaks into the tomb is analogous not only to the Christ who harrows hell but also to the Orpheus who tries to rescue Eurydice and to the figures in the nature myths who descend into the underworld to bring out goddesses of spring and rebirth. The continuing parallels to places where death is not absolute reinforce our awareness that Romeo could bring back life if only he could recognize his role. He could become a quester UR able to bargain with death or to wrest Juliet from his grasp. In triumphing over Juliet's two-day death, they would together achieve the fulfillment of an Easter-like dawn and spring.[13] But this resurrection is not to be for a complex of reasons connected with the imperfections of a fallen world. Romeo proves to be an ironic Christ or Orpheus who descends only for the purpose of adding his body to death's feast LC.

Romeo's handling of Paris reminds us that Romeo has a gentler side and that Paris is more than a caricature of a courtly fop. Although Romeo describes himself as a "desp'rate man" and a "madman" LC (5.3.59, 67), he also claims to be an older man UR looking out for an impetuous youth <UL>. He warns "Good gentle" Paris about a world of death that he does not understand: "think upon these gone, / Let them affright thee" (5.3.59–61). Then referring to Tybalt, he says that he does not want his "fury" LR to "Put . . . another sin upon my head" (5.3.62–63). But nothing will stop Paris from doing what he thinks he must. Paris's behavior is more plausible when we understand his code of honor <UR> and remember that he sees and hears everything that Romeo does and says earlier in the scene.[14] He assumes that Romeo plans "some villainous shame / To the dead bodies" (5.3.52–53). When he steps forward, he is acting in the name of order and decency to stop the man he thinks is indirectly responsible for his bride's death: "Condemned villain, I do apprehend thee. / Obey and go with me, for thou must die" (5.3.56–57). Paris expects obedience now and Romeo's death later by the process of law UR. Instead of being angry, Romeo grieves for him and treats him with respect UR. He thinks of the death of Paris, like those of Tybalt, Mercutio, Juliet, and soon his own, as a part of the lamentable waste LL brought on by the rush of uncontrollable events. They are all written in "sour misfortune's book!" LC (5.3.82).

The tomb Romeo enters is quite different from the horrible place both he and Juliet have imagined. The light of Romeo's torch, the calm confidence of his manner, and, most important, the still vital physical presence of Juliet transform the tomb at least temporarily from a place of death to a "feasting presence" <UC> (5.3.86) that suggests royal celebration, with ironic overtones of Christian communion [LC] recalling the imagery of the scenes leading up to Juliet's "death."[15] We should also note a comparison with the Capulet feast <UC>, where a place of potential disaster also turns into a setting where light and order seem to rule. First Romeo puns on the "lightning before death" (5.3.90) that doomed men are supposed to feel. Romeo thinks of a lightning flash, but his thoughts are now of light UC as the opposite of heavy, sad, and dark LC, all familiar to us from earlier imagery in the play. The Juliet who was light in all of these senses could still relume Romeo's world, and Romeo is for a moment drawn away from despair by Juliet's beauty and color. The death that was feminine as Romeo entered the tomb is once again masculine, at this point a soldier LR who has "suck'd the honey of thy breath" but "Hath had no power yet upon thy beauty" (5.3.92–93). Unfortunately, the respite of dwelling on her vitality serves primarily to remind Romeo of what might have been. He can joke sardonically about joining her so that "amorous" death, "the lean abhorred monster" LR, will not use her as his "paramour," but he is also aware of an obscene deception—that masculine "worms . . . are thy chambermaids" (5.3.103–05, 109) and corrupt her from within. The tomb has now become "a [palace] of dim night" LC, and his only satisfaction is to "shake the yoke of inauspicious stars / From this world-wearied flesh" LC (5.3.107, 111–12).

In Romeo's final lines, he uses traditional legal imagery to express his state of mind, but his views are based on cosmic pessimism LC. His lips, "The doors of breath," will "seal with a righteous kiss / A dateless bargain to engrossing death!" (5.3.114–15). Sealing the lips through a binding contract LR with "death" will prevent renewal in this world or the next through the Juliet who in his dream "breath'd such life with kisses in my lips / That I reviv'd and was an emperor" UC (5.1.8–9). The Romeo who has forced the "rotten jaws to open" denies this promising power and instead unknowingly justifies Juliet's parallel fear she will be "stifled" by a "foul mouth" LC that "no healthsome air breathes in" (5.3.47; 4.3.33–34). If we recognize an analogy of the lips to the mouth of hell, Romeo's cool courage reflects his despair about achieving anything beyond the body; in the Christian metaphor that is latent in the analogy, his lips will not feast on the body of Christ UR, who has opened the mouth of hell and provided the triumph of divine love UC over rigid law LR. Romeo has given control to death rather than life.

Romeo has followed a cycle of Cupids that define his changing views of love:[16] in the opening scenes he sees Cupid as a blind tormentor LR while Benvolio tries and eventually succeeds in persuading him that both he and Cupid can see UR; in the Queen Mab scene he gives the "steerage of my course" to an ambiguous Cupid he seems to think is celestial UR; in the party scene he views himself as a less exalted seeing and judging Cupid UR; in the balcony scene he speaks of a blind Cupid [LR] of an ascending higher "love" who "lent me counsel" to soar into Juliet's garden UC; after Mercutio's death he deserts Cupid and asks "fire[-eyed] fury" LR to "be my conduct"; now he turns to another blind Cupid (here poison) LR, an ambiguous god of death, as his "bitter conduct" and "unsavory guide" (1.4.112; 2.2.81–82; 3.1.124; 5.3.116). In describing Cupid as "bitter" and "unsavory" after earlier talking about "sour misfortune's book" (5.3.82), he describes the opposite LC of love's sweetness <UC>. Later Cupid is also the "desperate pilot" LR who will end Romeo's earthly voyage by taking the "sea-sick weary bark" of his body to "The dashing rocks" LC (5.3.117–18).

In the apothecary scene, Romeo used a gunpowder image to describe the effect he wants from the poison. The "life-weary taker" wants to "be discharg'd of breath / As violently as hasty powder fir'd / Doth hurry from the fatal cannon's womb" (5.1.62–65). This curiously phallic "womb" unites fire [UR] and powder [UL] in an explosion that "delivers" the breath in an ecstatic death LC. In the image of kissing the poisoned cup, the sexual reference is continued: an active UR Romeo raises the cup UL to his lips, kisses it, and drinks, but the powerful poison LR then controls his response. After an ambiguous salute to "my love" (Juliet, the cup, the poison, Cupid, and even the apothecary), he punningly suggests that the apothecary is "true" because his drugs are "quick;" the kiss that was to be coldly "righteous" (5.3.119, 120, 114) has the speed, vitality, and perhaps even the explosive and ecstatic power that Romeo wants in the kiss of death. There is a different passion as he turns to kiss Juliet: "Thus with a kiss I die" (5.3.120). The two kisses link the two ecstasies implicit in his final word, a pun on "die" soon repeated in Juliet's final word "die" (5.3.170).

Juliet's death is dignified and poignant. If Romeo's final kiss initiates her first stirrings, the timing can emphasize the ironic meeting of death and renewed life. After the Friar makes a hasty departure, Juliet quietly accepts her death with the simple recognition that life without Romeo would be meaningless. When she kisses Romeo, she is hoping for a literal kiss of death from the poison still on his lips. When she finds Romeo's dagger and makes her body its "sheath" (5.3.170), she is, like Romeo, at once active and passive. The dagger is the phallic weapon of a masculine death LR (and perhaps of Romeo since it is his dagger, and his death causes hers), but an active Juliet <UR> seeks out death and wields the dagger. There is a fusion of masculine and feminine in both lovers as the woman dies with a dagger LR and the man with a cup LL.[17]

That Romeo and Juliet die with so little hope does not necessarily imply that the audience will join them in cosmic pessimism. We know much more than Romeo does—primarily that Juliet is alive and that more patience UL would have led to her restoration to him. From one point of view, his despair LC is the inevitable product of the facts as he knows them, but from another he is giving up not only on God but on the cycles of nature that promise some sort of renewal, even if not the revival of Juliet. Juliet faces the same choice and makes the same decision. Nevertheless, we are drawn to the courage and nobility UR of lovers who are ready to die rather than live without each other. As Ruth Nevo has said, "Their death is an act of freedom and of fidelity; hence an affirmation of the reality, vitality, and value of their experience."[18] This combination of idealism about their love UC and despair about the world LC is particularly appealing to modern readers who assume the plight of the individual in an unfeeling cosmos. We must be wary of turning the play into either a romantic (or existential) celebration of love UC in a cruel (or meaningless) LC universe, a religious criticism UR of despair LC that gives up on God and nature, or a detached, almost postmodern, comment LC on the hollowness of both idealistic love and traditional religion. The Shakespearean vision includes all of these concepts and ends up somewhere in between.

Friar Lawrence's breakdown implies the inadequacy of extreme positions. The stable counselor UR identified with his garden and his cell and with a wisdom based on both nature and philosophy UR has become increasingly dogmatic LR in his views and impulsive LR in his actions. The signs of strain have been apparent as his plans become more complicated, his role more manipulative, and his sympathy for others less apparent. Now he is the opposite of what he once was. He asks for his saint's help UL to give him speed, but his old legs are earthbound: "Saint Francis be my speed! how oft tonight / Have my old feet stumbled at graves!" (5.3.121–22). He has warned

Romeo and Juliet about speed and stumbling, but now he himself is the stumbler LR, significantly on the graves that reveal the same power of death LC he knows threatens Romeo and Juliet. Beginning to panic, he is unable to think clearly or act wisely. In neglecting to tell Balthazar about his plans, the Friar has made a disastrous mistake LR. Now when Balthazar confronts him, he continues to treat him as an uninvolved observer. Learning that Romeo is already at the tomb, he implores Balthazar to go with him and then expresses fear LR directly when Balthazar refuses: "Fear comes upon me. / O, much I fear some ill unthrifty thing" (5.3.135–36). When his worst fears are confirmed as he discovers the bodies of Paris and Romeo, he refers for a second time to the forces LC working against him: "Ah, what an unkind hour / Is guilty of this lamentable chance!" (5.3.145–46). The Friar fails totally to provide the help and counsel that Juliet needs when she awakes and asks confidently for "my Romeo" (5.3.150). He has become the embodiment of fear and haste LR, while Juliet in her clear and controlled response <UR> is now settled on both her place and her course: "Go get thee hence, for I will not away" (5.3.160).

The exact nature of the Friar's fear is hard to pin down, but it seems connected to both his sense of supernatural forces LC and his practical concerns for his own future. His statement to the Prince that "a noise did scare me from the tomb" (5.3.262) is consistent with his warning to Juliet: "I hear some noise, lady. Come from that nest / Of death, contagion, and unnatural sleep" LC (5.3.151–52). His description recalls the contrasting "bird's nest" UC (2.5.74) of Juliet's room, the analogous "contagion" of the house of pestilence LC, and the "unnatural" sleeps LC, not just of Juliet, but also of the young men who have slept in death before their proper time. Now the Friar is unable to put these forces in a perspective that allows him to behave wisely. He also has selfish reasons LR for leaving. When he tells Juliet that "the watch is coming" (5.3.158) and seems to identify the noises with

them, he sounds more desperate. Putting Juliet in a re-
mote nunnery would cover up his role; leaving her alone
might allow him to escape without anyone except Juliet
knowing anything; but being found with a living Juliet in
the tomb would be hard to explain. The two dimensions
of fear are not inconsistent. If his confidence in moral
action breaks down, he would quite plausibly begin to
look out for himself.

Having the Friar fail under pressure has important thematic effects. The sharp contrast of the glib rationalism
and faith <UR> in his earlier statement to the Capulets
with his betrayal of Juliet and loss of confidence in himself LR casts doubt on his faith and on a certain kind
of religious belief. When he tells Juliet that a "greater
power than we can contradict / Hath thwarted our intents" (5.3.153–54), he is ostensibly reminding her that
people must accept with patience UL whatever happens
since no one is able to control fate <LC>. That is good
doctrine, but people may use it to accept fatalistically
what they might still control. The Friar seems to have
concluded that the "horrible conceit of death and night"
LC (4.3.37) Juliet has feared has taken over; instead of
stoically trusting his God, he panics.

A similar weakness is present in his final defense.
When he tells the Prince, "I entreated her come forth /
And bear this work of heaven with patience" (5.3.260–
61), we know that he was the one who lacked patience
UL. He admits that "a noise did scare me from the
tomb" but puts most of the blame on Juliet for not following: "she, too desperate, would not go with me, / But
as it seems, did violence on herself" (5.3.262–64). The
Friar is willing to grant some fault in himself, but his ad-
mission is couched in excuse and evasion: "and if aught
in this / Miscarried by my fault, let my old life / Be
sacrific'd some hour before his time, / Unto the rigor of
severest law" (5.3.266–69). In four lines he manages to
imply that he might not be guilty at all, that he will soon
die anyway, and that punishment would make him the

sacrifice of a severe Old Testament legalism LR that ignores New Testament mercy UL. Much of what the Friar
says in his last speech is an accurate summation of what
has happened, and the Prince says that Romeo's letter to
his father verifies the Friar's account. He neglects, however, to mention his long-range plan to bring the families
together and minimizes his responsibility for what has
happened. Despite his age and religion, he tries both in
the tomb and in his summation to find a solution that
will allow him to live. He may no longer be the "friar,
that trembles, sighs, and weeps" LL (5.3.184), but he is
neither a moral model nor a reliable commentator UR.

If, as I have been maintaining, the play is a literary
microcosm where each detail is important, the actions of
even the minor characters should be relevant. The servants, Balthazar and Paris's page, behave more worthily
than the Friar. They overcome their respective fears LR—
of the graveyard (the page) and of Romeo's wrath (Balthazar)—and do what they think they must. Paris asks his
page to lie down "under yond [yew] trees" (5.3.3) and lis-
ten for noises. Since the ground is "loose, unfirm, with
digging up of graves," he will be able to hear someone
coming if he keeps his "ear close to the hollow ground"
(5.3.6, 4). The unimaginative Paris sees no cause for fear
in such reminders of death, but the page is understand-
ably terrified: "I am almost afraid to stand alone / Here
in the churchyard, yet I will adventure" (5.3.10–11).[19]
Balthazar's description of the fight between Paris and
Romeo reiterates the yew reference and emphasizes a curiously dreamlike quality: "As I did sleep under this
[yew] tree here, / I dreamt my master and another fought,
/ And that my master slew him" (5.3.137–39). Balthazar
has some reason to justify his inaction, but more likely
the yew tree specifically and the churchyard atmosphere
generally have pulled him into a strange state of mind
<LC> between sleeping and waking, between reason and
a kind of madness. Romeo has a similar reaction upon
discovering that Paris is dead. He vaguely remembers

that Balthazar has told him Paris was to marry Juliet: "Said he not so? or did I dream it so? / Or am I mad, hearing him talk of Juliet, / To think it was so?" (5.3.79–81). Our sense of mysterious forces <LC> at work in the graveyard is increased. Dream and madness <LC> are somehow linked. Cool reason cannot explain everything.

The deaths of Paris, Mercutio, and Tybalt clearly contribute to our sense of the wasteful destruction LC of the youth of the society. That Shakespeare sees the final scene as broader than the tragedies of Romeo and Juliet is suggested by the fact that he at one time included Benvolio as well in the final carnage. In the first quarto, when Montague reports the death of his wife, he adds: "And yong Benuolio is deceased too."[20] While the need to double acting roles can explain Benvolio's absence, we can not be sure why this line was dropped. There is no plausible reason why the healthy young Benvolio should die, and Shakespeare may have decided that the thematic advantage of having all the young men die LC is outweighed by the distraction and implausibility of his death. At least Benvolio is not present in the last scene. Having no living young people on stage LC makes the point without having him killed.

The ladies have also moved toward death. Lady Montague has actually died of grief LC over Romeo's banishment, and on hearing of Juliet's second death Lady Capulet exclaims: "O me, this sight of death is as a bell / That warns my old age to a sepulchre" LC (5.3.206–07). We remember that Juliet was "my only life!" (4.5.19) and understand how a woman of about twenty-eight can feel old and ready for death. This movement toward death is analogous to the movement of the deeply distressed Helena and Hermia to a death-like sleep LC in *A Midsummer Night's Dream*. In *Romeo and Juliet* the movement toward tragedy LC is completed, while in *A Midsummer Night's Dream* the confused night LC becomes a dawn UL of revitalization and reconciliation. Having all the women dead or dying adds to the effect created by the death of the young people. Both the generative and the nurturing power of the society UC is lost, and the only ones still alive to try to rebuild are the Prince, the fathers, and the Friar. In a patriarchal society, men find ways to survive, and their tendency to overlook masculine faults LR is not reassuring. The only other woman who is not present in the last scene, or at least is not mentioned, is the Nurse, who is no doubt also absent because of the need to double roles. Perhaps having the Nurse there and somehow paired with Friar Lawrence, another old counselor who has failed LR at a crucial time and now has little to do except await death, would be thematically appropriate.

The maturity and wisdom of the leadership <UL> the Prince provides has been at least open to question, but in the last scene he has a neutral though somewhat superficial role: he is choric in pulling together themes and images from the play as a whole and monarchical in trying to find a basis for a new order UC. His comment to Montague relates time, light, and descent: "thou art early up / To see thy son and heir now [early] down" (5.3.208–09). The pun on son-sun accentuates the unnaturalness of a son dying before his father, an idea Montague picks up a few lines later. The Prince also asks someone to "Seal up the mouth of outrage for a while" (5.3.216). The reiteration of the mouth metaphor suggests again that death and the tomb have some monstrous or demonic power LC and makes more plausible the speculation that a recognizable Hellmouth was used. The Prince may share their sense of the mysterious, but he has the practical goal of getting rational explanations that will play down their fears and restore order. While the Prince's neat apportioning of blame and his moralizing about the punishments may seem oversimplified in contrast to the complexity of causes the audience by then should understand, he does recognize a guilt LR that includes himself. More important, he appreciates the paradox that "heaven" UC has used "love" <UC> to "kill" the individual and familial "joys" UC so inconsistent with the "hate" LC (5.3.293, 292) that has governed their interfamily relationship.

When Capulet and Montague pick up the cue and join hands <UC>, the feud is ended. When they pledge gold statues as "Poor sacrifices of our enmity!" (5.3.304), remembrance of the lovers is assured. The impulse on both sides is obviously genuine: the statues will serve as a reminder of an unnecessary tragedy LC and a noble love UC; if these "sacrifices" are purgative, a better society can emerge. But there is some role-playing to the very end; gold is the color of conspicuous glitter as well as of wisdom. The Shakespeare who has called attention to the ambivalence of metal symbolism,[21] particularly gold <UR>, would want us to be aware of continuing ambiguity. Establishing the degree of irony is subjective: the grand gesture in this ostentatious memorial <UC> points to but does not achieve ideal wisdom.

The Prince's final summation once again pulls together familiar patterns. Morning comes and brings "peace," but it is a "glooming peace," for this "morning" (5.3.305) also brings mourning LR. The transition to day of the fifth dawn of the play will be as uneasy and problematic as the previous four. Romeo flees the first dawn to return to the "artificial night" (1.1.140) of his room. On the second and third dawns, Romeo must leave Juliet in order to escape detection. At the fourth dawn, Juliet is found dead, a disaster for the Capulets and a false hope for the lovers. Now, before the fifth dawn, the Prince asserts cosmic sympathy UC in saying that "The sun," the emblem of cosmic order and analogous to both the Prince and God, "for sorrow, will not show its head" (5.3.306). In classical and Christian story the sun does stop,[22] but an overcast morning <UL> is as ambiguous an emblem as the gold statues. A time of mourning is essential, but something approaching wisdom will result only if dawn and life itself can be understood as being as complex as the Friar described them in his opening soliloquy.

The stage remains in partial darkness, and we are left with mixed hopes about the chances for meaningful revitalization.

Many of the cosmic issues of *King Lear* are present at least in embryo in this ending, but the questioning of the traditional order does not become explicit even though it remains a possible response. The Prince's final speech will be more ironic if we stress "talk" <UR> in his wish "to have more talk of these sad things" and contrast it with Edgar's final comment: "The weight of this sad time we must obey, / Speak what we feel, not what we ought to say" (*King Lear*, 5.3.324–325). The Prince, with his insistence on pardoning and punishing, seems more confident than Edgar about the possibility of transforming the tragic experience into something that can be described and explained. But to stress only the limitations of the Prince and the other survivors is to make the tragedy more ironic than it seems to be. While no one in Verona has achieved full wisdom, Shakespeare has presented his story in a way that suggests they have learned something. Having the tragic results far exceed what any of the participants deserves may imply the chaos of life itself LC, but we have been shown that life is full of mysteries that cannot be fully or easily explained.

The last couplet brings us back to the prologue, for there is something choric about the Prince's reference to "story" (5.3.309). Perhaps this final bit of distancing will encourage an audience to thoughtful reflection UR as well as emotional response UL. *Romeo and Juliet* is a play about people whose experience of "death and night" LC (4.3.37) makes a meaningful dawn difficult, if not impossible. Those who comprehend their story can expand their awareness of the complexities of existence, but Shakespeare wisely avoids formulations that require a uniform response.

PART 3

A Midsummer Night's Dream

SIX

Sharp Athenian Law
(*A Midsummer Night's Dream* 1.1–1.2)

LYSANDER. And to that place the sharp Athenian law
Cannot pursue us.

(1.1.162–63)

I n writing *A Midsummer Night's Dream* Shakespeare
may very well have started with the idea of doing a
comedy based on the "Pyramus and Thisby" story that
so closely resembles *Romeo and Juliet*. Instead of con-
centrating on Lysander and Hermia, the couple most parallel to the tragic couples, he develops analogous love
stories shaped by generic modes—classical legend, fairy
and folk tale, narrative romance, and low comedy—that
allow a more comprehensive study of masculine and
feminine interactions. The method is more symbolic
than realistic and leads to a more abstract analysis of
love than that in *Romeo and Juliet*, but the underlying
structures are similar.

171

Instructions for interpreting the charts in part 3:

Each chapter's chart combines features of part 1's charts on Metaphors of Cycles and Metaphors of Hierarchies. (See pp. 29, 31) Hierarchies provide the underlying structure, with the positive masculine and feminine principles at each analogous level—individuals, the family, society, art, and nature—linked by love at the top and by negative forces at the bottom. The cycles—of the humours, seasons and days, and the ages of life—are indicated in the inner and outer circles. Each chart suggests how gender and analogy shape the patterns of metaphor in that part of the play. When reference to the chart is helpful for clarification of my analysis, I use abbreviations in the text: UL = upper left; UC = upper center; UR = upper right; LL = lower left; LC = lower center; LR = lower right. Since each moment in time has potentially positive or negative overtones, further discriminations are needed. When metaphors contradict the basic up-positive and down-negative form, I use brackets—[ ] to indicate a reversal and < > a partial reversal. Readers should remember that metaphorical associations are suggestive and complex, not exact. The charts should be thought of as providing a rough outline of the plays' metaphorical structure that my analysis fills out and makes more precise. Shakespeare had no need to develop charts to communicate with his audience since the metaphorical patterns I describe were built into the Elizabethan understanding of the world.

PATTERNS
OF
METAPHOR

A MIDSUMMER NIGHT'S DREAM I
(1.1 – 1.2)

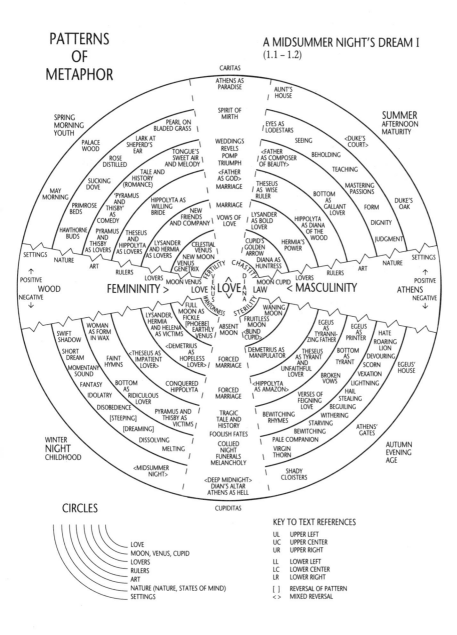

CIRCLES

LOVE
MOON, VENUS, CUPID
LOVERS
RULERS
ART
NATURE (NATURE, STATES OF MIND)
SETTINGS

KEY TO TEXT REFERENCES

UL UPPER LEFT
UC UPPER CENTER
UR UPPER RIGHT

LL LOWER LEFT
LC LOWER CENTER
LR LOWER RIGHT

[ ] REVERSAL OF PATTERN
<> MIXED REVERSAL

Both plays are literary microcosms that involve conflicts in hierarchical relationships, characterization based on the expectations of literary genre, and a framework of metaphor reflecting the analogies described in part 1. In analyzing how Shakespeare shapes the play's development, I again make use of charts, one for each chapter, based on my charts in part 1. In *A Midsummer Night's Dream*, Shakespeare uses Athens and the wood as overarching symbolic settings and sharpens the perspective through significant combinations of time and place. In the first part of the play, settings in the day at the Athenian court and at night in the wood help establish contrasting moods related to gender oppositions. In the later scenes, a movement toward resolutions takes place as Theseus brings the court to the wood at dawn and Oberon and the fairies come to the court at midnight. Shakespeare explores relationships through interlocking imagery, much of it based on the cycles of nature—day and night, the sun and the moon, and the months and seasons—and on polarities such as mutability and transformation, and death and renewal.

In the opening scene, Shakespeare introduces the central opposition between the rational, orderly world UR of Athens and the passionate, natural world UL of the lovers. The conflict is not simply between law and love but rather between two conceptions of how love UC, the vital principle in the traditional hierarchical system,[1] should function. Theseus and Egeus think that love must be governed by reason UR. (In my charts, this means shifting the upper right to the very top so that reason and the axis of ideal love coalesce.) The more passionate Lysander and the women think the feelings UL should be given more prominence (and for them the qualities of the upper left move toward the axis of love). Theseus and Egeus emphasize the love (traditionally *agape*) that comes down from a gracious and wise patriarch UC (analogous to God) to immature dependents LL in danger of making unwise decisions. In their view, lovers should stay within the framework of traditional institutions UC (the family, marriage, and the state) that give structure to their inevitably unruly impulses. Hermia and Lysander think that they can make their own decisions and see patriarchal interference as unjustified LR. For them, love is closer to the traditional *eros* that permits people to rise through their own efforts toward meaningful human and divine love. In such relationships, *agape* still has a place in the recurring exchange of roles: each lover is in turn the aspiring suppliant UL (*eros*) and the gracious giver (*agape*) UR. In the first scene (and in the play generally), we are given ample reason for doubts about the wisdom of both the patriarchs and the lovers. Achieving a balance of order UR and freedom UL that avoids both dogmatism LR and immaturity LL, although perhaps possible through the conventions of comedy <UC>, is apt to remain an unattainable ideal.

The shaping metaphor of the opening scene—Theseus's defeat of Hippolyta, queen of the Amazons—gets curiously little direct explication, no doubt partly because Shakespeare could assume knowledge of its main features but also because he seems to want to make Hippolyta more than an image of Amazonian revolt LR. The scene's imagery ties her to the conventional power of the moon <UR> and the night <LC>, not just to an attempt to seize power for women. By avoiding the details of her subjugation, Shakespeare is able to develop his own myth of masculinity and femininity without being restricted by the old story. From a patriarchal view, conquering Hippolyta is a legendary masculine feat: Theseus as man, ruler, and soon to be husband UR has subdued the woman, subject, and soon to be wife UL who has been threatening order. From a more feminine perspective, however, Hippolyta has the virtues and rights of an independent Diana UR, and her relationship to the masculine realm reflects the complex interactions of gender at every level of existence.

In Shakespeare's version of the story, a resolution has

already been achieved, and we inevitably wonder how Hippolyta has reconciled herself to the marriage. On the literal level, she has simply lost and may recognize the need to submit: perhaps she realizes the error of her ways and is genuinely happy, or she may be making the best of a bad situation. If the battle or war is taken as a metaphor of courtship, however, with an ardent male winning over a strong but independent woman, then Hippolyta's former life as a Diana-figure can be seen as a time of natural growth to personal maturity UR and her apparent defeat as a paradoxical victory. In the language of myth, she has fused her newly awakened Venus side UL with her Diana self UR and is ready for marriage UC. Shakespeare's metaphorical scheme contains some basic gender polarities in a hierarchical society: Theseus has fought Hippolyta both to establish legitimate masculine authority and to win the love of a great lady. Hippolyta is now happily accepting her approaching marriage but retains considerable power as a woman and as the object of his love. The first scene becomes a study of the various ways, both positive and negative, in which men and women try to work out the continuing problems of their relationships.[2] Success is not guaranteed. When we see Theseus's rigid handling LR of Hermia's marriage, we remember his use of force <LR> to win Hippolyta and must wonder about his qualities as both a ruler and husband. Although Hippolyta seems to be taking her subjugation with grace, understanding, and even love, she could easily disrupt the harmony of the approaching marriage.

Theseus's reputation as at once a wise ruler of Athens UR and a womanizer LR fits with Shakespeare's emphasis on polarities. In the first scene, however, Shakespeare reverses expectations by depicting Theseus as a devoted lover UL and a dogmatic ruler LR. That he wants to marry Hippolyta implies a more responsible love than he has exhibited in his frequent affairs, and he seems to be genuinely excited and loving as he tries to establish a good relationship with her. Aware of the significance of

cycles and perhaps wanting to define himself in relation
to Hippolyta's more natural rhythms, he has scheduled
his wedding for the time of the new moon UL, and he
uses the imagery of old and new moons to reinforce the
sense of the end of one order and the beginning of another.[3] Associating Hippolyta with the moon and the
night may at first seem surprising since in the myth her
link with Diana has been primarily with the huntress of
the wood, but Shakespeare apparently wants broader thematic implications. To make the association more clear
to an audience, she might be identified iconographically
on stage by the attributes of Diana as moon goddess as
well as huntress. If this identification is explicit, a playful Theseus may be suggesting that his possibly still reluctant "fair Hippolyta" should transform herself as the
moon itself changes: the "Four . . . days" before the wedding will be "happy" but not the nights since the "old
moon" (both the waning moon and a chaste Hippolyta)
"lingers my desires, / Like to a step-dame, or a dowager, /
Long withering out a young man's revenue" (1.1.1, 2,
4–6). To compare Hippolyta with a dying old moon-
dowager is wittily daring: when he grants the power of
her "fair" beauty UR over his suffering self LL, he recalls
Hippolyta's earlier independence while lamenting her
continuing chastity. For Theseus, that waning cycle cannot end too soon: he yearns, like the impetuous young
men of the play, to act now instead of waiting patiently
UL for the cycle of time to bring the right moment, and
he wants to establish an entirely new relationship UC in
which he can be both Hippolyta's servant UL and her
lord UR.

Hippolyta's perception of the interval before their marriage is reassuring both about its brevity and about the
role of the night. We should remember that the Hippolyta of North's Plutarch is described as a peacemaker UR
as well as a rebel LR.[4] She speaks with an almost god-
desslike authority on matters cyclical, especially on time,
the night, and the moon, as she defines with appropriate

irony a positive night [LL] that moistens and refreshes. The days, hot and moist like a young sunlike UR Theseus, will "quickly steep themselves in night" (1.1.7). No rejection will take place: "steep" implies that the midsummer night (and the moist moon) will satisfy the days' masculine "desires" instead of withering them away, so Hippolyta implies that she too will be much more like a receptive bride than an old "dowager." The passage is a shorter and more restrained version of the Juliet's epithalamium as she describes the progress of the horses of the sun toward the night (3.2). When sleep comes to the days, the nights, far from being threatening, will "quickly dream away the time" (1.1.7–8). They will be the agents of sleep and dream [LC], not of nightmare and death LC. When the moon returns, it will bring the full attention of "a silver bow / [New] bent in heaven" that "shall behold the night / Of our solemnities" (1.1.9–11). The image suggests not only a fresh new order but also an armed Diana UR, now at once a huntress, a moon goddess, and even a Cupid, ceremonially watching over the wedding night of her votaress Hippolyta.[5] All of these images imply the power and dignity of a feminine force that will balance male extremes: the marriage will embody, not the victory of the male over the female, but the union of two significant powers. For this strong woman, marriage is no capitulation. In the battle of the sexes that the whole episode represents, she has become, not a conquered Diana who continues to resist love and marriage, but a Venus who has won Theseus's love. Nevertheless, a threat of renewed rebellion LR by her Diana side remains implicit. The scene takes on a different tone if the largely silent Hippolyta remains a powerful feminine presence UR that supports Hermia's revolt [LR].

Theseus's enthusiasm UL seems healthy as he develops a new mood of amity and spreads it to Athens itself: "pomp," "triumph," and "revelling" UC will replace the "sword" <LR> (1.1.19, 16). Since a marital "key" UR will open a new time of harmony, Diana's "silver bow" UR

(1.1.18, 9) can remain ceremonial. Mirth UC needs wakening: "Stir up the Athenian youth to merriments, / Awake the pert and nimble spirit of mirth" (1.1.12–13). Melancholy, the "pale companion" LC, has no place in this fresh and active world: "Turn melancholy forth to funerals" (1.1.15, 14). Nevertheless, in this play about the need for balancing polarities, we need to be wary about Theseus's tendencies. As in Milton's "L'Allegro" and "Il Penseroso," mirth and melancholy have both positive and negative dimensions, and an effort must be made to fuse the positive sides of each. Theseus risks going from the violence of war LR to the revel of sport LR that allows no place for a richly positive "melancholy" [LC]. With no time to "steep" and "dream," "pomp" and "triumph" may easily become pretentious [UR] and sterile LC.

As the play develops we see other examples of mirth's polarities. Analogy links this "pert and nimble spirit of mirth" and the accompanying "merriments" not only to the festivities UC developed by Philostrate as master of the revels UR but also to Lysander's later comment that "quick bright things come to confusion" LC, to Helena's belief that "waggish boys in game themselves forswear" LC, to the purposeless sport <LR> that Oberon seems to prefer, and to the often irresponsible antics LR of the "merry wanderer" (1.1.13, 12, 149, 240; 2.1.43) Puck, the play's embodiment of the polarities of mirth and sport. A production should probably try to communicate a sense of Theseus's conception of mirth through some stage action. If Hippolyta were to seem skeptical, the dangers would be more apparent.

While trying to create a positive mirth, Theseus gets instead a choleric LR Egeus, whose anger brings the threat of approaching "funerals" and restores a mood of strife LC. Egeus's influence proves to be stronger than Hippolyta's. Theseus too must struggle to find the wisdom that will lead to order and happiness UC. When he supports Egeus's demands that Hermia marry Demetrius, we see a rigid Theseus LR who may be unwilling or unable to establish a renewal of love UC. He may support a traditional position in public while working something out in private since he later tells Demetrius and Egeus that he wants to "confer with you / Of something nearly that concerns yourselves" (1.1.125–26). But the threat of male tyranny LR would seem strong to an audience that might be expected to remember Theseus's long history of loving and leaving women. He may treat Hippolyta as he has Perigenia, Aegle, Ariadne, and Antiopa LL, all mentioned later (2.1.77–80) by Oberon. If some editorial speculation is correct, Theseus's comment—"Come, my Hippolyta; what cheer, my love?" (1.1.122)—suggests a Hippolyta who is visibly unhappy LL with what has been happening.[6]

Egeus's sharply defined attitudes put law UR and love UL into direct opposition. His insistence on dictating Hermia's choice of husband is a dogmatic version LR of the traditional view of marriage <UR>[7] and has a practical logic that fills out its idealistic rationale. Since marriage is a union of families and young love is unreliable, the presumably wiser father should choose the mate. With good will, people through marriage will direct their passions and develop mature love UC. In Egeus's view, all problems would disappear with proper respect for hierarchy. Hermia is his property LL and therefore has no rights: "As she is mine, I may dispose of her; / Which shall be either to this gentleman, / Or to her death" (1.1.42–44). He blames Lysander for Hermia's revolt. In defiance of hierarchical order, Lysander has "Turn'd her obedience (which is due to me) / To stubborn harshness" (1.1.37–38). He has "bewitch'd the bosom of my child" by a black art LR that uses the deceptions of "rhymes," "love-tokens," and "verses of faining love" "sung / With faining voice" "by moonlight at her window" (1.1.27–31). Like Montague and Capulet, Egeus thinks night is a time of disorder LC. Lysander has "stol'n the impression of her fantasy" through alluring gifts that are "messengers /

Of strong prevailment in unhardened youth" (1.1.32, 34–
35). What Egeus fails to realize is that he himself illustrates the processes he describes: he has allowed the illusions of his own disordered fantasy LL to develop into
obsessions.

When Theseus supports Egeus's position, he becomes
another image of the unyielding law of an Athens in danger of slipping from order to tyranny LR. Theseus extends Egeus's argument. Hermia is not only depriving
Egeus of his property rights, she is also rebelling against
an image of god UC: "To you your father should be as a
god" (1.1.47). To Theseus, the feminine is the passive
material of nature <LL> that a godlike male force UR
shapes into meaningful forms. The father is an artist UR
or, even more ominously, a printer [LR] who "compos'd
your beauties," while a daughter LL is "a form in wax, /
By him imprinted, and within his power, / To leave the
figure, or disfigure it" (1.1.48, 49–51).[8] By the end of the
speech, the analogous authorities of ruler, god, creator-
artist, judge, father, reason, law, and day <UR> are all
powerfully mounted against Hermia <LL>.

In the next part of the scene, Theseus assumes the role
of the still authoritarian but more approachable teacher
<UR>: he gives the fatherly advice that the angry Egeus
has failed to provide. Earlier he was the conqueror in sub-
jugating Hippolyta but modified that power with love.
Now he backs up Egeus's position on law but tries to balance that strength with concern UL for Hermia. Later
he has "private schooling" UR (1.1.116) for Egeus and
Demetrius as well. His third option for Hermia—entering a nunnery—seems totally unsatisfactory. Using imagery that recalls the opening speeches, he associates
marriage with growth and fulfillment UL, and life in a
nunnery with withering and unhappiness LR.[9] A sunlike
Theseus offers the heat and light of marriage UC and
threatens a return to the darkness of death or a nunnery
LC. While granting that chastity is a valid way of life, he
deplores the restriction of a "shady cloister" LC and the

"barren" sterility of "Chaunting faint hymns to the cold fruitless moon" LC (1.1.71–73). Whether the moon is "fruitless" LC and deceptive [UR], as Theseus and Egeus imply, or moist [LL] and vital UR, as Hippolyta thinks, is at issue. Later, Theseus is even more explicit in associating "austerity and single life" with "Diana's altar" LC (1.1.90, 89). Even though he is describing a nunnery, his images of a narrowly constricted feminine single life (and the moon and Diana) would presumably win little favor from Hippolyta (or from Diana or the Virgin Queen Elizabeth). If Hippolyta has taken a prominent position beside Hermia, the application of what he says to Hippolyta's own situation would be apparent, and we might even postulate a Theseus who slips into making his speech a lecture for Hippolyta as well. If Theseus is to rule wisely, he must find ways of using his power to promote both growth UL and order UR, but he may be overconfident about his ability to find that balance. His earlier neglect of the lovers' affairs and his failure to realize that young people in love are not likely to submit to law suggest his lack of understanding, and we must question whether he knows himself and Hippolyta well enough to make his own marriage work.

In contrast to Egeus, Hermia and Lysander believe in love UL and suspect law <UR>. In their view, love is an ennobling force UL that must be allowed natural expression, and marriage is too personal a matter to be decided by anyone except the people involved. Hermia is the more outspoken, perhaps partly because of the support she feels from Hippolyta. With "bold" UR "modesty" UL she asks "that I may know / The worst that may befall me" (1.1.59, 60, 62–63). She has felt the full force of male authority and knows that the woman's role is to be quiet and patient UL, but she also knows that a woman must be responsible UR for her own actions and state of mind. When Theseus asks her to "yield" and to consider whether she is like the nuns who can "master . . . their blood" (1.1.69, 74), he refers to the masculine control UR of passions UL that nuns above all people must have. People must be true to their natures, and claiming a control one does not have is courting disaster. Hermia is mastering UR her blood in a different way by trying to work out a marriage with Lysander that she sees as the only hope for her health and future happiness UC. She speaks also of her right UR not to "yield my virgin patent up" and of her refusal to "give sovereignty" to the "unwished yoke" LR (1.1.80–82) of Demetrius. Like Hippolyta and later Titania, she has a strong sense of her rights as a person, but the undefined and mysterious "power" UR (1.1.59) that leads her to speak also stems from her intuitive awareness of a force within her that is ultimately related to cosmic love UC. The Duke in *Measure for Measure* tells Isabella, "Virtue is bold, and goodness never fearful" (3.1.208).[10] Hermia's boldness UR is based on her awareness of the "Virtue" and "goodness" UC of her cause.

Hermia's belief that she must control her own life both reflects and determines her taste in art. She and Lysander try to see their lives as parallel to the young lovers of the romances who fall in love at first sight UL and must struggle to overcome obstacles raised by an unsympathetic society LR. Their reliance on their reading of "tale or history" (1.1.133) for both their knowledge and rhetoric of love suggests some immaturity LL. Hermia and Lysander may speak for natural emotion UL, but Shakespeare is well aware that they celebrate the natural in highly artificial ways. Nevertheless, he is not just satirizing <LR> young lovers. Their situation parallels exactly the tales <LL> that have shaped their views. Such tales are popular partly because they communicate accurately the fragile but sensitive lyricism of innocent and threatened young love <LL>. To some degree, life may mirror art in Lysander and Hermia's mannered responses, but art also mirrors life. As in *Romeo and Juliet*, Shakespeare "unmetaphors" the attitudes of a conventional genre and thereby goes beyond the satirical to the psychological.[11] Both plays reveal the foolish tendencies of conventional lovers but also lead to a fuller understanding of how they think, feel, and behave.

Hermia and Lysander's reading has taught them that "The course of true love never did run smooth" LC (1.1.134). When hierarchical considerations take precedence over love in setting up marriages, lovers are "enthrall'd," relationships are "misgraffed," and life becomes a "hell" LC (1.1.136, 137, 140). These images of servitude, perverted nature, and misdirected religion LC give the references a generalizing scope that a literary microcosm demands. If true lovers find each other, other uncontrollable forces LC—"War, death, or sickness"—interfere, and "The jaws of darkness do devour it up" (1.1.142, 148). The language recalls the imagery of feud, death, and pestilence LC so strong in *Romeo and Juliet*. The "jaws of darkness" image parallels the Hellmouth entrance to the Capulet tomb and through the personification implies that there are powerful and unfriendly forces not just in Athens but in the universe as a whole.

Lysander sees love as "swift," "short," and "Brief," like a "shadow," a "dream," or "lightning" in the night, but also suggests that, despite mutability, love can provide a glimpse that "unfolds both heaven and earth" (1.1.144–46): sounds communicate; shadows provide at least some definition of objects; dreams <LC> can be visions UC. What the lightning "unfolds" and man can briefly "Behold" is the transcendent truth UC that Petrarchan lovers like Romeo and Lysander seek despite the angry frustration ("in a spleen") LR of lacking the "power" UR (1.1.146, 147) to make it permanent.[12] Such ambiguity about motivations and causes—personal, societal, natural, cosmic—captures the complexity of cause and effect we examined in *Romeo and Juliet* and helps establish a fuller context for the play's consideration of love. Theseus has talked about waking "the pert and nimble spirit of mirth" but is partly responsible for bringing "quick, bright things" UL to "confusion" LC

(1.1.13, 149). The tragic note LC does not become dominant since Lysander is in part merely describing his reading and since Hermia quickly changes the mood back toward optimism UL. Nevertheless, Lysander's pessimism
<LC> remains a forceful impression of a view of love and
life that recurs throughout the play.

Hermia, who seems to share Hippolyta's positive vision of the night and love, is both more sensible in avoiding extremes and more hopeful about solutions. She suggests that the vision of "tale or history" that she and
Lysander have been discussing is not always gloomy:
"If ... true lovers have been ever cross'd" LC, (and we
think of the "star-cross'd" Romeo and Juliet), then lovers
should accept that "customary cross" (and we think of
the analogy to the divine cross) as an "edict in destiny"
LC inevitably accompanying love (1.1.150–53). They
must depend on "patience" UL to see them through;
time will transform the "thoughts and dreams and sighs,
/ Wishes and tears" <LC> that are "poor fancy's followers" <LL> (1.1.152, 154–55) into the fulfillment of love
UC. Since a destiny shaped by a beneficent divine force
UC will not continue to work against lovers, life will be
a romance with a happy ending UC rather than a romantic tragedy LC.[13] For a more detached audience, however,
their story is more likely to seem like comedy UC: we
can laugh as the story unfolds and avoid the emotional
engagement of the romance.

Hermia's conventional imagery helps define the fusion
of masculine and feminine impulses that she brings to
her perspective. She swears both "by Cupid's strongest
bow, / By his best arrow with the golden head," and by
"Venus' doves" (1.1.169–71). Paul Olson suggests that
these oaths have satirical and ominous overtones because of the associations of Venus and Cupid with disasters in love LC,[14] but we should also respond to a Venus
and Cupid *in bono*, associated with natural love and fecundity UL. (As we shall see, Helena invokes Cupid *in
malo* at the end of the scene.) Hermia seems to be aware

of both dangers and possibilities. She associates Venus and Cupid both with a force that "knitteth souls and prospers loves" UC (1.1.172) and with the threat of destruction LC. Perhaps remembering Demetrius's desertion of Helena, Theseus's long history of abandoning women, and her own father's tyranny, Hermia reminds Lysander that Dido was loyal UL to an untrue Aeneas LR and that "men have broke" more vows "than ever women spoke" (1.1.175–76). In recalling a tragic suicide LC that results from both an ambiguously passionate love <UL> and victimization LL of the female, Hermia becomes analogous to Dido. All the young lovers are "quick bright things" that glimpse something higher even while contributing to their own potential tragedies. We might wonder why Hermia goes ahead if she has such doubts: she has already learned something about the dangers of feminine loyalty and male fickleness, and we soon learn that she has good reason to worry about Lysander. Love apparently offers few choices. Like Lysander, she is dominated by its passion UL and can only trust UL in its positive power UR and hope UL for its immense rewards UC.

Demetrius and Helena's situation is very different, but Shakespeare finds ways of making the two sets of lovers seem more alike. Hermia and Lysander always act like the troubled young lovers [LL] of romance who somehow will have their problems solved, but Helena and Demetrius's plight at first seems much more serious. How can we sympathize with a Demetrius who has villainously deserted LR his love and with a Helena who can still love such a man? If you take them seriously as studies of rounded human beings, Demetrius is deeply flawed, but the impression that the play makes is quite different. Although Demetrius says very little in the first scene, he is apparently very much like Lysander in appearance and background, and his former love for Helena is described in terms that suggest its sincerity UL. Also, Helena's continuing devotion UL and Hermia and Lysander's support make us want her to get him back. Because of these factors we are more inclined to wonder what is wrong with Demetrius now and how he might be restored to Helena than to start probing for more tragic implications. From one perspective his recourse to Egeus is cynical and calculating LR, but his swing from worship <LL> to dominance LR is characteristic of the male and seems to result from lovesick desperation LL rather than Machiavellianism LR. We are slow to judge Helena because we see how totally she has committed herself to Demetrius. Once such a relationship UC has been established by a virtuous young woman UL, trying to change to someone else is and should be almost impossible.

As we watch Helena in the last part of the scene, her similarities to Hermia become more significant. Her bold pursuit <LR> of Demetrius parallels Hermia's revolt <LR> against Theseus and her father. Both must express their true feelings or submit unnaturally LL, and both are entering a metaphorical wood <LL> of uncertainty. Later in the play we hear more about their differences in size and disposition, but in the first scene both tend to understand themselves as specific illustrations of the woman in love UL rather than as unique individuals. When Helena tries to discover what attracts Demetrius to Hermia, she thinks about the causes of love and not, for example, about whether Demetrius now prefers short women. Also, both women speak in the same poetic style. Hermia's speech to Lysander just before Helena enters depends on a conventionally poetic use of rhymed couplets and mythological imagery that serves both as a coda to their exchange and a transition to the more artificial language of the scene with Helena. Helena's first speech makes clear that, like Lysander and Hermia, she has taken her reading very seriously. Life again seems to imitate art, but there has been a change from the themes and style of the romance ("tale or history" [1.1.133]) to that of the sonnet. Romances record the struggle of true

love UC against an unsympathetic world LC while sonnets characteristically consider the plight of the unrequited lover <LL>, in this case an "unmetaphored"
Helena.[15]

Both Hermia and Helena find themselves in unconventional but unmistakably Petrarchan situations with
Demetrius: Hermia is the adored but disdainful lady
<UR> who distrusts and tries to discourage her ardent
admirer <LL>, and Helena is experiencing the emotions
<LL> of loving someone who refuses her. We are invited
to think about the causes of love itself. In trying to discover whether love originates in the loved one or the
lover, Helena uses the elaborately poetic Petrarchan language appropriate for romance lovers. She sees love as a
force originating in physical beauty and the senses, particularly in hearing and sight. Hermia's eyes are "lode-
stars" UR that control Demetrius's love, and her tongue
produces a "sweet melody" UL (1.1.184, 190) that affects
him as a lark does a shepherd at dawn in the spring UL.
Helena wants to learn the "art" that gives Hermia this
power UR over Demetrius's "heart" UL (1.1.192, 193).
Like Egeus, Helena stresses art, only she sees art's power
in the woman, not the man, and associates it with positive images of pastoral nature UC, not with grim images
of an evil night LC. She is perceptive in recognizing the
woman's power but seems somewhat naive <LL> in
accepting the flattering praise of the Petrarchan courtier
as sincere. Egeus would no doubt see her comments as
further proof of the corrupting influence of such courtship and as justification for the father's careful control
over a daughter's courtiers.

The following exchanges between Helena and Hermia
emphasize paradoxes that complicate their world. The
paradoxes themselves are of course also Petrarchan: the
curses and frowns LR of the loved one <UR> lead the victim <LL> to even greater love, but worshiping love <LL>
elicits only stronger hate LR. Such results are not what
you would expect in an orderly world UC, and the

acceptance of paradox becomes an important part of the vision that leads not only Helena but also Hermia and Lysander away from Athens. Hermia maintains a friendly manner with Helena, and the sticomythia of their dialogue gives their answers an epigrammatic quality that suggests their joint effort to understand their experiences. Earlier, we noted Hermia and Lysander's awareness of the outside forces that have made any love difficult and Athens a place of confinement. Now Hermia develops the paradox that the "graces in my love" (1.1.206) (Lysander), which should at least parallel divine grace UC, have transformed the paradise UC of Athens into a hell LC. She seems to have an increasing awareness that forces within themselves LC as well as in Athens are responsible for their plight.

Both Lysander and Hermia are basically optimistic UL about themselves, their love, society, and nature, and neither is quite the rebel LR they both sometimes appear to be. Abstractions, settings, and imagery help communicate these attitudes. The patience, loyalty, dreaming, and sighing that Hermia associates with love may seem opposite to the quickness and brightness UL that Lysander describes, but it is the fusion of these gender-influenced attitudes that brings about successful love. They understand that the tyranny LR in Hermia's house and the city of Athens requires a strong UR, even militant [LR], response. Hermia was "to arm yourself / To fit your fancies to your father's will" but instead will "swear . . . by Cupid's strongest bow" UR (1.1.117–18, 169). She follows the spirit if not the letter of Theseus's advice when she refuses to be "mew'd" in a "shady cloister" LL (1.1.71) that seems analogous to her house in Athens, and references to their flight UL (1.1.203, 212, 246) continue the bird image. When openness is impossible because Egeus thinks Lysander has "stol'n" his daughter, he does steal [LR] her: she must "steal forth thy father's house," and together they must "steal" "through Athens gates" (1.1.32, 164, 213), emblematic of the city's restrictions

<LR>. But they refuse to see conflict and stealth as a way of life. They are ready to "unfold" their "minds" to Helena: friendship requires the openness UL of the times when they "were wont to lie, / Emptying our bosoms of their counsel [sweet]" (1.1.208, 215–16). Nor are they seeking total freedom: "that place" where "the sharp Athenian law / Cannot pursue us" is not the wood where the "mew'd" bird could be free but the house of Lysander's "widow aunt" (1.1.162–63, 71, 157). They seek a new home, a new parent, marriage, money, "new friends and [stranger companies]" UR (1.1.219). Their optimism about society's institutions and other people fits with their continuing trust in their love.

No doubt they are naive to believe that the night wood will be like the day wood UL they have known in happier times instead of like the frightening night world LC Lysander imagines. The wood where they will meet is the place UL where they have done "observance to a morn of May" and where Hermia and Helena "Upon faint primrose beds were wont to lie" (1.1.167, 215). The "collied night" with its "jaws of darkness" has become a helpful friend [LC] that "lovers' flights doth still conceal" (1.1.145, 148, 212). Its light comes not from lightning's brief illumination, which "unfolds" so quickly that not even the exclamation "Behold!" is possible, but from a gracious Phoebe UC who can both "behold / Her silver visage in the wat'ry glass" (1.1.146, 147, 209–10) and keep their secret. Phoebe's life-giving, natural role UL, "Decking with liquid pearl the bladed grass" (1.1.211), sounds like Titania's, but Phoebe is more like a relaxed Titania still in harmony with Oberon. Both recall the moist night [LL] Hippolyta described wherein "days quickly steep themselves" (1.1.7). In her final words to Lysander, Hermia dwells on another paradox: "we must starve our sight / From lovers' food till morrow deep midnight" (1.1.222–23). To the conventional metaphor— that to be deprived of the sight of the beloved is to lack the food of love—is added the idea that the next sight of each other will come at "morrow deep midnight," the darkest and most frightening time of the night. Phoebe's light makes the night less ominous, but their love does not depend on literal sight; "deep midnight" can become for them a time of loving communication [LC] that depends only secondarily on the senses. Athens is no longer a paradise, but "deep midnight" in the wood can become one through their love. In Hermia's plea that Helena "pray thou for us" and her wish that "good luck grant thee thy Demetrius" (1.1.220, 221), she implies acceptance of night forces <LC> beyond people's rational control. Prayers and luck belong to a spiritual universe that operates in mysterious and unpredictable ways, but Hermia and Lysander proceed with confidence and trust UL that such a universe can be orderly even if not always rational.

Helena's soliloquy at the end of the scene reflects a more pessimistic view of the possibilities for order. Earlier she thought Hermia's unconscious art <UR> was responsible for Demetrius's love, but now she has swung to the opposite extreme of granting no influence to the outer senses. She knows herself to be as beautiful as Hermia; therefore something irrational LC about love itself must bring about lovers' strange behavior. She shares Hermia's insight that love belongs to a world where Athenian values have little place, but she finds no positive dimension in "the mind" (1.1.234) that governs its object. From her perspective, the Athenian hope of somehow fusing love and reason is groundless. She perceives Demetrius to be "base and vile" LR and thinks that her illusion [UC] alone has given him "form and dignity" UR (1.1.232, 233); her wild plan to tell Demetrius what she knows and follow him to the wood, besides forwarding the plot, suggests her abandonment to an irrational night world LC. We sympathize since her attitudes and behavior result from her impossible situation, but we also understand that her insights are unbalanced. When she fails to consider that her revelation also betrays her friendship with Hermia and Lysander, love's power to overthrow civilized manners and morals becomes even more evident.

Many of the secondary image patterns related to love are pulled together in Helena's description of a blind Cupid LR who contrasts sharply with Hermia's earlier reference to a seeing Cupid with a golden arrow UR. Hermia distrusts her father's "judgment" but wants to look "with my eyes" UR, and both she and Lysander believe in the inner sight [LC] that will illuminate their love even at "deep midnight" [LC] (1.1.57, 56, 223). After Helena describes the Demetrius who "errs, doting on Hermia's eyes," she goes on, "Nor hath Love's mind of any judgment taste" LC (1.1.230, 236). Other contrasts follow: to have "Wings, and no eyes" suggests "unheedy haste" LR to Helena, but earlier metaphors suggest that wings UL can also belong to Venus's doves, the lark of Helena's first speech, or the "mew'd" Hermia, and can be used for "lovers' flights" (1.1.237, 71, 212). Speed can be the quality of someone "pert and nimble" UL or something "quick" and "bright" UL: just because results are "Swift . . . short . . . or brief" (1.1.13, 149, 144–45) does not mean that they are meaningless. Finally, Helena describes Cupid as a child, one of the "waggish boys" LR who do all "in game" LC; her Cupid "is perjur'd every where" LC (1.1.240, 241). Earlier, Hermia talks of a personified "poor fancy" [LL] (1.1.155) who is worth following. Like a natural force parallel to a devious Cupid LR, Demetrius has "hail'd down oaths" on Helena, but with "heat from Hermia" <UR> his "show'rs of oaths did melt" (1.1.243–45). His oaths were coldly destructive LR, and their moisture untrue LC. In contrast, Hermia's cheeks fade for lack of sustenance after her own "tempest" (1.1.131) of tears LL. Though Demetrius behaves like the false Cupid LR, we should also remember Hermia's Cupid, with his "best arrow with the golden head" UR (1.1.170).

By the end of the scene, we have met at least two sides

to almost every image, not only those of Cupid but also the earlier ones of night, day, the moon, the wood, Athens, law, and love. Shakespeare fills the play with specific mentions of natural objects and beings that help provide a sense of objective reality;[16] but every image has a context. Sorting out our responses requires recognizing polarities and thinking about the abstractions that lie behind them. From one perspective, Hermia's "obedience" and "modesty" UL have become "stubborn harshness" and "disobedience" LR (1.1.37, 60, 38, 87). From another, she rejects the "maiden pilgrimage" of "austerity and single life" <LC> and instead uses "patience" UL and "power" UR on a journey that risks "confusion" LC to achieve the "form and dignity" UC (1.1.75, 90, 152, 59, 149, 233) of love. Egeus finds "duty and desire" fused in following Theseus, but the "desires" (1.1.127, 67, 4) of Hermia and Lysander (and Theseus) lead them to love. Such patterns make clear once again that Shakespeare in the play uses metaphor, not in a realistic way that depends on subjective connotations, but in a formal and emblematic way that demands larger contexts.

Perhaps the most striking illustration of this complexity is the pattern of polarized references to the moon. As we have seen, Theseus associates the waning moon with withering LR, but Hippolyta connects both it and the absent moon with moisture, sleep, and dream [LL]. Hippolyta's new moon is associated with love and vitality UL, Hermia and Lysander's Phoebe with light UR, and with fecundity and the renewing moisture of dew [LL]. These references extend Diana's involvement in women's chaste independence (the armed UR new moon UL) to include the natural fulfillment of marriage UC and mothering UL. Male references to the moon tend to be demeaning. For Egeus, moonlight is also a powerful force, but its strength comes from bewitching LC. Theseus seems to see the moon itself (even the full moon) as always "cold" and "fruitless" LC (1.1.73), not just during the drying and ageing part of its cycle.

As the play develops, earlier references to the moon are filled out and new dimensions are added when we encounter different manifestations of femininity: we see the moon as the "governess of floods" UR (1.1.103), as a disruptive force connected to fickleness and fairy madness LC, as a watery moon that can be tearful LL or fecund UL, as a partly ungendered man in the moon who is old and withered LR, and finally as a primitive moon <UR> that the "wolf [behowls]" (5.1.372). The moon, like love, can be an image of chastity or fickleness, sterility or fecundity, madness or inspiration, and passivity or power.[17] It is a natural force that is destructive or generative depending on the circumstances. Like the moon, love is shown to be at once wondrous and foolish, magical and deceptive, elevated and absurd, and enriching and chaotic. Confusion is inevitable as young lovers make their way to marriage, and we are encouraged to see the comedy of love's problems and fulfillments as a part of nature's cycle.

In the second scene of act 1, we are introduced to characters—Bottom and his friends—who invite comparison in various ways to the first scene.[18] In contrast to the lovers, they have been caught up in the "revelling" <UC> proposed by Theseus; they may have little love in their own lives but are enthusiastically looking forward to their possible presentation of an "enterlude" (1.1.19; 1.2.6) about love for the wedding festivities. Like the lovers, they are fascinated by romances <LL>, in their case dramatic romances; their story of "Pyramus and Thisby" is another version of "quick bright things" coming "to confusion" LC (1.1.149), and the obvious parallels to *Romeo and Juliet* are made even closer by the casting of Pyramus's father and Thisby's parents. (In the actual production there are no parts for the parents, but the point has been made.) When Peter Quince says that Pyramus "kills himself most gallant for love" and Flute wonders whether Thisby is a "wand'ring knight" (1.2.23–24, 45), their taste in plays becomes more evident. For them there is something ennobling about a "gallant" "knight" UR willing to sacrifice himself in service [LL] to his love. For the artisans, as for the young lovers, a story of struggling lovers and autocratic parents reproduces many of these romance qualities, and Bottom may even believe the point of the story to be that sacrifice [LL] brings reconciliation UC.[19] That there might be trouble in making a story of revolt <LR> and tragedy LC fit a wedding atmosphere of societal and familial harmony UC does not occur to them.

Their planning for the performance leads to farcical humor [LC] and literary satire <LR> but also points to larger issues about the relationship between art and life. They plan their play as they do their work: as artisans (a weaver, a carpenter, a tailor, a tinker, a bellows mender, and a joiner), they are makers, builders, and renewers UR, and Bottom insists that they follow orderly procedures so they can "grow to a point" UC (1.2.10). For them a play is a noble undertaking UC whose scope includes all of life, and players are superior men UR who can take on any role. Bottom thinks of himself as a force of nature (or a god) UC who can "move storms" (1.2.27), not just tears, in his audience. Peter Quince proclaims pompously: "Here is the scroll of every man's name, which is thought fit, through all Athens, to play in our enterlude before the Duke and the Duchess" (1.2.4–6). If these men have been chosen, any man can be the Everyman that Quince unwittingly recalls. Though they may be just artisans escaping their class while playing their betters, their idea of a play both reflects and parodies the literary microcosm: they seem to think that a play can and should include everything—nobility and cruelty, passion and suffering, comedy and tragedy. When Peter Quince calls the play *"The most lamentable comedy and most cruel death of Pyramus and Thisby"* and Bottom calls it a "merry" "work" (1.1.11–14), they reveal not only their ignorance about genre and tone but also their grand intentions. Pyramus and Thisby are, for

them, representative figures whose tragedy is truly significant. Trying to get such diverse materials into one
play is an undertaking that burlesques Shakespeare's own
ambitious goals and methods in *A Midsummer Night's
Dream* (and *Romeo and Juliet*) and thereby adds a sense
of the potential absurdity of art as well as life.

Bottom, very much the artisan on holiday, is delighted
with the prospect of playing some great role. His claim
that he can take any part reflects both the bravado of the
ambitious actor and his role as an ironic Everyman: he
confidently asserts that he understands and can express
all human attitudes and feelings. He can play strongly
masculine parts <LR>—the tyrant and the lion—but also
the "more condoling" (1.2.40–41) roles of the lover UR
and his love UL. In acting out his fantasies, Bottom becomes the prototype of masculine attitudes. He thinks
his "chief humor is for a tyrant," and his Ercles is an image of power and control who rants about "raging rocks /
And shivering shocks" that "break the locks / Of prison
gates" (1.2.28–29, 31–34). The violence of this power is
presented, none too subtly, as a force for good [LR]: the
prison gates, presumably related to the gates of hell LC
as they are in an earlier version, will be broken, and the
sun UR ("Phibbus' car"), not "The foolish Fates" LC
(1.2.35, 38), will govern. To be at once all-powerful and
loving has been the traditional challenge for masculine
authority at all levels, not only for God but also for the
sun, rulers, fathers, husbands, and lovers. Even Romeo,
though primarily the lover, fits the pattern when he defies the stars and assaults the Hellmouth of Juliet's
tomb.[20] But Ercles, a confident blusterer, is more like
the tyrannical Egeus and the sun of the first scene,
Hercules's friend Theseus LR, than like the night lovers
[LL], Romeo and his counterpart Lysander. We see very
little of the sun in the play, and linking it, as well as
Egeus and Theseus, to Bottom's bombast continues the
implied criticism of Athenian values.

Fusing love UL with authority UR while avoiding both

excessive love [UL] and tyranny LR proves to be difficult. As we have seen, Theseus is transformed first from Hippolyta's conqueror to her ardent lover and then from Egeus's dogmatic backer to Hermia's sympathetic advisor. When Bottom learns that the ladies might be frightened by his roaring, he protests that his lion "will roar you as gently as any sucking dove" or "any nightingale" (1.2.82–84). The lover-tyrant Theseus can also be seen as roaring like a "sucking dove" in his attempt to persuade Hermia to marry Demetrius. Since the nightingale has explicit associations with love, both carnal and elevated,[21] Bottom's interest in both "roaring" and nightingales suggests once again the male tendencies toward domination LR and worship [LL]. With their lack of understanding of feminine sensibilities, both Theseus and Bottom run the risk of being too Athenian.

Peter Quince thinks that Bottom will be effective as Pyramus because he is "a sweet-fac'd man; a proper man as one shall see in a summer's day; a most lovely gentleman-like man" (1.2.86–88). That he sees Bottom as the perfect gentleman UR conflicts absurdly with Bottom's view that his "chief humor is for a tyrant." Ironically, Bottom later gets a chance to play diminished versions of all of these roles. With Puck's help, he becomes a singing ass who inadvertently frightens his friends; in Titania's company he comments on love and reason, and, though not "sweet-fac'd," tries to remain a gentleman while coping with his chances for both power and love. In their different ways, Theseus and Bottom try to play all the parts demanded of the male, but both have trouble finding the balanced wisdom necessary for success. There is hope for Theseus, but Bottom, despite having the right impulses and feelings within him, turns out to be an ass who can do nothing effectively. Nevertheless, he has redeeming features: along with Puck, a more "pert and nimble spirit of mirth" (1.1.13) to whom he is surprisingly parallel,[22] Bottom does much to establish the play's comic tone.

While the young lovers worry about tragedy, they hope to take part in a real-life chivalric or pastoral romance UC. The artisans, on the other hand, understand little of either love or art but have a natural instinct for farce <LC>. When they plan on going to the wood, they expect an orderly place that will be an extension of their Athenian world UR. They will meet "At the Duke's oak" "in the palace wood . . . by moonlight" (1.2.110, 101–02). Mentioning the palace UR and the "Duke's oak" UR seems to make them feel secure. Getting away means finding a quiet and secret place UL to make their plans, and the moon UR will provide the light. Like the lovers, what they find is completely different from what they expect.

SEVEN

Ill Met by Moonlight
(*A Midsummer Night's Dream*
2.1–2.2.83)

OBERON. Ill met by moonlight, proud Titania.

(2.1.60)

I n act 1, the literal story of Theseus and Hippolyta's approaching marriage, the young couples' problems with their elders and with each other, and the artisans' plans for their play take place in Athens but are put in the context of polarized metaphors of day, night, and nature. The masculine tendency illustrated in Theseus and Egeus is to see the night and the moon as bewitching and deceptive LC and the whole realm of Diana as constricted and sterile LR. A pessimistic Lysander thinks of himself and Hermia as "quick bright things" UL swallowed up by the "jaws of darkness" LC (1.1.149, 148). When Helena despairs at the end of the first scene, the mind itself becomes for her a dark place LC ruled by illusions [UC] of love. In contrast, Hippolyta associates the moon and the night with sustaining qualities of steeping and dreaming [LC] and of alertness and strength UR. Also, after Hermia has restored Lysander's confidence, they see nature itself as a pastoral and paradisal place UC lighted by Phoebe UR and removed from Athenian rigidities LR.

In act 2, this metaphorical world of the night and the wood becomes the play's reality, but its complexities need to be seen in relation to various conventions of the time. In order to explicate the meanings of the wood and the fairies more fully, I have used four images of the wood, two positive and two negative, that fit with the patterns on my charts and that are particularly important in the play. All are familiar from Renaissance sources, but the descriptive scheme is my own. The positive woods include: 1) *the wood of revel* UL, a festive place of revitalizing nature most strongly associated with the views and actions of Titania (and Hippolyta as Amazon); and 2) *the pastoral wood* <UC>, an idyllic setting whose idealized order links it to the patriarchal vision of Oberon (and the optimistic phase of the young lovers). These positive woods have strong paradisal overtones in that both Oberon and Titania believe that his or her version of Eden could be achieved if only the other would cooperate. The negative woods include: 3) *the chivalric wood* LL, a place of moral testing that reflects traditional views of the generalized state of mankind and nature after the Fall; it is described not only in chivalric romances but also in slightly variant forms (for example, as a wood of error) in morality plays and literary epics; it implies the patriarchal assumptions of Oberon and Theseus and, with some modifications, of the young lovers about the high ideals and individual effort needed to overcome challenges; and 4) *the nightmare wood* LC, a place where chance, deception, and illusion (forces most clearly embodied in Puck) resist efforts to impose order. Broadly speaking, people in a chivalric wood control their own destinies UR, while those in a nightmare wood LL do not.

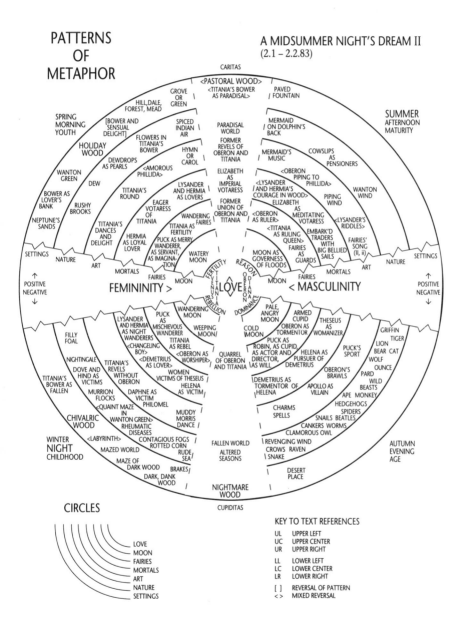

PATTERNS
OF
METAPHOR

A MIDSUMMER NIGHT'S DREAM II
(2.1 – 2.2.83)

CARITAS

<PASTORAL WOOD>
<TITANIA'S BOWER
AS PARADISAL>

GROVE
OR
GREEN

PAVED
/ FOUNTAIN

HILL, DALE,
FOREST, MEAD

SPRING
MORNING
YOUTH

SUMMER
AFTERNOON
MATURITY

[BOWER AND
SENSUAL
DELIGHT]

SPICED
INDIAN \
AIR

PARADISAL
WORLD

MERMAID
/ ON DOLPHIN'S
BACK

FLOWERS IN
TITANIA'S
BOWER

FORMER
REVELS OF
OBERON AND
TITANIA

MERMAID'S
MUSIC

COWSLIPS
AS
PENSIONERS

HOLIDAY
WOOD

DEWDROPS
AS PEARLS

HYMN
OR
CAROL

<AMOROUS
PHILLIDA>

ELIZABETH
AS
IMPERIAL
VOTARESS

<OBERON
PIPING TO
PHILLIDA>

WANTON
GREEN

DEW

TITANIA'S
ROUND

LYSANDER
AND HERMIA
AS LOVERS

<LYSANDER
/ AND HERMIA'S
COURAGE IN WOOD>

PIPING
WIND

WANTON
WIND

BOWER AS
LOVER'S
BANK

RUSHY
BROOKS

EAGER
VOTARESS
OF
TITANIA

FORMER
UNION OF
OBERON AND
TITANIA

ELIZABETH
AS
MEDITATING
VOTARESS

<LYSANDER'S
RIDDLES>

NEPTUNE'S
SANDS

WANDERING
FAIRIES

<OBERON
/ AS RULER>

TITANIA'S
DANCES
AND
DELIGHT

TITANIA AS
FERTILITY

<TITANIA
AS RULING
QUEEN>

EMBARK'D
TRADERS
WITH
BIG BELLIED
SAILS

FAIRIES'
SONG
(II, ii)

HERMIA
AS LOYAL
LOVER

PUCK AS MERRY
WANDERER,
AS SERVANT,
AS IMAGINA-
TION

WATERY
MOON

MOON AS
GOVERNESS
OF FLOODS

FAIRIES
AS
GUARDS

SETTINGS

NATURE

ART

MORTALS

FAIRIES

MOON

FERTILITY

REASON

MOON

FAIRIES

MORTALS

ART

NATURE

SETTINGS

↑
POSITIVE
NEGATIVE
↓

UNION

OBERON

DIANA

↑
POSITIVE
NEGATIVE
↓

FEMININITY >

LOVE

< MASCULINITY

OBERON

REBELLION

DOMINANCE

WANDERING
MOON

PALE,
ANGRY
MOON

ARMED
CUPID

PUCK
AS
MISCHIEVOUS
WANDERER

LYSANDER
AND HERMIA
AS NIGHT
WANDERERS

WEEPING
MOON>

COLD
MOON

OBERON AS
TORMENTOR

THESEUS
AS
WOMANIZER

FILLY
FOAL

GRIFFIN
TIGER

TITANIA
AS REBEL

ROBIN, AS CUPID,
AS ACTOR AND
DIRECTOR,
AS WILL

PUCK AS
HELENA AS
PURSUER OF
DEMETRIUS

PUCK'S
SPORT

LION
BEAR CAT
WOLF

<CHANGELING
BOY>

NIGHTINGALE

TITANIA'S
REVELS

<DEMETRIUS
AS LOVER>

QUARREL
OF OBERON
AND TITANIA

OBERON'S
BRAWLS

OUNCE
PARD
WILD
BEASTS

DOVE AND
HIND AS
VICTIMS

<OBERON AS
WORSHIPER>

TITANIA'S
BOWER AS
FALLEN

MURRION
FLOCKS

WITHOUT
OBERON

WOMEN
VICTIMS OF THESEUS

DEMETRIUS AS
TORMENTOR OF
HELENA

APOLLO AS
VILLAIN

APE MONKEY

DAPHNE AS
VICTIM

HELENA
AS VICTIM

QUAINT MAZE
IN
<WANTON GREEN>

PHILOMEL

HEDGEHOGS
SPIDERS
SNAILS BEATLES

CHIVALRIC
WOOD

RHEUMATIC
DISEASES

MUDDY /
MORRIS
DANCE /

CHARMS
SPELLS

CANKERS WORMS

WINTER
NIGHT
CHILDHOOD

<LABYRINTH>

CONTAGIOUS FOGS
ROTTED CORN

FALLEN WORLD
ALTERED
SEASONS

REVENGING WIND
CROWS RAVEN
SNAKE

CLAMOROUS OWL

AUTUMN
EVENING
AGE

MAZED WORLD

RUDE,
SEA/

MAZE OF
DARK WOOD

BRAKES/

DESERT
PLACE

DARK, DANK
WOOD

NIGHTMARE
WOOD

CUPIDITAS

CIRCLES

LOVE
MOON
FAIRIES
MORTALS
ART
NATURE
SETTINGS

KEY TO TEXT REFERENCES

UL   UPPER LEFT
UC   UPPER CENTER
UR   UPPER RIGHT

LL   LOWER LEFT
LC   LOWER CENTER
LR   LOWER RIGHT

[ ]   REVERSAL OF PATTERN
< >   MIXED REVERSAL

All four woods are feminine in that they describe human passion and its analogues, while only two (the pastoral wood and the chivalric wood) emphasize the importance of masculine order. The wood of revel and the nightmare wood do not usually appear as shaping or resolving forces in the literature of the time, which tends to be patriarchal. All relate to states of mind and attitudes toward nature and the world rather than to any literal reality. In real life, you do not need to go to a literal wood to find a metaphorical one, and Shakespeare's play is concerned with metaphorical reality presented in dramatic form. Richard Cody titles his valuable book on pastoralism in Tasso and Shakespeare *The Landscape of the Mind*. For a Renaissance audience, such a landscape would include not just the individual mind but also the analogous familial, societal, natural, and cosmic levels that my charts attempt to explicate.[1]

To interpret the Athenian wood adequately requires an understanding of these larger metaphorical contexts. Too often, scholars, like the characters in the play, have had too narrow a response and have thus tended to force the wood and consequently the play into one or two of the four categories. (Their terms are slightly different, but I have tried to be accurate in recounting their ideas.) Thus, C. L. Barber highlights the wood of revel (his festive "holiday" world), includes but downplays the pastoral wood, and largely ignores the chivalric wood and the nightmare wood.[2] Richard Cody describes a pastoral wood filled with neoplatonic overtones and tends to be critical of those who see the wood as festive or chivalric.[3] Paul Olson emphasizes the moral dimension of what I call the chivalric wood, with Oberon representing a higher Christian neoplatonic reality. To him, Athens is the archetypal city of wisdom, law, and reason UR, and the wood is identified with sin, folly, and illusion LC.[4] The problem with the Olson view and a danger in applying a specifically Christian framework is that the play's wood, though irrational and chaotic, seldom seems immoral. In calling this wood the chivalric wood instead of the wood of error, I mean to imply that Shakespeare is more concerned with the illustration of often foolish chivalric ideals <UC> than with the moral issues raised by the traditional temptations of the dark wood LL. The lovers usually get into trouble by applying their high ethical standards inappropriately. Other recent scholars have been more interested in the nightmare wood,[5] but reducing the whole wood to this one image does not square very well with the text or with Elizabethan views. Modern readers are often inclined to see psychological or cosmic breakdown where most Elizabethan playgoers would see the inevitable aberrations of a fallen world.

The Barber reading associates the wood and nature in general with many of the positive features of the left side of my Metaphors of Hierarchies chart. Barber describes not just a wood but a whole set of attitudes linked to the holiday revel of the folk festivals of actual English experience UL. At such times, people are free of the usual restraints of the patriarchal society UR and function in an atmosphere of misrule [LC] that turns the hierarchies upside down. Only from a narrowly patriarchal perspective LR are such revels suspect, and their popularity at all levels of Elizabethan society suggests not only the significance of this dimension in the culture but also the ease with which it was assimilated. It is the world of Mayday UL, midsummer night <LC>, and wedding festivities UC, with deeper implications of archetypal fertility patterns UL that celebrate the vitality and fullness of life. According to this view, the wood is a primary symbol UL in the play of a state of mind that we associate with the natural, emotional, and imaginative side of human lives.

There is considerable specific evidence of this festive world in each of the plots (and not just in the scenes in the wood): the holiday atmosphere of revel and mirth associated with Theseus's wedding which opens and closes the play (to say nothing of the actual wedding that provides a framework for the whole play); the revels that form an important part of Oberon and Titania's activities and the folk traditions that lie behind Robin Goodfellow; the holiday mood of Bottom and the artisans as they plan and put on their play; and the young lovers' memories of going-a-Maying and hopes for future weddings. The characters themselves would recognize that holiday and festivity play an important role in their lives, and other deeper though less obvious manifestations should be apparent to an audience if not fully to the characters: the connection of Oberon and especially Titania to the natural rhythms of life, the ceremonial progress of Theseus to the forest, and the participation of all elements of the society in the celebration at the end. As Barber points out, even the troubles of the young lovers in the wood provide not only a revel for the audience but also for the lovers themselves, who participate in an experience that frees, enlarges, and vitalizes their lives.[6] This positive dimension, however, needs to be understood in a larger metaphorical context that also presents the dangers of excess [UL].

The pastoral image of the wood is more literary and philosophical, based on associations with pastoral poetry and other traditional forms.[7] This wood is less robust and more idyllic, almost Edenic UC, in its innocence. It is associated with freedom and the natural, with detachment and contemplation, and with love and poetry. It usually includes an at least implied contrast with the fallen world, and in Oberon it has overtones of the masculine power UR that he believes would restore its values. He sees Titania's bower as potentially paradisal, and his impersonation of Corin in his idyll with Phillida seems to be in part an attempt to recover pastoral innocence. The pastoral fuses uneasily with revel in Puck's mischievous sport <LC> with the milkmaids and villagers of a simple rural world while Oberon's festivity tends to degenerate to manipulative sport LR that lacks the vitality UL so apparent in Titania's revels. (As we have seen in 1.1, such attitudes represent a danger for Theseus as well.) Hermia and Lysander's assumption that the pastoral wood exists is at once a state of mind associated with their idealism <UC> and an expectation based on their earlier experience of May morning in the wood. When Hermia and Helena question men's faith, Hermia says Athens no longer seems like a paradise, but she reverts to pastoral optimism UC as she talks of the wood's "faint primrose beds" (1.1.214). When Helena longingly describes Hermia's control over Demetrius, she puts it in a pastoral context: "your tongue's sweet air" is "More tuneable than lark to shepherd's ear / When wheat is green, when hawthorn buds appear" (1.1.183–85). But by the end of the scene she has abandoned that view of love and also her pastoral language.[8] All of the pastoral references describe a state of mind that links idealism, friendship, and love with an escape to an idyllic and curiously artificial nature. In general, the pastoral wood, while pointing to a genuine ideal, is associated in the play with the illusion [UC] of patriarchal visions and with a dream of what perhaps once was or what might be rather than with a mature vision of what is.

The fairy wood is neither quiet nor orderly, but Shakespeare chooses to introduce the fairies, not through action that mirrors the chaos, but through various mythic overtones.[9] The relationship between Oberon and Titania parallels that between Theseus and Hippolyta, although in their case the battle is still going on during the play. If Theseus represents order on the level of society, then Oberon can be seen as the figure of order UR at the level of the natural, which in the Elizabethan view includes a supernatural dimension. Shakespeare's audience may not believe in fairies, but most would believe in a spiritual universe filled with unseen realities. Shakespeare carefully limits Oberon's functions to the night and thereby precludes associating him with fire, the highest UC and most masculine UR of the elements. Theseus, a sunlike ruler whose realm includes not only Athens but also the daytime wood, has much more power UR over his political and social realm than Oberon has over the night.

By not invoking a larger structure in which Oberon could easily seem analogous to God UC, Shakespeare makes him a less consequential "king of shadows" (3.2.347), not a monarch of all nature. With no direct access to the active forces of the day (the sun, light, and heat) UR, and with an active Titania responsible for ordering the moisture and growth UL governed by the moon, Oberon occupies himself primarily with sport <LR>, magic <LC>, and ceremony <UC>. While Shakespeare grants Oberon more dignity UR and power UR as the play proceeds, he does not develop the analogy with God, at least not until near the end of the play. The image of ruling the night <UR> invokes the complexities of metaphor and myth without requiring theological, philosophical, and political resolutions. Shakespeare studies the forces operating within the self and in relationships among people and suggests the analogical overtones in the natural world and the cosmos. His metaphors elaborate mysteries; they do not explicate philosophies.

Providing a mythical Greek setting helps make the personifications of forces of nature more familiar, but the often comic handling of their roles suggests an atmosphere more Ovidian than Greek. Since the Renaissance Ovid was commonly allegorized to explicate the physical and moral structures of the cosmos, the Ovidian atmosphere would be an invitation to look for deeper meanings.[10] Ovid lowers gods and elevates animals to a human level, thereby creating a cosmos full of strange juxtapositions and metamorphoses. The name Titania is taken from Ovid, who uses it for both Diana and Circe; her rebellious attitudes LR make her perhaps the most Ovidian character in the play. Oberon's name comes from romance; in his use of magic to maintain authority in the wood, he reflects the patriarchal assumptions UR of a chivalric world.[11] By presenting their conflict over how to manage the natural world as the marital quarreling of beings who do not fully understand either themselves or the larger structure of the cosmos, Shakespeare removes the heavy overtones of good and evil. Since Oberon and Titania are both well-meaning rather than evil, we sense an optimistic atmosphere appropriate for a comedy without being forced to consider whether there are other fairies who are evil LC or how our view relates to what many Elizabethans would see as the universal struggle between God and Satan. Puck, both because he delights in being totally irresponsible <LC> and because he refers specifically to more threatening forces in the wood LR (3.2.382–87; 5.1.371–82), comes closest to presenting an evil dimension, but his approach is more amoral than immoral and the powers he alludes to never take an active role. By keeping these references vague, Shakespeare avoids the larger moral issues and encourages a speculative frame of mind in his audience.

Shakespeare also explores the psychological, even the epistemological, implications of the fairies' relationships. Like Theseus, Oberon reflects the male tendency to both worship <LL> and dominate LR: he responds to the beauty of women UC but believes that order in love and marriage comes from masculine reason and control UR that keep femininity in a subservient place LL. Through all of the references to Titania's close ties to the lower elements, earth and water, she becomes a kind of earth goddess <LL>, and Oberon is depicted as the masculine principle that should bring order and direction UR to her femininity. Titania, though, is preoccupied with fecundity UL and, like Hippolyta in her Amazonian phase <LR>, sees little need for masculine direction. From her point of view, she has the essential role in the natural world, and Oberon's interference LR is what causes their problems. He should either leave her alone altogether or else learn to "patiently dance in our round" UL (2.1.140). If we think of nature as having, like a person, a tripartite soul that gives it vitality, Oberon is the rational soul UR and Titania the vegetative soul <LL>, but one source of their difficulties is that neither admits that they both have a share in the sensitive soul <UL> that expresses their common animality.

The set speeches of act 2, scene 1 help fill out our understanding of the fairies and of nature itself. Titania's long speech on the disruption of the elements and seasons rests on an awareness, shared by Oberon, that their broken relationship has resulted from events analogous to the Fall LC. The renewal of their proper marriage would lead to peace in nature UC, but that would require overcoming basic conflicts about their roles. Titania's description of the chaos LC produced by their quarrel stresses the male disruption LR of the typical orderly and productive cycles of nature. Allusions to the four elements suggest that their meetings involve the interactions of powerful natural forces: Puck says that they meet "in grove or green, / By fountain clear, or spangled starlight sheen" (2.1.28–29). When Oberon began to disturb Titania's revelers with what Titania calls his "brawls" (2.1.87), he initiated a quarrel between the winds UR and the moon that parallels the squabble between Oberon and Titania. In retaliation for not being able to participate in Titania's harmonious dance <UC>, "the winds, piping to us in vain, / As in revenge, have suck'd up from the sea / Contagious fogs" (2.1.88–90). The fogs in turn cause the rivers to flood and upset the earth's natural cycle. As a result, "the moon (the governess of floods)" UR, the powerful force that controls both the water and the fecundity of the earth, turns, "Pale in her anger" LR, on the wind and "washes all the air, / That rheumatic diseases do abound" (2.1.103–05). This disruption of the elements causes the seasons, associated by personification with the ages of life, to lose their natural order LC. Winter is usually a time for holiday "cheer" (following Theobald's emendation) [LC] and night a time for "hymn or carol blest" UC (2.1.101, 102), but these traditional ways of overcoming cold and darkness LC no longer function.

When Titania describes herself and Oberon as the

"parents and original" of this personified "progeny of evils" LC (2.1.117, 115), she links their problems to the Fall LC. References to mazes invite our attention to the world as a labyrinth full of intricate delights UC enveloped by corruption LC after the Fall.[12] The seasons "change / Their wonted liveries, . . . and the mazed world / . . . now knows not which is which;" earlier Titania says that the "quaint mazes in the wanton green" formerly used for holiday festivities now "are undistinguishable" (2.1.112–13, 99–100). Titania believes in the natural pleasures of the mazes and in festive rituals UC of purgation, renewal, and celebration that will restore the natural progression of the seasons; but the "quaint mazes" that she regrets losing may already belong to a bawdy labyrinth of moral temptation LL if "quaint" punningly recalls the old meaning of "queynte" (female genitalia), as Olson suggests.[13] Certainly Oberon takes a high moral stand when he explains the disorder as the result of Titania's disobedience LL: "Do you amend it then" (2.1.118). We may also associate these mazes of Oberon and Titania's world with the labyrinth from which Theseus saves the youths and maidens of Athens by killing the minotaur. Anyone who negotiates the maze of the fallen world and, like Theseus, overcomes the lusty minotaur LC would achieve a personal triumph and a restoration of order UC. The lovers strive heroically <UR> but are "amazed" LC (3.2.220, 344), while for much of the play Oberon proves to be no Theseus but a King Minos LR who torments young people of Athens in his labyrinth. In this comic version, however, the minotaur is a "bully" (4.2.19) ass <LC> who never meets the lovers and whose affair with Titania, ludicrously parallel to the affair of the minotaur's parents, a bull and Queen Pasiphae, is encouraged by Oberon. An Elizabethan audience would be more alert to these parallels than we are, but they are more important for creating a general atmosphere than as specific allusions. Shakespeare develops his own myths.

Puck's diverse roles in the play contribute richly to our

understanding of the metaphorical associations of the fairies, the wood, and the night.[14] Except as Oberon's "servant" and "messenger" UL (2.1.268; 3.2.4), he is detached from all ties—from the masculine values of the hierarchical system UR, from the passions of feminine rebellion LR, and from the elements and the senses. He has no concern about moral, social, or cosmic order, no emotional, loving, or sexual impulses, and little relationship to the natural world. Nevertheless, he is an irrepressible force <LC> that seems to be present everywhere—in fairies, in people, and in nature itself. If we study his roles in relation to the levels of meaning described on my charts, his qualities emerge as crucial for understanding the play. Puck has analogous emblematic roles: as Robin Goodfellow, he is associated with folklore traditions of luck, chance, and disorder <LC> in nature and the cosmos; as "the merry wanderer of the night," he parallels Theseus's "pert and nimble spirit of mirth" and serves as an unofficial Lord of Misrule <LC> of the night and wood; as Oberon's servant, he is a court jester <LC>, master of Oberon's revels <UR>, and actor-director of his own shows UR; as the vehicle for Oberon's potions, he is a Cupid <UR> who governs love; and as a messenger who gathers information and carries out commands, he functions as Oberon's imagination UL and will UR. Remarkably, Shakespeare fuses all of these roles into a believable dramatic character who, as simple Puck, has transcended all attempts at definition and become his own emblem. While he often disrupts the orderly structures of traditional morality and of conventional literary form UC and thereby makes the play's literary microcosm more complex, the stress of his role is on irony and humor <LC>, not profound questioning. Puck fits naturally in a comedy dealing with life's follies in a satiric but basically positive way.

Puck's interests on the cosmic and natural levels reflect Oberon's interests and limitations, though he retains his own qualities. Although Oberon's plotting includes some nastiness LR, Puck is never a devil or evil angel. Their pleasure in tormenting others could link them both to evil, but Puck's tricks do no irreparable damage, and he tempts no one, except perhaps Oberon himself. His victims make no moral choices in falling under his spell and indeed have no awareness of his power. Since Oberon is not a God-figure, Puck is not a good angel, either. When Oberon seeks harmony in the last part of the play UR, Puck helps him reconcile the lovers but continues to make undercutting comments <LC>. On the level of nature, Puck as Robin introduces the world's uncertainties <LC> as he disrupts the expected results of people's labors, but he seems interested in the processes of nature only when they affect people. Although Oberon uses Puck to "overcast the night" "With drooping fog" <LL> (3.2.355, 357) and prevent a fight between Lysander and Demetrius, Puck has no role in the disruptions of nature caused by Oberon and Titania's quarrel. Nor does he exert control over the animal world: he assumes animal shapes only to deceive people. Identifying Puck with Robin leads to seeing luck and chance <LC> as explanations for life's difficulties and makes more tragic views LC of fortune and fate seem overblown. He is responsible for mistakes and absurdities, not for deaths and disasters. People can laughingly dismiss their problems as Robin's practical tricks and get some relief for the sense of guilt or helplessness they may feel in a chaotic world <LC>. And they can propitiate him by treating him well.

On the societal level, he is Oberon's servant, like Philostrate a master of the revels whose job is to bring mirth UC rather than melancholy LC. Oberon is a surrogate dramatist UR who delights in planning complicated love plots, and Puck is the actor-director who stages and takes part in the stories. He embodies the "pert and nimble spirit of mirth" (1.1.13) that for both Theseus and Oberon should contain a strong element of sport <LR> but stop short of chaos LC. Puck, however, becomes a court jester whose actions hilariously disrupt Oberon's patriarchal attempts to create productions that teach moral lessons UR and end happily. Oberon refers to him as "gentle" and "good" when he is pleased with him, calls him "mad spirit" when Puck is obediently promoting chaos, but then is quick to charge him with "negligence" and even "knaveries" LR (2.1.148; 4.1.46; 3.2.4; 3.2.345–46) when he makes mistakes. Farce <LC> is Puck's natural medium: he inadvertently transforms Oberon's plans into "things" that "befall prepost'rously" (3.2.120–21). His comedy is often physical, as when the old aunt mistakes him for a stool and falls to the floor. Time is for laughter—"A merrier hour was never wasted there" (2.1.57)—not for reform or redemption. But while the emphasis is on fun as an end in itself, Puck as court jester has some of the qualities of a comic spirit that unmasks the pretentious and the ridiculous. If people cannot laugh at themselves and at life's absurdities, Puck will be interested in them. The young lovers and the artisans deserve Puck's attention, and his fooling helps restore the sanity that ultimately controls our sense of the play's atmosphere of chaotic delight.

On the interpersonal level, Puck is also related to the mischievous Cupid who influences loves and hates.[15] While he sprinkles a potion instead of shooting arrows, the potion is from a flower struck by Cupid's arrow. Puck's love-magic can be turned to constructive ends when directed by Oberon, but both the Cupid who shot the arrow and the Puck who gets the potion seem closer to Helena's "wing'd," "blind," "waggish," and "perjur'd" "child" LR than to Hermia's Cupid "that . . . knitteth souls and prospers loves" UR (1.1.235, 240, 241, 238, 172). Puck as Cupid embodies love's mysteries. When we speculate about how the potion works, our questions are apt to be similar to those Helena raises in 1.1 about whether Demetrius in love is affected by Hermia's power or by something within himself. Is love an outside force or an inner passion? Does Puck or Cupid strike at random or only at those who have made themselves vulnerable? The play's metaphorical structure suggests the questions are unanswerable, but the implication is that all lovers share the same sense of being beyond their own control. The interpretive ambiguity proves to be useful: Shakespeare does not need to be explicit about whether people do crazy things because of their own madness, because of outside forces, or because of some combination of the two.

On the intrapersonal or psychological level, Puck functions like the imagination <LL> that reports to the reason or judgment UR (the rational soul identified with Oberon) and like the will <LR> that carries out the dictates of the understanding UR (again connected to Oberon).[16] (In contrast, Titania's fairies, like the external senses <UL>, are preoccupied with the elements and with nature itself.) As Oberon's "messenger" (3.2.4), Puck brings him what turn out to be confused reports (the product of fantasy LL, a more negative term for the process of imagination) of his encounters with the lovers and artisans. After Oberon has decided what to do, Puck is the unreliable will <LR> that finds it difficult to complete what Oberon's reason has ordered. If the journey to the wood is on one level a revelation of the inner self, the fairies can be seen as revealing the structures and processes that shape responses. What happens to each of the characters is appropriate to his or her imagination, experience, and expectations. Rather than introducing some mind-expanding confrontation with the supernatural, Shakespeare fits the madness to the individual's state of mind and thereby keeps the emphasis comic and psychological. Thus, the young lovers struggle with love potions, the milkmaids, gossips, and travelers with appropriate tricks, and the artisans with apparitions of animals they would know well and later with "senseless things" (3.2.28) that grab at their clothes.

The interchange between Puck and the fairy that opens the fairy section reveals opposed approaches to life that reflect the quarrel between Oberon and Titania. Like

Titania, the fairy takes his job very seriously. Among his responsibilities UR are "To dew her orbs upon the green" UL (2.1.9) and in general to spread the moisture that will permit the growth that Titania supervises. We should be reminded of Phoebe's watery tasks, cited by Lysander (1.1.209–11). The imagery of valuable minerals—the "gold coats" of the cowslips, spots on the coats seen as "rubies" that then become "freckles" with "savors," and "dewdrops" used to "hang a pearl in every cowslip's ear" (2.1.11–15)—suggests an atmosphere of magical transformation in which a continuum exists between the vegetative and the mineral. Puck, probably played by an adult actor, tries to ridicule and frighten LR the eager young fairy and to demonstrate his stature UR in Oberon's entourage, but the fairy UR refuses to be intimidated: when he recognizes Puck as Robin Goodfellow, he calls him "shrewd and knavish" LR (2.1.33). Earlier, he described Puck contemptuously as "thou lob [that is, bumpkin] of spirits" LL (2.1.16). The fairy even adopts a lecturing tone UR when he deplores Robin's terrorizing LR of workers and charges him with favoritism.

The scene not only introduces us to Puck but also helps define metaphorical polarities that dominate the fairy scenes. References to wandering are particularly significant. While wandering usually has negative overtones LL in conventional metaphor, Puck and the fairy give it opposite positive meanings as well. Chivalric metaphor praises the high purposes of knights errant (wandering knights) UR, but such wandering becomes futile or, in the Christian trope, immoral LC if the knight (or fairy) is lured into a wood of error LL or sin LC. (When Flute asks if Thisby is a "wand'ring knight" [1.2.45], he is impressed by such knights and the literary genre that goes with them, but we recognize the ironies.) Positive wandering usually belongs to the active day, though Titania's fairies work at night and knights often quest in the maze of a dark wood LL. Puck also associates wandering with a night world of merriment that he understands as a maze of delight <LC> rather than confusion.

Polarities abound. The fairy wanders, foolishly from Puck's perspective, to help Titania make nature more abundant, while Puck wanders, irresponsibly in the fairy's view, for the fun of playing tricks on people. Whether the fairy is analogous to noble wandering knights UR or is another of the confused "night-wanderers" LL (2.1.39) that the fairy accuses Puck of tormenting remains ambiguous. Puck as "that merry wanderer of the night," Robin Goodfellow, tries to sound more like the "the pert and nimble spirit of mirth" UC that Theseus has called for than the "knavish" LR (2.1.43, 33; 1.1.13) Robin that the fairy describes. Later references keep the wandering metaphor in our minds. Oberon greets Puck with apparent approval as "wanderer" when he returns from getting the potion; Lysander refers naively to "wand'ring" LL from the "way" in the forest; and Puck talks about "Damned spirits" LC who, after "wand'ring here and there" LL during the night, must "Troop home to churchyards" (2.1.247; 2.2.35–36; 3.2.381–82) with the coming of the dawn. The last reference suggests a more ominous context in which sinners, perhaps including wandering lovers, find no dawn.

Oberon's attitudes toward women become a way of defining his approaches to life. For him the ideal female seems to be, not Titania, but a chaste UR and passive UL figure who, like the mermaid and the vestal of 2.1, controls passions and like the shepherdess Phillida, quietly accepts male adoration [LL]. A contemptuous Titania describes Oberon's escape to a daytime pastoral world [UC] where, in the shape of Corin, he sat all day "Playing on pipes of corn, and versing love, / To amorous Phillida" (2.1.67–68). From his perspective, such piping no doubt celebrates a pastoral ideal UC of love, art, and stability, but Titania sees this interlude as a self-indulgent daydream that reflects an inadequate conception of the feminine and of the active processes of nature. For Oberon fecundity is a by-product of masculine control UR, but

Titania refuses to be an "amorous Phillida" <UC> who passively LL accepts masculine worship <LL> and domination LR. If we are to believe a jealous Titania, Oberon has also had a relationship with Hippolyta, "the bouncing Amazon, / Your buskin'd mistress, and your warrior love" (2.1.70–71). Titania sees Hippolyta as an active, even seductive, earthly Venus LL and Obcron as a typically lusty male [UR]. Since Amazons were not always known for Diana-like chastity and since we learn later that Oberon is a forester-hunter who "with the Morning's love have oft made sport" (3.2.389),[17] her charge is plausible. If, as I have been suggesting, Oberon is analogous to Theseus (and indeed to men in general), he might very well have had affairs that began with protestations of elevated love UC and ended with abandoning LR the woman, and Titania's shrewd analysis of his male proclivities should be taken seriously. His present interest in Hippolyta, however, seems to be more that of a cosmic blesser of marriages UC than a former lover. Again like Theseus, he is a promoter of marriage as a means of furthering societal order UC. Even Titania stresses the ceremonial role when she says that he has come "To give their bed joy and prosperity" UC; but when she says that Hippolyta "must be wedded" (2.1.73,72) to Theseus, she suggests that Hippolyta has had no choice LL and implies her own uneasiness about the marriage.

A parallel reading of Titania's love for Theseus is convincing. She may be a lover with whom Theseus has had an intermittent relationship, but she seems also to be an earthly Venus LL, almost a symbolic force, who encourages his natural instinct for change LC. Oberon describes "thy love to Theseus" (2.1.76) as a cause of Theseus's infidelity LR: "Didst not thou lead him through the glimmering night / From Peregenia, whom he ravished? / And make him with fair [Aegles] break his faith, / With Ariadne, and Antiopa?" LL (2.1.77–80). Theseus's fickleness may result from Titania's seductive charms and / or from an effeminizing force LC within himself. In

Oberon's view, chaos results from Titania's obsession with fecundity; that symbolic role seems more important than whether or not Titania and Theseus have had an actual affair. At this point a quadrangle seems possible, with Titania once again leading Theseus away from a commitment in love, and she may imply a threat when she answers Oberon's question about her plans by saying that she will stay "Perchance till after Theseus' wedding-day" (2.1.139). But the matter drops when Oberon goes on to ask about the changeling. That Shakespeare avoids a quadrangle analogous to that of the young lovers suggests his dramatic tact about mixing levels of reality and further highlights the greater importance of a mythical reading of Theseus and Hippolyta's previous relationship. In the first scene, Shakespeare plays down their larger-than-life legendary or mythic quality by ignoring the countless stories of their past, but here he invites us to think of these stories and to seek out their various implications.

The quarrel about the changeling reflects similar issues. From Oberon's perspective, Titania [UR] is at fault. Puck also blames Titania: "But she, perforce, withholds the loved boy, / Crowns him with flowers, and makes him all her joy" (2.1.26–27). Since Titania has "forsworn his [Oberon's] bed and company" (2.1.62) because of the boy, some see her as playing Venus <UL> to the boy's Adonis. But since Titania seems to have at least temporarily forsworn Venus and since tradition and some references suggest that he is a little boy <LL>, her obsession is more likely maternal <UL>. Having the boy grow up with Titania encourages effeminacy LL in the boy and rebellion LR in Titania, thereby offending Oberon's highly developed sense of hierarchy.[18] If we see Titania as a Mother Earth figure who has maternal responsibilities UR as vegetative soul for the whole world, the conflict over the boy becomes an appropriate symbol of the larger unresolved issues between them. Titania has lost interest in men and the masculine, while Oberon desperately wants both his wife and nature once again under his control.

Titania's description of her relationship with the boy's mother expresses her essentially Amazonian ideal for women: they must relate to men sexually but should retain the freedom, spontaneity, and joy UC of their own natural revels. Her imagery expresses a fullness UC present most obviously in the votaress's pregnancy but also in the women's friendship, in the natural setting—the "spiced Indian air" and "Neptune's yellow sands" beside "the flood" (2.1.124, 126, 127)—and even in society's mercantile enterprises. The pregnant woman UL "rich with my young squire" is like a merchant ship whose sails are "big-bellied with the wanton wind"; the woman's playful imitation of the ship when she goes forth "to fetch . . . trifles" and returns "rich with merchandise" UC parallels "the embarked traders" (2.1.131, 129, 133, 134, 127) journeying to find riches for themselves and their society. The independence of the feminine ships from their home port and the purposefulness of the venturing (wandering) suggests the rewards of getting beyond constricting masculine control LR.[19] Here is the harmony UC of the "spiced Indian air" and the masculine wind (air) with the feminine sea (water) and earth not found in the present disorderly weather LC. Titania does not invoke the moon in this speech, but she refers to her planned "moonlight revels" (2.1.141) in the passage that immediately follows. She believes that when natural impulses UL can be freely expressed, harmony results between the masculine and feminine forces within people, nature, and society.

From a male perspective, however, the absence of men is a danger sign and the harmony a feminine fantasy [UC]. Puck's earlier reference to the boy as "stolen from an Indian king" (2.1.22) suggests that Titania LR took him from the king after the mother's death and therefore did not raise a helpless, orphaned child LL. Although a

defender of Titania could legitimately argue the importance of feminine nurturing UL, Titania says that her
preoccupation has been her responsibility UR to the
mother, not the boy: "And for her sake do I rear up her
boy; / And for her sake I will not part with him"
(2.1.136–37). If Titania is an Amazon <LR> in spirit, the
atmosphere she would create could be particularly un-
suitable, and Oberon has a reason besides jealousy to be
concerned. The mother's early death may also be a reminder that mortality results from the Fall and that
Titania's prescription for feminine independence reflects
the same male-female quarrel that caused the original
Fall. I have suggested that males are likely to focus on
moments that define experience in relation to hierarchies. Women, too, celebrate such moments but are apt
to see them as times defined by natural cyclical processes, most prominently reflected in paradisal spring and
harvest imagery.[20] Titania understands and accepts the
transformations of mutability in nature but seems to
blame corruption at all levels on the male.

After Titania's departure, Oberon, reacting against these
images of blissful fecundity by the sea, cites two examples of feminine power and restraint UR—"a mermaid on
a dolphin's back" and "the imperial vot'ress" of the
"wat'ry moon" (2.1.150, 162–63). Titania and her votaress on the one hand and the mermaid and the moon's
votaress on the other are contrasting sea or water maids,
with the first pair linked to fecundity UL and the second
to restraint UR. The mermaid UR has not only, like
Orion UR, gotten the dolphin to carry her but has, like
Orpheus[21] UR, succeeded in charming the sea itself: "the
rude sea grew civil at her song" (2.1.152). The mermaid
has parallels to Queen Elizabeth in being able to control both her own and others' passions, but an ironic danger exists: that "certain stars shot madly from their
spheres, / To hear the sea-maid's music" (2.1.153–54)
may suggest the admiration [LL] of the lords of the court

for Elizabeth's goddess qualities UC.[22] We should also think of an adoring <LL> Oberon, who "upon a promontory" (2.1.149) was also looking down on the mermaid UC. Paradoxically, what subdues UR baser instincts LL may overthrow what is higher, but the resulting love is likely to be ennobling UC rather than degrading LC.

The description of the "imperial vot'ress" (2.1.163), transparently Queen Elizabeth on one level,[23] again contrasts with Titania's "vot'ress" speech and continues the mermaid passage's unfinished story. If an identification with Elizabeth provides a link between the mermaid and the votaress, then Cupid's interest in the votaress parallels the attraction of the shooting stars to the mermaid's music. That Puck sees the mermaid but not the vestal may signal a shift to more personal praise. While Oberon usually links chastity and marriage, he sees a place for virginity as well. (Certainly, Shakespeare sees a place for complimenting the Queen.) The story describes how Cupid took aim "At a fair vestal throned by [the] west" but had his "fiery shaft / Quench'd in the chaste beams of the wat'ry moon" (2.1.158–62). With the help of a moon both chaste UR and fertile ("wat'ry") UL, the vestal, like the mermaid an image of personal restraint UR, is able to control her passions LL. Her maiden strength contrasts with the vulnerability LL of the "milk-white" flower, which when hit turns "purple with love's wound," and her "maiden meditation" UR contrasts with the fanciful thoughts LL of the "maidens" who "call" the flower "love-in-idleness" LL (2.1.167, 164, 168). The potent force of the arrow of fire UR is made fecund by the "wat'ry" feminine moon <LL> so that the passive, wounded flower <LL>, by analogy both the female heart and genitalia, becomes a potion of love <UC> with power over sight and sexuality.

By this point in the play we have two sets of polarized images of women that relate to Diana. The chaste UR "imperial vot'ress" UC is a "wat'ry" UL version of Theseus's "barren sister" LR who in a "shady cloister"

chants "faint hymns to the cold fruitless moon" LC and
worships at "Diana's altar" LC (2.1.163, 162; 1.1.71–73,
89). Another set includes differing images of feminine independence within marriage. Hippolyta and Titania are
moving in opposite directions: the former rebel LR Hippolyta UL has now accepted male sovereignty UR and
wants marriage UC, while Titania and her pregnant votaress are struggling to maintain their independence UR after marrying. Finding a proper balance that will allow
women to find and be their natural selves within marriage requires the reconciliation UC of Diana and Venus.
The two votaresses serve opposite but potentially harmonious goddesses; they play Amoret UL and Belphoebe UR
to a Titania whose Venus *genetrix* role has become ambiguous <UL> and to an unnamed Diana UR.[24] (The moon
is named as the vestal's protector but is not personified.)
Although there is no need for marriage if the person can
control his or her passions, only a few, including an idealized Elizabeth UR, can manage it. Hermia, Helena,
Titania, and Hippolyta are more typical females UL. In
Hermia and Helena, the absence of love would mean
withering LR and death LC. In Titania and Hippolyta,
independence from the masculine can lead to destructive rebellion LR. In all four women, we see the threat
of rebellion LR but also the possibility of mature marriage UC.

Natural imagery associated with Titania reflects a
similar split between the promising and the threatening.
No doubt Oberon's beautiful description of the bower
will remain in our minds when the scene changes and is
thus dramatically functional, but the iconographical significance is more important. The bower reflects, on the
one hand, the almost Edenic perfection UL that Oberon
hopes to restore and, on the other, his male fantasy of a
sensual paradise <UL> full of beautiful flowers. The Titania "Lull'd in these flowers with dances and delight"
(2.1.254) sounds as subdued and receptive LL as Oberon
could wish, not at all like the rebellious Titania LR we

have met earlier in the scene. When Oberon mentions "the snake" who "throws her enamell'd skin, / Weed wide enough to wrap a fairy in" (2.1.255–56), the mood changes. He seems to be referring to the snake as an emblem of fertility and regeneration UL and to believe that he could bring that renewal to nature if Titania would only be cooperative, but he may also imply that an evil serpent LR has contributed to Titania's corruption.[25] Oberon apparently thinks of the snakeskin, an image of the snake's discarded old life, as an appropriate straitjacket LR for any fairy who interrupts what to him is justified punishment of Titania. Titania's bower, like Athens for Hermia, can no longer be a paradise for either Oberon or Titania, and a balanced reading suggests that both have brought the snake to the garden.

In the following scene, Titania introduces us to a bower that seems completely different from the place Oberon has described. Her version of the fallen world gets the emphasis, with Titania imploring her fairies to do their best to protect their bower against threatening masculine forces LR. The fairies' song that follows is a catalogue of the beings, many traditionally associated with evil LC,[26] that threaten Titania's world, including "spotted snakes with double tongue" and "Weaving spiders" (2.2.9, 20). Calling on Philomel, a victim LL of male violence LR turned nightingale [LL], accentuates the antimasculine implications. Titania seems to treat herself as a goddess of the natural world UL or as a personification of the vegetative soul [LL] who should reject the crude animality LR of masculinity. Jan Kott proposes an obsessed Titania fearful of her own sexuality LL.[27] That reading can properly be pursued at a personal level, but Titania at this point seems more concerned with a destructive male dominance LR that threatens her independence UR and the fecundity UL of nature itself.

While specific evidence of Oberon's motives for wanting Titania to love an animal is lacking, his general attitudes permit some plausible speculations. In different moods he wants to adore [LL] or dominate <LR> his women, and he finds Titania's rebellion LR an affront to both impulses. Instead of loving and serving UL her lord, she seems to wonder if male sexuality has any role at all. In contrast, Oberon believes that to repudiate love is to deny both the sexuality that women share with men (and animals) UL and the higher reason UR that raises people toward the divine. To force Titania to love a male animal both requires her to recognize her own sexuality UL and offers her a chance to change through experiencing the humbling but paradoxically ennobling [LL] suffering of love. At this point in the play, Oberon's motivations are mixed, but he seems more interested in torment LR than order UR. On the one hand, he will make Titania forget her maternal obsession [UL] with the Indian boy and with nature and will lead her to love the masculine. On the other, he will delight in seeing her suffer the humiliation LL of loving an animal LR. He thinks she deserves to love something "vile" LR (2.2.34) since she views masculinity itself as vile and has allowed her preoccupation with fecundity to supersede her natural relationship with him. An ironic contrast exists between the small size of the intruders Titania fears and the much larger animal—"ounce, or cat, or bear, / Pard, or boar"—that Oberon plans as her "true-love" (2.2.30–31, 28).[28] To Titania, masculine animality is small, corrupt, and threatening LR and must be resisted at every opportunity; to Oberon, it is large, natural, and aggressive <UR>, even though it lacks the higher virtues. Since Oberon is not in full control of either himself or the world around him, hilarious chaos <LC> is almost sure to result from his plans.

While my main consideration of the young lovers in the wood will be in the next chapter, their brief appearances in act 2 also need analysis here since they extend some major patterns of the early fairy scenes. Oberon's treatment of Titania needs the context of his response to Demetrius and Helena. Oberon is sympathetic to a

young woman who is both frankly physical UL and properly submissive UL, and he is upset with "a disdainful
youth" LR (2.1.261) who refuses to show proper courtesy
UR to his love and therefore deserves to suffer LL. The
potion is to restore the traditional roles, with the overly
dependent Helena <LL> becoming the object of adoration
UC, just as Phillida, the mermaid, and the vestal have
been for Oberon and as a wild beast LR will be for
Titania. Helena's image of herself as a small animal
(a hind) LL pursuing a large, uncaring, and bewildered
male animal (a tiger) LR that, like Demetrius, runs away
(2.1.232–33) introduces a parallel that helps explain Oberon's plans for Titania. What Oberon wants is Titania's
degradation before a male animal who, like a Petrarchan
lady <UR>, will care as little for Titania as Demetrius
does for Helena and as Titania has for Oberon. Titania
will experience the passionate animality <LL> and worshiping subservience <LL> that Helena embodies. Oberon, like the other lovers, will himself need to reconcile
extremes in order to find meaningful solutions. There is
some hope: his pity UL for Helena is the first instance of
a sympathy that becomes more prominent as the play
proceeds. We should see a parallel with Theseus's behavior in 1.1. After conquering Hippolyta, he woos [UR]
her; after being dictatorial with Hermia, he counsels UR
her; and after he hears of Helena's plight, he becomes
sympathetic UL to her and critical UR of Demetrius. In
his treatment of Titania, however, Oberon has returned
to the stage LR Theseus experienced when he went out
to conquer Hippolyta. He will use a potion, not a sword,
as an instrument of subjugation <LR> to bring about
Titania's capitulation, but he cannot escape the inherent
polarities of his masculine impulses.

If we have developed any sense of place, Lysander
and Hermia's approach toward Titania's bower just after
Oberon puts the potion on Titania is significant. The
paradisal bower <UC> that Oberon wants to restore and
Titania to protect becomes the approximate setting for

their own ironic fall LC. That subjective impressions determine outlooks is strongly implied when Puck soon after refers to this place (earlier Oberon's lost paradise,
Titania's threatened bower, and the lovers' bank) as
"dank and dirty ground" LC (2.2.75). An audience that
has had its imagination pulled to such contradictory impressions of the bare stage in such a short period of time
is perhaps most likely to accept Puck's cynical realism
and laugh. When Puck invades this bower with a potion
that will induce passion, and when Hermia dreams of a
serpent eating her heart, we should note the comparison
with the snakeskin in Oberon's description of the paradisal bower, with Titania's attempt to keep the "spotted
snakes" (2.2.9) away, and with her failure to prevent
Oberon's entry. Like Oberon and Titania, the young lovers naively assume their own virtue and good intentions
UR. When Puck mistakes Lysander for Demetrius, his
mistake is understandable. Seeing Hermia lying apart
from Lysander, he concludes that she does not dare lie
near "this lack-love, this kill-courtesy" LR (2.2.77). In
their different ways, both of the young men have failed
to care for their women with the true courtesy UR that
goes beyond courtly manners. Puck and Oberon would be
less interested in them if they were more attuned to the
natural, and no doubt they would be less open to the influence of potions. Puck is only gradually learning "what
fools these mortals be!" (3.2.115).

By the end of this section of the play, the focus has begun to shift from the first three woods to the nightmare
wood LC. The differences between the wood of revel UL
championed by Titania and the pastoral wood <UC>
envisioned by Oberon have been defined. With Titania
herself in love, her perspective is submerged, just as
Hippolyta's was by Theseus's victory in war. Neither
has an opportunity to proselytize among the young
women, as they might if Shakespeare wanted to pursue
the Amazon theme. Having established the framework
in which love relationships develop, Shakespeare in the

next section of the play makes the behavior of lovers the primary topic. While the chivalric wood of romance <LL> still governs most of the responses of the mortals, the audience has a fuller vision that allows us to see how "night-rule" (3.2.5) transforms conceptions of heroic order into a nightmare wood of chaos and bewilderment LC.

EIGHT

Night-rule
(*A Midsummer Night's Dream* 2.1.188–end; 2.2.34–4.1.45)

OBERON. How now, mad spirit?
What night-rule now about this haunted grove?

(3.2.4–5)

T he Athenians' awareness of the remarkable wood they experience is severely limited. Except for Bottom, they see no fairies, and Oberon's magic insures that Bottom will remember only "the fierce vexation of a dream" and the young lovers only a "fruitless vision" (4.1.69; 3.2.371). Later, Theseus misreads the significance of the lovers' reports of their night, and only Hippolyta and, to a lesser degree, the lovers and Bottom have some understanding of what has taken place. Any audience has a distinct advantage,[1] but that advantage is sacrificed if we are so preoccupied with fairy magic that we lose sight of what it represents. The night scenes should delight us but should also lead us to a fuller understanding of the psychology of love and the nature of the passions. Fascination with the fairies can lead to the misleading impression that the "night-rule" is brought about entirely by the fairies and that the play's unreality should be enjoyed primarily on the level of wonder and incident.

While the fairies cause the fundamental shifts (and the later reversals) in Titania, Lysander, and Bottom that propel the plot, their presence functions as a metaphor for the night-spirit LC that infuses itself into everything that takes place in the "haunted grove" LC of the characters' passionate lives. Rewriting the lovers' plot without the fairies would be quite possible since what the fairies bring about and what the lovers and artisans themselves do and think are so similar. The fairies do not influence the lovers and artisans' first scenes in the wood: Demetrius and Helena's quarrel (2.1) and Hermia's dream would happen without them, and the Ovidian atmosphere of mixed levels of reality (animals, humans, nature) owes much to the extravagant use of animal imagery in that section of the play. When Demetrius tells Helena, "do not haunt me thus" (2.2.85), Helena for him is no spirit but a chaotic presence LC that threatens his sanity. When in the next scene Peter Quince calls out, "We are haunted" (3.1.104), the fairies are active, but haunting has become a general condition. Shakespearean metaphor leads to richer connections within the context of his complex analogical polarities: the wood of Oberon, Titania, and Puck embodies a metaphorical version of reality in its human, natural, and supernatural dimensions.

In chapter 7, I described four metaphorical woods that sum up various responses to the world in the play: the wood of revel UL and the pastoral wood UC reflect Titania and Oberon's opposing views of the relative importance of fecundity and patriarchy; the chivalric wood LL and the nightmare wood LC govern the responses of the lovers. The first scenes of the play establish the broader context of masculine and feminine relationships

PATTERNS
OF
METAPHOR

A MIDSUMMER NIGHT'S DREAM III
(2.1.188 – END; 2.2.44 – 4.1.45)

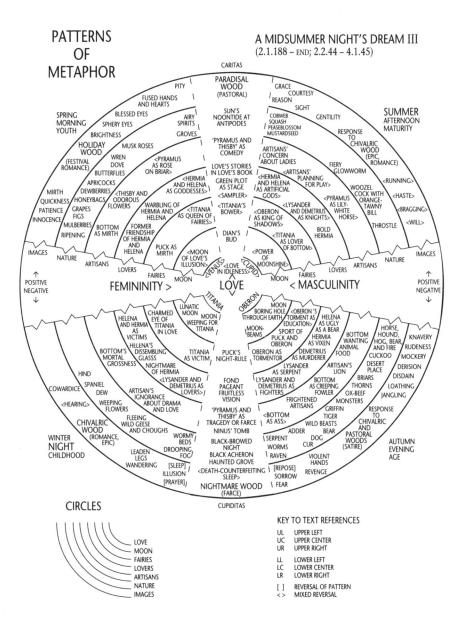

CIRCLES

LOVE
MOON
FAIRIES
LOVERS
ARTISANS
NATURE
IMAGES

KEY TO TEXT REFERENCES

UL   UPPER LEFT
UC   UPPER CENTER
UR   UPPER RIGHT

LL   LOWER LEFT
LC   LOWER CENTER
LR   LOWER RIGHT

[ ]   REVERSAL OF PATTERN
< >   MIXED REVERSAL

in the day-world of Athens and the night-world of the wood, and the central scenes in the wood illustrate how love actually affects people. The lovers never lose their belief in the pastoral and chivalric ideals of reason, order, and harmony UC even when they are faced with experiences that threaten to turn their lives to nightmare LC. Demetrius envisions a chivalric wood where he can defeat Lysander in battle and thereby win his Hermia. Lysander and Hermia have overcome Lysander's initial pessimism and expect a friendly pastoral wood. Even Helena, who has described love as illusion [UC] at the end of the opening scene, reverts to increasingly desperate but more conventional attitudes after her initial exchanges with Demetrius. We see a nightmare wood of illusion and disorder LC, but various forces working toward harmony UC (including the comic form itself) keep us optimistic about resolutions.

The short scene between Helena and Demetrius in 2.1, discussed from Oberon's perspective at the end of chapter 7 above, introduces much of the metaphorical language that dominates the wood scenes. Since they are "unmetaphored" characters from the romances, their assumption of these dramatic roles and of the imagery that goes with them is at once inevitable and comic. Hierarchical conceptions of love provide the structure, but their language of love repeatedly inverts what a watching Oberon regards as appropriate behavior. In her aggressive worship of Demetrius, a despondent but sardonic Helena switches between polarities of abject dependence LL and desperate action LR. In his quixotic pursuit of Hermia, a frustrated Demetrius uses a Petrarchan rhetoric full of troubled sentiments and strained puns as he tries to balance the conflicting roles of bold knight UR and suffering lover LL. He will literally kill Lysander even though he is metaphorically being killed by Hermia: "The one I'll [slay]; the other [slayeth] me;" being "wode within this wood" (2.1.190, 192) reflects his fear of madness LC brought on by unreciprocated love.

The confusion caused by adding an importunate Helena to Demetrius's torment over Hermia proves to be more than he can assimilate. He tries to play the honest knight UR who must deny a lovesick suppliant LL because he loves elsewhere, but Helena refuses to accept his indifference. A contrast between active pursuing LR (referred to three times in the scene) and more subservient following LL (referred to five times) helps define their attitudes. After first telling her to "pursue me not," he later orders her to "follow me no more" (2.1.188, 194). Helena responds by claiming to "follow" only because he is "hard-hearted adamant" <LC> with "power to draw" her heart UL, which is "true as steel" UR (2.1.195–97). By implication, he has been a false lord LR destroying her virtue, not an analogue to the loving God UC who draws the "hard-hearted" sinner LC toward Him. Appropriate gestures might also develop the sword imagery implicit in "draw" and "steel" (and in Demetrius's previous speech about slaying and being slain) to suggest that he has stabbed her heart earlier and now torments her by drawing out both his masculine "steel" sword UR and her "true as steel" feminine heart UL. When "in plainest truth" he says he cannot love her, she echoes a paradox of love from the opening scene (1.1.193–99) in lamenting that "The more you beat me, I will fawn on you" LL, and then descends further when she asks only to be a "spaniel" LL (2.1.200, 204, 205) that he can mistreat as he pleases. That would at least mean a relationship.

When Demetrius goes against courtesy UR by talking crudely of his "hatred" LR and of being "sick" LR (2.1.211, 212) when he looks at her, she has at last won a passionate reaction. From that point on, he is on the defensive, and he becomes increasingly desperate LC as he fails to find a satisfactory way of dealing with her. In threatening her with rape LR, he recognizes her virtue but associates himself with vague personifications of nature's evil LC: the "opportunity of night" LC and "the ill counsel of a desert place" LC would allow "the hands of one that loves you not" LR to take "the rich worth of your virginity" UL (2.2.216–19). But Helena ridicules his pretense of evil and outdoes him metaphorically by returning to her Petrarchism. For her, he remains an idealized microcosm UC fusing the sun UR and the world UL; his face is an implied sun that lights the night, and he provides "worlds of company" UC in this "desert place" LC (2.1.223, 218). When she says that this paragon who is "all the world" will "look on me" (2.1.226), she postulates a restored relationship with an adoring Demetrius [LL] looking up to her as an idealized woman UC.

When Demetrius quits talking of rape but threatens to leave Helena "to the mercy of wild beasts" LR (2.2.228) who presumably would eat her, Helena cleverly takes advantage of his animal reference by switching from a Petrachan to an Ovidian mode. In Ovid's *Metamorphoses*, fables about lusty gods in animal form chasing after humans express sexually charged masculine-feminine interactions at various levels of meaning.[2] Helena first turns the literal-minded Demetrius, who is talking of real "wild beasts," into a metaphorical beast by replying that "the wildest hath not such a heart as you" (2.2.229). As a chivalric knight UR, Demetrius will not rape her, but his "wild" heart [UL] endangers her even though his peaceful hands UR do not. Then Helena goes on to talk of "wild beasts" LR whose interest in small animals LL *is* aggressive. Earlier, she was a "spaniel" LL to a human master UR. Now, by comparing herself not only to a Daphne [LL] who must chase Apollo <LR> but also to a "dove" [LL] that "pursues the griffin" LR and to a "mild hind" [LL] that "Makes speed to catch the tiger" LR (2.1.232–33), she invokes the Ovidian sexuality that Demetrius has been avoiding. A love-starved Helena [LL] claims to welcome masculine aggression LR and laments that nothing will happen if "valor flies" from "cowardice" (2.2.234). Demetrius may be her sun-Apollo UR, but she will not need to be transformed into a laurel tree if he ignores her.

Demetrius's obviously hollow threat—"if thou follow me, do not believe / But I shall do thee mischief in the wood"—results in Helena's twisting of his vaguely sexual "mischief" to yet another telling metaphorical charge: "Ay, in the temple, in the town, the field, / You do me mischief" LR (2.1.236–39). Such mental abuse from men like Demetrius recalls the irresponsible side of Puck and Cupid and of the "waggish boys" LR (1.1.240) that Helena mentions in her soliloquy. When Helena says "Fie, Demetrius!" (2.1.239), she has assumed a control that seems partly maternal and partly masculine <UR>. When she continues—"We cannot fight for love, as men may do. / We should be woo'd, and were not made to woo" (2.1.241–42),—the disruption of order is apparent. Her boldness <UR> has led her, not to Hippolyta or Titania's self-assurance, but instead to unsatisfying preaching <LR> at her humiliated lord LL. He has no response and flees LL with his masculinity in doubt. In calling out that she will "follow thee and make a heaven of hell, / To die upon the hand I love so well" (2.1.243–44), she has become aggressively LR passive LL. To die upon his "hand" (now metonymically both sword and phallus) LR would fuse hellish death LC and heavenly love UC in an ecstasy that would at least return them both to conventional gender roles. His magnetic power UC, which swordlike <UR> drew out her heart UL in the opening lines of their scene, has become her analogous power <LC> to force him to return his sword to her body in love and death.

In contrast to this nightmarish wood-world of Petrarchan and Ovidian chaos, Hermia and Lysander's conception of the wood in the next scene (2.2) combines the two patriarchal woods—the pastoral wood UC that will remain friendly even in darkness and the chivalric wood LL that reassures them that with good will and moral effort UR they can overcome any obstacles. Their expectation of an easy journey to Lysander's dowager aunt does not change, even when they lose their way. Lysander's reference to "wand'ring" from the "way" (2.2.35, 36) recalls the earlier cluster of references to wandering: Lysander may be thinking of wandering knights UR, but our perspective also includes the conventional Christian trope LL and Puck as a wanderer and a misleader LR of "night-wanderers" LL (2.1.39). By insisting on inappropriate chivalric standards that ignore the real perils of the wood, Lysander and Hermia become "night-wanderers" LL vulnerable to a Puck <LC> interested in folly, not sin. Hermia's elevated notion of what is suitable for "a virtuous bachelor and a maid" (2.2.59) specifically recalls the romance since "bachelor" would retain some of its meaning of "young knight" <UR>. Lysander in his somewhat archaic language and forms—his use of "troth" (2.2.36) to mean both "truth" and "a vow of faith," his elaborate courtly riddle of friendship, and his prayers for faith and vows of loyalty—is the image of the aspiring knight. But to Puck, whose standards are less artificial, he is a "kill-courtesy" LR (2.2.77) who fails to take proper care of his lady.

Athens has already become a "hell" (1.1.207) to Hermia, but she resists her earlier doubts about Lysander's love. As we have seen in chapter 7, the juxtaposition of their belief in an idyllic wood UC with Oberon's invasion of Titania's bower and with Puck's comment that they are sleeping on "dank and dirty ground" (2.2.75) LC calls attention to their naivete. They speak of beds and pillows in the wood, and Lysander refers confidently to the "comfort of the day" and to a helpful "sleep" that will "give thee all his rest" (2.2.38, 64). When Hermia asks him to "lie further off yet; do not lie so near" (2.2.44), Lysander rejects the implications of her inadvertent pun on "lie" and launches into a naive celebration <UC> of their love as a non-physical friendship. Friendship is an appropriate accompaniment to marriage, as Juliet realizes when she calls Romeo "friend" (3.5.43), but it is not the primary motivation of young lovers.

Hermia better understands the dangers, but she too wants to believe in the forms of chivalric behavior UC. Both are unprepared for their coming experience of a nightmare wood LC, a part of themselves and the world that they have never known.³

Demetrius and Helena are already in their nightmare but are trying to hang on to their sanity. Helena now gives up her belief that love is a mad illusion LC beyond her control and returns to the rational self-analysis of conventional love theory. Her delusion LC has, she thinks, come from the "wicked and dissembling glass" LR that tempted her to compare herself "with Hermia's sphery eyne" (2.2.98, 99). Love is based on heavenly beauty UC after all, and she has acted both foolishly and immorally LC. Demetrius reinforces her sense of an evil force within her when he tells her "do not haunt me thus" (2.2.85). In trying to ascend, she has descended: her unnaturally masculine behavior LR has destroyed her femininity and revealed her as a monstrous animal LR. The scene becomes a kind of beast fable built on the Ovidian atmosphere of animal allusion in 2.1. Helena imagines herself as being "ugly as a bear" LR and associates Demetrius with the "beasts that . . . run away for fear" LL (2.2.94, 95). Ironically, she has a masculine will to pursue when she sees herself as a "spaniel," "dove," or "mild hind" LL (2.1.203, 232) but loses it along with her self-confident femininity when she thinks of herself as a "monster" or "bear" (2.2.97, 94). The circle of the image pattern is completed when Helena, who by this time lacks all self-esteem, wakens the potion-struck Lysander and he calls her among other things a "dove" UL (2.2.114). The Helena who has yearned to be a dove pursued by Demetrius no longer believes that she could be attractive to anyone. To be subjected to the "keen mockery" and "scorn" LR of a Lysander pretending she is not a bear is to "be abus'd" once again by a "lord" without "true gentleness" (2.2.123, 124, 134, 132). In this new love chase, the dove Helena will be the pursued, and

Hermia, who earlier swears by "Venus' doves" UL, will be ignored as a "raven" LC (1.1.171; 2.2.114).

Throughout the play, Demetrius and Lysander define themselves by their aspirations to a higher love. When they are most crazy LC, they claim to be most rational UR. When Lysander receives the potion, he changes the object of his affections but not the style of his rhetoric. Helena, preoccupied with love and death, looks for the "blood" or "wound" of an actual injury, but Lysander is "purple with love's wound" LL (2.2.101; 2.1.167). He claims that "being young" he was "ripe not to reason" <UL> but now has reached "the point of human skill" UC; now "Reason" UR is "the marshal to my will" and makes him understand that Helena is "the worthier maid" (2.2.118–20, 116). He is of course unaware that the feeling of having achieved the metaphorical high point he describes may be an illusion [UC]. Similarly, at the start of the play, Demetrius is convinced that it is Lysander's "title" that is "crazed" LC and that reason would mean granting him his "certain right" UR (1.1.92). Man's position as the supposed voice of reason lures him to make the claim. The young women are more sensible, at least partly because they by nature depend on the heart UL more than the reason.

Lysander's use of eye imagery UR reflects his overconfidence in the male's ability to distinguish between the illusion and the reality of love. The conventional view of male love suggests that power exists both in the woman's beauty UC that elicits male wonder and passion [LL] and in the man's rational ability UR to move from the beauty to something higher. Female love works in analogous though different ways: beauty gives her power UR while love leads her to recognize and accept UL male reason and authority UR. Gender bias inevitably functions as each sex minimizes the power of the other: Helena sees women's eyes as a magnetic force UR that controls men, and Lysander sees them as an opening to the wonders of the cosmos UC. As Helena struggles to explain

Hermia's power over Demetrius, she speaks of her "blessed and attractive" "sphery eyne" UR (2.2.91, 99). In contrast, Lysander describes Helena's "eyes, where I o'erlook
/ Love's stories written in Love's richest book" (2.2.121–
22). In Lysander's view, the woman remains passive as
man finds ways of seeing, reading, and understanding
love with the help of a masculine art or intelligence UR.
He now realizes the "heresy" LC of his former worship
[LL] of Hermia and becomes the "knight" UR (2.2.141,
144) of his true lady UC. In referring to heresies that "deceive" (2.2.140) and in describing Hermia as overly sweet
food, he implies a progression from the deceptions of illusion [UC] and the appetites of the lower senses [UL] to
an elevated love UC. When Puck puts the potion on
Lysander's eyelid and comments on "the power this
charm doth owe" (2.2.79), he seems to support the view
that love is in the eye of an active beholder UR, but his
explanation is much closer to Helena's earlier view of
love's irrationality LC (1.1.226–45) than to Lysander's
courtly Platonism UR.

The animal images LR in Hermia's dream parallel
those in Helena's scene with Demetrius and accentuate
our sense of the degradation the women are undergoing.
She awakes just after Lysander's grotesque speech about
how the "surfeit of the sweetest things / The deepest
loathing to the stomach brings" and about the "heresy"
(2.2.137–38, 141) of his love for Hermia. Like the serpent
LR of her dream, he is a false worshiper LL whose eating
and devotion are both unnatural. Hermia's dream seems
in part to be a vision [LC] of what was happening while
she slept.[4] The Lysander who earlier "knit" "my heart
unto yours" so that they have "one heart" UC has become at once a "crawling serpent" LR destroying their
Eden by eating her heart and an unconcerned observer
LR "smiling at his [that is, the serpent's] cruel prey"
(2.2.47, 48, 146, 150). The dream may also relate to
what Hermia was feeling before she went to sleep. On
the simpler level she may subconsciously fear LR that

the Lysander who "riddles very prettily" (2.2.53) will be unable LL to protect her in the wood; on a deeper level the serpent may be phallic LR: she may feel both threatened by LL and guiltily attracted to <UL> Lysander's sexuality. Through the dream these doubts about herself, Lysander, and the world of the wood find indirect expression, but her proper self somewhat naively <UL> tries to return to a world where love and sense perceptions can be trusted: if he is "out of hearing" and will not "Speak," then "I well perceive you are not nigh" (2.2.152, 153, 155). She is fearful but her practical solution UR is to look for him. Her grim alternatives—"Either death, or you, I'll find immediately"—ominously echo her earlier courtly comment: "Thy love ne'er alter till thy sweet life end!" (2.2.156, 61). We should note the parallel to Helena's obsessive desire to have Demetrius either love her or kill her. Shakespeare, no Freudian but a shrewd psychological observer, manages to use conventional methods and images to develop incisive portraits.

The visual images of the stage reinforce our responses to the characters' states of mind. The alternate running and resting of the lovers suggest the quality of their wandering and repose. While Lysander and Hermia at first have some idea of why they are running (or flying) <LR>, by the end of the night they are wanderers without much purpose LL. Nevertheless, their sleep [LL] in 2.2 indicates a certain security about their relationship, misguided though it may be. In contrast, Demetrius and Helena's chases LR are more frantic from the start, and their rests—a pause for Helena in 2.2 and sleep for Demetrius in 3.2—reflect their increasing despair LC about their chances for love. Stage images are particularly effective in revealing the sudden shifts in each lover's situation near the end of 2.2. When Puck enters with the potion, his comment "Night and silence" <LC> (2.2.70) calls attention to the atmosphere of apparent calm in which Titania and the lovers are resting but also implies that a mischievous Puck, already identified with an unruly night LC, is about to destroy that calm. (Later in the play [4.1.80–86] a contrasting silence [LC] precedes the triumphant music and dance UC of Oberon and Titania's reconciliation.)

In the final 70 lines of the scene, running (and chaos) begin again. All is reversed: the despairing Helena finds herself chased by the newly transformed Lysander, and Hermia, made insecure by her dream of a serpent, starts after the departed Lysander. What was a confused diamond with a neglected Helena at the bottom LC, an aspiring Demetrius and hopeful Lysander in the middle UL, and an admired Hermia at the top UC has a new configuration—a vertical line with Lysander at the bottom and with Helena, Demetrius, and Hermia in turn above him. But because of Hermia's pursuit of Lysander, an image of a circle of chasers fits the nonhierarchical irrationality LC better, with Lysander after Helena after Demetrius after Hermia after Lysander in a cycle without meaning.[5] While Helena no longer chases Demetrius, she retains her love, and her aimless wandering LL becomes an image of her despair LC as well as of her flight from Lysander.

The return to the Bottom plot in 3.1 provides an abrupt change from Shakespeare's ingenious staging of his love plots to the artisans' obtuse planning for their parallel romance. We might expect a comparison between Thisby's tragic journey to the wood and Hermia's brave search <UR> for death or Lysander, but the artisans' earlier anticipation of taking on gallant roles UR has given way to worry about stage techniques and audience response. Their problems in staging "Pyramus and Thisby" encourage our attention to playwright-directors UR at work, most obviously to the Shakespeare who is also trying to find an appropriate form for a play about lovers to be presented at a wedding. The solutions worked out by the artisans at once mirror and parody Shakespeare's dramatic methods. When Bottom and Starveling worry about the ladies' reaction to swords and deaths, and Bottom proposes a prologue of explanation, the method recalls the prologue to *Romeo and Juliet*, which also has the effect of distancing Shakespeare's audience from the swordplay and tragic deaths.

At the very start of the scene, Peter Quince points to the physical surroundings in a way that accentuates the bare Elizabethan stage: "This green plot shall be our stage, this hawthorn brake our tiring-house" (3.1.3–4). Some members of the audience might reflect that *this* bare stage we must imagine is a wood will serve as *their* stage, which they will transform into other imagined settings, one of them a wood! Shakespeare himself has just been making a virtue of stage necessity by suggesting that his characters' very different impressions of this same "green plot" (near Titania's bower) reflect their own subjective views of love and life.[6] When the artisans consider making use of the actual moon but decide they must "present . . . the person of Moonshine" (and also "Wall") (3.1.61, 67), they solve their practical problem by moving from realism to symbolism but turn one of the play's key images into comic pedantry. Shakespeare also opts for the symbolic over the realistic in his contradictory presentation of the moon: he wants a new moon UL for the wedding but also an impression of moonshine <UR> in the wood. Throughout the play Shakespeare invites us to remember that his play is a fiction and to think about the meanings and methods of drama itself.

The other major concern of the artisans—that the lion LR may frighten the ladies—recalls the animal imagery that is so prominent in 2.2 and is to become even more significant in the beast fable of Bottom's transformation. Helena has defined herself, Demetrius, and Lysander through images of beasts, birds, and serpents. Bottom tells Snug to tell the ladies he is "a man as other men are" (3.1.44). What "men are" is a recurring theme, and paradoxically one of the primary metaphors for describing them is animal and bird imagery. In a play in which characterization is governed more by types than individuality, stereotypes of animal behavior provide the characters with conventional metaphors that accurately reflect their natures. As hidden, nonrational, and amoral qualities over which there seems to be little or no control, such stereotypes relate personal identity to the analogous ambiguities of the natural world.[7] Bottom's transformation gives him quite literally the head of an ass but also reflects his asslike nature LR, and Oberon uses Titania's love LL for an ass as a way of humbling her before an image of masculinity. Later, Bottom, not realizing that he has terrified the others, thinks they "make an ass of me, to fright me, if they could" (3.1.120–21) and introduces bird imagery as he tries to fortify his courage by singing. The aspiring Bottom's dream of becoming a loving knight through art has been destroyed as he is "translated" (3.1.119) instead into a lowly ass LR and a fearful singing bird LL. Bottom thinks that singing in itself will prove his harmonious composure UC and apparently that a song about the bravery UR of little birds will fit his situation.[8] Unfortunately, the song is dreadfully discordant LC, and having a man with a donkey head singing about and like small birds makes his position even more absurd LC.

Bottom's role permits both artistic pretensions <UR> and magical possibilities UC, but his actual performance undercuts his illusions of grandeur. Asses, the epitome of priapic sexuality and / or stupid sterility LR, are fit symbols of human inadequacy and therefore apt candidates for transformation; and Bottom, "the shallowest thickskin of that barren sort" (3.2.13), rises through both art and magic. We have seen that in his claim of being able to play every part—lover and tyrant, gentle lady and gallant knight—he becomes a kind of everyman who contains within himself all human aspirations and emotions. In his transformation, he calls to mind the opportunities granted to the lowly asses <LR> of biblical and literary tradition who rise toward the divine UC—the talking Balaam who had a vision of an angel and became a communicator between God and man, the suffering beast of burden who humbly bore Christ into Jerusalem and became a symbol of both Christ's human dimension and his divine sacrifice, the golden ass of Apuleius who is eventually elevated by a love commonly allegorized as divine, the Erasmian (and Pauline) ass whose folly about the temporal world accompanies a divine wisdom, and, in immediate memory for an audience of 1595, the ass who bore Una in *The Faerie Queene*.[9] The description of Pyramus that immediately precedes the transformation suggests his chivalric, and ultimately Christlike, virtues of strength and purity UR ("Most radiant Pyramus, most lily-white of hue"), sacrificial love [LC] ("the red rose on triumphant brier"), and devoted service UL ("As true as truest horse, that yet would never tire") (3.1.93, 94, 96). But pricking love also has a profane dimension, and to become the horse <UL> comically inverts conventional sexual roles. Bottom may also bring to mind beasts of classical legend who come to unsatisfactory ends—notably the minotaur LR that Theseus kills in the labyrinth and the Actaeon LR who is transformed into a deer and killed by his own hounds after he sees Diana bathing. Shakespeare develops his own myths in a wildly comic style, with the Ovidian (and biblical) overtones of transformation implying an ironic commentary on both aspiration UC and inadequacy LC.

The scenes in which Bottom meets Titania and the fairies provide a juxtaposition of opposites that shows us a different dimension of both Bottom and Titania. Until this point, the fairies have drawn us to an imaginative world depicting the unseen realities that lie behind the chaotic but magical forces <LC> of nature and love, but the "rude mechanicals" (3.2.9) and their play have pulled us back to stolid lives LR and unimaginative art [UR]. Now Shakespeare uses Bottom as ass and Titania as lover of an ass to illustrate that being animal-like has surprising implications. When Titania awakes and calls him "angel," Bottom is at once an emblem of divine beauty and the vehicle of a divine revelation <UC>: Titania stresses both her own eyes UR and ears UL as the means of recognizing and rising toward love (*eros*) UL and Bottom's "fair virtue's force" UC (3.1.129, 140) as a divine power (*agape*) that acts upon her (much as Juliet as a masculine angel communicates to Romeo) [2.2.25–32].) If Bottom were still Pyramus or Endymion, her love and her rhetoric would almost be appropriate. Pyramus would have been comfortable with such language, but Bottom is not. Apparently because of his new donkey nature UR (in part a return to his Athenian self), Bottom now has little of Pyramus in him and is consequently less vulnerable to Titania's blandishments. He has enough sense and self-knowledge UR to wonder why Titania would fall in love with him and concludes that there must be something about love itself and not his person that has won her: "And yet, to say the truth, reason and love keep little company together now-a-days. The more the pity that some honest neighbors will not make them friends" (3.1.143–46).

A whole series of masculine-feminine references enriches the section, not only Bottom's reference to reason and love but also Titania's claim to have been influenced by both her eyes and ears, her belief that he is both wise and beautiful, and Bottom's wish that he had "wit enough to get out of this wood" (3.1.149–50). (The "wood" here refers at once to the wood itself, to madness, ["wode"] and perhaps to his new wooden head.) When Titania continues her attentions, Bottom becomes more gentlemanly UR. He may be lower in class, but he loves being treated as someone important and responds graciously, if a little pompously. Gentility proves to be much easier for the Athenian Bottom to achieve and maintain than for the young lovers, whose experiences in the wood lead them to cast away most of their civilized manners. When Titania woos him, Bottom seems oblivious both to material pleasures and to what he now seems to regard as the nonsense [UC] of romantic and physical love. That he is more interested in having his head scratched and in munching dry oats and hay is only partly due to his asshead. Once again, polarities of interpretation coexist. If we accept the paradox that love is a wise folly [LC], the passionate lovers, if not Titania, are closer to genuine wisdom than Bottom and the "honest neighbors" who would make "reason and love" only "friends." Not being able to love is to be less than fully human and truly an ass, but if love is as foolish <UC> as love in these woods tends to be, then not being interested in Titania may be a sign of genuine wisdom.

When Titania reveals herself as "a spirit of no common rate" and promises Bottom, "I will purge thy mortal grossness so, / That thou shalt like an aery spirit go" (3.1.154, 160–61), she has switched from doting lover LL to a goddess <UC> offering a mere mortal an experience of transcendent love. Like all lovers, she is caught up in a dream LC or illusion [UC] that disguises the animal side LR of sexuality. From Oberon's perspective, she has gone to one extreme of repudiating love LR and now should suffer and learn by going to the other extreme of passionately dependent love LL. Her rhetoric may be elevated, but she seems primarily interested in getting Bottom to her bower: "mortal grossness" can be purged by satisfying physical desire as well as by transcending it.[10] Her link to the fullness of nature UC remains—"The summer still doth tend upon my state" (3.1.155)—but is reduced and debased as the queen of nature serves Bottom. She appeals to Bottom's lower instincts by promising him "jewels from the deep" and fruits to satisfy his taste: "apricocks and dewberries, / . . . purple grapes, green figs, and mulberries" (3.1.158, 166–67). The Titania who has made the fecundity of nature her primary goal now directs it all to Bottom.

Even the moon seems disturbed by what is happening: "The moon methinks looks with a wat'ry eye; / And when she weeps, weeps every little flower, / Lamenting some enforced chastity" (3.1.198–200). Apparently an unconcerned and even mildly contemptuous Titania LR is accurately describing a sorrowful moon's reaction to Titania's degradation. Earlier, Oberon has referred to the "wat'ry moon" that protected the chastity of the "imperial vot'ress" (2.1.162, 163). That cool and moist moon promoted both chastity UR and fecundity UL; this moon's moisture is tears LL as it laments a love that would be both unchaste and unproductive. Oberon used a flower's potion on Titania and thereby forced her to love; now "every little flower" laments the unnatural behavior of Titania, who mistakenly thinks Bottom's "fair virtue's force" UC (3.1.140) is responsible for her love.[11] The moon's tears for Titania's "enforced chastity" are the passive equivalent LL of the "anger" LR of the "governess of floods" UR (2.1.103–04) with the wind, an image of the natural chaos caused by Titania's earlier battle with Oberon. The "enthralled" Titania, far from depending on help from the moon, will have her fairies "fan the moonbeams from his [Bottom's] sleeping eyes" (3.1.139, 173). She will force an "enthralled" Bottom to her bower, but the comic tone is maintained when she asks her fairies to "Tie up my lover's tongue" so the loquacious Bottom will come "silently" (3.1.201).

Despite his earlier grandiose claims, Bottom proves incapable of participating in Titania's world. When he becomes an ass, he becomes most fully himself LR, and we begin to understand that he is willing to take risks only with the protection of art's fantasy. When the situation seems real, he retreats to his own nature. He could play the potent ass but seems uninterested; he could have sensual delights but settles for peas and hay; he could be treated like a lord but remains a friendly would-be gentleman; he could rise above his mortal state but becomes even more earthly. He finds it difficult to understand or participate in love: he will never achieve the elevated wisdom of the Athenian (or Christian neoplatonic) philosophy of love either through reason or inspiration, and he remains a "true Athenian" <UR> (4.2.30–31) in his doubts about all that happens in the wood. As an ass who imitates lions and birds, he illustrates varieties of masculinity: Bottom roars like a lion, but he lacks the lion's extremes of majesty UR and cruelty LR; he wants to sing like a bird UL, but his song is foolish and discordant LC. His polarities of aspiration and limitation define his very real physical presence as a man, but his enthusiasm and vitality make him a delightful stage character. His pretensions to be gentlemanly may be possible only because of the surprising respect he gets from Titania, but he has a natural grace and decency about him that enable him to stumble through crises. He is optimistic, friendly, well-meaning, and good-natured; in short he is "bully Bottom" (4.2.19), a "sunny" figure of daytime Athens <UR> who would always be out of place in the wood. Harmony and marriage are as far from him as his various songs are from being genuinely musical and his love from being either passionate or divine.

The lovers have no awareness of either the artisans or the fairies, but the two groups establish a context that allows us to understand the lovers' experience more fully than they can themselves. Bottom, whose very presence in the wood at night is a reversal of his ordinary life, can be seen as the opposite of Puck, the "merry wanderer of the night" (2.1.43). Although, like Puck, Bottom has characteristics that have overtones at several levels of meaning,[12] and both reveal Shakespeare's epistemological interest in the processes of the mind, Puck embodies imagination or fantasy (the often chaotic night world of mind), while Bottom belongs to the disturbed world of the senses (the day world of body). Bottom's confused accounts of experience record mixups of perception and language and suggest once again that being Athenian does not in itself guarantee understanding of the world. He wants to develop a night side of love and adventure UL but instead experiences Puck's "night-rule" (3.2.5) of chaos LC. Puck, having been spared the human foibles of the sensory world, can laugh at Bottom's enthusiasms, but Bottom's warm humanity becomes in turn an implicit comment on the limitations of Puck's detached intelligence. Both are or want to be actor-directors UR, but Puck is a jester whose comic impulse is satiric <LR> and tends toward sport, while Bottom is an unwitting clown <LC> who can generate only humor and fun. The "spirit of mirth" in Puck's art is full of the improvisation of commedia dell'arte that lets the preposterous develop on its own, while the mirth of the artisans' pretentious play is unintentional. Bottom, in straining for drama that includes everything—tragedy and comedy, epic and romance, the emblematic and the realistic, all with implications at every level of meaning—creates a parody <LC> of the literary microcosm that Shakespeare himself is writing.[13]

In act 3, scene 2, the descent to chaos LC accelerates, and a countermovement toward reconciliation UC begins. Puck's surprisingly detailed recapitulation of Titania's encounter with Bottom allows us to evaluate Oberon's response: he is delighted with the effects of Puck's "night-rule" LC (3.2.5) on Titania, but when he discovers Puck's mistake with Lysander, his pity for the suffering young women and distaste for disorder begin to lead him toward the resolutions of his own patriarchal "night-rule" UR. The scene moves toward apparent disaster for the lovers, but our sense of comic form directs us to laugh and remain optimistic. Puck establishes a dramatic context when he describes the "fond pageant" LC (3.2.114) that he and Oberon have set up and now will watch. Oberon, the "king of shadows" (3.2.347), (with "shadows" suggesting the fairies and the actors as well as the night), is an author-director whose potions permit art as well as magic: he has already turned his conflict with Titania into the sport <LR> of low comedy and is about to try to shape a romantic comedy UC of reconciled lovers. Countering his efforts and thereby helping Shakespeare avoid a conventional patriarchal structure are the farcical instincts LC of Puck. He is pleased when the absurd situation works itself out in ways that seem to be almost as surprising for them as for the lovers. Though the scene is their play, it takes on Puck's form, commedia dell'arte, in which the lovers improvise within a framework that Oberon only thinks he can control. Like Oberon, the lovers are struggling for resolutions. The young men self-consciously try to embody the noble love of chivalric romance UR, and each of the women fears that the others are involved in a drama of mockery LR in which she is at once the help-less audience and the object of scorn LL. Uncertainties about dramatic form mirror the characters' doubts about their lives.

In a series of skillfully contrived encounters involving each of the lovers in relation to each of the others, Shakespeare shows the young men getting more lunatic LC and the women more troubled LL. Hermia is at first furious LR with Demetrius for killing Lysander, then be-wildered LC with Lysander for being fickle, and finally outraged LR with Helena for stealing Lysander's love. Demetrius at first courts [UR] the angry Hermia, then, influenced by the potion, adores [LL] Helena, and finally fights LR with Lysander. Lysander coldly rejects LR Hermia, then worships [LL] Helena, and finally fights LR with Demetrius. In 2.2, Helena thinks Lysander is mock-ing LR her, then in 3.2, thinks first Demetrius and then Hermia are joining him. Identities and relationships be-gin to disintegrate LC. Hermia asks, "Am not I Hermia? Are not you Lysander?" (3.2.273). While the men are una-ware of their lunacy, the women are all too conscious that their worlds are crumbling around them. The plot's ironic contrasts are sharpened by having both young women for opposite reasons refuse to accept the men's transformations. Hermia responds with a courage UR that becomes more and more desperate as the night pro-ceeds, while Helena is unable to recover from the despair LC that first overtakes her when she stops chasing Demetrius.

In the first encounter of the scene, Hermia, frantically

searching for Lysander, uses an exaggerated image that accentuates her conventional faith in Lysander. In describing the sun as "not so true unto the day / As he to me" (3.2.50–51), Hermia reverses her earlier suspicion of the rigid law [UR] of Theseus and Egeus's daytime Athens. Now Hermia seems troubled about a night that has brought her trouble rather than secrecy. Nevertheless, she still believes that the moon side of Lysander would not "displease / Her brother's noontide with th' Antipodes" (3.2.54–55)—her paradisal time UC with the former Lysander. If that happened, the analogy in nature would be the dislocation of the natural cycles that would occur if the moon left its regular circular orbit to "creep" (3.2.54) through the center of the earth and produce an eclipse.[14] For her, such a cosmos and such a Lysander are equally impossible, even though she has dreamed of a split Lysander (2.2.145–56) and has in the opening scene warned him about deserting.

To Hermia's mind, the destructive force is Demetrius. A part of the fun is to watch the characters using metaphorical patterns that reflect confidence in their own values. When a self-righteous <UR> Hermia charges that Demetrius is "oe'r shoes in blood," "dead" (deathly pale), and "grim" through murdering LR the sunlike Lysander and disrupting their bright day, a Petrarchan Demetrius claims the bloodiness and paleness of a metaphorical victim LL, not a murderer, and protests that she, far from losing her brightness UC, still compares with "Venus in her glimmering sphere" (3.2.48, 57, 61). When an exasperated Demetrius bluntly tells Hermia, "I had rather give his [Lysander's] carcass to my hounds" than give him to her, she assumes a murder and calls him a "dog" and "cur" (3.2.64, 65), thereby associating him with his hungry hounds. If he has killed Lysander, he should "be never numb'red among men!" (3.2.67). If he has killed him while sleeping, he would be a cowardly "worm" or lying "adder," or even worse a "serpent" LR (3.2.71, 73). If we remember her dream of Lysander as a serpent, we can appreciate the desperation in her assertion that

Demetrius is the evil serpent who has destroyed her paradise.

When Demetrius declares that there is no use in chasing her and sinks to the ground, the image of repose seems hopeful after his frantic chasing. But he has now swung to the opposite extreme of despair LC: he describes sleep as a bankrupt who will not pay his debt of rest to Demetrius's sorrow, thus making sorrow even heavier. Since "heavier" (3.2.84) puns on drowsiness, Demetrius speculates that some slight offer of payment has been made and decides to take advantage of it. He sees sleep, not as a means of rejuvenation—"Nature's soft nurse" that "knits up the ravell'd sleeve of care"[15] [LL]—but as a temporary escape. Only through Oberon's potion will his despair be overcome and his impulse to love restored. Oberon's imagery is of the blood of renewal, not murder: love-in-idleness is "purple with love's wound" (2.1.167). Now Helena is "pale of cheer / With sighs of love, that costs the fresh blood dear;" the "purple dye" of the love potion, "Hit with Cupid's archery," will restore sanguinity UC to the "apple of his [Demetrius's] eye" and will make her "shine as gloriously / As the Venus of the sky" UC (3.2.96–97, 102–07).

Even though Hermia remains courageous and Helena despairing, they agree in questioning whether men who behave as Demetrius and Lysander do can properly be considered men. On the one hand, Bottom is an ass who behaves like a gentleman and Snout a stage lion who must explain that he is "a man as other men are" (3.1.44); on the other, Demetrius and Lysander make grand claims but are accurately described by the women's animal imagery LR. Their reprimands are now replaced by pleas to be as gentlemanly UR as they claim to be. Helena tells them they would not mock her "If you were men, as men you are in show" (3.2.151). Both Hermia and Helena struggle to maintain their feminine virtues and to get the men to recognize the contradiction between their fine speeches and their actual behavior. Helena argues that "If you were civil and knew courtesy, / You would not do me thus much injury" (3.2.147–48). Hermia tells Demetrius: "thou driv'st me past the bounds / Of maiden's patience"; and Helena tells Lysander and Demetrius that "None of noble sort / Would so offend a virgin" (3.2.65–66;159–60).

The women's pleas for courtesy UR and loyalty UL, however, risk pulling them to their own version of chivalric excess. Lysander and Hermia attracted Puck's attention in the first place partly because of Hermia's insistence on sleeping apart. Now Helena laments that Hermia is going against the "sisters' vows" (3.2.199) of their childhood friendship.[16] The "childhood innocence" (3.2.202) that she celebrates parallels the paradise <UC> of Athens that Hermia experienced before she fell in love and the pastoral wood <UC> the naive lovers expected to find. Their art in producing the sampler is charming but dangerously static, and their "double cherry" (3.2.209) of unity is vulnerable. Chiding "the hasty-footed time" (3.2.200) is a futile gesture if it does not lead to a mature recognition of mutability. Only through adjusting to change and finding new patterns of relationships can there be true love and friendship UC.[17]

The major movement of the scene is toward disintegration LC—the active conflict LR of the men and the weariness and despair LC of the women. When Oberon has Robin "overcast the night" "With drooping fog as black as Acheron" (3.2.355, 357), the night becomes a dark pseudo-hell <LC> that protects the men from actual encounters but also serves as a symbol of how chaotic their lives have become. Both sight and hearing are now unreliable. Earlier, a naive Hermia has praised the "Dark night" (3.2.177) for doubling the power of hearing to allow her to find Lysander, but Puck now makes the men's hearing as deceptive as their sight. The wandering of the women in the last part of the scene has become purposeless. The slight indications that Helena is trying to get away from Hermia and that Hermia is pursuing Helena seem like barely plausible, conscious reasons for wandering that fail to disguise their underlying lack of direction. They are to chase "Till o'er their brows death-counterfeiting sleep / With leaden legs and batty wings doth creep" (3.2.364–65). This grotesque linking of sleep with death controls the mood of the scene's ending. Both women have talked about finding death if they do not find love (2.2.156; 3.2.244).

All of the lovers mention the coming day, but their attitudes toward it are twisted. The men see it as a time for continuing their conflict. Lysander calls it "gentle day" but will use it to "find Demetrius and revenge this spite;" Demetrius says, "Thou shalt buy this dear, / If ever I thy face by daylight see" (3.2.418, 420, 426–27). The women are despondent. Helena asks for "comforts, from the east" but wants to get away not only "From these that my poor company detest" but also through sleep "from mine own company" (3.2.432, 434, 436). She recalls "sleep, that sometimes shuts up sorrow's eye" (3.2.435), but, like Demetrius earlier (3.2.84–87), sees little hope of a restorative sleep [LL] for herself. Hermia maintains her love for Lysander, but she too sounds despairing, with even the dew <LL>, usually the image of a watery moon's concern, now contributing only to her misery (3.2.443). Their sleep is a death-in-life UC that returns them to the earth without much hope for a dawn of renewal.

Our view is different: their wood of nightmare and illusion must be measured against our fuller knowledge. Going to the wood proves to be the beginning of the solution even though chaos is the first result. In Shakespeare's drama, a part of the healthy wonder of human nature is that we are and should be incapable of going against what our deepest selves tell us is right. Love may be irrational but can also be magical. Shakespeare seems to understand Freud's point that people who try to be fully rational end up repressing feelings that will break out somewhere. Seen from this perspective, people's problems are also their strength, and the solutions could not have been worked out if the lovers had not thrown themselves fully into their experience. Helena has no idea what the result of chasing Demetrius into the wood will be; Lysander and Hermia's plan is probably no solution, but they all act as they do because there is nothing else they can do if they are to be true to their natures. Such a view is not fatalistic. Shakespeare is not showing that people have no control over their actions but only that emotions are powerful and potentially beneficial. Understanding ourselves turns out to be as complicated as understanding the universe: in the Shakespearean world, to understand the microcosm of ourselves is to understand the macrocosm of the cosmos. Love is a mystery best described by the artist's symbolic methods.

If the fairy world is Shakespeare's attempt to depict the deeper reality of nature, then the fairies' concern suggests the presence of some beneficent force—Oberon's version of "night-rule"—in the universe despite all the tendencies toward conflict and disorder. What this might be is never spelled out, but it has something to do with love. Maybe we should call it *caritas* and link it to the Augustinian tradition of the power of divine love UC. Or maybe we should simply say it is parallel to the force that brings the spring and makes the sun come up. It is the opposite of the entropy that modern physicists see as characteristic of the physical world and has some similarities to the chaos theory that postulates a deeper pattern under the surface manifestations of disorder.[18] Whatever it is, it leads Oberon to strive for peace with Titania and to bring order to the mortals as well. We should not see it in narrowly religious terms: Oberon is not simply a God-figure or a grace-figure, and we should recognize that people are in constant danger of accepting the illusion <UC> of love and order as a reality: in a fallen world genuine order is impossible. Nevertheless, Shakespeare seems to see a force within nature and within people that works toward health and stability. In drama, that force can be expressed through the vehicle of comedy.

NINE

The Concord of This Discord

(*A Midsummer Night's Dream* 3.2.366–end)

THESEUS. How shall we find the concord of this discord?

(5.1.60)

I n the last section of the play, Puck's "night-rule" LC (3.2.5) is replaced, first by order and harmony UC in the wood and then by an analogous "concord" UC in Athens. The key scenes in the movement toward renewal take place at dawn in the wood and in the evening at court. Symbolically that is appropriate. We have gone from the disorder of day in the court to the disorder of night in the wood. Now we find proper fusions—the order of day in the wood and of night in the court, and the harmony of mystery and revel with authority and hierarchy. The sleep of the lovers as the dawn begins to appear

PATTERNS
OF
METAPHOR

A MIDSUMMER NIGHT'S DREAM IV
(3.2.366 – 5.1)

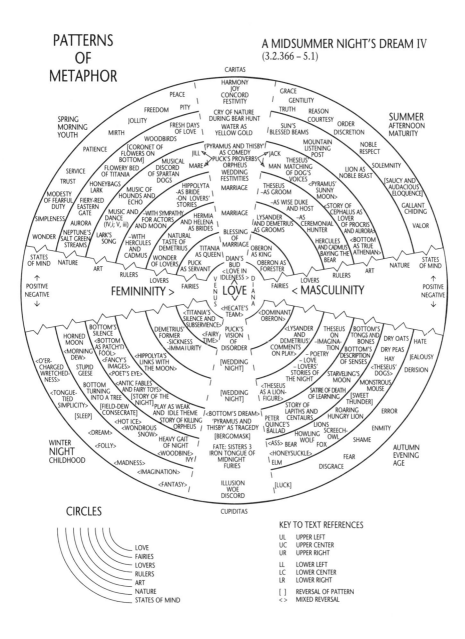

CARITAS

CUPIDITAS

CIRCLES

LOVE
FAIRIES
LOVERS
RULERS
ART
NATURE
STATES OF MIND

KEY TO TEXT REFERENCES

UL   UPPER LEFT
UC   UPPER CENTER
UR   UPPER RIGHT

LL   LOWER LEFT
LC   LOWER CENTER
LR   LOWER RIGHT

[ ]   REVERSAL OF PATTERN
< >   MIXED REVERSAL

is restorative, and their participation in the revels of the ending moves from wonder to festivity. The image of dawn joins that of May morning as images of the new time beginning for the lovers. Oberon and Theseus serve as analogous rulers as they preside benevolently over both wood and court. They are also surrogate playwrights who through their power shape the resolutions of comedy.

Shakespeare produces a complex ending by suggesting both the value of order UR and the danger of domination LR. Both Oberon and Theseus—embodiments of the masculine in nature and society—continue to reflect not always appropriate attitudes and methods. Putting the stress on the "discord" LC of their control leads some to deplore their heavy-handed application of power LR and to explain Shakespeare's need to bow to patriarchal ideology.[1] This approach is deconstructionist in its conclusion that pressures lead the work away from coherent form. From such a perspective, comedy itself becomes a reductive instrument that supports patriarchal ideology. My contention is that Shakespearean irony undercuts patriarchal assumptions while still recognizing the need for responsible leadership that will balance gender polarities. Comedy points to ideals but also reveals limitations. If we are to find "the concord of this discord" without minimizing either, we must seek it in the analogous, often ironic, polarities and fusions of Renaissance art and culture.

Oberon's idealistic hopes for the world and his image of his own virtues always seem partly illusory <UC>. He blames Puck (3.2.345–46) for all his problems with the young lovers even though his own motives and planning have been suspect. The promised release of Titania comes only after another quarrel: he later tells Puck that when he met her he "did upbraid her, and fall out with her" (4.1.50) before eventually having compassion. He has created the illusion of a hellish night <LC> in order to reconcile the lovers but may misjudge the nature of evil itself. When Puck urges haste because of the approaching day, he makes the night that has been disorderly, even chaotic, seem more conventionally evil. Morning is so close that "ghosts, wand'ring here and there, / Troop home to churchyards" and "Damned spirits" return to their "wormy beds" (3.2.381–82, 384). In Puck's description, the stress falls on the mental suffering of despairing wanderers LC who can find no way to escape the consequences of their sins. They "willfully themselves exile from light" rather than face a day that reveals their "shames" and so, in contrast to the permanence in love promised by Oberon a few lines earlier, "must for aye consort with black-brow'd Night" (3.2.385–87). The "Damned spirits" are most obviously parallel to the young lovers whose fight in a hell-like fog suggests one potential destination; but Oberon and Puck are themselves spirits of the night whose actions in creating an atmosphere of hell and tormenting the lovers LR might also attract the attention of judging day UR.

In his reply to Puck, Oberon identifies their difference—"we are spirits of another sort" (3.2.388)—and celebrates their compatibility with the day. But even here a troublesome allusion intrudes: Oberon speaks of "sport" with "the Morning's love" (3.2.389), probably a deliberately ambiguous reference to the disastrous love affair UC between a naive Cephalus and a seductive, jealous Aurora.[2] Since Oberon has shown himself to be particularly susceptible to women and since "sport" has taken on unfavorable connotations, the reference encourages a nagging doubt about Oberon's activities. Nevertheless, his description is impressive when viewed in a paradisal context UC. The lines suggest that the night can still be active in the early morning and that the dawn remains properly feminine in its relationship with both the still rising sun and early morning hunters. The overarching marriages UC of the masculine day and sun to the feminine night and moon are in the background, and when the sun itself appears at "the eastern gate" (3.2.391), the

masculine gods of the night (Oberon) and sea (Neptune)
take on properly passive roles [LL]. This sun transmits
"fair blessed beams" (3.2.392), in contrast to the judging day <UR> of Puck's speech and to "Titan's [fiery]
wheels" <UR>, which threaten the "drunkard" "darkness" in the Friar's dawn speech in *Romeo and Juliet*.
Day and night need each other: here, day's fire is added to
night's water and earth with spectacular results. The
heat and light of the "fiery red" (3.2.391) dawn (itself the
result of the sun's union with Aurora) combine with the
moisture of the sea to produce the conditions for growth
as well as beauty; more specifically, heat and moisture
together suggest the sanguinity of youth and the renewal
of the day and the year UC. In alchemy, the mysterious marrying of fire and water produces first a salt base
and ultimately gold UC. Here, the "fiery red" dawn's
"blessed beams" turn the "salt green streams" to "yellow gold" (3.2.391–93). The further suggestion of harvest
in green becoming gold may remind us that Eden UC
combines the fullness of autumn and the freshness of
spring.[3] The paradisal overtones of these natural marriages—sun and moon, day and night, and fire and water—presage the joyful unions of the lovers at the end of
the play.

In the last part of the scene, Puck returns to his role as
a force whose effect on the lovers has as much to do with
his own spirit as with Oberon's commands. On the one
hand, he seems to have forgotten the need for haste and
to delight in the power LR he has: "I will lead them up
and down; / I am fear'd in field and town," and later he
seems pleased that "Cupid is a knavish lad, / Thus to
make poor females mad" (3.2.397–98, 440–41). Another
side of his nature UR, though clearly connected to his
role as Oberon's servant, seems to want a happy resolution for the lovers. His allusion to the "country proverb"
about getting Jack and Jill, and the man and his mare, together by applying "remedy" (3.2.458, 452) belongs to the
language of folklore. In the popular imagination, Robin

Goodfellow is a bringer of joy as well as misery. Puck is more mischievous than Oberon, but he is not just a bringer of chaos.

In 4.1, both the conflict and the reunion of Oberon and Titania are presented through patterned nature imagery. Oberon watches Titania and Bottom's version of paradisal living, which seems to involve becoming as much a part of nature itself as possible. If we see a Titania who is still a force of nature as an influence on this change, the scene makes more sense. When Titania gets Bottom to "sit thee down upon this flow'ry bed," she begins to "stick musk-roses in thy sleek smooth head" (4.1.1, 3). As the scene proceeds, he asks for food and pleasures that reflect his increasingly limited awareness LR as he moves toward sleep. His lively opening speech about getting Cobweb to "bring me a honey-bag" degenerates to shorter requests for "dry oats," "sweet hay," and finally for "a handful or two of dried peas" (4.1.13, 32, 33, 37–38). When he falls asleep, he becomes a metaphorical tree and an aggressive Titania the ivy around it: "Sleep thou, and I will wind thee in my arms;" "So doth the woodbine the sweet honeysuckle / Gently entwist; the female ivy so / Enrings the barky fingers of the elm" (4.1.40, 42–44). To have ivy instead of the usual vine around the elm makes the image one of illicit passion LC rather than marriage UC, thereby suggesting the quality of Titania's interest in Bottom.[4] Bottom, in turn, is at least metaphorically transformed again, as his animal asshead (possibly wooden) seems to be taking on a wooden body as well. He is descending from animal to inert tree LC under Titania's influence, and a fertility rite beyond Titania's powers will be needed to rouse him.

This ludicrous image of adulterous love evokes pity rather than jealousy in Oberon as Titania's earlier devotion to the vegetative takes precedence over her more recent passion for the animal. To Oberon, the "coronet of fresh and fragrant flowers" UL Titania has put on Bottom's "hairy temples" is a further affront that offends even the flowers' dew which "Stood" "Like tears that did their own disgrace bewail" (4.1.52, 51, 55, 56). Dew in the play can be either the life-giving moisture of nature's renewal UL or the tears LL or excessive moisture that retard growth. Oberon's "round and orient pearls" and Lysander's "liquid pearl" UL (4.1.54; 1.1.211) contrast with these tears, with the tears of the flowers and the moon when Titania takes Bottom to her bower (3.1.198–200), and with the morning dew that contributes to Hermia's suffering.[5] The image pattern comes to a meaningful conclusion with the "field-dew consecrate" (5.1. 415) that Oberon uses to bless the marriages at the end of the play. Here, the natural dew takes on a supernatural dimension, obliquely suggesting a sacred grace UC analogous to that of God.

Oberon restores Titania through the "force and blessed power" of "Dian's bud o'er Cupid's flower" (4.1.73). Both goddesses have positive and negative dimensions. As we have seen, Diana can be associated with the cold chastity of unfulfilled femininity LR or with a natural growth UL to mature self-confidence UR. Here, the latter is clearly implied. The bud's moisture is as natural as dew but, like communion wine or divine *caritas* UC, purges and transforms higher beings than plants. The renewal restores Titania to an unfallen condition and suggests an Oberon with the power of grace UC even though he continues to be motivated partly by his desire to reassert a rigid patriarchal control LR.[6] Significantly, the impulse that breaks the impasse comes from Titania, who "in mild terms begg'd my patience" and quickly gave up the "changeling child" (4.1.58–59). Feminine emotion UL has its impact on masculine severity UR, as it does with Eve and Adam in *Paradise Lost*, book 10. Cupid's flower, love-in-idleness, while often connected to foolish and irrational love [UC], error associated with *cupiditas*, can also have a positive function UC, as its application to Demetrius in 3.2 makes clear. In using love-in-idleness instead of Dian's bud, Oberon implies an uncertainty about whether Demetrius ever loved Helena. He needs to be touched by love, not just restored to his previous state. Apparently, the way in which the potion is applied—its spirit and the words accompanying it— also makes a difference.[7] When Oberon orders it for Demetrius in 2.1, he is thinking more about torment LR than reconciliation UC: he cautions Puck, "Effect it with some care, that he may prove / More fond on her than she upon her love" (2.1.265–66). When he applies it to Demetrius in the later scene, he wants Helena to "shine as gloriously / As the Venus of the sky" (3.2.106–07). Here, the love will be elevated rather than doting, with this noble Venus being understood as the polar opposite of the illusory "Venus in her glimmering sphere" (3.2.61) to whom Demetrius has just compared Hermia. There is a difference between foolishly destructive love and love that positive forces move toward marriage.

In the scene of Oberon and Titania's reconciliation, imagery of music and dance functions analogously to the potions.[8] After first using music to put the young lovers into a charmed state, "more dead / Than common sleep" <LC>, Oberon asks Titania to "take hands with me, / And rock the ground whereon these sleepers be" (4.1.81–82, 85–86). The harmony of the music and dance UC communicates something mysteriously renewing to the dormant lovers, and Oberon suggests that the same harmony will be present at the wedding festivities that they will bless. When Oberon tells Titania to be quiet—"Silence a while"—and later speaks of their departure "in silence sad [that is, serious]" (4.2.80, 95), he is creating the necessary atmosphere for the remarkable music and for their journey. This expectant quiet at dawn UL is opposite the "Night and silence" LC (2.1.70) that Puck mentions just before initiating the chaos LC by putting the potion on Lysander by mistake. On a more mundane level, Oberon also seems to fear that Titania's talk will renew their quarrels. As they leave, his control remains in doubt: she is anything but silent as she tells him that

he can explain "in our flight" (4.1.99) what has happened. Nevertheless, Oberon seems certain that the renewal that brings the lovers to themselves will bring
marriage as well. The sound of the lark, nature's herald
of the morning <UL>, here more beneficent than in
Romeo and Juliet,[9] sends Oberon and his company off.
Another sound of the morning, the winding of horns UL,
announces the coming of Theseus and the hunters.
Oberon and Theseus do not meet, both because they
function on different planes of reality and because one
actor is most likely playing both parts, but a promising
though fragile harmony <UC> exists.

Theseus's journey to the wood parallels in various
ways Oberon's experience with the dawn. He comes to
the wood primarily as a lover and worshiper [LL], not as a
soldier or hunter. His morning progress has included an
"observation" (4.1.104), a ritual celebration of the dawn
UL, and is about to become a ceremonial hunt UR in
which charming Hippolyta is more important than hunting. Hunts can suggest pursuit of the physical LR or a
search for something higher UL.[10] Theseus would no
doubt identify with the loftier goal, but our memory of
the passion-ridden Theseus of the first scene implies that
some question still remains. From his own perspective,
the hunt extends his realm to include the natural UL as
well as the civilized UR and illustrates how order and
freedom can be made harmonious UC. On another level,
the hounds' harmony suggests the orderly passion of his
love. The dogs' barking, "match'd in mouth like bells,"
when heard from the mountain top will produce "the
musical confusion / Of hounds and echo in conjunction"
(4.1.123, 110–11). The freedom UL suggested by the order
to "let them go" (4.1.107) and the transcendence UC implied by the mountain top listening point contribute to
the effect.

Hippolyta describes a hunt with Hercules and Cad-
mus where the harmonious barking of the dogs UL was a
part of the baying UR of a bear LR. Hippolyta gives full

recognition to the stature of the hounds and the hunters UR, and implies that the harmony involved reflects both the ordered passions of the self and a just venture against the bestial. It affects all of nature: the "discord" LC became "musical" UC and the "thunder" LR "sweet" UC (4.1.118) through mysterious sympathy with the heroic cause. The bear is analogous to the lion LR of "Pyramus and Thisby" and to the various wild beasts of the wood scenes.[11] If we pursue the analogy, Theseus would be like the bear if he were to renew his aggression against Hippolyta, and a Diana-like Hippolyta UL would legitimately resist him.

In this setting and time—the wood at dawn in spring UL—a sense of mysterious powers dominates, but there is room for playfulness as well. We see a new Theseus who seems to want to illustrate the relaxed ease of his rule. Instead of taking offense at Hippolyta's mention of Hercules, whose heroic activities frequently parallel those of Theseus himself, he uses humor that implies a modestly ironic perspective. While his dogs are also musical and "of the Spartan kind" (4.1.119), he describes their faintly absurd characteristics in a way that allows him to deflect but not deny the high seriousness of Hippolyta's speech: they are "Crook-knee'd, and dewlapp'd like Thessalian bulls" and "Slow in pursuit" <LR> (4.1.122, 123).[12] That their "ears . . . sweep away the morning dew" (4.1.121) sounds like a mild gibe at their imperfection. When Theseus and Hippolyta come upon the lovers, Theseus continues his festive mood of good-natured amity as he jokes about "wood-birds" UL that "couple" when "Saint Valentine is past" (4.1.140, 139). He also sounds pleased with the change from "hatred" and "hate" LR to "gentle concord" UC (4.1.143–45). Only Egeus proves to be a discordant figure LR in this holiday atmosphere, and his objections are quickly overruled.

The lovers' and later Bottom's responses to their experiences, as well as Theseus and Hippolyta's responses to the lovers' "story of the night" (5.1.23), become the major topic in the next part of the play. The reactions fall into two broad categories—a masculine suspicion <LR> based on belief in rationality and order UR and a feminine willingness UL to explore and accept the mysterious. Oberon has told Puck that "When they next wake, all this derision / Shall seem a dream and fruitless vision" (3.2.370–71). His motives are benevolent, but his implication that dreams can be dismissed as unimportant LR is analogous to Theseus's later skepticism LR about imagination. On the other hand, women and lovers follow their impulse to raise questions, express feelings, and explore mysteries. An analogy develops among various subjective experiences—dream, love, poetry, madness, illusion, and fantasy <LC>—as exploration of the metaphorical night leads to deeper insights about life and love.

When the lovers awake, they are full of sleepy wonder [LL] at the miracle of a renewal that we know has come through the potion. Lysander has changed his attitude not only toward Hermia but also toward truth. In the first scene, he and Hermia stole off to escape patriarchal authority. Now, after insisting on his openness UL—"for truly would I speak" (4.1.149)—he tells the whole story of their escape. The potion, designed to remove "all error" (3.1.368), has restored their innocent trust UL in themselves and their society. When Egeus, failing this trust by once again trying to impose his will LR, charges that "They would have stol'n away" (4.1.156) and asks for Demetrius's support, a transformed Demetrius also tells the whole truth. For Demetrius, the potion has changed the whole period of his love for Hermia into a "fruitless vision" LC (3.2.371). Now he speaks of his love for Hermia as snow that has melted, as a childish "idle gaud" LL, and as a "sickness" LL that has led him away from his "natural taste" (4.1.167, 173, 174). Earlier images of snow and hail LR (1.1.243–45; 3.2.141–42), of childishness LL and "gawds" (1.1.240, 33), and of disease

LL, (1.1.142, 186; 2.1.212–13; 2.2.137–38), all in the context of immature love, have prepared us for these references. Demetrius may still be under the influence of the potion, but the potion itself has become a metaphor for the mystery of harmonious love UC.

In overruling Egeus, Theseus reveals a wisdom based partly on his knowledge of what will bring order UR but also on his own love UC (and emblematically on being in the wood). After the rulers leave, the strange mood continues. Helena thinks of Demetrius as a "jewel" she has "found" that is "Mine own, and not mine own" while Demetrius wonders if "yet we sleep, we dream" (4.1.191–94). When the lovers decide to "recount our dreams," their openness UL recalls Hermia and Helena "Emptying our bosoms of their counsel [sweet]" (4.1.199; 1.1.216). Without truth and trust UL, love and friendship lack a solid basis, as all of the lovers now instinctively realize. Without these qualities, the order UR of the society is also endangered.

Bottom is less successful at discovering and communicating what has happened in the wood, but he too knows that he has experienced something remarkable, something beyond the ability of the senses to comprehend. As he puts it in his unconscious parody of 1 Corinthians 2.9, "The eye of man hath not heard, the ear of man hath not seen, man's hand is not able to taste, his tongue to conceive, nor his heart to report, what my dream was" (4.1.211–14). The passage from St. Paul, itself a paraphrase of Isaiah 64.4, reads: "Eye hath not seen, nor ear heard, neither have entered into the heart of man, the things which God hath prepared for them that love him." Bottom lacks this ability to understand a deeper spiritual or imaginative reality [LC]. The attributes of mind and soul that would lead him to appreciate what has happened are analogous to a more profound approach to religious mystery. He says that "man is but [a patch'd] fool, if he will offer to say what methought I had" (4.1.209–11). Perhaps to reveal that he has had an asshead would be folly in Athens, but we should remember the Pauline injunction to become a "fool for Christ" and the traditional association of the ass with divine inspiration and of the fool [LC] with wisdom. In becoming a "[patch'd] fool," Bottom might take on some of the imaginative qualities of Puck as jester. In refusing such a role, though, Bottom remains one of the "crew of patches, rude mechanicals" LR (3.2.9), that Puck describes earlier and thereby limits himself to an earthly and not very profound reality.[13] In the Geneva Bible, which Shakespeare probably knew, the passage from Corinthians goes on: "for the Spirite searcheth all thinges, yea, the botome of Goddes secretes."[14] God's secrets have a bottom even though Bottom's dream does not. This Bottom is not likely to get to the bottom of anything.

Nevertheless, Bottom's instinct that art UC may be the means of expressing such an experience is sound, even though a ballad by Peter Quince would not be likely to penetrate beneath any surfaces.[15] Nor would singing such a ballad just before Thisby's death make much sense, unless it could somehow reveal a deeper unity behind life and death. Bottom may have caught a glimpse of some deeper truths about life and about art's role in interpreting it, and his jumbled report, like his confusions in other scenes, may reflect the discord LC of life even more accurately than scientific analysis, but the Bottom who is fully awake in the next scene is reluctant to risk ridicule through telling such a wild story. His initial impulse to "discourse wonders" [LC] is restrained by his awareness LR that "if I tell you, I am [no] true Athenian"; he next considers factual reporting—"I will tell you every thing, right as it fell out"—and finally decides to keep quiet altogether—"Not a word of me" (4.2.29–32, 34). Unlike the lovers, Bottom and the other artisans are never shown discussing their night: their silence tells us something about both them and the Athens <LR> that shapes their values. Before Bottom arrives, Snug laments that "If our sport had gone forward, we had all been made men," and Flute regrets that Bottom has "lost sixpence a day during his life" (4.2.17–20). That practical concern provides an ironic context for their part in the final act.[16]

In contrast to the artisans, the reunited lovers do talk among themselves and then go on to share their "story of the night" (5.1.23) <LC> with Theseus and Hippolyta. This story is omitted from the play; Shakespeare apparently decided that the generic conventions of romance and Theseus and Hippolyta's comments could communicate the underlying significance. In telling their "story," the trusting, truthful lovers UL would shape another version of what we have just seen. By transforming their memories of what happened from actuality to dream, Shakespeare makes their dream <LC> parallel to his play <UC> and encourages our attention to literary form. While Shakespeare has produced a sophisticated fusion of generic forms in his play, the lovers apparently fit the experience into their own favorite form, the romance <LL>. Their open wonder and their eagerness to "recount our dreams" (4.2.199) suggest the enthusiasm UL with which they approach their discussion. As we saw in chapter 6, their assumptions about love and life so closely parallel their self-conscious reading of "tale or history" (1.1.133) that we can see them as "unmetaphored" characters.[17] Lysander has worried that "quick bright things come to confusion" LC, but Hermia has insisted that "patience" UL can bring "poor fancy's followers" [LL] through their "trial" (1.1.149, 152, 155). Now they have gone through a dream experience that restores their faith that romances can end happily UC. In contrast to "Pyramus and Thisby" (and *Romeo and Juliet*), their story is to end in "jollity" (4.1.92). Theseus says the lovers are "full of joy and mirth" (5.1.28). A "joy" UC based on the optimism appropriate to romance lovers and "mirth" that avoids excessive sport LR govern their genial participation in the revels that follow.

Shakespeare uses Theseus and Hippolyta's responses

to the lovers' story as a way of emphasizing the opposite responses that such attitudes and stories evoke. At issue is not just the lovers' experience but, by analogy, all of the qualities and perspectives of the feminine night. While the lovers' earlier passive wonder [LL] seems to have delighted Theseus, he has a much cooler reaction LR to their accounts of their dreams. His skeptical words to Hippolyta imply something about both the form and content of their recollections: "I never may believe / These antic fables, nor these fairy toys" (5.1.2–3). Since no one except Bottom has actually seen fairies (and he has not talked to Theseus), we might wonder what he means. Unless we postulate a slip by Shakespeare (always a dangerous supposition), the lovers have explained the odd conjunctions of their dreams by referring to the fairies and fables appropriate to romance. Theseus and Hippolyta agree that what they report is "strange," but Theseus thinks of it as "more strange than true" while Hippolyta sees it as "strange and admirable" (5.1.1, 2, 27). Theseus seems to be objecting not only to explanations that go beyond what the reason can accept but also to stories of this kind, while Hippolyta notes that "all their minds transfigur'd so together, / More witnesseth than fancy's images, / And grows to something of great constancy" (5.1.24–26). While a philosophical Theseus moves quickly to generalizations, a more art-oriented Hippolyta brings the question back to the form of the lovers' story.

If we see Theseus as picking his specific examples of love and madness from the lovers' story, then he may also be ridiculing them directly. (A production could help make the point by having the lovers on stage before their entrance at line 28.) When he mentions that the lunatic "sees more devils than vast hell can hold" (5.1.9), the charge has more point if he has heard the phenomena of the lovers' night explained as the work of "devils." His description of a lover's ability to see "Helen's beauty in a brow of Egypt" (5.1.11) makes more sense if Theseus is punning on the young men's ability to see Helena's fair beauty in the darker Hermia. (If Hippolyta is also fair, the point would have flattering overtones as well.) "The poet's eye, in a fine frenzy rolling" sounds suspiciously like Lysander's eyes in Oberon's command that Puck "make his eyeballs roll with wonted sight" (5.1.12; 3.2.369). The elaborately poetic young men may very well provide the examples for Theseus's image of the poet. A specific reference to the fleeing artisans (3.1.105–11), may be present when Theseus concludes: "Or in the night, imagining some fear, / How easy is a bush suppos'd a bear!" (5.1.21–22). He has no way of knowing that, but the parallel is close and also makes the other allusions more likely. If Hippolyta has implied a veiled threat to Theseus as being potentially like the bear that she and her companions have bayed,[18] then Theseus may also be suggesting that she is imagining things if she thinks he is an aggressive bear.

Whether or not the examples are this specific, they illustrate the qualities of imagination that Theseus criticizes UR and Hippolyta respects UL. The lovers have the poet's ecstatic vision [LC] that glimpses a higher reality UC even though not always achieving it: dream, the "tale or history" (1.1.133) of romance, love tragedy like *Romeo and Juliet*, Petrarchan sonnets, indeed any creation in art or life that reflects or encourages such responses, are analogous ([LL] or [LC]).

Theseus, the most Athenian character in the play, makes telling criticisms of the excesses of the lovers but fails to get a broad enough perspective.[19] For him, there is little possibility that the lunatic, the lover, and the poet—and the young lovers—will see deeper truths that the reason cannot reach. With his masculine, rational, and orderly perspective UR, he will dismiss as illusion [UC] everything that cannot be described precisely and analytically. When Theseus describes the lover, he criticizes experience that may be based on wonder [LL] rather than illusion. When he describes the poet, he provides a perceptive account of what Shakespeare has accomplished in the play. Only one change is needed: the "forms of things unknown" that the "imagination bodies forth" (5.1.14–15) should be seen as reflecting the intangible, but nevertheless real [LC], feminine dimension of the natural order. Theseus believes in the "forms of things" UR, but his hierarchies have little place for "things unknown" LC. Recent criticism has given full value to Hippolyta's deeper vision [LC]. Within the context of the play Hippolyta is right: something did happen in the wood, and Theseus is shortsighted not to see that. But privileging her version denies us the advantage we have in experiencing Shakespeare's more balanced account. What Theseus says about illusion <UC> also includes much that is true: the play's reconciliations do provide some reason for optimism but not for much confidence in the processes of love.

Throughout the last act, Theseus and Hippolyta's exchanges continue to reflect how gender affects attitudes to life. Though Hippolyta can tell Theseus about the wood, she has something to learn about the court. Theseus's dogmatism LR exacerbated conflict in the opening scene; now he rules with a lighter UL touch and encourages everyone to feel a part of the revels. He understands that illusion brings the lovers "joy" UC (5.1.29) and that even the artisans' bad play can have a function: "never any thing can be amiss, / When simpleness and duty tender it" (5.1.82–83). When Hippolyta worries that the artisans will fail, Theseus reassures her: "Our sport shall be to take what they mistake; / And what poor duty cannot do, noble respect / Takes it in might, not merit" (5.1.90–92). They will make sport <LR> of the production in such a way that the participants will be flattered, not offended. As illustration of his skill in avoiding bad feelings, Theseus explains that he prefers "the modesty of fearful duty" [LL] to "the rattling tongue / Of saucy and audacious eloquence" LR (5.1.101–03). When Hippolyta is "a-weary of this moon," Theseus replies that "courtesy" and "reason" UR (5.1.251, 254, 255) require them to stay until the end. One pattern of the last act is Hippolyta's gradual relaxation as she realizes that authority can be gracious UC. Hippolyta injects several comments that suggest her attempt to get more involved and even sounds like Theseus <LR> when she describes the prologue's speech as "like a child on a recorder—a sound, but not in government" (5.1.122–24).

The philosophy that lies behind Theseus's ability in governing has inherent limitations, however. He may exhibit superficial "respect" <UR> (5.1.90) for his subjects, but any relationship based on illusion and deception LR risks destroying the deeper trust upon which their traditional values are grounded. Art itself can easily drift toward a glorification of patriarchal power that prefers order to truth. When Hippolyta turns critic and calls the play "the silliest stuff that ever I heard," Theseus counters with a defence of the imagination that he has earlier criticized in a different context: "The best in this kind are but shadows; and the worst are no worse, if imagination amend them" (5.1.210, 211–12). While this positive claim for imagination has the virtue of inviting audience involvement, it also suggests that art's "shadows" <LL> and "imagination" <UL> itself are acceptable only if they serve reason and order [UR].

When Theseus chooses the artisans' production of "Pyramus and Thisby," he rejects three other possibilities that have direct relevance to themes in the play. Two illustrate extremes of masculine and feminine behavior. The first—"'The battle with the Centaurs, to be sung / By an Athenian eunuch to the harp'" (5.1.44–45)—concerns unruly passion, indeed the attempted rape LR of a bride and the bloody prevention of that act by the brute force <UR> of Hercules, Theseus, and others.[20] Such a crushing illustration of masculine power might seem a little too relevant to what has led up to this wedding, particularly since Theseus himself was involved. That he has already told the story to Hippolyta has ominous overtones even though the violence was in support of the bride. The opposite extreme would be present in "'The riot of the tipsy Bacchanals, / Tearing the Thracian singer in their rage'" (5.1.48–49). What would be shown is the murder of Orpheus, a figure who symbolizes both order and inspiration UC, by passionate women LR.[21] While Hippolyta was no "Bacchanal," she was the leader of a group of women with violent inclinations and might be offended. The third possible presentation is also about death, with an apparent topical reference to Tasso or Greene included;[22] the "Muses" would be "mourning for the death / Of Learning, late deceas'd in beggary" (5.1.52–53). Theseus states directly that this "satire, keen and critical" <LR> would be inappropriate for a "nuptial ceremony" (5.1.54–55). Shakespeare's audience may also recognize that satire <LR> of any kind would be improper at their own aristocratic wedding.

In "Pyramus and Thisby,"[23] Shakespeare gets another opportunity to explore the relationships between comedy and tragedy, masculinity and femininity, and illusion and reality. The play will be "'A tedious brief scene of young Pyramus / And his love Thisby; very tragical mirth'" (5.1.56–57). Theseus calls attention to both the paradox and the humor of such an undertaking: "Merry and tragical? Tedious and brief? / That is hot ice and wondrous strange snow" (5.1.58–59). He also asks: "How shall we find the concord of this discord?" (5.1.60). His witty use of the language of paradoxes and polarities may encourage the Shakespearean audience to expect a comic version of a literary microcosm and to compare it with both the larger play and with *Romeo and Juliet*. Shakespeare has used the artisans' antics for his own ends from the beginning, and now like them he needs something appropriate for a wedding. In the first scene involving the artisans (1.2), he wants the parallels with the play's opening scene to be apparent. Planning parts for Pyramus and Thisby's parents recalls Egeus's opposition LR to the lovers (and *Romeo and Juliet*), and Bottom wants to play not only the young lovers but also a tyrant and a roaring lion LR that remind us of Theseus and Egeus. In 3.1, allusions to parents and tyranny are set aside as attention shifts to lovers and artisans struggling to find appropriate styles of behavior and art for dealing with situations that challenge their assumptions about life and genre. The lovers apply chivalric values <UR> in a nightmare LC context while the artisans seek a courteous UR way to tell a grim LC story. In 5.1, festive comedy UC dominates as overarching gender analogies continue in the parallels of Lion and Moonshine to Theseus and Hippolyta and of Pyramus and Thisby to the young lovers.

The connections of "Pyramus and Thisby" to the rest of the play and to *Romeo and Juliet* would have been particularly amusing to Shakespeare's first audience. As Noel Purdon has pointed out, part of the fun is that the actors have just enough idea of court drama to find language and symbols that unconsciously parody, not just other drama (and poetry) of the time, but also Shakespeare's own topics and methods in the play as a whole.[24] Their jumbled allusions to Lysander and Helen and to Cephalus and Procris recall the main plot but are ironically inaccurate and inappropriate.[25] Pyramus repeatedly exaggerates images that have been important in *Romeo and Juliet* as well as in *A Midsummer Night's Dream*. He swings from the naive optimism UL of his eulogy of the moon to a diatribe <LR> against the Furies, the Fates LC, and Nature itself. In his account of these forces acting against him and in his impatient misjudgment that his love is dead, we recognize parallels to *Romeo and Juliet* (1.4.106–11; 5.1.24). The feud between the families of *Romeo and Juliet* seems to be alluded to when Bottom answers Demetrius's jesting comment that Wall must help bury the dead: "No, I assure you, the wall is down that parted their fathers" (5.1.351–52). Bottom sounds frustrated that their point has not gotten across: his comment makes sense only to someone who understands more about the old story than they have been shown in this version. Bottom's reading suggests that he thinks the tragic story is suitable because of the reunion of the families UC. Theseus, too, has referred indirectly to the wall being down "between the two neighbors" (5.1. 206–07).[26]

But Shakespeare goes beyond literary satire to examine again what causes the breakdown LC of harmonious polarities. The artisans' version describes a "grim-look'd" night along with a friendly moon and a "vild" but "gentle" (5.1.170, 292, 227) lion. Even Wall switches from being "sweet," "lovely," and "courteous" to being "wicked" and "vild" (5.1.174, 178, 180, 200). When Pyramus says, "O, wherefore, Nature, didst thou lions frame?" (5.1.291), his grand apostrophe restates a major question: why is masculine power so destructive LR in a world supposedly governed by an orderly Nature UC? In the story it is, of course, not Lion's fault, but Shakespeare has to be careful in handling the link between the king of the beasts and the monarch, particularly since this lion is a lioness. When Theseus refers to Lion and Moonshine as "two noble beasts," "a man and a lion," Snug identifies himself as a man and says, "'twere pity on my life" "if I should, as lion, come in strife / Into this place" (5.1.217–18, 225–26). He seems to be recognizing that such pretensions would threaten the Duke as well as the ladies and elicits Theseus's reassurances. Joking about what makes a good monarch (or man) follows: a denial of "valor" UR may be due to foxlike "discretion" <UR> (5.1.231, 232), but a secure Theseus instead attributes it to gooselike stupidity LL.[27] Snug's lion belongs to the tired allegory of a beast fable, as the spectators imply by developing their ironically moralized emblems of this lion, a fox, and a goose. The Shakespeare who has used an ass and what I have called beast-fable metaphors thus calls attention to methods hilariously close to his own.[28]

The rich associations of the moon with Hippolyta and with the feminine dimension <UL> of experience get

similarly ludicrous development in the presentation of
Moonshine. Possible emblematic readings of the moon's
attributes—the link of the lantern with Diana's light, the
dog with Diana as huntress, the crescent horns with the
moon's renewal, and the man in the moon with Endymion or Cain—are left unexplained. This company can
only burlesque such symbolism, as the spectators once
again point out. Having the iconography explained by a
thin, apologetic old man "in the wane" LR (5.1.254) with
a lantern, and perhaps even a real dog, and with no idea
of what the moon has to do with this story, trivializes
the moon's mystery and reduces symbolism to ridiculous
pedantry LR.[29] Associating the "horned" (5.1.239) moon
with a man allows additions to the moon's already rich
iconography in the play through inevitable jokes about
the tumescence of the crescent moon and the horns of an
old moon, the necessary entry of the man into the moon,
and the previously lighted and now snuffed candle that
has beaten him into the feminine lantern. If Hippolyta is
identified iconographically with the moon by her cos-
tume, we can better understand why she is "a-weary of
this moon" and wants it to "change" (5.1.251–52). Theseus has taken part in the sport but draws back with a
"courtesy" and "reason" UR (5.1.254–55) that seem to be
directed at both Starveling and Hippolyta. In the comic
exchange that follows, Hippolyta makes amends for her
earlier criticism by praising the moon when it aids
Thisby's escape: "Well shone, Moon. Truly, the moon
shines with a good grace" (5.1.267–68). Theseus responds
with mock praise for the lion: "Well mous'd, Lion"
(5.1.269). When Pyramus eulogizes the moon that has
been so diminished by Starveling's presentation, he not
only parodies the principles of duality and analogy with
his talk of the moon's "sunny beams" (5.1.272) but may
also be trying to compliment Hippolyta. When the moon
follows a confused Pyramus's order to "take thy flight"
(instead of to "lose thy light")[30] and thereby to join
Pyramus's soul "in the sky," Hippolyta jokingly notes

this mild insult to femininity by asking pointedly, "How chance Moonshine is gone before Thisby comes back and finds her lover?" (5.1.303–05, 312–13). Responding that "She will find him by starlight" (5.1.314), Theseus may imply an allusion to them as "star-crossed" LC lovers. Shakespeare himself seems to want to reassert the stature of both masculine and feminine power <UR> that have been much diminished in this lion and moon. Puck's first lines after the fairies arrive remind us of nature's primitive power: "Now the hungry [lion] roars, / And the wolf [behowls] the moon" (5.1.371–72).[31] Nature's stark polarization of the masculine and the feminine once again define the complex interactions of gender.

At the start of the last scene, Theseus has called for "revels" to help them all "wear away this long age of three hours / Between [our] after-supper and bed-time" (5.1.36, 33–34). This need "To ease the anguish of a torturing hour" is ironic in light of the wedding night ahead, but a cycle-conscious Theseus knows that the festive art UC of a civilized community UR counteracts the decline of the day.[32] Bottom in his awkward way tries to make his tragedy fit such a mood: "Will it please you to see the epilogue, or to hear a Bergomask dance between two of our company?" (5.1.352–54). But Theseus and the others have already made sufficient use of the unintentionally uproarious play: "The heavy gait of night" LC is "well beguil'd" by this "palpable-gross play" (5.1.368, 367). The rough Bergomask of the artisans, like an antimask, gives way to the more graceful dance of the aristocrats.

Now day, artificially maintained for the evening revel, must pass suddenly into the depth of night. When Theseus refers to the "iron tongue of midnight" LC (5.1.363), we sense the inexorable passing of time; "iron" suggests not just the clang of a personified but still metallic midnight's "tongue" but also the end of the revels that have given "this long age," also iron, some sanguine UC moments. The transition, like the dawn of act 4, is rich and orderly. When Theseus says "'tis almost fairy time," night seems more magical than dangerous, though he may intend an ironic reference to the previous night when "fairy toys" (5.1.364, 3) disturbed the lovers. Theseus's only worry now seems to be too much sleep: "I fear we shall outsleep the coming morn" (5.1.365). He is aware of the longer range dangers of not taking full advantage of new days, but for a fortnight they will have "nightly revels and new jollity" [LC] (5.1.370). The three couples depart, going to their marriage beds UC, where passion will be ordered and regeneration will begin.

In this transformed world of love UC, an unchanged Puck becomes the foil who reminds us of the disorder LC still all around. As we have seen, the "hungry lion" and the wolf howling at the moon remind us of the powerful and unruly forces LR that the artisans have described so ludicrously. The sleep of the "heavy ploughman" after "weary task fordone" (5.1.373, 374), conventionally an image of hard but productive work, prepares him only for another thankless day. The fire is dying, and the "screech-owl, screeching loud, / Puts the wretch that lies in woe / In remembrance of a shroud" LC (5.1.376–78). We remember the "clamorous owl" LR that Titania's fairies are to "keep back" (2.2.6, 5) and realize that the order is fragile. Puck goes on to mention the spirits of the dead who are released from their "graves, all gaping wide" LC and says the fairies who "run / By the triple Hecat's team / From the presence of the sun, / Following darkness like a dream, / Now are frolic" <LC> (5.1.380, 383–87). The context emphasizes the opposition of day and night and implies that the fairies are a part of the disorder LC.

Puck seems to be celebrating the freedom and irresponsibility <LC> of a night world where the "frolic" of "dream" is possible. We may recall the "Damned spirits" (3.2.382) that made Puck worry that fairies too need to depart before a judging <UR> sun rises; and the mention of Hecate's "team" may imply a role for the dark Hecate <LC>, whose influence Oberon (and Shakespeare, in the spirit of comedy UC) has minimized. When Puck switches abruptly from these metaphysical speculations to his role in Oberon's ritual, he has become a mere servant who must control the mice and sweep the floor: "Not a mouse / Shall disturb this hallowed house. / I am sent with broom before, / To sweep the dust behind the door" (5.1.387–90). Lion has referred to ladies' fear of a "monstrous mouse," and an ironic Theseus has undercut the lion's power with a reductive image: "Well mous'd, Lion" (5.1.220, 269). Puck has talked expansively of a "hungry lion" (5.1.371) but now must concern himself with mice.

When Oberon, Titania, and their train enter to bless the marriages, harmony returns as Puck again serves Oberon's higher causes. As Barber points out, Puck with his broom has the role of the traditional presenter of a mummers' group and of the housewife's friend who sweeps out both dust and evil spirits.[33] Oberon has been able to sport with the dawn and now moves easily from his place in the wood to Theseus's court. Oberon at midnight in the court parallels Theseus at dawn in the wood. In 4.1, Theseus enters as Oberon departs, and here Oberon enters soon after Theseus leaves. Both have orderly, not disruptive, purposes, and their harmonious rule points to an ideal order UC. With the help of the fairies, this house and its offspring can be protected. Folk custom and Christian ceremony unite. Barber suggests that the use of "field-dew consecrate" (5.1.415) as an exorcism parallels the blessing of the bridal couple with holy water UC in some marriages of the time. This "may . . . be an ecclesiastical adaptation of a more primitive bridal lustration, a water charm of dew-gathering on May Day is one variant."[34]

Dream and night can be both free and orderly: the fairies' "frolic" in "Following darkness like a dream" can be parallel to Hippolyta's image in the first scene: "Four nights will quickly dream away the time" (5.1.386; 1.1.8). The fairies Oberon asks to "Hop as light as bird from brier" and "dance it trippingly" are the image of the "pert and nimble spirit of mirth" UC (5.1.394, 396; 1.1.13) Theseus was seeking. Their "light" "gait" will continue the revels' resistance to "the heavy gait of night" LC; and their "glimmering light" will reflect and spread the remaining light in the "dead and drowsy fire" (5.1.416, 368, 391–92). As they "stray" through the house "until the break of day" (5.1.402, 401), they will embody the purposeful wandering UR that Titania ordered and Puck lacked. As they join hands to "sing, and bless this place" so that the residents will find "sweet peace," they guarantee the "peace" UC (5.1.400, 418; 3.2.377) that Oberon has promised.

Even though Oberon brings about an orderly and harmonious conclusion, Shakespearean metaphor continues to develop the scene's inherent polarities. Some ambiguous patriarchal tendencies remain in Oberon. Titania, whose silence was twice commanded by Oberon when she awoke at dawn (4.1.80, 95), has only four lines, but the first two make her sound like a subordinate: "First, rehearse your song by rote, / To each word a warbling note" (5.1.397–98). She is one member of the group, not a leader: "Hand in hand, with fairy grace, / Will we sing, and bless this place" (5.1.399–400). While a transformed Titania seems to be happy with this traditional role, at least some members of the Elizabethan audience might detect irony and wonder if Oberon's plan is one more instance of his wanting to lock in permanence <UC> in an imperfect LC world. Shakespeare is able to suggest the dualities of the Fall while still pointing to an eternal moment UC that transcends earthly limitations. The resolution is generic in pulling together the threads of comedy UC and theological in pointing to the paradisal ideals UC possible if behavior can be unfallen. When the inevitable quarrels develop, the marriages will lose their paradisal innocence, but such doubts are temporarily subsumed in the mood of celebration that belongs to both comedy and marriage.

Puck's epilogue returns to polarities familiar from earlier speeches of Oberon, Bottom, Theseus, and Hippolyta. Puck, now in his role as actor, treats his fellow actors as "shadows" that present only an image <LC> of reality and tells the audience to "Think" they "have but slumber'd here" if they have been "offended" (5.1.423–26). The irony functions in complex ways. Earlier, Oberon has led the lovers to think of what happened as a dream: "When they next wake, all this derision / Shall seem a dream and fruitless vision" <UC> (3.2.370–71). But we know that in the terms of the play it all actually happened. If we respond by dismissing the play as a "weak and idle theme, / No more yielding but a dream" (5.1.427–28), we are following Theseus in dismissing the lovers' reports. Instead, we should remember Oberon's plan and see with Hippolyta that "the story of the night" resulted in "something of great constancy" (5.1.23, 26). The equation can be put in this way: the young lovers' dream vision is to what actually happened as the play *A Midsummer Night's Dream* is to reality itself. But works of art, even a Shakespearean play, do not always succeed in getting at deeper reality; we remember "Pyramus and Thisby" and Bottom's plan for Peter Quince's ballad. By including an epilogue, Shakespeare implies his own detachment or at least his ability to laugh at his own pretensions. He has described an inclusive and ambitious vision but now draws back from grand claims. Each character's hopes and expectations are realized in accordance with the assumptions of the genre that formed them. The lovers are happy in their romance ending UC and Theseus and Oberon in their restored patriarchy UR. The women can be happily acquiescent since their men are behaving properly. Bottom and his company are full of the triumph of their production. In a play that deals with transformations, no one changes very dramatically (though some are restored to an earlier vision). A detached actor with the qualities of a slightly cynical Puck is the perfect spokesman for skepticism <LR>. Puck as actor (and Shakespeare as author) knows that some in the audience will respond like Theseus to "Pyramus and Thisby" and take Shakespeare's *Dream* as merely an entertainment or sport, while others may find deeper meanings.

The play has been an imperfect presentation, just as all human activity after the Fall is imperfect. People do not earn their reconciliation and happiness, and the actors have not earned "luck" [LC] to "scape the serpent's tongue" LC (5.1.432–33), but to hiss now would be a destructive condemnation LR that prevents improvement. Puck's mention of luck recalls Hermia's wish for "luck" (1.1.221) for Demetrius. Finally, when all is explained, an element of mystery and wonder remains, and "luck" with its folk overtones captures this sense of forces beyond our control. Life includes both triumph UC and tragedy LC; in a mutable world we can never be altogether sure which will result. All we can do is try, as the actors are trying, to "make amends" (5.1.434).

Epilogue

Like the poet Theseus criticizes, Shakespeare in these plays attempts to describe the "forms of things unknown," but he does so by relating these mysterious "forms" to what was familiar to an Elizabethan audience. In retrospect, we can see that the Renaissance was giving birth to the modern world. From one perspective, Shakespeare's stress on the cycles is a return to an older "residual" structure that predates the "dominant" theological and patriarchal framework, but from another and, I would argue, more valid point of view, the more narrowly theological perspective is becoming residual where as the emphasis on nature in all of its manifestations is a vital and workable if not dominant way of avoiding divisive conflict.[1] In contrast to the still primarily traditional orientation in these plays, the "emergent" would include the forces that we associate with the religion of the Puritans, the science of Bacon, the politics of Machiavelli, the skepticism and fideism of Montaigne, and the materialism of a changing economic system. In their indirect ways, these forces affect audience responses, but in the world of 1595 do not have a controlling influence on the plays' metaphorical structures.

People supporting change were likely to think that they were renewing and reforming traditional structures even as their world moved away from them. The English church was shaping a via media between Catholic and Protestant, philosophers were still seeking a synthesis of Plato and Aristotle, experimenters on the edge of chemistry were dabbling with alchemy, and poets were exploring the subtleties of love with the aid of Petrarchism and neoplatonism. In these plays, Shakespeare tries to balance a day world of reason, power, and order—the foundations of Renaissance patriarchy—with a night world of love and personal relationships and of the inner self and nature. The latter world has always resisted systematic analysis but has been described metaphorically by an analogical framework of cycles and hierarchies that developed gradually over the centuries and was attracting renewed interest from writers in the early 1590s. A confident Theseus thinks he knows the important forms and regards exploring "the forms of things unknown" as both futile and dangerous. Shakespeare, though not denying the patriarchal paradigm that includes God, the sun, the monarch, the father, and the husband, explores the more subjective feminine night and its relationship to masculine realities.

Shakespeare emphasizes metaphor that describes life's patterns and avoids religious and philosophical questions that require dogmatic answers. The conventional struggle between good and evil recedes in importance as characters are defined by their stages in cycles and their places in hierarchies. In both plays, young lovers struggle with their humours and passions, their shifting masculine and feminine roles, their rebellious relationships with parents and others in authority, and the confusing influence of natural forces and cosmic powers. The factors that function at each of these levels operate analogously at the other levels with the result that action, theme, and metaphor all fit into a larger framework. The plays' individuals, families, and societies all find it difficult to direct the metamorphoses of life into meaningful patterns that fuse natural expression and orderly control. When *Romeo and Juliet* is seen in this context, interpretations that reduce causation to fate or fortune, or to character faults, or to the feud, or even to some combination expressed in these terms, seem oversimplified, and *A Midsummer Night's Dream* becomes a more abstract study of the same themes but with less emphasis on story and more on the cyclical patterns that shape life's rhythms.

As examples of early Shakespearean comedy and tragedy, the plays prove to be different but congruent manifestations of a refreshingly nonjudgmental way of looking at the world. Comedy expresses the ongoing vitality that both individuals and societies need to function effectively. While *A Midsummer Night's Dream* reveals the folly and illusion of people in the grip of love's madness, it also promotes continuity through its celebration of marriage as a personal, social, and political institution.[2] Tragedy's use of more individualized characters encourages our involvement in what happens to *these* people: it reminds us that living in a structured society is not always easy and that death is an ever threatening reality. Conventional tragedy finds its primary cause in human sin or error and thereby explains, even justifies, the resulting deaths. The disaster of the young lovers in *Romeo and Juliet* mocks facile confidence in orderly patterns by revealing the deeper oppositions and continuities that neither tragedy's horrific nor comedy's paradisal closure can fully define. *Romeo and Juliet* ends in tragedy before dawn, but the remaining characters seem ready to begin again with what they think is a new wisdom. *A Midsummer Night's Dream* ends in celebration at midnight but retains a sense of the vulnerability of the confident lovers and rulers. Both plays imply that although individual actions affect immediate situations, their effect is temporary since the pattern of cycles and hierarchies and the structures based on them do not themselves change.[3] When positive changes occur, they restore characters to what they once were or to an accepted role in the larger society rather than to some radically different outlook. When disasters happen, the hope for the future is simply that people will do better in shaping events toward constructive ends. The moment of stasis in the resolutions can be only temporary since time itself is both ongoing and fallen.

In Shakespeare's literary microcosms, genre structures gender: dramatic form defines and heightens the polarities of masculinity and femininity that govern all levels of existence. Subgenres within the larger framework of comedy and tragedy—the sonnet, pastoral, romance, epic, satire, farce, and their variations—express divergent impulses of life and help contribute the subtleties that illuminate character, theme, and action. The sonnet can define the aspiration but also the lunacy of the tormented lover. Pastoral can express a paradisal goal but also a vulnerable naivete. Romance can describe the idealism, patience, and courage that motivate the struggles of noble love but can also depict the excesses of love's illusions. By mixing genres and tones, Shakespeare avoids forcing a single shape on the plays as a whole and thereby leaves considerable latitude for interpretation to the company and in turn to the audience. Defining the Shakespearean balance will always be problematical because the framework itself is open. One person or one period sees elevation where another sees illusion, but understanding the structures allows us to state the issues in a meaningful way.

Approaching *Romeo and Juliet* and *A Midsummer Night's Dream* with an awareness of this intellectual and artistic context leads to a clearer recognition that Shakespeare is telling different versions of the same story. *Romeo and Juliet* concentrates almost exclusively on the lovers and their immediate situation while *A Midsummer Night's Dream* develops another set of young lovers and three other only tangentially connected plots; but parallels abound. The story of Lysander and Hermia may seem reduced to stylized unreality, but someone seeing *A Midsummer Night's Dream* after *Romeo and Juliet* could easily fill in with associations from the other play. Since the roles of tyrannical father and rebellious lovers are so conventional, they would need no specific knowledge to understand the issues, but the parallels are striking enough to encourage comparison. Lysander and Hermia resemble Romeo and Juliet not only in their mutual devotion and elevated language but also in their characteristic imagery of generational conflict, most obviously when Lysander laments that "quick bright things come to confusion" (1.1.149) after a speech full of light-dark imagery emphasizing cosmic disorder. We learn nothing about why Lysander is unacceptable to Egeus, but if we postulate family tensions like those between Capulet and Montague, Egeus's opposition is more explicable. Many suggest that Romeo and Juliet should have told Capulet of their marriage, but if he were to respond like Egeus, Romeo and Juliet would also have had to flee to escape his wrath. Fathers are omitted in the final version of "Pyramus and Thisby," but Bottom's reading—"the wall is down that parted their fathers" (5.1.351–52)—suggests the importance of the families.

The study of plot differences also helps clarify what is most significant in each story. In *Romeo and Juliet*, Shakespeare avoids distraction from his tragic love story by ignoring many plot possibilities he pursued in *A Midsummer Night's Dream*. Paris, like Demetrius, is a suitor spurned by his love but advanced by her father, but he knows nothing of Juliet's love for Romeo and fails to realize that Juliet would never marry him. Rosaline, like Helena, is loved and then forgotten, but she remains a shadowy figure whose own love interests are never considered. If Rosaline were linked to Paris by love and to Juliet by friendship, the quadrangle would be close to that of *A Midsummer Night's Dream*, but Shakespeare avoids such symmetries. The conflict between Romeo and Paris parallels that between Lysander and Demetrius. If Paris were to know that Romeo is Juliet's lover, indeed husband, he would have additional motivation for the fight at the tomb. Tybalt, a figure structurally analogous to Paris in opposition to Romeo, is also ignorant of Romeo's relationship to Juliet. With some shifts that would actually improve motivation for the two fights, Tybalt or Paris, or both combined into a single character, could find out about Romeo's love for Juliet and be outraged. Such a conflict with Romeo would be structurally parallel to the frantic chasing that passes for a fight between Demetrius and Lysander and would give the play a powerful countering force, but that story would stress the feud rather than the misunderstandings of well-meaning but impetuous young people. The fights between Mercutio and Tybalt and between Romeo and Paris have no clearly defined cause, and the fight between Romeo and Tybalt is a tragic mistake that goes against Romeo's peace-loving nature. Tight plotting can sharpen issues but endanger important thematic effects.

Lysander and Hermia are as influenced by "tale or history" (1.1.133) as Romeo is by the sonnet, and all their stories work out according to their generic expectations. Lysander briefly considers a "script" (in both a literary and the modern psychological sense) that includes a Romeo-like disaster, but Hermia persuades him that their story will be like a romance that tests their patience and love but ends happily. Neither loses this conception despite the wild happenings in the wood. Romeo begins in a sonnet-influenced preoccupation with joys and woes. As the play proceeds, he takes on new roles—the chivalric hero rescuing Juliet from "bondage" and carrying her off to marriage, the sophisticated Renaissance man jesting with Mercutio, the peacemaker trying to resolve his conflict with Tybalt and establish family peace, the avenger seeking justice by killing Tybalt, the exiled husband waiting hopefully for his return, and finally, though he is unaware of it, the redeemer-hero who could rescue Juliet from death itself.

Some would say that these different Romeos suggest his lack of stature: he reacts to situations instead of shaping them and might win our pity but not our admiration. This view fits with either a "medieval" reading that blames Romeo or with a postmodern reading that deconstructs the values of both Romeo and his patriarchal society, but Romeo's success as a character suggests that audiences of his time and through the centuries have found a person behind the shifting images. It may be that Shakespeare's story encourages an audience to "fashion" a new kind of hero and heroine who are at once sensitive and rebellious, victims of a feuding society and passionate initiators of a tragic love.[4]

Such figures cannot be accounted for by traditional metaphor but may succeed in a society in which many are perhaps subconsciously looking for ways to express emerging values of individualism and love. In that open-ended context, historical criticism stumbles in the realization that drama ultimately defies reduction to categories. Analogy, however, does function. In *Romeo and Juliet*, Romeo's inability to find measured responses is matched by analogous disruptions at the familial, societal, and cosmic levels. In *A Midsummer Night's Dream*, conflict evaporates in dream that broadens the sense of life's complexities and in laughter that calls into question many old assumptions. Understanding metaphor historically brings us closer to Renaissance responses but finally does not unravel the subjective mystery of *Romeo and Juliet*.

The older couples—Theseus and Hippolyta, Oberon and Titania, the Montagues, the Capulets—and the other older people—Egeus, the Prince, the Friar, the Nurse—have roles that invoke the levels of family, society, and nature. In their various relationships, all are made to seem misguided or unfortunate rather than villainous. We learn nothing about what has caused the feud between the Montagues and the Capulets or its earlier consequences (or about the apparent rift between Egeus and Lysander's family); we get only a brief allusion to the former affairs of Theseus and Titania and of Oberon and

Hippolyta, and hear almost nothing of Theseus's subjugation of Hippolyta or of his history as a womanizer. As a result, we have no specific case to make against any of them and can judge them only by what they do in the present. The current relationships of Theseus and Hippolyta and of Oberon and Titania help establish the social and natural contexts in which the young lovers function. Theseus and Oberon are father figures to the lovers, with Theseus joining Egeus as a harsh parental figure of authority in Athens and with Oberon playing an analogous, ultimately more helpful (though hidden) role in the wood. There is some attention to the Capulet marriage, but they are seen primarily as well meaning but dictatorial parents. The Nurse takes on a motherly role, and the Friar replaces Montague as Romeo's father figure. As with Romeo and Juliet, these characters take on an independent vitality that makes them seem more individual and that allows considerable diversity of presentation and response, but their roles are more circumscribed than Romeo and Juliet's by the framework of the plays' metaphorical structures.

Theseus and Oberon also have roles that invoke the societal and natural orders, with Theseus having the governing function of the Prince. Theseus's failure to resolve the deeper conflict in the family dispute in act 1, scene 1, directly parallels the Prince's only temporary resolution of the Capulet-Montague conflict. Neither the Prince nor Oberon is effective in limiting the chaos in the street or wood. In the endings, the generic difference between comedy and tragedy shapes the presentations as Theseus and Oberon preside over hopeful marriages while an unmarried and still bewildered Prince presides over death, broken families, and uncertain renewal. Our sense that the world of Athens could work comes largely from comedy's expectation that Theseus, with the essential addition of Hippolyta's perspective, will support a balance of the masculine and feminine in all of life's areas. Oberon and Titania's reconciliation adds more evidence for the possibilities for a natural harmony. Nevertheless, our awareness of cyclical natural processes that make all moments impermanent brings us closer to Puck, who with his more detached wisdom reminds us of threats that will always exist. In *Romeo and Juliet*, the natural at all levels is more obviously fragmented: Montague bases his naive conception of the world on the "all-cheering sun" (1.1.134) and Capulet on fruition through an arranged marriage, while only the earthy old Nurse is comfortable in Juliet's balcony-orchard. Their misguided efforts lead finally to the tomb, but the ending, nevertheless, provides some hope to balance the gloom.

Friar Lawrence's active role in relation to the lovers begins more positively than Oberon's analogous role. Even though the Friar belongs to a more realistic mode, he reveals in his dawn speech that he both understands and has power over nature. When he later introduces his potion, his role and the play as a whole take on an aspect of fairy tale romance. Interpreted symbolically, the Friar's magical potion reflects a larger-than-life wisdom that links him to natural powers. Oberon and the fairies are also in this deepest sense natural rather than magical. Despite their power, neither Oberon nor the Friar can control all of the variables. The Friar cannot change the attitudes of the Capulets or Montagues, or prevent Romeo from responding impulsively to the death of Mercutio, or guarantee that Romeo will get his message about Juliet's "death." Similarly, Oberon cannot manage the rebellious Titania, or be sure that the irresponsible Puck will put the potion on the right young man, or even persuade the fun-loving Puck to take life seriously. The Friar starts well as a wise advocate of love and a bold opponent of the society's rigidities, but he slips gradually into dogmatism, desperation, and fear. Oberon starts as an insensitive, sport-loving patriarch but recovers enough to preside over the resolutions of the ending. The outcomes, however, have more to do with the difference between comedy and tragedy than with the superiority of fairy kings to friars.

When we look at the plays as symbolic structures, other parallels appear. Puck's wood, governed by "night-rule," is analogous not only to Queen Mab's "sleep-rule" of dreams but also to Verona's disorderly streets and to the force behind the characters' precipitate actions and the Friar's unfortunate mistakes. The servants and families express this chaos in *Romeo and Juliet*'s opening scene, but the real embodiment of that spirit is in Mercutio and Mab. In their different ways, Puck, Mab, and Mercutio all serve to expose absurdities and reveal underlying desires. The Cupid-like Puck, through love-in-idleness, governs Demetrius and Lysander's physical and idealizing love impulses and, through his tricks, pokes fun at housewives and artisans. Mab, through her sexual and fanciful night-journey, rules the dreams of would-be lovers and aspiring lawyers, courtiers, and preachers. Mercutio, in his mad "noon-rule" in the street, exposes the folly of the lover (Romeo), the courtier (Tybalt), and the moralist (Benvolio). Mab, Mercutio, and Puck all have fun with lovers' unruly emotions and with stuffiness and pretense wherever they find them, but in their lack of seriousness they are in danger of standing for nothing worthwhile. In contrast, Romeo repudiates Mab and Mercutio and believes in dreams and love; and Oberon, with the help of a grudging Puck and of potions that go beyond Mab's scope, helps bring about the reconciliation of lovers and the renewal of life. Puck's vitality and energy are controlled, but Mercutio's are not. As a result, there are disastrous fights in Verona's streets but only a comic nonclash in the wood.

The parallels in the two plays go deeper than plot and characterization. Settings and times in the two plays prove to be mirror images of each other. Both plays deal with love on four midsummer days and nights. In Renaissance metaphor, day is a time either for constructive activity or for ambition and conflict, while night is a time either for love, renewal, and spiritual understanding or for breakdown and disorder. Day in *Romeo and Juliet* is usually chaotic, from the opening morning scene to the later scenes of fighting in the streets, but night is at first associated with positive settings—the Capulet party, the balcony scene, and the wedding night. The second night—the wedding night—in itself seems positive, but the dawn scene of parting is ominous because of the tragedies that have occurred and because of Romeo's banishment. The third night is notable for Capulet's hasty preparations for the wedding and for Juliet's entrance into a nightmare world of death and madness as she takes the potion. On the final night, horror takes over and the dawn is delayed. Thus there are four nights—two positive and two negative—with the first positive and the second negative nights getting by far the most emphasis.

The overall pattern is cyclical, beginning in Romeo's despair and the society's disorder, rising to hope and transcendent love on the first two nights, and then descending through unfortunate deaths and Romeo's banishment to a disaster from which no new rise seems likely for some time. Transitions from night to day are always difficult in *Romeo and Juliet*, with the oppositions being clarified by the Friar's dawn speech with its polarized imagery that suggests both dangers and opportunities. First threats and then tragedy dominate: the approach of dawn brings partings on the first two nights and the discovery of deaths on the last two. The early positive settings—the Capulets' hall, Juliet's orchard, the Friar's garden—shift in the final scenes to horrible reminders of death—an apothecary's lifeless shop, a house of pestilence, and finally a graveyard and tomb.

In *A Midsummer Night's Dream*, the pattern is reversed. Although the opening daytime scene at court features a squabble about Hermia's marriage, all of the main characters remain hopeful that solutions for their problems can be found. Theseus and Hippolyta have overcome their previous conflict and anticipate a wedding-night celebration watched over by a new moon. The lovers expect that the night will aid their flight from their troubled daytime world in Athens and that the pastoral wood they have known by day will be just as idyllic by night. Even the artisans have high hopes for their play and expect their night rehearsal in the wood to be free from the interruptions of the city. In the first scenes at night, Oberon and Titania's conflict is threatening, but Oberon asserts his masculine power and Titania is confident that her fairies will be able to protect her bower, a place of love analogous to Juliet's balcony and orchard. This first night, in contrast to *Romeo and Juliet*, turns out to be a nightmare of shifting loyalties and identities. Most of the characters end the night in despair and confusion that they see as reflecting a larger chaos in nature itself.

When Oberon invokes a "fog as black as Acheron" for the wood and "death-counterfeiting sleep" (3.2.357, 363) for the lovers, there is an exact parallel to Juliet's death-sleep in a tomb described in images of hell. The dawn, however, brings a rising pattern that does not occur in *Romeo and Juliet*. With restored order between Oberon and Titania and among the young lovers, and with harmony between the night world of the fairies and the day world of Theseus, dawn and later midnight bring orderly transitions. Morning in the wood, and evening and night in the court become times of celebration. That the comedy ends in marriages at midnight and the tragedy in deaths before the dawn reflects the plays' preoccupation with opposing principles within the feminine night. Achieving a proper fusion of day and night proves to be as difficult as marrying the masculine and feminine at every other level.

The imagery of the plays fits analogous dualistic patterns. In the potion that the Friar gives to Juliet are both the appearance of death and the promise of renewed life. Juliet depends on the potion's promise, but Romeo turns to another natural potion, the apothecary's poison. The poignancy of the final scene comes because we sense, partly through Romeo's imagery of light and life in the tomb, how close the lovers are to renewal instead of death. In *A Midsummer Night's Dream*, the potion "love-in-idleness" can lead to the craziest passion while "Dian's bud" (2.1.168; 4.1.73) and a properly directed love-in-idleness restore true and natural love. The principles of Diana and Venus that match the potions are finally reconciled even though much of the play has illustrated love's inconsistencies and absurdities. The moon itself is associated at different times with chastity, barrenness, fecundity, power, fickleness, madness, and romance while the sun can be "all-cheering" or "burning" (*Romeo and Juliet*, 1.1.134; 2.3.5). In both plays, nothing is good if not turned to proper ends. The morning dew of *A Midsummer Night's Dream* can be associated with growth or with tears, and the gardens of *Romeo and Juliet* with "medlars" and a "pop'rin pear" (2.1.36, 38) or with pomegranates and singing birds. The Friar's secluded and earthy cell and the dark wood are appropriate places for hopeful hiding or woeful despair and for escape to a genuine or illusory spiritual illumination. The senses and the language describing them can reflect the beauty of Juliet or the confusion of Bottom's attempts at communication. Motion can suggest the wild wanderings of the lovers in the night wood or the harmonious movements of the dancers in the morning wood and at court. Music can be as unpleasant as Bottom's singing or as satisfying as that at the Capulet feast and at Theseus's wedding. Art itself can be as lacking in meaning as "Pyramus and Thisby" and Peter Quince's putative ballad or as profound as the two plays themselves.

What is our final impression of the world of the two plays? If we could overhear a discussion between a husband and wife—ideal playgoers with both knowledge and sensitivity—who have just returned from the wedding at which *A Midsummer Night's Dream* was presented, we would get a sense of the play as a cultural document that both reflects and influences the society. Their sense of occasion would be strong, with both perhaps sharing anecdotes about the responses of old lords and young ladies to the "weak and idle theme" of the fairy scenes or perhaps commenting on the fun of having a play at the wedding that included a comic version of the recent success, *Romeo and Juliet*, at still another wedding. There might be wise talk about Lyly, emblems, and myth; about Ovid, Apuleius, and animal imagery; about Petrarchism, neoplatonism, and Christianity; about Bottom, St. Paul, and Erasmus; about Diana, Venus, and Queen Elizabeth; about Puck, Robin Goodfellow, and Cupid; and about the various parallels with *Romeo and Juliet*. Predicting what they would say about such questions as the degree of illusion and elevation in the young lovers, and in Romeo and Juliet, and the extent of the undercutting of authority figures like Theseus, Oberon, the Montagues, and the Capulets is more difficult. Since Shakespeare utilizes the conventional forms of his culture in order to communicate and please (or in more traditional terms, to instruct and entertain), he himself has an uncertain relationship to his own work. Even if we could see the production itself, we might still have trouble with such matters as its presumably tactful handling of authority figures or its sophisticated and often ironic treatment of genres whose tone we recover only through an effort of an often deceptive historical imagination. We are so far removed from that world that we can say little that is conclusive about how an Elizabethan audience would respond.

What can we say? I can offer only some speculations. When I postulate an ideal couple who would appreciate ambiguities and enjoy heated exchanges and disagreements about what Shakespeare meant to imply and what they themselves believed, I am in danger of making them modern readers in Elizabethan dress. Actually, I suspect that many in the audience would experience some frustration in that Shakespeare leaves more questions open than most Renaissance artists do. For an audience of 1595, the plays' most significant qualities may have been the scope of Shakespeare's vision of the night and his reluctance to invoke the usual theological and philosophical categories. Conservative Christians in the audience might object to the absence of a moral context of good and evil (and to the breakdown of the Friar at the end of *Romeo and Juliet*) and might also question how little control the lovers, especially Romeo and Juliet, have in what happens to them. Political conservatives might object to the subtle undercutting of Theseus, Oberon, Montague, and Capulet. Some men might object to the importance of women in the plays and to the repeated emphasis on balancing masculine and feminine dimensions. Some women might feel that what we get is the old patriarchal vision in an only slightly more palatable form.

All of these responses are possible, even likely. But perhaps more people would see *A Midsummer Night's Dream* as a comic presentation of conventional ideas that is appropriate for the wedding festivities and *Romeo and Juliet* as an exciting dramatic version of an old poem. Every member of any audience will have his or her own personal perspective. All I can say with some confidence is that the framework of the Elizabethan response would be the patterns of metaphor that have been the subject of this study. Attention to these patterns helps us identify the ways in which the plays would be complex for their Elizabethan audiences.

NOTES

Notes to Introduction

1. All references to the plays are to *The Riverside Shakespeare*, ed. G. Blakemore Evans (Boston: Houghton Mifflin, 1974). For Sidney's role in formulating these issues, see S. K. Heninger, Jr., *Sidney and Spenser: The Poet as Maker* (University Park: Penn State University Press, 1989); and my discussion on 49–51.

2. W. R. Elton, "Shakespeare and the Thought of His Age," in *A New Companion to Shakespeare Studies*, ed. Kenneth Muir and S. Schoenbaum (Cambridge: Cambridge University Press, 1971), 193. See also S. K. Heninger, Jr., *The Subtext of Form in the English Renaissance: Proportion Poetical* (University Park: Pennsylvania State University Press, 1994). For a discussion of the importance of nature that stresses contrariety and hierarchy as complementary but competing principles, see T. McAlindon, *Shakespeare's Tragic Cosmos* (Cambridge, Cambridge University Press, 1991), 1–13. See also Robert Grudin, *Mighty Opposites: Shakespeare and Renaissance Contrariety* (Berkeley, University of California Press, 1979).

3. No adequate history of the scholarship on either play seems to exist. For a start on *A Midsummer Night's Dream*, see Antony W. Price, introduction to Shakespeare: *A Midsummer Night's Dream* Casebook (London: Macmillan, 1983), 11–21. On the relationships between the plays and the arguments for their dating, see the Arden editions: Harold Brooks, introduction to *A Midsummer Night's Dream* (London: Methuen, 1979), xxxiv–lvii; and Brian Gibbons, introduction to *Romeo and Juliet* (London: Methuen, 1980), 26–31. For the case that

Romeo and Juliet was first, see also Amy J. Reiss and George Walton Williams, "'Tragical Mirth': From *Romeo* to *Dream*," *Shakespeare Quarterly* 43 (1992): 214–18. For the relationship of the plays' literary forms, see Northrop Frye, *Fools of Time: Studies in Shakespearean Tragedy* (Toronto: University of Toronto Press, 1967), 59–60; Frye, *The Myth of Deliverance: Reflections on Shakespeare's Problem Comedies* (Toronto: University of Toronto Press, 1983), 74–82; and *Northrop Frye on Shakespeare*, ed. Robert Sandler (New Haven: Yale University Press, 1986), 15–50.

4. For analyses of criticism that call attention to these three readings of the play, see Franklin Dickey, *Not Wisely But Too Well* (San Marino: The Huntington Library, 1957), 63–64; A. C. Hamilton, *The Early Shakespeare* (San Marino: The Huntington Library, 1967), 203–04; and Virgil Whitaker, *The Mirror up to Nature: The Technique of Shakespeare's Tragedies* (San Marino: The Huntington Library, 1965), 109–10. For summaries that recommend balancing the contradictory readings, see Robert Metcalf Smith, "Three Interpretations of *Romeo and Juliet*," *The Shakespeare Association Bulletin* 23 (1948): 60–77; and Douglas Cole, introduction to *Twentieth Century Interpretations of Romeo and Juliet* (Englewood Cliffs, New Jersey: Prentice-Hall, 1970), 13. On the possible confusion of fortune and fate in the play, see Frederick Kiefer, *Fortune and Elizabethan Tragedy* (San Marino: The Huntington Library, 1983), 183–84; and T. J. B. Spencer, "Introduction," *Romeo and Juliet*, New Penguin Shakespeare (London: Penguin Books, 1967), 21.

5. Standard studies of Shakespearean imagery include G. Wilson Knight, *The Shakespearian Tempest* (Oxford: Oxford University Press, 1932); Caroline F. Spurgeon, *Shakespeare's Imagery and What It Tells Us* (Cambridge: Cambridge University Press, 1936); and Wolfgang H. Clemen, *The Development of Shakespeare's Imagery* (London: Methuen, 1951). For the importance of dramatic images on the stage, see Alan C. Dessen, *Elizabethan Stage Conventions and Modern Interpreters* (Cambridge: Cambridge University Press, 1984).

6. See particularly Jacques Derrida, "White Mythology: Metaphor in the Text of Philosophy," *New Literary History* 6 (1974–75): 7–74. See also George Lakoff and Mark Johnson, *Metaphors We Live By* (Chicago: Chicago University Press, 1980); and Lakoff and Johnson, *More than Cool Reason* (Chicago: Chicago University Press, 1989); Robert Weimann, "Shakespeare and the Study of Metaphor," *New Literary History* 6 (1974–75): 149–67; and Ann Thompson and John O.

Thompson, *Shakespeare: Meaning & Metaphor* (Iowa City: University of Iowa Press, 1987).

7. Derrida, "White Mythology," 22.

8. Gaston Bachelard, *The Psychoanalysis of Fire*, tr. A. C. Ross (London, 1964), as quoted in Derrida, "White Mythology," 67.

9. For Foucault's concept, see particularly *The Order of Things* (New York: Pantheon, 1970) and *The Archeology of Knowledge* (London, Tavistock, 1972). See also Frank Lentricchia, *After the New Criticism* (Chicago, Chicago University Press, 1980), 193-98.

10. Raymond Williams, *Marxism and Literature* (Oxford: Oxford University Press, 1977), 121–27.

11. Derrida, "White Mythology," 13. See also Barbara Freedman, *Staging the Gaze: Postmodernism, Psychoanalysis, and Shakespearean Comedy* (Ithaca: Cornell University Press, 1991), 163, 167.

12. The phrases, describing the views of Foucault, are from Lentricchia, *After the New Criticism*, 201.

13. Most of these approaches are conveniently available in *Alternative Shakespeares*, ed. John Drakakis (London: Methuen, 1985). For the political overtones of the Bottom plot, see James H. Kavanagh, "Shakespeare in Ideology," in *Alternative Shakespeares*, 152–56; and Malcolm Evans, "Deconstructing Shakespeare's Comedies," in *Alternative Shakespeares*, 75, 80–81. For a Marxist approach to Shakespeare, see Jonathan Dollimore, *Radical Tragedy: Religion, Ideology and Power in the Drama of Shakespeare and his Contemporaries*, second edition with a new introduction (Durham: Duke University Press, 1993). For a Marxist reading of *A Midsummer Night's Dream*, see Elliot Krieger, *A Marxist Study of Shakespeare's Comedies* (New York, 1979), 37–69. On feminist approaches, see Catherine Belsey, "Disrupting Sexual Difference: Meaning and Gender in the Comedies," in *Alternative Shakespeares*, 188–89. Readings that draw on both psychoanalysis and rhetorical theory in explaining the impulses of young love include Rene Girard, "Myth and Ritual in Shakespeare: *A Midsummer Night's Dream*," in *Textual Strategies: Perspectives in Post-structuralist Criticism*, ed. Josue V. Harari (Ithaca: Cornell University Press, 1980), 189–212; and Joel Fineman, "The Turn of the Shrew," in *Shakespeare and the Question of Theory* (New York: Methuen, 1985), 138–59. For an anthropological and psychological approach to death and renewal, see Kirby Farrell, *Play, Death, and Heroism in Shakespeare* (Chapel Hill: University of North Carolina Press, 1989). For

interactions between conventional genres and Renaissance ideologies, see Michael Hall in *The Structure of Love: Representational Patterns and Shakespeare's Love Tragedies* (Charlottesville: University Press of Virginia, 1989). On Shakespeare's drama as play with language, see Keir Elam, *Shakespeare's Universe of Discourse: Language-Games in the Comedies* (Cambridge: Cambridge University Press, 1984). For a reading with nihilistic overtones, see Jan Kott, "Titania and the Ass's Head," in *Shakespeare Our Contemporary*, tr. Boleslaw Taborski (Garden City, New York: Doubleday, 1964), 207–28. For a new historical analysis of *A Midsummer Night's Dream* in the context of issues of gender and power, see Louis Adrian Montrose, "'Shaping Fantasies': Figurations of Gender and Power in Elizabethan Culture," *Representations* 1 (1983): 61–94, reprinted with some changes as "*A Midsummer Night's Dream* and the Shaping Fantasies of Elizabethan Culture: Gender, Power, Form," in *Rewriting the Renaissance* (Chicago: University of Chicago Press, 1986), 65–87, 329–34. On gender in *Romeo and Juliet*, see Edward Snow, "Language and Sexual Difference in *Romeo and Juliet*," in *Shakespeare's "Rough Magic": Renaissance Essays in Honor of C. L. Barber*, ed. Peter Erickson and Coppelia Kahn (Newark: University of Delaware Press, 1985), 168–92.

14. Jonathan Culler, *On Deconstruction: Theory and Criticism After Structuralism* (Ithaca: Cornell University Press, 1982), 153–54.

15. The phrase describing male participation in gender studies on the interaction of masculine and feminine in both sexes comes from Tania Modleski, *Feminism Without Women: Culture and Criticism in a "Postfeminist" Age* (New York: Routledge, 1991). See particularly part 2, "Masculinity and Male Feminism," 59–111.

16. Recent feminist studies of "woman" as a social construct include two books by Judith Butler: *Gender Trouble: Feminism and the Subversion of Identity* (New York: Routledge, 1990); and *Bodies That Matter: On the Discursive Limits of "Sex"* (New York: Routledge, 1993). On the difficulty of avoiding essentialism in such discussions, see: Diana Fuss, *Essentially Speaking: Feminism, Nature, & Difference* (New York: Routledge, 1989). For the cultural influences on gender theory, see Thomas Laqueur, *Making Sex: Body and Gender From the Greeks to Freud* (Cambridge: Harvard University Press, 1990). On the more general issues of essentialism, see Dollimore, *Radical Tragedy*, particularly 153–81, 249–71.

17. Leonard Tennenhouse, *Power on Display: The Politics of Shakespeare's Genres* (New York: Methuen, 1986), 6. On the revision of older views of the age, see Jonathan Dollimore, "Introduction: Shakespeare, Cultural Materialism and the New Historicism," *Political Shakespeare: New Essays in Cultural Materialism* (Ithaca: Cornell University Press, 1985), 2–17.

18. Tennenhouse, *Power on Display*, 40–41, 73–75.

19. The standard works, most of which tend to ignore gender issues, include: Lily B. Campbell, *Shakespeare's Tragic Heroes: Slaves of Passion* (Cambridge: Cambridge University Press, 1930); Hardin Craig, *The Enchanted Glass: The Elizabethan Mind in Literature* (New York: Oxford University Press, 1936); Arthur O. Lovejoy, *The Great Chain of Being*, Harper Torchbook (New York: Harper and Brothers, 1960); Theodore Spencer, *Shakespeare and the Nature of Man*, 2d ed. (New York: Macmillan, 1949); E. M. W. Tillyard, *The Elizabethan World Picture* (London: Chatto and Windus, 1943); Herschel Baker, *The Image of Man* (Cambridge, Harvard University Press, 1947); C. S. Lewis, *The Discarded Image* (Cambridge: Cambridge University Press, 1964); S. K. Heninger, Jr., *Touches of Sweet Harmony: Pythagorean Cosmology and Renaissance Poetics* (San Marino: The Huntington Library, 1974); Leonard Barkan, *Nature's Work of Art: The Human Body as Image of the World* (New Haven: Yale University Press, 1975); and John Erskine Hankins, *Backgrounds of Shakespeare's Thought* (Hamden, Connecticut: Archon Books, 1978). For political thought, see James Daly, *Cosmic Harmony and Political Thinking In Early Stuart England, Transactions of the American Philosophical Society*, vol. 69, part 7 (Philadelphia, 1979). For an application to the 1590s, see Marion Bodwell Smith, *Dualities in Shakespeare* (Toronto: University of Toronto Press, 1966), particularly the first chapter.

20. The Yates thesis is pervasive in her many books. See particularly *Giordano Bruno and the Hermetic Tradition* (Chicago: University of Chicago Press, 1964); *Theatre of the World* (Chicago: University of Chicago Press, 1969); *Shakespeare's Last Plays* (London: Routledge and Kegan Paul, 1975); and *The Occult Philosophy in the Elizabethan Age* (London: Routledge and Kegan Paul, 1979). See also John S. Mebane, *Renaissance Magic and the Return of the Golden Age: The Occult Tradition and Marlowe, Jonson, and Shakespeare* (Lincoln: University of Nebraska Press, 1989); and Stevie Davies, *The Feminine Reclaimed: The Idea of Woman in*

Spenser, Shakespeare, and Milton (Lexington, University of Kentucky Press, 1986), particularly 1–36. On the continuing importance of Augustine, see John D. Cox, *Shakespeare and the Dramaturgy of Power* (Princeton: Princeton University Press, 1989), particularly 3–21.

21. For the traditions of holiday and carnival, see C. L. Barber, *Shakespeare's Festive Comedy* (Princeton: Princeton University Press, 1959); M. M. Bakhtin, *Rabelais and his World* (Cambridge: Harvard University Press, 1968); Robert Weimann, *Shakespeare and the Popular Tradition* (Baltimore, Johns Hopkins University Press, 1968); Michael Bristol, *Carnival and Theater: Plebeian Culture and the Structure of Authority in Renaissance England* (New York: Methuen, 1985); Jan Kott, *The Bottom Translation: Marlowe and Shakespeare and the Carnival Tradition* (Evanston: Northwestern University Press, 1987), particularly "The Bottom Translation," 28–68; and Richard Hillman, *Shakespearean Subversions: The Trickster and the Play-text* (London: Routledge, 1992).

22. For a balanced account that stresses Sidney as an Aristotelean, see S. K. Heninger, Jr., *Sidney and Spenser: The Poet as Maker*; for his Christian context, see Thomas P. Roche, Jr., *Petrarch & the Sonnet Tradition, Studies in the Renaissance* 18 (New York: AMS Press, 1989); on his Protestantism, see also Mark Rose, *Heroic Love: Studies in Sidney and Spenser* (Cambridge: Harvard University Press, 1968). On imagery of microcosm and macrocosm in *Astrophil and Stella*, see Leonard Barkan, *Nature's Work of Art*, 175–200. For the relationship of the Petrarchan mode to Queen Elizabeth, see Tennenhouse, *Power on Display*, 17–36.

23. On Marlowe in the context of the Yates views, see James Robinson Howe, *Marlowe, Tamburlaine, and Magic* (Athens, Ohio: Ohio University Press, 1976). On Dr. Faustus, see Mebane, *Renaissance Magic and the Return of the Golden Age*, 113–36.

24. The phrase is Northrop Frye's. See "The Structure of Imagery in *The Faerie Queene*," *Fables of Identity: Studies in Poetic Mythology* (New York: Harcourt, Brace, and World, 1963). See also Thomas P. Roche, Jr., *The Kindly Flame: A Study of the Third and Fourth Books of The Faerie Queene* (Princeton: Princeton University Press, 1964); and James Nohrnberg, *The Analogy of The Faerie Queene* (Princeton: Princeton University Press, 1976).

25. For Donne's Petrarchism, see Donald Guss, *John Donne: Petrarchist* (Detroit: Wayne State University Press,

1965); and Rosalie Colie, *Paradoxia Epidemica: The Renaissance Tradition of Paradox* (Princeton: Princeton University Press, 1966).

PART 1

Notes to Chapter 1: Cycles and Hierarchies

1. For a discussion of the inconsistencies in Renaissance cosmologies, see S. K. Heninger, Jr., *The Cosmographical Glass: Renaissance Diagrams of the Universe* (San Marino: The Huntington Library, 1977), xvi–xvii. On inconsistencies in Renaissance psychological treatises, see Lawrence Babb, *The Elizabethan Malady: A Study of Melancholia in English Literature from 1580–1642* (East Lansing, Michigan State University Press, 67–72. For the importance of analogy as a habit of mind, see Elton, "Shakespeare and the Thought of his Age," 180–88. On the modern tendency to split the creative impulse of poetic "suggesting" from scientific "naming," see Rosemond Tuve, *Elizabethan and Metaphysical Imagery* (Chicago: University of Chicago Press, 1961), 105. On the importance of metaphorical constructs in modern science, see Angus Fletcher, *Allegory: The Theory of a Symbolic Mode* (Ithaca: Cornell University, 1964), 116. On the "'humour' metaphor of the Elizabethans as intrinsically closer to the truth as we understand it than was the 'drive' metaphor of the early twentieth century," see Melvin Konner, *The Tangled Wing: Biological Constraints on the Human Spirit* (New York, Harper Colophon Books, 1983), 92–93. See also David Edge, "Technological Metaphor and Social Control," *New Literary History* 6 (1974–75): 135–47.

2. Studies of Renaissance views of time include: Ricardo J. Quinones, *The Renaissance Discovery of Time* (Cambridge: Harvard University Press, 1972); Douglas L. Peterson, *Time, Tide, and Tempest* (San Marino, The Huntington Library, 1973); G. F. Waller, *The Strong Necessity of Time: The Philosophy of Time in Shakespeare and Elizabethan Literature* (The Hague: Mouton, 1976); Wylie Sypher, *The Ethic of Time: Structures of Experience in Shakespeare* (New York: Seabury Press, 1976); and David Scott Kastan, *Shakespeare and the Shapes of Time* (Hanover, New Hampshire: University Press of New England, 1982). The standard studies of the history of love include Anders Nygren, *Agape and Eros*, tr. Philip S.

Watson (Chicago: University of Chicago Press, 1982); M. C. D'Arcy, *The Mind and Heart of Love* (New York: Henry Holt, 1947); and Irving Singer, *The Nature of Love*, 3 vols. (Chicago: University of Chicago Press, 1967–1987). See also Julia Kristeva, *Tales of Love*, tr. Leon S. Roudiez (New York: Columbia University Press, 1987). For a fuller discussion of Renaissance views of love, see my discussion on 44–47 and the references in note 35 below.

3. For the general background, see John F. Callahan, *Four Views of Time in Ancient Philosophy* (Cambridge: Harvard University Press, 1948). See also Heninger, *The Cosmographical Glass*, 7–8.

4. A. E. Taylor, *A Commentary on Plato's Timaeus* (Oxford: The Clarendon Press, 1928), 221, quoted by Callahan, *Four Views of Time in Ancient Philosophy*, 24.

5. For Christian views of time, see Callahan on Augustine, 149–87. See also Oscar Cullman, *Christ and Time: The Primitive Christian Conception of Time and History*, tr. Floyd V. Filson (Philadelphia: Westminster Press, 1950).

6. For these medieval views, see Ernst H. Kantorowicz, *The King's Two Bodies: A Study in Medieval Political Theology* (Princeton: Princeton University Press, 1957), 273–84.

7. For the four periods, see Harry Levin, *The Myth of the Golden Age in the Renaissance* (Bloomington: Indiana University Press, 1969), particularly 3–31; see also A. Bartlett Giamatti, *The Earthly Paradise and the Renaissance Epic* (Princeton: Princeton University Press, 1966), 15–33.

8. For similar preoccupations in other cultures, see S. G. F. Brandon, "Time and the Destiny of Man," in *The Voices of Time*, ed. J. T. Fraser, 2d ed. (Amherst: University of Massachusetts Press, 1981), 140–57.

9. The naming of the days of the week was determined by the ruling deity (planet) during the first hour of each day. Following the cycle (Saturn, Jupiter, Mars, Sun, Venus, Mercury, Moon) through the 24 hours (7 times 3 + 3 = 24) means that the fourth on the list (the Sun) will rule the first hour of the next day. Thus, Sunday follows Saturday, Monday follows Sunday, etc.

10. For the relationship of Saturn and melancholy, see Raymond Klibansky, Erwin Panofsky, and Fritz Saxl, *Saturn and Melancholy: Studies in the History of Natural Philosophy, Religion, and Art* (London: Nelson, 1964).

11. For variations on the basic analogy of humours and seasons suggested on my chart, see Erwin Panofsky on Durer in

The Life and Art of Albrecht Durer (Princeton: Princeton University Press, 1971), 157. On the disagreements about which season and age are melancholy, see also Babb, *The Elizabethan Malady*, 10. For the view that "the tradition was allowed to degenerate," see Heninger, *The Cosmographical Glass*, 110.

12. See Campbell, Shakespeare's Tragic Heroes, 51–92; Babb, *The Elizabethan Malady*, 1–72; Heninger, *Touches of Sweet Harmony*, 158–77; Klibansky, Panofsky, and Saxl, *Saturn and Melancholy*, 1–123; Hankins, *Backgrounds of Shakespeare's Thought*, 119–45.

13. For an analysis of the physiological and psychological interactions summarized in this paragraph, see Babb, *The Elizabethan Malady*, particularly 1–20.

14. For an illustration of the blending of these factors, see Leuine Lemme, *The Touchstone of Complexions*, Englished by Thomas Newton (London, 1581), D4r.

15. For the activities of the spirits, see Campbell, 84–92. For an illustration of the working of the spirits with reference to the humours and the passions, see Lemme, *The Touchstone of Complexions*, C7v. For a summary of the theory, see Samuel C. Chew, *The Pilgrimage of Life* (New Haven: Yale University Press, 1962), 3.

16. For other references to fortune, see note 48 below. On the relationship of the wheel of time to the wheel of fortune, see Chew, *The Pilgrimage of Life*, 26. On holiday festivities, see the references in note 21 of my introduction.

17. For Lemme's analysis of the cycles, see *The Touchstone of Complexions*, D5r–v. See also Campbell, *Shakespeare's Tragic Heroes*, 60.

18. On the different rates of a person's progress through the humours, see Babb, *The Elizabethan Malady*, 9. On the connection of women with moisture and the phlegmatic, see Klibansky, Panofsky, and Saxl, *Saturn and Melancholy*, 105, 111.

19. On the humours of the body and times of the day, see T. Bright, *A Treatise of Melancholie* (London, 1586), H1v–H2r; and the scholarly discussions in Campbell, *Shakespeare's Tragic Heroes*, 59–60; Heninger, *The Cosmographical Glass*, 151; and J. W. Draper, "The Star-Crossed Lovers," *The Review of English Studies* 15 (1939): 21–22.

20. For discussions of the ages of life and their relationship to other cycles, see Chew, *The Pilgrimage of Life*, 144–73; Hankins, *Backgrounds of Shakespeare's Thought*, 61–67; Heninger, *Touches of Sweet Harmony*, 166–73, 223–25, 332–34; Babb, *The Elizabethan Malady*, 11–12. For the applications

to Shakespeare, see Marjorie Garber, *Coming of Age in Shakespeare* (London: Methuen, 1981). For a Renaissance example, see Henry Cuffe, *The Differences of the Ages of Man's Life* (London, 1607), 120–21, quoted by Alan Taylor Bradford, "Jaques' Distortion of the Seven-Ages Paradigm," *Shakespeare Quarterly* 27 (1976): 172–73. For illustrations of the seven ages, see Maurice Hussey, *The World of Shakespeare and his Contemporaries: A Visual Approach* (New York: Viking, 1972), 31; and Klibansky, Panofsky, and Saxl, *Saturn and Melancholy*, illustration 79. For the four ages, see *Saturn and Melancholy*, illustrations 75, 76; and Heninger, *The Cosmographical Glass*, figures 65, 67, and 88. All of these illustrations include a wheel of life.

21. Edmund Spenser, "February," *The Shepherd's Calendar and Other Poems*, ed. Philip Henderson (London: J. M. Dent and Sons, 1956), 17–25.

22. Don Cameron Allen, *The Star-Crossed Renaissance* (Durham: Duke University Press, 1941), 147–89.

23. For astrology as a reflection of Renaissance scientific thought, see Wayne Shumaker, *The Occult Sciences in the Renaissance: A Study in Intellectual Patterns* (Berkeley, University of California Press, 1972), 1–59; and Robert K. De Kosky, *Knowledge and Cosmos: Development and Decline of the Medieval Perspective* (Washington: University Press of America, 1979), 65–71. For a summary and evaluation of Renaissance works on astrology, see Allen, *The Star-Crossed Renaissance*. For the relationship of astrology to occult thought, see D. P. Walker, *Spiritual and Demonic Magic From Ficino to Campanella* (Notre Dame, University of Notre Dame Press, 1975); Yates, *The Occult Philosophy in the Elizabethan Age*; Yates, *Giordano Bruno and the Hermetic Tradition*; and Mebane, *Renaissance Magic and the Return of the Golden Age*. On Mercury (Hermes) and Hermetic thought, see also Elam, *Shakespeare's Universe of Discourse*, 148–59. For a general outline of the history of astrology, see Christopher McIntosh, *The Astrologers and their Creed: an Historical Outline* (New York: Praeger, 1969).

24. For general discussions of the sun, see Mircea Eliade, "The Sun and Sun-Worship," *Patterns in Comparative Religion*, tr. Rosemary Sheed (Cleveland: World, 1963), 124–53; and Jacquetta Hawkes, *Man and the Sun* (New York: Random House, 1962). For Renaissance views, see Hankins, *Backgrounds of Shakespeare's Thought*, 25–27.

25. For discussion of the moon, see Mircea Eliade, "The Moon and Its Mystique," *Patterns in Comparative Religion,*

154–87; Hankins, *Backgrounds of Shakespeare's Thought*, 27–30. For a link of the phases of the moon to the qualities of the elements, see James Wilson, *A Complete Dictionary of Astrology* (Boston, 1885), 319.

26. For the positive reading of the gods-planets, see Yates on Pico and Giorgio in *The Occult Philosophy in the Elizabethan Age*, particularly 33–34.

27. For discussions of alchemy, see John Read, *Through Alchemy to Chemistry: A Procession of Ideas & Personalities* (London: G. Bell, 1957); C. G. Jung, *Psychology and Alchemy*, *The Collected Works of C. G. Jung*, vol. 12 (Princeton: Princeton University Press, 1953); Allen G. Debus, *The English Paracelsians* (New York: Franklin Watts, 1966); Debus, *The Chemical Philosophy: Paracelsian Science and Medicine in the Sixteenth and Seventeenth Centuries*, vol. 1 (New York: Science History Publications, 1977); Heninger, *The Cosmographical Glass*, 182–90; De Kosky, *Knowledge and Cosmos*, 97–105; and Shumaker, *The Occult Sciences in the Renaissance*, 166–200.

28. Read, *Through Alchemy to Chemistry*, 19. For the importance of analogical thinking for alchemy, see Shumaker, *The Occult Sciences in the Renaissance*, 193–97.

29. On the huge and controversial subject of Elizabethan attitudes toward love, see Franklin M. Dickey, *Not Wisely But Too Well: Shakespeare's Love Tragedies* (San Marino: The Huntington Library), 3–45; John Vyvyan, *Shakespeare and Platonic Beauty* (London: Chatto and Windus, 1961); Rose, *Heroic Love: Studies in Sidney and Spenser*, 5–34; Barbara L. Parker, *A Precious Seeing: Love and Reason in Shakespeare's Plays* (New York: New York University Press, 1987), 44–66; and Mary Beth Rose, *The Expense of Spirit: Love and Sexuality in English Renaissance Drama* (Ithaca: Cornell University Press, 1988). See also the references to gender studies in note 35 below, and the references in note 2 above. On the links among love, mutability, and metamorphosis, see William C. Carroll, *The Metamorphoses of Shakespearean Comedy* (Princeton: Princeton University Press, 1985), 7–32. On the importance of daemons both as agents of cosmic forces and as parallels to the abstractions of allegory, see Fletcher, *Allegory*, 25–69. See also my discussion of fairies in *A Midsummer Night's Dream* in chapter 7.

30. For modern views of androgyny, see June Singer, *Androgyny: Toward a New Theory of Sexuality* (Garden City, New York: Anchor Press, 1976); and Ellen Piel Cook, *Psychological Androgyny* (New York: Pergamon Press, 1985). For Jung on the

animus and anima, see *The Collected Works of C. G. Jung,*
vol. 6, 467–72; vol. 7, 198–211; vol. 9, pt.2, 11–22. For neo-
Freudian views of gender and love, see Julia Kristeva, *Tales of
Love;* and Nancy Chodorow, *The Reproduction of Mothering:
Psychoanalysis and the Sociology of Gender* (Berkeley, University of California Press, 1978). See also Madelon Gohlke, "'I
wooed thee with my sword': Shakespeare's Tragic Paradigms,"
in *Representing Shakespeare: New Psychoanalytic Essays,* ed.
Murray M. Schwartz and Coppelia Kahn (Baltimore: Johns
Hopkins University Press, 1980), 170–87. On similarities be-
tween Renaissance Christian and Freudian views of love, see
Arthur Kirsch, *Shakespeare and the Experience of Love* (Cambridge: Cambridge University Press, 1981), particularly 1–9.

31. On images of Cupid, Venus, and Diana, see particularly
Erwin Panofsky, *Studies in Iconology: Humanistic Themes in
the Art of the Renaissance* (Oxford: Oxford University Press,
1939); Edgar Wind, *Pagan Mysteries in the Renaissance* (New
Haven: Yale University Press, 1958); Nohrnberg, *The Analogy
of The Faerie Queene,* 562–66; and Kott, "The Bottom Translation," 29–30, 45–50.

32. For a fuller analysis, see Babb, *The Elizabethan Malady,*
2–5. See also my discussion of Davies's views in *Nosce
Teipsum* on 55–56. On the animal spirits, see Hankins, *Backgrounds of Shakespeare's Thought,* 82–83. On the five senses,
see Hankins, *Backgrounds of Shakespeare's Thought,* 76–89;
and Chew, *The Pilgrimage of Life,* 192–95. On the eye and the
ear, see William G. Madsen, *From Shadowy Types to Truth:
Studies in Milton's Symbolism* (New Haven: Yale University
Press, 1968), 145–80. On the link of sight and reason, see Pico
della Mirandola, *A Platonick Discourse upon Love,* ed.
Gardner (Boston, 1914), 27. See also Peter de la Primaudaye,
The French Academie (London, 1586), H5r. On the internal
senses (common sense, phantasy, imagination, judgment, and
memory), see Hankins, *Backgrounds of Shakespeare's Thought,*
89–101.

33. See de la Primaudaye, *The French Academie,* N2v.

34. For discussions of Medieval and Renaissance views on
the virtues and vices, see Rosemond Tuve, "Allegory of
Vices and Virtues," *Allegorical Imagery* (Princeton: Princeton
University Press, 1966), 57–143; and Adolf Katzenellenbogen,
Allegories of the Virtues and Vices in Medieval Art (London:
Warburg Institute, 1939).

35. For Shakespeare's treatment of gender issues, see particularly Juliet Dusinberre, *Shakespeare and the Nature of*

Women (New York: Barnes and Noble, 1975); Coppelia Kahn, *Man's Estate: Masculine Identity in Shakespeare* (Berkeley: University of California Press, 1981); Irene G. Dash, *Wooing, Wedding, and Power* (New York: Columbia University Press, 1981); Linda Bamber, *Comic Women: Tragic Men: A Study of Gender and Genre in Shakespeare* (Stanford: Stanford University Press, 1982); Marilyn French, *Shakespeare's Division of Experience* (New York: Summit Books, 1983); Marianne Novy, *Love's Argument: Gender Relations in Shakespeare* (Chapel Hill: University of North Carolina Press, 1984); Marilyn L. Williamson, *The Patriarchy of Shakespeare's Comedies* (Detroit: Wayne State University Press, 1986); Diane Elizabeth Dreher, *Domination and Defiance: Fathers and Daughters in Shakespeare* (Lexington: University of Kentucky Press, 1986); and Edward Snow, "Language and Sexual Difference in *Romeo and Juliet*," 168–92. On the difficulty of becoming adult in a patriarchal society, see Kahn, *Man's Estate*, 82–103. On that theme, see also Garber, *Coming of Age in Shakespeare*. For the tendency in recent studies to take an extreme patriarchal position as the Elizabethan norm and to see views more favorable to women as evidence of contradiction and / or a developing feminism, see Kahn, *Man's Estate*, 12–17; and Montrose, "*A Midsummer Night's Dream* and the Shaping Fantasies of Elizabethan Culture: Gender, Power, Form.*" For the view that a more traditional "Idea" of woman was "reclaimed" even though day-to-day life for women did not change dramatically, see Davies, *The Feminine Reclaimed*, 6–7.

36. See Leonard Barkan, "The Human Body and the Commonwealth," *Nature's Work of Art*, 61–115.

37. For the metaphor of the world as a stage, see Anne Righter, *Shakespeare and the Idea of the Play* (New York, Barnes and Noble, 1962), 64–86.

38. For the significance of *Defence of Poesie*, see Heninger, *Sidney and Spenser*, a revised and expanded version of his chapter on "The Poet as Maker" in his *Touches of Sweet Harmony*, 287–324. See also Andrew D. Weiner, *Sir Philip Sidney and the Poetics of Protestantism: A Study of Contexts* (Minneapolis: University of Minnesota Press, 1978). For Sidney's influence on *A Midsummer Night's Dream*, see Weiner, "'Multiformitie uniforme': *A Midsummer Night's Dream*," *English Literary History* 38 (1971): 328–49; and Michel Poirier, "Sidney's Influence Upon *A Midsummer Night's Dream*," *Studies in Philology* 44 (1947): 483–89. See

also Diana Akers Rhoads, *Shakespeare's Defense of Poetry: A Midsummer Night's Dream and The Tempest* (Lanham, Maryland: University Press of America, 1985).

39. Heninger, *Sidney and Spenser*, 223–306.

40. Sir Philip Sidney, *Selected Prose and Poetry*, ed. Robert Kimbrough (New York: Holt, Rinehart, and Winston, 1969), 108.

41. For a much fuller discussion of cosmic metaphor and the literary microcosm, see Heninger, *Touches of Sweet Harmony*, 325–97. See also Tuve, *Elizabethan and Metaphysical Imagery*, 155–64; and Fletcher's discussion of "The Cosmic Image" in *Allegory*, 70–146.

42. For the Augustinian and Medieval backgrounds, see D. W. Robertson, Jr., *A Preface to Chaucer: Studies in Medieval Perspectives* (Princeton: Princeton University Press, 1962), particularly 292–300; and Patrick Grant, *Images and Ideas in Literature of the English Renaissance* (Amherst, University of Massachusetts Press, 1979), 1–26. On the implications of a shift to a more Aristotelean emphasis, see Heninger, *Spenser and Sidney*, 64–65. See also Fineman, *Shakespeare's Perjured Eye*, 342–45.

43. Heninger, *Touches of Sweet Harmony*, 325. On the place of metaphor, see also *Sidney and Spenser*, 286–91; Madsen, *From Shadowy Type to Truth: Studies in Milton's Symbolism*, 54–84; Fineman, *Shakespeare's Perjured Eye*, 95–121; and Fletcher, *Allegory*, 135.

44. For a general discussion, see Northrop Frye, *The Anatomy of Criticism: Four Essays* (New York: Atheneum, 1966). On the conventions of romance, see also Peterson, *Time, Tide, and Tempest*, 3–70.

45. For Venus and Diana, see the references in note 31 above. For Renaissance works utilizing mythological themes, see Douglas Bush, *Mythology and the Renaissance Tradition in English Poetry*, New Revised Edition (New York: Norton, 1963).

46. A convenient introduction to these matters from a mythological point of view is Alan W. Watts, *Myth and Ritual in Christianity* (New York: Grove Press, 1960), 27–47.

47. See Peterson, *Time, Tide, and Tempest*, 19–44. See also Frye, *Fools of Time*, 88–95.

48. For discussions of fortune, see Russell A. Fraser, *Shakespeare's Poetics in Relation to King Lear* (London: Routledge and Kegan Paul, 1962), 46–60; and Kiefer, *Fortune and Elizabethan Tragedy*, particularly 1–29, 193–231. See also Peterson, *Time, Tide, and Tempest*, 26–32; Leo Salingar, *Shakespeare*

and the Traditions of Comedy (Cambridge: Cambridge University Press, 1974), 129–74; Klibansky, Panofsky, and Saxl, *Saturn and Melancholy*, 202 and illustrations 19–23; Frye, *Fools of Time*, 13–14, 88–95, 116; and Chew, *The Pilgrimage of Life*, 22–69. On the tendency to overemphasize the importance of fortune and fate in *Romeo and Juliet*, see H. A. Mason, *Shakespeare's Tragedies of Love* (New York: Barnes and Noble, 1970), 3–23.

49. On Machiavelli's attitudes, see Kiefer, *Fortune and Elizabethan Tragedy*, 198–203.

50. Sir John Davies, *Nosce Teipsum, in Some Longer Elizabethan Poems: An English Garner* (New York: Cooper Square Publishers, 1964), 83.

51. Davies, 47.

52. Davies, 43, 92.

PART 2: *ROMEO AND JULIET*

Notes to Chapter 2: Every Thing in Extremity

1. For an approach in some respects similar to mine, see Marion Bodwell Smith's chapter on *Romeo and Juliet* in her *Dualities in Shakespeare*, 79–109. See also the chapter on *Romeo and Juliet* in Joan Hartwig's *Shakespeare's Analogical Scene: Parody as Structural Syntax* (Lincoln: University of Nebraska Press, 1983); and McAlindon, *Shakespeare's Tragic Cosmos*, 56–75. On the language of Romeo and Juliet in relation to gender roles, see Snow, "Language and Sexual Difference in *Romeo and Juliet*," 168–92.

2. For the double meanings of "fearful passage," see M. M. Mahood, *Shakespeare's Wordplay* (London: Methuen, 1957), 56. See also James L. Calderwood, *Shakespearean Metadrama* (Minneapolis: University of Minnesota Press, 1971), 113–16. For a fuller discussion of literary microcosms, see my discussion on 50–52. For the view that knowledge of the ending gives the audience a sense of fate's control, see Bertrand Evans, *Shakespeare's Tragic Practice* (Oxford: Oxford University Press, 1979), 22–24.

3. We learn later in the scene that it is 9 A.M.

4. Gregory is named but Sampson is not, unless in some program list. See also Roy Battenhouse, *Shakespearean Tragedy: Its Art and Its Christian Premises* (Bloomington: Indiana University Press, 1969), 116.

5. For choler as the humour that governs the time between 6 A.M. and noon (or in a variant scheme from 3 A.M. to 9 A.M.), see my discussion on p. 35 and note 19 on p. 305.

6. See Eric Partridge, *Shakespeare's Bawdy* (London: Routledge and Kegan Paul, 1955), 199.

7. On the presence of comedy in this opening, see Dickey, *Not Wisely But Too Well*, 73–74; Nicholas Brooke, *Shakespeare's Early Tragedies* (London: Methuen, 1969), 88–89; and Susan Snyder, *The Comic Matrix of Shakespeare's Tragedies* (Princeton: Princeton University Press, 1979), 59–60.

8. On the Prince as the image of proper authority, see G. K. Hunter, "Shakespeare's Earliest Tragedies," *Dramatic Identities and Cultural Tradition: Studies in Shakespeare and His Contemporaries* (New York: Barnes and Noble, 1978), 324–25. More negative readings are presented by Battenhouse, *Shakespearean Tragedy*, 118–19; and Kirby Farrell, *Shakespeare's Creation: The Language of Magic and Play* (Amherst: University of Massachusetts Press, 1975), 119.

9. See Gibbons's note in the Arden *Romeo and Juliet*, 88.

10. See Norman Rabkin, *Shakespeare and the Common Understanding* (New York: The Free Press, 1967), 162–64; Clemen, *The Development of Shakespeare's Imagery*, 63–73; Smith, *Dualities in Shakespeare*, 100–09; Calderwood, *Shakespearean Metadrama*, 85–119; Ralph Berry, *The Shakespearean Metaphor* (Totowa, N. J.: Rowman and Littlefield, 1978), 37–47; David Laird, "The Generation of Style in *Romeo and Juliet*", *Journal of English and Germanic Philology* 63 (1964): 204–13; E. C. Pettet, *Shakespeare and the Romance Tradition* (London: Staples Press, 1949), 114–22; Philip Edwards, *Shakespeare and the Confines of Art* (London: Methuen, 1968), 76–77; and Garber, *Coming of Age in Shakespeare*, 96–97. Less negative accounts of the Petrarchan tradition's influence are found in Inge Leimberg, *Shakespeares Romeo und Julia von der Sonettdictung zur Liebestragodie* (Munich, 1968), 67–79, 131–45; Rosalie L. Colie, *Shakespeare's Living Art* (Princeton: Princeton University Press, 1974), 135–46; and Gibbons, introduction to *Romeo and Juliet*, 42–52. See also Winifred Nowottny, "Shakespeare's Tragedies", in *Shakespeare's World*, ed. James Sutherland and Joel Hurstfield (London: E. Arnold, 1964), 49–51; Joseph S. M. J. Chang, "The Language of Paradox in *Romeo and Juliet*," *Shakespeare Studies* 3 (1967): 22–42; and Robert O. Evans, *The Osier Cage: Rhetorical Devices in Romeo & Juliet* (Lexington: University of Kentucky Press, 1966).

11. Colie, *Shakespeare's Living Art*, 11.

12. Colie, *Shakespeare's Living Art*, 145.

13. For the plant image, see Gibbons, *The Arden Shakespeare*, 91n. For the smoke and fume passage, see S. K. Heninger, Jr., *A Handbook of Renaissance Meteorology* (Durham: Duke University Press, 1960), 214.

14. J. Leeds Barroll, *Artificial Persons: The Formation of Character in the Tragedies of Shakespeare* (Columbia: University of South Carolina Press, 1974), 67–73.

15. On contrariety as a reference to irreconcilable oppositions, see Grudin, *Mighty Opposites*, 35–40.

16. For the iconography of Cupid, see Panofsky, "Blind Cupid," *Studies in Iconology*, 95–128; on the blind Cupids, see Wind, *Pagan Mysteries in the Renaissance*, 57–77, 129–41.

17. For the tradition of the harmony of Diana and Venus, see Wind, *Pagan Mysteries in the Renaissance*, 73–77; see also the bibliography in note 2 of chapter 6.

18. For Renaissance attitudes toward the parental role in selecting husbands for daughters, see Dreher, *Domination and Defiance*, 16–75, particularly 48–51 on Capulet.

19. On Lady Capulet's support for her husband as an image of the "Law of the Father," see Gail Kern Paster, *The Body Embarrassed: Drama and the Disciplines of Shame in Early Modern England* (Ithaca: Cornell University Press, 1993), 225–27. For negative readings of Lady Capulet, see Harry Levin, "Form and Formality in *Romeo and Juliet*", *Shakespeare and the Revolution of the Times* (Oxford: Oxford University Press, 1976), 105–07; and Farrell, *Shakespeare's Creation*, 122–23.

20. See also Bassanio's image of Portia as a "golden fleece" in *The Merchant of Venice*, 1.1.170; and Snyder, *The Comic Matrix of Shakespeare's Tragedies*, 61.

21. On the judgment of Paris, see Hallett Smith, *Elizabethan Poetry: A Study in Convention, Meaning, and Expression* (Cambridge: Harvard University Press, 1952), 3–9.

22. On the analogous cosmic disruption, see Smith, *Dualities in Shakespeare*, 82. See also Everett, "*Romeo and Juliet*: The Nurse's Story," *Critical Quarterly* 4 (1972): 129–39; Chang, "The Language of Paradox in *Romeo and Juliet*," 25–26; Farrell, *Shakespeare's Creation*, 130–31; Snow, "Language and Sexual Difference in *Romeo and Juliet*," 181–85; Farrell, *Play, Death, and Heroism in Shakespeare*, 141–42; and Paster, *The Body Embarrassed*, 220–31.

23. On the emphasis on coming of age caused by changing

the age of the Juliet of the sources, see Hankins, *Backgrounds of Shakespeare's Thought*, 64–65. See also Bullough, introduction to *Narrative and Dramatic Sources of Shakespeare*, vol. 1: *Early Comedies, Poems, Romeo and Juliet* (London: Routledge and Kegan Paul, 1957), 279; and my discussion of the ages of life on 35–36.

24. Barbara Everett, "Romeo and Juliet: The Nurse's Story," 132.

25. See my discussion of astrology on 36–41. See also Gibbons's introduction, 52–62; Chang, "The Language of Paradox in *Romeo and Juliet*," 35–39; and T. J. Cribb, "The Unity of 'Romeo and Juliet'," *Shakespeare Survey* 34 (1981): 93–104, particularly 97–98.

26. On the mask tradition, see Enid Welsford, *The Court Masque* (New York: Russell and Russell, 1927); and Kott, "The Bottom Translation," 45–52.

27. On the planet Mercury, see my discussion on 41. For Mercutio in Brooke, see Geoffrey Bullough, introduction to *Narrative and Dramatic Sources of Shakespeare*, 1: 279–81. On the contradictory elements in Mercutio, see Harley Granville-Barker, *Prefaces to Shakespeare*, vol. 2 (Princeton: Princeton University Press, 1947): 335–38; Norman N. Holland, "Mercutio, Mine Own Son, the Dentist," in *Essays on Shakespeare*, ed. Gordon Ross Smith (University Park: Penn State University Press, 1965), 3–14; and Derick R. C. Marsh, *Passion Lends Them Power: A Study of Shakespeare's Love Tragedies* (Manchester, Manchester University Press, 1976), 56–57, 59. For the background of the god Mercury, see Joseph A. Porter, *Shakespeare's Mercutio: His History and Drama* (Chapel Hill: University of North Carolina Press, 1989). For the moral weaknesses of Mercutio, see Harold C. Goddard, *The Meaning of Shakespeare* (Chicago: University of Chicago Press, 1951), 120–31.

28. On the internal senses, see part 1, note 32; and my discussion of Puck and Oberon on 213.

29. See the note in *The Riverside Shakespeare*, 1064.

30. Sigmund Freud, *A General Introduction to Psychoanalysis* (New York: Liveright, 1964), 162.

31. On the speech's "cynical, promiscuous, and even nasty" tone, see Brooke, *Shakespeare's Early Tragedies*, 94.

32. For the conventional association of the winds with the humours, see Heninger, *A Handbook of Renaissance Meteorology*, 114.

33. For a discussion of dream in the play, see Marjorie Garber, *Dream in Shakespeare: From Metaphor to Metamorphosis* (New Haven: Yale University Press, 1974), 35–47.

See also K. M. Briggs, *The Anatomy of Puck: An Examination of Fairy Beliefs among Shakespeare's Contemporaries and Successors* (London: Routledge and Kegan Paul, 1959), 47; Frye, *Fools of Time*, 59–61; Calderwood, *Shakespearean Metadrama*, 104–05; Jerome Mandel, "Dream and Imagination in Shakespeare", *Shakespeare Quarterly* 24 (1973): 61–68; Gibbons's introduction, 67–68; Brooke, *Shakespeare's Early Tragedies*, 86–87; and Chang, "The Language of Paradox in *Romeo and Juliet*," 35–36.

34. Peterson, *Time, Tide and Tempest*, 54. For his discussion of the image in *Romeo and Juliet*, see 56–58, and his article, "*Romeo and Juliet* and the Art of Moral Navigation", *Pacific Coast Studies in Shakespeare*, ed. Thelma Greenfield and Waldo F. McNeir (Eugene: University of Oregon Press, 1966), 33–46. See also Smith, *Dualities in Shakespeare*, 94.

Notes to Chapter 3: Extreme Sweet

1. On Shakespeare's use of techniques of comedy, see Snyder, *The Comic Matrix of Shakespeare's Tragedies*, 56–73.

2. For the view that Will Kempe played not only Peter and Sampson but also the clownish servants in 1.2 and 4.2, see Giorgio Melchiori, "Peter, Balthazar, and Shakespeare's Art of Doubling," *The Modern Language Review* 78 (1983): 777–92.

3. For the view that the feud is about to end, see Evans, *Shakespeare's Tragic Practice*, 30–31.

4. See Alan Brissenden, *Shakespeare and the Dance* (Atlantic Highlands, New Jersey: Humanities Press, 1981), 64–66.

5. Romeo and Juliet speak only about 255 lines directly to each other, about 220 of them in the balcony scenes. For the importance of the imagery of the religion of love, see Paul V. Siegel, *Shakespeare in his Time and Ours* (Notre Dame: University of Notre Dame Press, 1968), 69–107; and Dusinberre, *Shakespeare and the Nature of Women*, 137–75. For the sonnet and its context, see Brooke, *Shakespeare's Early Tragedies*, 95–96; Leimberg, *Shakespeares Romeo und Julia*, 149–50; and Marsh, *Passion Lends Them Power*, 59.

6. See note, *The Complete Works of Shakespeare*, ed. Irving Ribner and George Lyman Kittredge (Waltham, Massachusetts: Ginn, 1971), 977. See also John Erskine Hankins, *Shakespeare's Derived Imagery* (Lawrence: University of Kansas Press, 1953), 156.

7. For the identification of the garden with Juliet's femininity, see Sherman Hawkins, "The Two Worlds of Shakespearean Comedy," *Shakespeare Studies* 3 (1967): 74; Garber,

Coming of Age in Shakespeare, 163–65; and Snow, "Language and Sexual Difference in *Romeo and Juliet,*" 182–85. For the metaphorical traditions of gardens, see Giammati, *The Earthly Paradise and the Renaissance Epic,* 11–93; and Stanley Stewart, *The Enclosed Garden: The Tradition and the Image in Seventeenth Century Poetry* (Madison: University of Wisconsin Press, 1966).

8. See Dusinberre, *Shakespeare and the Nature of Women,* 156. On mutuality in love in *Romeo and Juliet,* see Novy, *Love's Argument: Gender Relations in Shakespeare,* 100–09.

9. Significant discussions of the scene's poetic language include: Spurgeon, *Shakespeare's Imagery,* 310–16; Clemen, *The Development of Shakespeare's Imagery,* 66–68; Dickey, *Not Wisely But Too Well,* 84–87; Mason, *Shakespeare's Tragedies of Love,* 42–49; Leimberg, *Shakespeares Romeo und Julia,* 150–60; and Marsh, *Passion Lends Them Power,* 60–64.

10. See Garber, *Coming of Age in Shakespeare,* 25–26. On Juliet's "verbal nominalism," see Calderwood, *Shakespearean Metadrama,* 85–119, particularly 87–95. On her superior maturity, see Evelyn Gajowski, *The Art of Loving: Female Subjectivity and Male Discursive Traditions in Shakespeare's Tragedies* (Newark: University of Delaware Press, 1992), 26–50. For a discussion of neoplatonic beliefs about names, see Elam, *Shakespeare's Universe of Discourse,* 122–25. See also Brooke, *Shakespeare's Early Tragedies,* 96–98; and Manfred Weidhorn, "The Rose and its Name: On Denomination in *Othello, Romeo and Juliet, Julius Caesar,*" *Texas Studies in Literature and Language* 11 (1969–1970): 671–86.

11. On Romeo's language in relation to his masculinity, see also Snow, "Language and Sexual Difference in *Romeo and Juliet.*"

12. On Romeo's association with Cupid and the importance of the myth of Cupid and Psyche, see Garber, *Coming of Age in Shakespeare,* 166–70. For Renaissance interpretations of the myth, see Wind, *Pagan Mysteries in the Renaissance,* 134–35, 145–46; and Davies, *The Feminine Reclaimed,* 91–93.

13. For the cosmic overtones of sea imagery, see Peterson, *Time, Tide and Tempest,* 44–51. See also Smith, *Dualities in Shakespeare,* 92–93. On the timeless quality in the middle part of the balcony scene, see Emrys Jones, *Scenic Form in Shakespeare* (Oxford: Oxford University Press, 1971), 35. For the link of such moments to the eternal, see Stewart, *The Enclosed Garden,* 131–32. On the changing attitudes toward love reflected in Juliet's garden, see Hall, *The Structure of Love,* 25–30.

14. On the associations of Cupid with death, see the

chapter on "Amor as a God of Death" in Wind, *Pagan Mysteries in the Renaissance*, 129–41; and Nohrnberg, *The Analogy of The Faerie Queene*, 486–90.

15. Among those who see the speech as a significant statement of Renaissance attitudes are Dickey, *Not Wisely But Too Well*, 106–09; Roland Mushat Frye, *Shakespeare and Christian Doctrine* (Princeton: Princeton University Press, 1963), 216–19; Whitaker, *The Mirror up to Nature*, 113–14; Smith, *Dualities in Shakespeare*, 86–87; Pettet, *Shakespeare and the Romance Tradition*, 118–21; Grudin, *Mighty Opposites*, 36–40; and McAlindon, *Shakespeare's Tragic Cosmos*, 59–60. For more negative judgments, see Battenhouse *Shakespearean Tragedy*, 121; Gibbons's introduction, 66; and James C. Bryant, "The Problematical Friar in *Romeo and Juliet*," *English Studies* 55 (1974): 340–50.

16. Q2–3 and the Folio print these lines twice, once here and once with some variations for Romeo near the end of the preceding scene. For the view that the lines should be Romeo's, see George Walton Williams, note to *The Most Excellent and Lamentable Tragedie of Romeo and Juliet: A Critical Edition* (Durham: Duke University Press, 1964), 119–21; and Gibbons, *The Arden Shakespeare*, 136n.

17. See my discussion on 31–36.

18. On the association of rosemary with both love and death and with both weddings and funerals, see Philip Williams, "The Rosemary Theme in *Romeo and Juliet*," *Modern Language Notes* 68 (1953): 400–03. See also Dessen, *Elizabethan Stage Conventions and Modern Interpreters*, 131–32; and Hartwig, *Shakespeare's Analogical Structure*, 82–84.

19. See 2.4.140–41. See also Goddard, *The Meaning of Shakespeare*, 122.

20. For a somewhat more optimistic view, see Smith, *Dualities in Shakespeare*, 90–91. The gunpowder image recurs in 3.2.132–34 and 5.1.63–65. For the similar imagery of alchemy, see my discussion on 41–42.

21. Lysander uses a similar image: "a surfeit of the sweetest things / The deepest loathing to the stomach brings" (2.2.137–38). See my discussion on 237–38.

Notes to Chapter 4: Mortal Paradise

1. For interconnections among love, death, and fortune in Elizabethan tragedy, see Kiefer, *Fortune and Elizabethan Tragedy*, 158–92.

2. See my discussion on 66–67. See also Honor Matthews,

Character and Symbol in Shakespeare's Plays (New York: Schocken Books, 1969), 93–94.

3. For Juliet's soliloquy as an ironic epithalamium, see Gary M. McCown, "Runnawayes Eyes and Juliet's Epithalamium," *Shakespeare Quarterly* 27 (1976): 150–70. See also Gibbons's introduction, 57–59; Rabkin, *Shakespeare and the Common Understanding*, 181–83; Battenhouse, *Shakespearean Tragedy*, 108–09; and Hall, *The Structure of Love*, 91–93.

4. For a discussion of the Phaethon image in this scene and in relation to the Queen Mab coach, see Brooke, *Shakespeare's Early Tragedies*, 83–85; Chang, "The Language of Paradox in Romeo and Juliet," 35–36. See also Smith, *Dualities in Shakespeare*, 91–92; and my discussion on 79–81.

5. For the argument that the eyes belong to Cupid, see McCown, "Runnawayes Eyes and Juliet's Epithalamium," 156–65.

6. For a possible sexual reading of Juliet's death and the "little stars," see Gibbons, *The Arden Shakespeare*, 170n.

7. For the view that this visual metaphor reinforces Romeo's "womanish" behavior, see Dessen, *Elizabethan Stage Conventions and Modern Interpreters*, 3–5.

8. For the haste theme, see Granville-Barker, *Prefaces to Shakespeare*, 2: 313–17; and Brents Stirling, *Unity in Shakespearean Tragedy: The Interplay of Theme and Character* (New York: Columbia University Press, 1956), 10–25.

9. For discussions of the second balcony scene, see Marsh, *Passion Lends Them Power*, 74–76; Calderwood, *Shakespearean Metadrama*, 101–02; Evans, *Shakespeare's Tragic Practice*, 36; and Battenhouse, *Shakespearean Tragedy*, 109–10. For parallels between the two balcony scenes, see Mark Rose, *Shakespearean Design* (Cambridge: Harvard University Press, 1972), 69–72; on visual parallels, see James Black, "The Visual Artistry of *Romeo and Juliet*," *Studies in English Literature* 15 (1975): 246–48. On the aubade form, see Levin, "Form and Formality in *Romeo and Juliet*," 118. On the hunt imagery, see *Romeo and Juliet: A New Variorum Edition*, ed. Horace Howard Furness (New York: American Scholar Publications, 1963), 193–95n.

10. See Goddard, *The Meaning of Shakespeare*, 124.

11. For the view that bigamy was common and therefore less outrageous to an Elizabethan audience, see Garber, quoting Lawrence Stone, *Coming of Age in Shakespeare*, 120.

12. See Farrell, *Shakespeare's Creation*, 128–32. For more sympathetic views of Juliet, see Wolfgang Clemen, "Shakespeare's Soliloquies," *Shakespeare's Dramatic Art* (London:

Methuen, 1972), 155–56; Goddard, *The Meaning of Shakespeare*, 135–36; Leimberg, Shakespeares *Romeo und Julia*, 190–93; Garber, *Coming of Age in Shakespeare*, 219–20; and Marsh, *Passion Lends Them Power*, 79–80.

13. For the mandrake plant as a cause of madness and death, see Gibbons, *The Arden Shakespeare*, 205n. For the sexual associations of the mandrake, see D. C. Allen, "Donne on the Mandrake," *Modern Language Notes* 74 (1959): 393–97.

14. For Juliet's subconscious guilt over her revolt against her patriarchal family and her fantasy of a redeeming self-sacrifice, see Farrell, *Play, Death, and Heroism in Shakespeare*, 141–42.

Notes to Chapter 5: Womb of Death

1. For a discussion of the impact of discrepant awareness, see Evans, *Shakespeare's Tragic Practice*, 44–45.

2. For the negative reading, see particularly Rabkin, *Shakespeare and the Common Understanding*, 165–74; S. L. Bethell, *Shakespeare and the Popular Dramatic Tradition* (New York: Octagon Books, 1970), 134–37; Charles B. Lower, "*Romeo and Juliet*, IV, v: A Stage Direction and Purposeful Comedy," *Shakespeare Studies* 8 (1975): 177–94; and Hartwig, *Shakespeare's Analogical Structure*, 81–84. For a discussion of Shakespeare's problem in not being able to dramatize the truth, see Evans, *Shakespeare's Tragic Practice*, 42–43.

3. For imagery linking love and death, particularly death as a personified competitor for Juliet, see Smith, *Dualities in Shakespeare*, 82–88; and Kiefer, *Fortune and Elizabethan Tragedy*, 176–82. See also Nohrnberg, *The Analogy of The Faerie Queene*, 489–90.

4. Battenhouse notes this parallel between Peter and the Friar. See *Shakespearean Tragedy*, 125. Scholars critical of the scene include: Snyder, *The Comic Matrix of Shakespeare's Tragedies*, 69; Evans, *Shakespeare's Tragic Practice*, 43–44; Levin, "Form and Formality in *Romeo and Juliet*," 117–18; and Hartwig, *Shakespeare's Analogical Structure*, 84–90. On the practical reasons for the scene, see Granville-Barker, *Prefaces to Shakespeare*, 2: 325–26.

5. For a discussion of attitudes toward law, Catholicism, monasticism, and friars, see Darryl J. Gless, Measure for *Measure, the Law, and the Convent* (Princeton: Princeton University Press, 1979), 27–89.

6. See my discussion on 266–67.

7. For the traditional metaphorical readings of metals and their relation to alchemy, see my discussion on 41–42.

8. On the dream, see Evans, *Shakespeare's Tragic Practice*, 44; Norman N. Holland, "Romeo's Dream and the Paradox of Literary Realism," in *The Design Within: Psychoanalytic Approaches to Shakespeare* (New York: J. Aronson, 1970), 43–54; Battenhouse, *Shakespearean Tragedy*, 111; Hartwig, *Shakespeare's Analogical Structure*, 91–93; and Garber, *Dream in Shakespeare*, 44–47. See also my discussion on 132–33 of Lady Capulet's plan for killing Romeo.

9. Hartwig, *Shakespeare's Analogical Scene*, 93–105. On the apothecary and death, see Marsh, *Passion Lends Them Power*, 81–82. On the Friar as parallel to the apothecary, see Battenhouse, *Shakespearean Tragedy*, 125.

10. On the possible symbolic significance of pestilence, see Gibbons's introduction, 61. On the insignificance of Friar John's failure, see Evans, *Shakespeare's Tragic Practice*, 46–47.

11. See Battenhouse, *Shakespearean Tragedy*, 126–27.

12. On the use of a dragon's mouth for the entrance to Hell on the medieval stage, see Glynne Wickham, *Shakespeare's Dramatic Heritage* (London: Routledge and Kegan Paul, 1969), 214–24, and plates X and XI. See also Doebler, *Shakespeare's Speaking Pictures*, 124–25, 132, and plate 28; and Hartwig, *Shakespeare's Analogical Structure*, 108–09. On the Hell-mouth in Henslowe's listings of the inventory of the Lord Admiral's Men, see Wickham, *Early English Stages*, 2, pt.1 (New York, 1963), 310–14. See also 218–19, 224, 226. For the biblical references to death and hell as mouths, see Hankins, *Shakespeare's Derived Imagery*, 146. On the parallels between Romeo and Christ, see Battenhouse, *Shakespearean Tragedy*, 115.

13. For a review of the controversy about whether Juliet awakes on Thursday or Friday morning, see G. Thomas Tanselle, "Time in *Romeo and Juliet*," *Shakespeare Quarterly* 15 (1964): 349–61; Gibbons's introduction, 54n, and *The Arden Shakespeare*, 200n. For a possible Christ parallel in the number 42, see Battenhouse, *Shakespearean Tragedy*, 125.

14. For a defense of Paris's nobility, see Evans, *Shakespeare's Tragic Practice*, 39–40.

15. For the possible references to communion and to a royal presence chamber, see Smith, *Dualities in Shakespeare*, 95n.

16. On the various faces of Cupid, including the Blind Cupid of this final passage, see the references to Panofsky and Wind in part 2, chapter 2, note 16. See also Nohrnberg, *The Analogy of The Faerie Queene*, 489–90; Smith, *Dualities*

in Shakespeare, 93–94; and Peterson, *Time, Tide and Tempest,* 58.

17. On the gender overtones, see Michael Goldman, *Shakespeare and the Energies of Drama* (Princeton: Princeton University Press, 1972), 43; Garber, *Coming of Age in Shakespeare,* 144; and Hartwig, *Shakespeare's Analogical Structure,* 111.

18. Ruth Nevo, "Tragic Form in *Romeo and Juliet,*" *Studies in English Literature* 9 (1969): 257. See also Marsh, *Passion Lends Them Power,* 82–88.

19. On yew trees as a cause of death, see John Maplet, *A Green Forest: Reprinted from the Edition of 1567* (London: The Hesperides Press, 1930), 111–12.

20. *The Riverside Shakespeare,* 1098n. See also Chang, "The Language of Paradox in *Romeo and Juliet,*" 32; Black, "The Visual Artistry of *Romeo and Juliet,*" 253–54. On the possible need for the actor to play another part, see Granville-Barker, *Prefaces to Shakespeare,* 2:212n.

21. See my discussion on 148–50. Conflicting readings of the statues' worth have been presented, from highly favorable (Calderwood, *Shakespearean Metadrama,* 118; and Gibbons's introduction, 76) to highly negative (Battenhouse, *Shakespearean Tragedy,* 117–18; Goddard, *The Meaning of Shakespeare,* 138–39; Marsh, *Passion Lends Them Power,* 88; and Hartwig, *Shakespeare's Analogical Structure,* 112). For a more balanced reading, see Farrell, *Play, Death, and Heroism in Shakespeare,* 145. On the importance of the Capulet tomb as the final setting, see G. K. Hunter, "Shakespeare's Earliest Tragedies," 332.

22. Gibbons notes that the sun stops for a day in Ovid's *Metamorphoses* to "mock the fall of Phaeton," 60. In Joshua 10.12–14, the sun stops so that the destruction of the Amorites can be completed.

PART 3: *A MIDSUMMER NIGHT'S DREAM*

Notes to Chapter 6: *Sharp Athenian Law*

1. For the influence of Lyly on the debate between love and law, see G. K. Hunter, *John Lyly: The Humanist as Courtier* (Cambridge: Harvard University Press, 1962), 319–30; and David Young, *Something of Great Constancy: The Art of A Midsummer Night's Dream* (New Haven: Yale University

Press, 1966), 107–08, 151–55. See also R. A. Zimbardo, "Regeneration and Reconciliation in *A Midsummer Night's Dream*," *Shakespeare Studies* 6 (1970): 35–50.

2. See Olson, "A Midsummer Night's Dream and the Meaning of Court Marriage," 101–02. For the reputation of the Amazons, see Celeste Turner Wright, "The Amazons in Elizabethan Literature," *Studies in Philology* 37 (1940): 433–56. For their Greek origins, see Page duBois, *Centaurs and Amazons: Women and the Pre-History of the Great Chain of Being* (Ann Arbor: University of Michigan Press, 1982); and William Blake Tyrrell, *Amazons: A Study in Athenian Mythmaking* (Baltimore: Johns Hopkins University Press, 1984). On the danger of associating Hippolyta with Queen Elizabeth, see Winfried Schleiner, "*Divano Virago*: Queen Elizabeth as an Amazon," *Studies in Philology* 75 (1978): 163–80. See also Montrose, "*A Midsummer Night's Dream* and the Shaping Fantasies of Elizabethan Culture: Gender, Power, Form," 77–81. For Elizabeth as the moon fighting the sun of Europe and the papacy, see Frances A. Yates, *Astraea: The Imperial Theme in the Sixteenth Century* (London: Routledge and Kegan Paul, 1975), 76–78, 216. For the association of Theseus with civilization, see Alvin Kernan, "The Plays and the Playwrights," *The Revels History of Drama in English*, 3: 311–12. See also Calderwood, *Shakespearean Metadrama*, 124–25, and *A Midsummer Night's Dream*. Twayne's *New Critical Introductions to Shakespeare*, no. 14 (New York: Twayne Publishers, 1992), 10; Brooks's introduction, cii–cvi; and Rhoads, *Shakespeare's Defense of Poetry*, 31–35, 49–51, 85. For Shakespeare's awareness of positive interpretations of Theseus, see *The Two Noble Kinsmen*, in *The Riverside Shakespeare*, 1.1.77–85. See also Olson, "*A Midsummer Night's Dream* and the Meaning of Court Marriage," 101–02. For Chaucer's influence, see Olson, 99, 101, 114–17; Larry S. Champion, *Evolution of Shakespeare's Comedy: A Study in Dramatic Perspective* (Cambridge: Harvard University Press, 1970), 50–59; Ann Thompson, *Shakespeare's Chaucer: A Study in Literary Origins* (New York: Barnes and Noble, 1978), 88–92; Brooks's introduction, lxxvii–lxxviii; and E. Talbot Donaldson, *The Swan at the Well: Shakespeare Reading Chaucer* (New Haven: Yale University Press, 1985), 30–49. For the more negative side of Theseus's reputation, see D'Orsay Pearson, "'Unkinde' Theseus: A Study in Renaissance Mythography," *English Literary Renaissance* 4 (1974): 276–98. For the sources of Theseus and Hippolyta, see Bullough, *The Narrative and Dramatic Sources of Shakespeare*, 1: 368–69; and Muir, *The Sources of Shakespeare's Plays*, 66–67. On the harmony of

Venus and Diana, see Richard Cody, *The Landscape of the Mind: Pastoralism and Platonic Theory in Tasso's "Aminta" and Shakespeare's Early Comedies* (Oxford: Oxford University Press, 1969), 129–30. For their union in Spenser, see Roche, *This Kindly Flame*, 109–14; and Nohrnberg, *The Analogy of The Faerie Queene*, 453–62.

3. On the moon references in relation to "triple Hecat's team" (5.1.384), see Olson, "*A Midsummer Night's Dream* and the Meaning of Court Marriage," 103. See also Dent, "Imagination in *A Midsummer Night's Dream*," 128n.; Noel Purdon, *The Words of Mercury: Shakespeare and English Mythography of the Renaissance*, Salzburg Studies in English Literature, Elizabethan and Renaissance Studies, 39 (Salzburg, Austria: Institut fur Englische Sprache und Literatur, Universitat Salzburg, 1974): 179–80; Brooks's introduction, xci; French, *Shakespeare's Division of Experience*, 91–94; and Kott, "The Bottom Translation," 47.

4. Plutarch, in Brooks, appendix I, 136. For the possibility that using the name "Hippolyta" instead of "Antiopa" is intended to recall the disastrous future of Hippolytus, see Calderwood, *A Midsummer Night's Dream*, 5.

5. Kott, "The Bottom Translation," 47.

6. See Cody, *The Landscape of the Mind*, 130; and Brooks, *The Arden Shakespeare*, 12n.; and his introduction, xcvi, civ.

7. For the traditional views, see Olson, "*A Midsummer Night's Dream* and the Meaning of Court Marriage," particularly 99–101; Brooks's introduction, cxxx–cxxxii; and Dreher, *Domination and Defiance*, 16–75.

8. On Lysander and Egeus as artist figures, see Farrell, *Shakespeare's Creation*, 101–03. For the analogical relationship between life and art, see my discussion on 49–51.

9. On the nunnery as the wrong choice for young women, see Garber, *Coming of Age in Shakespeare*, 39.

10. See also Young, *Something of Great Constancy*, 155–56.

11. See my discussion of the mutual influences of art on life and life on art on 68–70. For negative readings of the lovers' dependence on convention, see Pettet, *Shakespeare and the Romance Tradition*, 113–14; Farrell, *Shakespeare's Creation*, 105, 112–13; J. Dennis Huston, *Shakespeare's Comedies of Play* (New York: Columbia University Press, 1981), 103–04; and Calderwood, *A Midsummer Night's Dream*, 20–22.

12. The spleen is the "seat of sudden impulsive feelings and actions" (*The Riverside Shakespeare*, 224n.).

13. On the associations with romance, see Barber, *Shakespeare's Festive Comedy*, 126; and Young, *Something of Great Constancy*, 89–90.

14. Olson, "*A Midsummer Night's Dream* and the Meaning of Court Marriage," 104–05. For the view that they celebrate a neoplatonic love, see Cody, *The Landscape of the Mind*, 130.

15. For the view that mocking the devices does not mean rejecting the reality of the emotions, see Barber, *Shakespeare's Festive Comedy*, 141.

16. For readings that stress the play's realistic treatment of nature, see Elizabeth Sewell, *The Orphic Voice: Poetry and Natural History* (New Haven: Yale University Press, 1960); Young, *Something of Great Constancy*, 75–85, 142–51; and Brooks's introduction, cxxv–cxxix. For the more traditional understanding of Renaissance imagery, see Olson, "*A Midsummer Night's Dream* and the Meaning of Court Marriage," 97–98; and Tuve, *Elizabethan and Metaphysical Imagery*, 382–410.

17. The variety of moon references has been discussed most fully by Rabkin, *Shakespeare and the Common Understanding*, 201–05; Brooks's introduction, cxxviii–cxxx; and Ernest Schanzer, "The Moon and the Fairies in *A Midsummer Night's Dream*," *The University of Toronto Quarterly* 24 (1955): 234–46. See also my discussion of the moon on 37–39.

18. For a discussion of "mirroring" between different characters and plots, see Young, *Something of Great Constancy*, 97–106; on the mechanicals, see Young, 100–06.

19. See John A. Allen, "Bottom and Titania," *Shakespeare Quarterly* 18 (1967): 107–17.

20. For the parodic link to Jaspar Heywood's translation of *Hercules Furens*, see Young, *Something of Great Constancy*, 35–37. On the ambiguity of the sun itself, see my discussion of general attitudes on 37, and of sun references in *Romeo and Juliet* on 67–68, 167–68. On Bottom and theater, see particularly Huston, *Shakespeare's Comedies of Play*, 103–08. For more parodic references to the Fates, see the speeches by Pyramus (5.1.277–79) and Thisby (5.1.327–32). See also Muir, *The Sources of Shakespeare's Plays*, 71.

21. On the nightingale, see Beryl Rowland, *Birds with Human Souls: A Guide to Bird Symbolism* (Knoxville: University of Tennessee Press, 1978), 105–11.

22. See my discussion on 246–47.

Notes to Chapter 7: Ill Met by Moonlight

1. See Cody, *The Landscape of the Mind*. For the wood as a metaphor for the self, see Calderwood, *Shakespearean Metadrama*, 131, 137; and Brooks's introduction, xcv. On the link

between dream and art, see also Young, *Something of Great Constancy*, 115–26. On the wood as a metaphor for the stage, see Huston, *Shakespeare's Comedies of Play*, 108–09.

2. Barber, *Shakespeare's Festive Comedy*, 119–62.

3. For criticism of the Barber and Olson approaches, see Cody, *The Landscape of the Mind*, 105, 127.

4. Olson, "*A Midsummer Night's Dream* and the Meaning of Court Marriage," 95–119. On the wood as a wood of error in the tradition of Dante and Spenser, see Olson, 106–07; and Nohrnberg, *The Analogy of The Fairie Queene*, 135–39. For the possible association of the chivalric overtones of the lovers' scenes with the tilts held annually to celebrate Elizabeth's accession, see Yates, "Elizabethan Chivalry: the Romance of the Accession Day Tilts," in *Astraea*, 88–111. For criticism of Barber, see Ornstein, *Shakespeare's Comedies*, 17.

5. See Farrell, *Shakespeare's Creation*, 104. For a more extreme statement of this position, see Kott, *Shakespeare our Contemporary*, 207–28. See also David Selbourne, *The Making of A Midsummer Night's Dream: An Eye-witness Account of Peter Brook's Production from First Rehearsal to First Night* (London: Methuen, 1982), 13. For the parallel between the belief in daemonic agents and modern psychologists' analyses of compulsive behavior, see Fletcher, *Allegory*, 286–89. See also Calderwood, *Shakespearean Metadrama*, 144. For the view that nightmare overtones are insignificant, see Brooks's introduction, cvii–cix.

6. Barber, *Shakespeare's Festive Comedy*, 124–31.

7. For the more intellectual version of the pastoral tradition, see Cody, *The Landscape of the Mind*. For an introduction to pastoral, see Frank Kermode, introduction to *English Pastoral Poetry* (London: Harrap, 1952). For a pastoral reading of *A Midsummer Night's Dream*, see Thomas McFarland, *Shakespeare's Pastoral Comedy* (Chapel Hill: University of North Carolina, 1972), 78–97.

8. For a parallel treatment of pastoral metaphor, see the opening scene of *The Winter's Tale*.

9. For discussion of various symbolic overtones, see Olson, "*A Midsummer Night's Dream* and the Meaning of Court Marriage," 107–12; James E. Robinson, "The Ritual and Rhetoric of *A Midsummer Night's Dream*," *PMLA* 83 (1968): 380–91; Calderwood, *Shakespearean Metadrama*, 137–38; Farrell, *Shakespeare's Creation*, 107–09; Kernan, "The Plays and the Playwrights," 3: 312–14; Brooks's introduction, cvi–cix; Frye, *The Myth of Deliverance*, 79–81; Carroll, *The Metamorphoses of Shakespearean Comedy*, 167–85; and Rhoads, *Shakespeare's Defense of Poetry*, 54–59, 75–77. For

the sources of the fairies, see Bullough, *Narrative and Dramatic Sources of Shakespeare,* 1: 370–72; and Muir, *The Sources of Shakespeare's Plays,* 67–68. For a more general discussion of Shakespeare's fairies, see K. M. Briggs, *The Anatomy of Puck,* 44–47; Minor White Latham, *The Elizabethan Fairies: The Fairies of Folklore and the Fairies of Shakespeare* (New York: Octagon Books, 1930); Barber, *Shakespeare's Festive Comedy,* 143–48; and Purdon, *The Words of Mercury,* 180–82.

10. For Renaissance readings of Ovid, see Don Cameron Allen, *Mysteriously Meant: The Rediscovery of Pagan Symbolism and Allegorical Interpretation in the Renaissance* (Baltimore: Johns Hopkins University Press, 1970), 163–99. For a discussion of changing attitudes toward metamorphosis from Ovid to Shakespeare, see Leonard Barkan, *The Gods Made Flesh: Metamorphosis & the Pursuit of Paganism* (New Haven: Yale University Press, 1986).

11. For the sources of the names, see Brooks's introduction, lix. For the Ovidian influence, see Walter F. Staton, Jr., "Ovidian Elements in *A Midsummer Night's Dream,*" *The Huntington Library Quarterly* 26 (1962–63): 165–78. See also Barkan, *The Gods Made Flesh,* 251–70.

12. On labyrinths and wandering, see Angus Fletcher, *The Prophetic Moment: An Essay on Spenser* (Chicago: Chicago University Press, 1971), 24–34. See also Nohrnberg, *The Analogy of The Faerie Queene,* 136–39; and Penelope Reed Doob, *The Idea of the Labyrinth from Classical Antiquity through the Middle Ages* (Ithaca: Cornell University Press, 1990). On the connections with the myth of Theseus and the minotaur, see David Ormerud, "'A Midsummer Night's Dream': The Monster in the Labyrinth," *Shakespeare Studies* 11 (1978), 39–52; and Mary Ellen Lamb, "'A Midsummer Night's Dream': The Myth of Theseus and the Minotaur," *Texas Studies in Literature and Language* 21 (1979): 478–91. On Bottom as a victimized Actaeon and Titania as an unchaste Diana, see Leonard Barkan, "Diana and Actaeon: The Myth as Synthesis," *English Literary Renaissance* 10 (1980): 317–59.

13. See Olson, "*A Midsummer Night's Dream* and the Meaning of Court Marriage," 111. The last citation of such a usage of "queynte" in *The Oxford English Dictionary* is from 1598.

14. On Puck, see Burroughs, *Narrative and Dramatic Sources of Shakespeare's Plays,* 1: 371–72; Muir, *The Sources of Shakespeare's Plays,* 67–68; Briggs, *The Anatomy of Puck,*

97; Enid Welsford, *The Fool: His Social and Literary History* (London: Faber and Faber, 1935), 48–51; Schanzer, "The Moon and the Fairies in *A Midsummer Night's Dream*," 234–46; Young, *Something of Great Constancy*, 27; Barber, *Shakespeare's Festive Comedy*, 143–44; Calderwood, *Shakespearean Metadrama*, 137–38; Farrell, *Shakespeare's Creation*, 103; John Weld, *Meaning in Comedy: Studies in Elizabethan Romantic Comedy* (Albany: State University of New York Press, 1975), 197–99; Kernan, "The Plays and the Playwrights," 3: 313–14; and Brooks's introduction, cix–cx. For parallels to the roles of Mercury, Cupid, the trickster of folklore, Harlequin, the Fool, and the Lord of Misrule, see Kott, "The Bottom Translation," 49–50. For allegorical abstractions as daemonic agents, see Fletcher, *Allegory*, 25–69, and my discussion on 44–45.

15. On Puck and Cupid, see Kermode, "The Mature Comedies," 206–07; Cody, *The Landscape of the Mind*, 132–33; and Purdon, *The Words of Mercury*, 181–94. For the meaning of the potion, see Dent, "Imagination in *A Midsummer Night's Dream*," 118–20; Kernan, "The Plays and the Playwrights," 3: 315; Brooks's introduction, cxxxiv; Farrell, *Shakespeare's Creation*, 106; Burroughs, *Narrative and Dramatic Sources of Shakespeare*, 1: 372; and Kott, "The Bottom Translation," 45–50.

16. On the imagination and the will, see Hankins, *Backgrounds of Shakespeare's Thought*, 89–108; and my discussion of Mercutio's comments (1.4.46–47) on 81–82.

17. On the possible affairs, see Calderwood, *Shakespearean Metadrama*, 124; and Farrell, *Shakespeare's Creation*, 108.

18. See Barber, *Shakespeare's Festive Comedy*, 137; Calderwood, *Shakespearean Metadrama*, 125; Farrell, *Shakespeare's Creation*, 108; and Brooks's introduction, xciii, cvi. On the possible love relationship of Titania and the changeling, see Donald C. Miller, "Titania and the Changeling," *English Studies* 22 (1940): 66–70; and Cody, *The Landscape of the Mind*, 135.

19. For the view that the pregnancy references are parodies of male endeavors, see Louis Montrose "'Shaping Fantasies': Figurations of Gender and Power in Elizabethan Culture," 72.

20. For the view that Titania tries to lock in the permanence of summer by denying mutability, see Zimbardo, "Regeneration and Reconciliation in *A Midsummer Night's Dream*," 39–40.

21. For the Orpheus allusion in the passage, see Madeleine Doran, "'Yet am I inland bred'," *Shakespeare Quarterly* 15

(1964): 110–11. For the general importance of Orphic themes of mysterious transcendence, see Sewell, *The Orphic Voice*, and Cody, *The Landscape of the Mind*.

22. On the possible references to Elizabeth, see Brooks's introduction, lxvii–lxviii.

23. For the historical implications, see Barber, *Shakespeare's Festive Comedy*, 121–22; and Brooks's introduction, lxviii. For an iconographical reading of Oberon's two emblematic images, see Purdon, *The Words of Mercury*, 188–92.

24. On the links between Venus and Diana, see Cody, *The Landscape of the Mind*, 132; Purdon, *The Words of Mercury*, 167–204; and Lyly's *Gallathea*, which is explicitly about the reconciliation of Venus and Diana. For possible Ovidian parallels, see Walter F. Staton, Jr., "Ovidian Elements in *A Midsummer Night's Dream*," 165–78. For Amoret and Belphoebe, see Roche, *The Kindly Flame*, 96–149.

26. On the snake, see Beryl Rowland, *Animals with Human Faces: A Guide to Animal Symbolism* (Knoxville: University of Tennessee Press, 1973), 142–47; and Garber, *Dream in Shakespeare*, 72–73.

27. On the hedgehogs, see Beryl Rowland, *Animals with Human Faces*, 101–02. On the bats and the owl, see Rowland, *Birds with Human Souls*, 6–9, 115–20. See also Peter J. Seng, *The Vocal Songs in the Plays of Shakespeare: A Critical History* (Cambridge: Harvard University Press, 1967), 28–32.

28. Kott, *Shakespeare Our Contemporary*, 218–21.

29. On the fairies' size, see Barber, *Shakespeare's Festive Comedy*, 145; and Brooks's introduction, cxxv–cxxvi.

Notes to Chapter 8: Night-rule

1. On the importance of discrepancies in awareness, see Bertrand Evans, *Shakespeare's Comedies* (Oxford: Oxford University Press, 1960), 33–46; and Young, *Something of Great Constancy*, 90–97.

2. For Renaissance readings of Ovid's *Metamorphoses*, see particularly Allen, *Mysteriously Meant*, 163–99.

3. For the view that the incident indicates Hermia's prudery, see Garber *Coming of Age in Shakespeare*, 134–35; and Huston, *Shakespeare's Comedies of Play*, 161, n15.

4. On Hermia's dream, see Garber, *Dream in Shakespeare*, 72–73; Norman N. Holland, "Hermia's Dream," in *Representing Shakespeare: New Psychoanalytic Essays*, ed. Murray Schwartz and Coppelia Kahn, 1–20; Young, *Something of*

Great Constancy, 115–20; and Dent, "Imagination in *A Midsummer Night's Dream*," 120n.

5. On the parallels with Montemayor's *Diana*, see *A Critical Edition of Yong's Translation of George of Montemayor's Diana and Gil Polo's Enamoured Diana*, ed. Judith M. Kennedy (Oxford: Oxford University Press, 1968), xlvi–l.

6. See Dent, "Imagination in *A Midsummer Night's Dream*," 126; and Huston, *Shakespeare's Comedies of Play*, 111–13.

7. For the view that the play's animal imagery implies the lovers' metamorphosis to a monstrous sexuality, see Carroll, *The Metamorphoses of Shakespearean Comedy*, 141–77.

8. For the symbolic contrast between animals and birds, see Knight, *The Shakespearian Tempest*, 154–56. See also Seng, *The Vocal Songs in the Plays of Shakespeare*, 33–35.

9. For Bottom as an everyman, see my discussion on 195–96. For the influence of *The Golden Ass* on Bottom's transformation, see Kott, "The Bottom Translation," 32–40. For the negative reading, see Helen Adolf, "The Ass and the Harp," *Speculum* 25 (1950): 49–57; Olson, "*A Midsummer Night's Dream* and the Meaning of Court Marriage," 113–15; and Deborah Baker Wyrick, "The Ass Motif in *The Comedy of Errors* and *A Midsummer Night's Dream*," *Shakespeare Quarterly* 33 (1982): 432–48. For the more positive reading, see Kermode on Apuleius's *The Golden Ass*, "The Mature Comedies," 207–10; K. M. Scoular, *Natural Magic* (Oxford: Oxford University Press, 1965), 112; and Cody, *The Landscape of the Mind*, 136–38.

10. For the views that purging also suggests a literal purging with fruit as the laxative and that Titania's interest in Bottom is both erotic and maternal, see Paster, *The Body Embarrassed*, 125–43.

11. For the view that "enforced" in "enforced chastity" means "forced upon" rather than "violated," see Purdon, *The Words of Mercury*, 193; and Carroll, *The Metamorphoses of Shakespearean Comedy*, 152–53.

12. On the contrast between Bottom and Puck, see Brooks's introduction, cxiv; Goddard, *The Meaning of Shakespeare*, 79; and Kott, "The Bottom Translation," 49–50. For Bottom as an ironic Hermetist, see Elam, *Shakespeare's Universe of Discourse*, 135–36. For Bottom as the embodiment of the play's robust humor and optimism, see Robert Ornstein, *From Romance Farce to Romantic Mystery* (Newark: University of Delaware Press, 1986), 85–86.

13. For the play as a "literary microcosm," see Heninger, *Touches of Sweet Harmony*, 325–97. On the use of theatrical metaphor, see Calderwood, *Shakespearean Metadrama*, 120–48, particularly 130–32 on Oberon as playwright and on the comedy in the wood as commedia dell'arte; and Huston, *Shakespeare's Comedies of Play*, 94–121.

14. For the backgrounds of this passage, see Hankins, *Backgrounds of Shakespeare's Thought*, 23–24.

15. See *Henry IV, Part 2*, 3.1.6; and *Macbeth* 2.2.34.

16. See Laurens J. Mills, *One Soul in Bodies Twain: Friendship in Tudor Literature and Stuart Drama* (Bloomington: Indiana University Press, 1937). On the link of the friendship theme to *The Two Gentlemen of Verona*, see Hamilton, *The Early Shakespeare*, 218–19. On the symmetry of the roles, see Brooks's introduction, xcviii.

17. On their friendship as an innocent twinning that threatens here and earlier to be destructive, see Garber, *Coming of Age in Shakespeare*, 33.

18. On chaos theory, see James Gleick, *Chaos: Making a New Science* (New York: Viking, 1987). For an application to cultural theory, see N. Katherine Hayles, *Chaos Bound: Orderly Disorder in Contemporary Literature and Science* (Ithaca: Cornell University Press, 1990). See also French, *Shakespeare's Division of Experience*, 98.

Notes to Chapter 9: The Concord of This Discord

1. On Shakespeare's support of patriarchal hierarchy in the play, see Freedman, *Staging the Gaze*, 154–91. On the need to reassert patriarchal authority in an atmosphere of disorder, see Tennenhouse, *Power on Display*, 73–76. On the plays as reflections of the woman's role in a patriarchal culture, see Bamber, *Comic Women, Tragic Men*, 27–30. See also Madelon Gohlke, "'I wooed thee with my sword': Shakespeare's Tragic Paradigms," reprinted in *Representing Shakespeare: New Psychoanalytic Essays*, 170–87.

2. See *The Riverside Shakespeare*, 238n. For other references to Cephalus, see 5.1.198–99, and note 25 below.

3. Spenser's Garden of Adonis (*The Faerie Queene*, 3.6.42) is such a place.

4. For the background of the allusion, see Peter Demetz, "The Elm and the Vine: Notes Toward the History of a Marriage Topos," *PMLA* 73 (1958): 521–32; for the substitution of ivy for the vine, see *The Comedy of Errors*, 2.2.173–

80; and Demetz, 528–30. See also Brooks, The Arden Shakespeare, 88–89n.; and Foakes, *The New Cambridge Shakespeare*, 106n.

5. For the belief that pearls are crystallised dew, see Heninger, *A Handbook of Renaissance Meteorology*, 68.

6. On Oberon's use of the potion for his own patriarchal ends, see Freedman, *Staging the Gaze*, 154–91.

7. See also Calderwood, *Shakespearean Metadrama*, 132.

8. For the importance of music and dance, see Brooks's introduction, cxx–cxxv; and Olson, *"A Midsummer Night's Dream* and the Meaning of Court Marriage," 115. See also Brissenden, *Shakespeare and the Dance*; and Leo Spitzer, *Classical and Christian Ideas of World Harmony* (Baltimore: Johns Hopkins University Press, 1963).

9. For the symbolism of the lark, see Olson, *"A Midsummer Night's Dream* and the Meaning of Court Marriage," 115.

10. On the general importance of the scene, see Goddard, *The Meaning of Shakespeare*, 74–76; and Kott, "The Bottom Translation," 52–53. On the background of the hunting motif, see Marcelle Thiebaux, *The Stag of Love* (Ithaca: Cornell University Press, 1974). See also *Titus Andronicus*, 2.1.112–19.

11. On the symbolic importance of the bear, see Farrell, *Shakespeare's Creation*, 100–01; Brooks, *The Arden Shakespeare*, 93n.; Richard Marienstras, *New Perspectives on the Shakespearean World*, tr. Janet Lloyd (Cambridge: Cambridge University Press, 1985), 203, n. 1; and Calderwood, *A Midsummer Night's Dream*, 90–91.

12. On Theseus's dogs, see Brooks, *The Arden Shakespeare*, 92–93n. On traditional views of the hounds, see Thiebaux, *The Stag of Love*, 103–04, 151–59. For the association of dogs with both the destructive and the sublime in readings of the Actaeon myth, see Barkan, "Diana and Actaeon: The Myth as Synthesis," 357–58. See also *Twelfth Night*, 1.1.16–22.

13. On Bottom's relationship to St. Paul, Erasmus, and the Christian tradition, see Thelma N. Greenfield, *"A Midsummer Night's Dream* and The Praise of Folly," *Comparative Literature* 20 (1968): 236–44; R. Chris Hassel, Jr., *Faith and Folly in Shakespeare's Romantic Comedies* (Athens: University of Georgia Press, 1980), 52–76; Kermode, "The Mature Comedies," 208–09; Rhoads, *Shakespeare's Defense of Poetry*, 79–83; and Kott, "The Bottom Translation," 29–43, 57–58.

14. On Shakespeare's possible use of the Geneva Bible, see Dent, "Imagination in *A Midsummer Night's Dream*," 121n.

15. On Bottom and Peter Quince's artistic instincts and abilities, see Young, *Something of Great Constancy,* 123–26; Calderwood, *Shakespearean Metadrama,* 138–41; Farrell, *Shakespeare's Creation,* 110; and Huston, *Shakespeare's Comedies of Play,* 96–102, 110–12.

16. On the practical concerns of other performers, see my discussion of Peter's scene with the musicians on 147–48.

17. For the case that the lovers learn something, see Hassel, *Faith and Folly in Shakespeare's Romantic Comedies,* 65–66; on their failure to understand very much, see Farrell, *Shakespeare's Creation,* 111.

18. See my discussion on 262–63.

19. On Theseus's need for Hippolyta's perspective, see Kermode, "The Mature Comedies," 219; Young, *Something of Great Constancy,* 137–41; Calderwood, *Shakespearean Metadrama,* 121–24; Farrell, *Shakespeare's Creation,* 98–101; Brooks's introduction, cxl–cxliii; Sidney Homan, *When the Theater Turns to Itself: The Aesthetic Metaphor in Shakespeare* (Lewisburg, Pa., Bucknell University Press, 1981), 79–103; Frye, *The Myth of Deliverance,* 75–79; and Rhoads, *Shakespeare's Defense of Poetry,* 33–35, 49–51, 61–75, 85–90. On the soundness of Theseus's theory of imagination, see Hankins, *Backgrounds of Shakespeare's Thought,* 91–94.

20. See *Shakespeare's Ovid: Being Arthur Golding's Translation of the Metamorphoses,* ed. W. H. D. Rouse (Carbondale: Southern Illinois University Press, 1961), 12, ll. 236–599. See also Burroughs, *Narrative and Dramatic Sources of Shakespeare,* 1: 373; and Kott, "The Bottom Translation," n. 47 on 66–67.

21. On the possible importance of Bacchus in the play, see Cody, *The Landscape of the Mind,* 133–34. For a fuller discussion of Orpheus, see Cody, 23–43; Sewell, *The Orphic Voice;* Kott, "The Bottom Translation," 56–57; and Burroughs, *Narrative and Dramatic Sources of Shakespeare,* 1: 373. On the Orpheus parallel in Romeo's descent into the tomb, see my discussion on 155–57.

22. See Brooks's introduction, xxxviii–xxxix; Cody, *The Landscape of the Mind,* 147; and *Shakespeare's Ovid,* 11, ll. 1–59.

23. For Shakespeare's treatment of "Pyramus and Thisby," see Muir, *The Sources of Shakespeare's Plays,* 66–77; Young, *Something of Great Constancy,* 38–48, 104–05; Madeleine Doran, "Pyramus and Thisbe Once More," *Essays . . . in Honor of Hardin Craig,* ed. Richard Hosley (Columbia: University of

Missouri Press, 1962), 149–62; J. W. Robinson, "Palpable Hot Ice: Dramatic Burlesque in *A Midsummer Night's Dream*," *Studies in Philology* 61 (1964): 192–204; John A. Allen, "Bottom and Titania," 107–17; Purdon, *The Words of Mercury*, 197–204; Farrell, *Shakespeare's Creation*, 110–15; Brooks's introduction, cxviii–cxx; Carroll, *The Metamorphoses of Shakespearean Comedy*, 157–67; and Kott, "The Bottom Translation," 53–56. For the view that "Pyramus and Thisby" reflects a nonanimist vision that looks toward modern materialistic philosophy, see Virgil Hutton, "*A Midsummer Night's Dream*: Tragedy in Comic Disguise," *Studies in English Literature* 25 (1985): 289–305; and T. Walter Herbert, *Oberon's Mazed World* (Baton Rouge: Louisiana State University Press, 1977).

24. Purdon, *The Words of Mercury*, 197.

25. See Foakes, *The New Cambridge Shakespeare*, 124n. The story of Cephalus and Procris, reprinted in *Shakespeare's Ovid*, 7, ll. 851–1123, shares many characteristics with the story, themes, and imagery of "Pyramus and Thisby."

26. "Most editors follow Pope in emending *moon vsed* to *mural* (i.e. wall) *down*", *The Riverside Shakespeare*, 244n. But see Brooks, *The Arden Shakespeare*, 159–62. For Bottom's view of the play, see Allen, "Bottom and Titania," 107–17.

27. Brooks notes the allusion to the qualities of a good monarch. See The *Arden Shakespeare*, 116n.

28. See my discussion on 231–38, 239–43.

29. His age suggests Endymion, who still loved the moon after sleeping for 40 years and who had "a gray beard, hollow eyes, withered body, and decayed limbs" (*Endymion*, 5.1.70–71, in *Elizabethan and Stuart Plays*, ed. Baskervill, Heltzel, and Nethercot [New York: Henry Holt, 1934]). For the satire of Lylyan iconography, see Purdon, *The Words of Mercury*, 198–201.

30. See *The Riverside Shakespeare*, 245n.

31. On Shakespeare's return to a revitalized version of the myth, see Sewell, *The Orphic Voice*, 89–91.

32. On the fusion of the fairies' mythical world with Athens's social world, see Robinson, "The Ritual and Rhetoric of *A Midsummer Night's Dream*," 380–91. On the theme of *discordia concors*, see Young, *Something of Great Constancy*, 61–108; R. A. Zimbardo, "Regeneration and Reconciliation in *A Midsummer Night's Dream*," 35–50; and Leon Guilhamet, "*A Midsummer Night's Dream* as the Imitation of an Action," *Studies in English Literature* 15 (1975): 257–71.

33. Barber, _Shakespeare's Festive Comedy_, 138–39. On sweeping as a ritual that symbolizes the end of one cycle and the beginning of another, see Kott, "The Bottom Translation," 59. On Puck as related to both "the light and the somber" (61) elements in the ending, see Kott, 58–61.

34. Barber, _Shakespeare's Festive Comedy_, 139.

Notes to Epilogue

1. For these terms, see Williams, _Marxism and Literature_, 121–27; Jonathan Dollimore, "_Introduction_ Shakespeare, cultural materialism and the new historicism," in _Political Shakespeare. New essays in cultural materialism_, ed. Dollimore and Alan Sinfield (Ithaca: Cornell University Press, London, 1985), 2–17; Dollimore, _Radical Tragedy_, 5–8; and my discussion on 7.

2. For discussion of the impulses behind comedy and tragedy, see Suzanne K. Langer, _Feeling and Form: A Theory of Art Developed from Philosophy in a New Key_ (New York: Charles Scribner's Sons, 1953), 306–66; Northrop Frye, "The Argument of Comedy," _English Institute Essays: 1948_, ed. D. W. Robertson, Jr. (New York, 1949), 58–73; Frye, _A Natural Perspective: The Development of Shakespearean Comedy and Romance_, 1–33; Robinson, "The Ritual and Rhetoric of _A Midsummer Night's Dream_," 380–91; Hawkins, "The Two Worlds of Shakespearean Comedy," 62–80; and Salingar, _Shakespeare and the Traditions of Comedy_, 1–27.

3. For the view that Shakespeare in his plays reflects the political and social instabilities of his time, see Dollimore, _Radical Tragedy_, 3–28, 83–108, 153–81, 249–71.

4. For these impulses, see particularly Stephen Greenblatt, _Renaissance Self-Fashioning: From More to Shakespeare_ (Chicago: University of Chicago Press, 1980).

INDEX

ABOUT THE AUTHOR

MARK STAVIG was an undergraduate at Augustana College (S.D.), read English as a Fulbright Scholar at Lincoln College, Oxford (B.A., M.A.), and completed his Ph.D. at Princeton. He has taught at the University of Wisconsin, Madison, and at Colorado College, where he is currently Professor of English. He is the author of *John Ford and the Traditional Moral Order* (The University of Wisconsin Press, 1968), as well as of an edition of Ford's *'Tis Pity She's a Whore* and various articles and reviews. He has done post-doctoral work at Harvard and has spent sabbatical years in London and Oxford. He is a member of the Shakespeare Association of America.